(Re-)Writing the Radical

spectrum Literaturwissenschaft / spectrum Literature

Komparatistische Studien / Comparative Studies

Herausgegeben von / Edited by
Moritz Baßler · Werner Frick · Monika Schmitz-Emans

32

De Gruyter

(Re-)Writing the Radical

Enlightenment, Revolution and Cultural Transfer in 1790s Germany, Britain and France

Edited by
Maike Oergel

De Gruyter

The editor wishes to thank the University of Nottingham and the British Comparative
Literature Association for their generous financial support.

ISBN 978-3-11-028985-5
e-ISBN 978-3-11-029011-0
ISSN 1860-210X

Library of Congress Cataloging-in-Publication Data

A CIP catalog record for this book has been applied for at the Library of Congress.

Bibliographic information published by the Deutsche Nationalbibliothek

The Deutsche Nationalbibliothek lists this publication in the Deutsche
Nationalbibliografie; detailed bibliographic data are available in the Internet
at http://dnb.dnb.de.

Table of Contents

Foreword

Elinor Shaffer

This book represents a gathering movement to show a comparative European picture of the information and opinion-making media that linked all parts of Europe even during times of strife and war, such as the French Revolutionary period. We have all been aware of certain major journals, beginning with the *Spectator* and the *Rambler*, that is those that went out from Britain carrying the names of Addison and Dr Johnson abroad in the eighteenth century, followed by the *Edinburgh* and the *Quarterly Reviews* in the early nineteenth century; we may also have been aware in the Romantic period of *The Monthly Review*, that did so much to bring new German writing to Britain in the 1790s; we may even have been aware of some European journals, such as the *Revue des Deux Mondes*, which was so widely read across Europe by anyone aspiring to general culture throughout the nineteenth century. But our awareness and our knowledge of the way in which ideas travel has been expanding rapidly in recent years. We now know, for example, through our Series on the *Reception of British and Irish Authors in Europe* (Continuum 2004–) that journals based in Switzerland, especially Geneva, played a powerful role in making the work of British women writers known – Jane Austen's *Pride and Prejudice* was translated in part in *La Bibliothèque britannique* (1813), *Mansfield Park* in part in the same Genevan journal by 1815, that is, within her lifetime. Full translations followed into French and then into German.[1] As the Series Editor of *The Reception of British and Irish Authors in Europe*, now numbering over twenty volumes, I have seen much evidence of intellectual and journalistic communication across Europe. But in the volume before us we find not just the power of certain major journals emanating from dominant centres and languages, but the beginnings of the sense of a cultural and intellectual network passing significant news and cultural responses back and forth across Europe, and of the growth of a local press with international concerns. This is a genuinely comparative insight, and introduces us to the strength and variety of regional and local organs of opinion that vied with the main currents of power and

---

1   *The Reception of Jane Austen in Europe*, ed. by Brian Southam and Anthony Mandal (London and New York: Continuum, 2007).

influence. This insight shifts us away from the obfuscating concern shown by sociologists like Pierre Bourdieu and his followers with centres of cultural power still based on nationalist models and towards the complex reality of mutual opinion-making. The major nations or powers are not necessarily the originating centres, nor do the cultural centres necessarily follow them or their model. This book offers examples of other models, perhaps consciously extreme or fringe, or governed by new or individual ambitions, which nevertheless achieved success. For example, the journal *London und Paris* (1798–1815), bringing illustrated news and political and social caricatures from the opposed capitals, is edited from neither city. These papers were high-priced, yet achieved a good circulation; the editors, correspondents, and critics could rely both on an independent Weimar tradition for which both London and Paris were equally objects of interest but not necessarily of respect. The political caricatures by Gillray which the paper reproduced were in effect being used by third parties against both France and the England from which they emanated. The small but autonomous duchy of Weimar also serves as a testing-ground for claims for independence of individuals within it, and since it was home to both Schiller and Goethe, is often seen as less subject to the exercise of arbitrary power by its rulers; the writers may well have been less independent than they appear, but the duchy and its renowned inhabitants nevertheless represents a distinct political entity with a view of its own as against the larger warring nation-states.

Other examples given here also reveal the paradoxical power of an unusual position or sidelight on political or cultural centrality. The viewpoint and position of women is rendered in several forms: the importation of German literature of sensibility, whether Goethe's immensely popular novel, *The Sorrows of Young Werther*, or its imitators, and the drama of sensationalism, gave opportunities to women translators, writers and readers, not only practical openings in the world but new modes of feeling which were suspect but empowering. These are shown to have embraced or implied a wide swathe of society, from Georgiana, Duchess of Devonshire, supporter and patroness of the leading Whig politician Charles James Fox, to Mary Wollstonecraft, the author of *The Rights of Woman,* and Isabelle de Charrière, author of *Trois Femmes* and its sequel, a black slave woman's tragedy. These also serve to point up the inadequacies even of a leading philosopher of moral theory, Kant, who omitted or excluded slaves, women, children and the lower, property-less orders from the claim to freedom. These spokeswomen are themselves only very partially empowered even when well-placed socially and often work by indirection from positions very far from the centre.

The stability of power claims in small states or communities is also tested by the extreme case of the absolute rule of the naval captain over his ship and his men, shown in the famous case of Captain Bligh to have been successfully challenged by mutineers, yet who in the circumstances of challenge to his authority spectacularly survived through weeks at sea in a small dinghy, though public opinion was divided in the political climate of 1794 between reasserting the traditional right of the captain and glorifying the renegade Fletcher Christian who led the mutiny against him. Here there is the further question of how far the sovereign power of any state extends overseas, which would be examined only much later, and is still far from resolved. How far did Europe extend? Other examples also reveal very special points of view: for example, the extreme Tory politics of the *Anti-Jacobin*, a journal which paradoxically succeeds in setting up the idea and the model of cosmopolitanism (a negative concept coined by Burke even before his fight against the French Revolution), in order to oppose it. Thus translation itself becomes a suspect activity, together with other forms of cultural importation, which may vitiate the native product. In fact, it is through the special interests of such journals or the personal perspectives and circumstances of individual writers, and the potentially special eccentric positions and viewpoints of either, that paradoxically they create a model of freedom from the domination of the centralizing cultural entities and their organs. If the *Anti-Jacobin* itself employed some borrowed, translated and imported models, that is only another sign of the increasing mobility and range of available models.

The same effect may be seen to characterize today's internationalism or 'globalism'. This book thus reveals the capacity of European culture to generate a variety of successful internal models from its own wide range of national, regional, and local models; the Romantic movement stressed their variety, and their potential (conflicting) claims to value and independence. Importing and exporting them sometimes enhanced their viability as independent positions. Paradoxically, this created a rich, shared culture across Europe. Only by studying these micro-cultures within the larger apparent political and national movements of the time can we achieve a just picture of cultural activity and the dissemination of ideas.

(Re-)Writing the Radical

Enlightenment, Revolution and Cultural Transfer in 1790s Germany, Britain and France

Introduction

Maike Oergel

It is a commonplace that the French Revolution had a stimulating impact on the development of political and cultural ideas in the 1790s. Not least, the Revolution affected the familiar paradigm shifts of the period around 1800, which transformed the notions of experience and thinking. To varying degrees, most of those shifts were rooted in the dialectic of the Enlightenment, its optimistic belief in the emancipating realization of reason coupled with a despotic blindness to the possibly unfathomable complexity of human understanding and existence, which emerged during the second half of the eighteenth century and which also found expression in the events of and following the Revolution. The first recognition of the one-sidedness of reason is evident in German *Sturm und Drang*, British pre-romanticism, and the work of Jean-Jacques Rousseau. Here those new conceptions that saw experience and thought as fluid and contingent were prepared and began to destabilize the established concepts of universal values. These developments contributed to bringing about the unusually fertile international intersecting of different discourses – aesthetic, intellectual, and political – which characterizes the 'revolutionary' decade and which is the subject of this volume. Crucially, all three discourses are marked by a need to deal with the 'radical', an approach dedicated to seeking truth by pursuing a path, political, aesthetic or philosophical, to its extreme end, which takes its legitimacy from the Enlightenment tenets of emancipation and autonomy. The fluidity of parameters and the openness of discursive areas presented a unique intellectual context for responding to the radical, affirmatively or negatively, and created the unique cultural and political launch pad that the 1790s present.

The Enlightenment notion of reason had promised individual and communal autonomy and perfectibility, while demanding moral as well as social responsibility. Based on this notion, the eighteenth century had produced a variety of new concepts, of art, politics, education, and society, all of which paved the way for the events of 1789. However, the Revolution also brought in its wake developments that increased the already existing doubts

regarding the efficacy of reason and the reliability of individual and communal judgement. This in turn triggered a thorough-going critique of Enlightenment values, building on the earlier recognition of the Enlightenment's
internal dialectic that dates back to the mid-eighteenth century. More often
than not, however, this critique[1] aimed at *revising* Enlightenment values,
rather than at abandoning them, as earlier scholarship has tended to claim.
But even a revision had powerful intellectual effects: these efforts reinforced
not just the *conditions* of fluidity in experience and thought, but also created
the reflexive *understanding* of this fluidity that is commonly associated with
the emerging Romanticisms of the 1790s, but which is equally pervasive in
the emerging new philosophies, in Kantian and German Idealist thought.

    The essays in this collection illuminate the *interdisciplinary nature* of these
late eighteenth-century discourses on aesthetics, politics, and philosophy, by
discussing the overlap between philosophical, aesthetic, and political concerns either in the work of individuals, or comparatively, in the transfer of
contemporary cultural materials and the changes these materials undergo in
the processes of reception, adaptation, and transformation. Each essay
contributes to the understanding of how progressive-revolutionary and con-
servative-reactionary impetuses interact in the fields of literature and
thought, as the latter engage with the political. What emerges is a clearer
understanding of the 'fate' of the Enlightenment, its radicalization and its
'overcoming' in aesthetic and political terms, and of the way in which political 'paranoia', generated by the fear of a spreading revolutionary radicalism,
facilitated and influenced the cultural transfer of the 'radical'. The comparative approach of the collection as a whole cuts across English literary and
historical studies on the relation between Enlightenment thought, political
and public culture,[2] including political and aesthetic theories,[3] current German approaches which readily foreground an essential link between the Enlightenment and the Revolution, but tend to be either interested in presenting histories of the period[4] or investigating local contexts,[5] and recent

---

1   Whether by Friedrich Schiller, Friedrich Schlegel or F.W.J. Schelling, by S.T. Coleridge or Mary
    Wollstonecraft.
2   Such as Tim Blanning's *The Culture of Power and the Power of Culture: Old Regime Europe 1660–
    1789* (Oxford: Oxford University Press, 2002) or James van Horn Melton's *Politics, Culture and
    the Public Sphere* (Cambridge: Cambridge University Press, 2001).
3   Such as Kennan Fergusen, *Politics of Judgement: Aesthetics, Identity and Political Theory* (Lanham:
    Lexington Books,1999) or Robert Porter's *Deleuze and Guattari: Aesthetics and Politics* (Cardiff:
    Wales University Press, 2009). Also Stephen White's *Edmund Burke: Modernity, Politics and Aes-
    thetics* (Thousand Oaks CA and London: Sage, 1994).
4   *Absolutismus, Aufklärung und Revolution*, ed.by Johannes Ebert, vol 11 of *Die große Chronik-Welt-
    geschichte* (Gütersloh, Munich: Chronik Verlag, 2008) or *Geschichtlichkeit, Aufklärung und Revolu-
    tion: Literatur im Gang der Zeiten*, ed. by Roland Opitz (Leipzig: Rosa Luxemburg Verlag, 2007).
5   Such as Jörg Schweigard's work on Mainz, e.g. *Die Liebe zur Freiheit ruft uns an den Rhein: Auf-
    klärung, Reform und Revolution in Mainz* (Gernsbach: Katz, 2005) or earlier *Auklärung und Revolu-
    tionsbegeisterung: Die katholischen Universitäten Mainz, Heidelberg und Würzburg im Zeitalter der Fran-*

French approaches which tend to focus on the implication of (European) Enlightenment thought in modern evils, such as hegemonic approaches to culture, thought, and global politics.[6] In its cross-cutting approach the collection presents a newly configured research field, and begins a comparative and interdisciplinary investigation that is likely to yield new insights into the origins of modern culture, politics, and aesthetics, both in terms of regional-national distinctions and common European legacies. Currently there are no comparative studies that investigate the Revolution's intellectual and aesthetic impact and influence on different countries *in conjunction* or that focus on the *reciprocity* of cultural and political transfers.[7] Studies in the development of conservatism, of which political paranoia is one aspect, have become more numerous over the past decade and a half, and in some respects this volume is also a contribution to the existing scholarship in this area. But while existing studies tend to focus on either the *reception* in *one* national context, or one specific literary or political issue,[8] the essays presented here combine to illuminate the international *exchange* driven by 'negative' factors, such as paranoia and xenophobia, and suggest a complex chain of reactions, triggered by receptions and adaptations of revolutionary ideas, events, or texts.

At first glance the connection between the fate of the Enlightenment and the reciprocity of cultural transfer fuelled by an interest in the radical may appear tenuous. But it is the very kaleidoscopic fluidity of values – the 'fate of reason', to use Frederic Beiser's term, in an historically aware world – that makes possible the shifts in the meaning, and in the use, of ideas and storylines, which so typically occur in the transfers of cultural material at this time. The recognition of the fluidity of the meaning(s) encoded in texts opened the door to their adaptation and transformation. The collection makes clear how thinkers and artists across 1790s Europe wrestled with the

---

zösischen Revolution (Frankfurt a. M.: Peter Lang, 2000). Also Hanns-Jürgen Geisinger, *Aufklärung und Revolution: Die Freiheitsbewegung in Bonn am Ende des 18. Jahrhunderts* (Stuttgart: Hochschulverlag, 1978).

6   Such as Michel Foucault's and Jean-François Lyotard's work, and more recently French postcolonial studies.

7   One classic comparative analysis, now nearly 40 years old and specifically dealing with the run-up to the Revolution rather than its impact, is *Towards the French Revolution: Europe and America in the 18th-century world*, ed. by Louis Gottschalk and Donald Lach (New York: Scribner, 1973).

8   Such as Lisa Wood's *Modes of Discipline: Women, Conservatism and the Novel after the French Revolution* (Lewisburgh: Bucknell University Press, 2003), which looks at British women writers, or Matthew O. Grenby's *The Anti-Jacobin Novel: British Conservatism and the French Revolution* (Cambridge: Cambridge University Press, 2001). Michael Wagner's *England und die französische Gegenrevolution 1789–1802* (Munich: Oldenbourg, 1994), on the other hand, focuses specifically on political culture. One exception as far as comparative approaches are concerned is Pekka Suvanto's survey *Conservatism from the French revolution to the 1990s* (1st 1994, English translation: Basingstoke: Macmillan, 1997), which compares conservatism in Britain, Germany, France, and the United States, but is focused on political history.

new ambiguities and instability that the historically aware critique of reason was creating. It no longer allowed unquestionable absolutes or reliable realities, but instead detached existential dichotomies, such as order and chaos, freedom and necessity, (de-)construction and immutability, mind and matter, from value systems, creating multiplicity, perspectivism, and relativism.

The discussion contained in this volume contributes to highlighting the difficulties of the interpretation of 'Enlightenment'. On the one hand, there are clear international trends in this interpretation, i.e. a swing from the 'liberal' interpretation of the Enlightenment as the foundation of modern Western political and intellectual culture (Hayes) towards more dialectical approaches in the later twentieth century that highlighted the darker and intolerant sides of Enlightenment notions of reason. On the other hand, there are equally clear differences in national critical traditions, which have evolved in different contexts and focus on different issues. In German criticism, *Aufklärung*, after it had in the late eighteenth and nineteenth centuries frequently been identified as foreign and set in contrast to *German* Romanticism, was post-1945 reclaimed for key eighteenth-century thinkers. In more recent assessments it has been increasingly defined by a complexity of thinking that critiques its own thought pre- and post-Revolution in a way that pre-empts the twentieth-century 'discovery' of the dialectic of the Enlightenment (and of reason) by the Frankfurt School. French criticism has traditionally celebrated the efforts of the eighteenth-century *philosophes* as a French achievement closely related to French classicism and responsible for French cultural hegemony in eighteenth-century Europe, protecting it from implication in the negative aspects of the Revolution. With the advent of postmodernist critical theory, however, French criticism has come to critique Enlightenment ideas as responsible for nineteenth- and twentieth-century beliefs in and practices of domination and intolerance. In Britain attitudes to the Enlightenment are less marked by changes in appreciation, not least because seventeenth- and eighteenth-century British thought made seminal contributions to Enlightenment thinking, while eighteenth-century British intellectual activities paved the way for European Romanticism, in which British literature then fully participated. So in Britain there was little need to minimize, maximize, or reclaim the importance of this movement. In contrast, Germany's contribution to Romanticism is traditionally seen as much stronger than the involvement of German thought in the Enlightenment, while France's contribution to the Enlightenment outweighs its intellectual input certainly into early Romanticism. This collection provides material to critique and modify such national critical traditions, which contribute to national stereotyping. It places studies of revolutionary responses to new radical ideas in Germany, Britain and France, which sought to *break out* of old (Enlightened) epistemologies, philosophies, aesthetics, and political structures, side by side with investigations into conservative responses that aimed at containing the revolutionary impact in stable structures based on traditional, often Enlightened, models. Such cross-referencing brings national, political and aesthetic similarities and differences into relief. The resulting picture reveals not only the complexity and self-awareness of these contemporary responses, but also provides clear markers of the departures of a number of varied developments in nineteenth- and twentieth-century aesthetic, philosophical and political discourses.

The notion of the 'radical' inevitably provoked strong conservative reactions. In all three countries, the conservative responses frequently presented the new political ideas or literary trends as 'foreign' and attached blame and notions of degeneracy to revolutionary ideas or fashionable cultural products, such as the 'Jacobin', the 'over'-sentimental and the 'Gothic'. Yet at the same time these responses had to deal with the considerable popularity that appertained to these destabilizing entities, whether they were notions of social equality or of intense sentimentality. The essays show that, despite (and because of) their suggested notoriety and outlandishness, these 'imported' entities were not just eagerly received, but also creatively adapted.[9] In dealing with such imports – news or texts – which were perceived on the one hand as threatening or in bad taste, yet exciting, interesting, or of popular appeal on the other, different approaches towards 'treating' them can be identified. One approach prefers to 'domesticate and publish', whereby domestication can take any form from neutralizing radical or disconcerting content (i.e. elimination by re-writing) to naturalizing it (re-interpreting it as something relating to or already existing in the native context). Another approach 'appropriates and denigrates (as a negative other)', which helps to establish a stable notion of the 'home' identity or situation, while yet another approach uses the imports to stimulate a domestic public debate after materials have undergone some sanitizing, i.e. limiting the destabilizing moment by reduction or diversion. These approaches are by no means mutually exclusive; evidently the first and third approach overlap. In this respect the collection pinpoints the elusive nuances between reception and adaptation and the dynamics of cultural transfer under 'negative conditions'.

But beyond the field of reception the essays show, through the triangulation of the material they cover, not just transfers, but *exchanges* – e.g. how notions of the Gothic were passed back and forth – and crucially highlight the reciprocity of these transfers – e.g. how notions of the Gothic are adapted and re-interpreted dependent on local circumstances, as they move back and forth. By presenting the responses and adaptations from Germany, Britain, and France side by side, an intriguing picture of re-interpreta-

---

9 Insights into the processes of adaptation in Britain can be gleaned from Peter Mortensen, *British Romanticism and Continental Influences: Writing in the Age of Europhobia* (Basingstoke: Palgrave Macmillan, 2004).

tion and creative mis-representation of key elements emerges: notions of
the Gothic, ideas of Jacobinism, and concepts of appropriate political culture receive different interpretations in the different national contexts, depending on where they are considered to 'come from' politically or aesthetically, and what status they are given. In Britain, German *Sturm und Drang*
ideas are presented as over-sentimental Gothic excesses that are in league
with dangerous revolutionary Jacobinism, which need defusing into safe (i.e.
existing) artistic and political channels, as Imke Heuer demonstrates for the
Whig-ist writings of the Duchess of Devonshire, and Susanne Kord for the
English *Werther*-reception. It is evident that the materials' popularity prohi-
bits their outright rejection, and requires their neutralization instead. Such
strategies of adaptation, rather than rejection, suggest the tacit admission of
their political and aesthetic relevance, which becomes clear in Barry Murnane's analysis of Gothic and sentimental features in the contributions to
the arch-conservative *Anti-Jacobin Review,* where 'German radicalism' is
adapted by British conservatism. In Germany radicalism tends to be identified as French in origin, and seen as mainly political in nature. Daniel Wilson's examination of the measures taken by the aristocratic government of
the Duchy of Saxe-Weimar shows to what extent the intellectual-aesthetic
project of *Weimar classicism*, by which a new German high culture was to
fend off political radicalism from France, was shaped by repression and intimidation. On the other hand, by examining the German current affairs
periodical *Minerva*, Birgit Tautz is able to demonstrate through the example
of the slavery debate to what extent liberal economic and emancipatory political concerns influenced the 'classical' projects of the aesthetic sublimation
of the political. German periodicals culture itself affords insights into the
politicizing of the aesthetic, as Renata Schellenberg's examination of the developing bourgeois public sphere in Germany, stimulated by the proliferation of periodicals shows: among the late eighteenth-century *Bildungsmania*
prevalent in much periodic print-media, which sought to elevate the individual above the mundane, two different approaches to the 'radical' political,
which divide high and low culture publications, can be identified: the (re)di-
rection of mental and cultural energies towards either the intellectual-aesthetic or the populist joys of consumer culture. However, the aesthetic and
consumerist redirection of political energies was not thorough-going. One
such periodical, *London und Paris*, while clearly belonging to the consumerist-
populist end of the market, finds a way of adapting French political radicalism and the British culture of political satire to contribute to the creation of
a moderate public arena in Germany. In his analysis of *London und Paris*
Christian Deuling identifies political engagement, albeit without political
radicalism, as the driving force behind this journal, despite its avowed apolitical intentions.

The changing reception of French political radicalism and the gradual adaptation of (German) over-excited sentimentalism in Britain is demonstrated by Maike Oergel in her examination of the contemporary treatment of the story of HMS *Bounty*: the changing public images of William Bligh and Fletcher Christian reflect the rejection of French radicalism as well as the gradual acceptance of the radical individual in the shape of the emerging Romantic hero. On the other hand, French criticism of radical (Kantian) German philosophy and French revolutionary politics with their focus on male-dominated autonomy and moral self-reliance as intolerant and repressive against other groups (women and slaves) is presented in Judith Still's analysis of Isabelle de Charrière's sequel to her novel *Trois Femmes*.

Explicit links between the political and the aesthetic in literary works are investigated by Melissa Deininger in her essay on the Marquis de Sade's *La Philosophie dans le boudoir* and presented by Jakob Ladegaard in his new interpretation of Friedrich Hölderlin's novel *Hyperion*. While de Sade uses revolutionary political language for a complex aesthetic critique of the yet to be overcome failings of the Revolution in his novella, Ladegaard demonstrates how Hölderlin's contradictory concerns regarding political and aesthetic reform (and revolution) interlink closely in his novel and pinpoint the problems of modern aesthetics and modern democracy, thus questioning the notion of the German priority of aesthetics over politics from a new perspective. Like many contemporary writers, Hölderlin elected to discuss the political and aesthetic revolution through the medium of classical materials. The fundamental importance of the classical tradition, both in aesthetic and political terms, for legitimizing both conservative and revolutionary aims, and in different (inter)national contexts, is discussed by Ian Macgregor Morris and Uta Degner.

Finally, the impact of political and intellectual instability and openness – the new presence of the radical, which results from (radically) questioning reason and traditional authorities – is also discussed in relation to encoding meaning in text. The German Romantic thinker Novalis, the German Romantic writer and critic Jean Paul, the French counter-revolutionary Xavier de Maistre, and the English poet-artist William Blake all engage differently with this instability and openness, created by the radical. Peter Krilles delineates the complex interactions of Novalis's project of a new historically dynamic epistemology, which is based on a synthetic inclusion of the aesthetic in conceptions of knowledge, with Enlightened concepts of encyclopaedic and scientific knowledge, while Dirk Göttsche highlights, through examining Jean Paul's poetic approach to the temporality and historicity of human existence and understanding, the intersections of his complex critical handling of *both* the Enlightenment and the Revolution in his satirical novel *Quintus Fixlein*, which critiques the time-driven revolutionary impetus alongside notions of historical stability. David McCallam outlines the challenges the newly fluid dichotomies present to the politically reactionary writer by analyzing the literary devices used in Xavier de Maistre's novel *Voyage autour de ma chambre*, which seem to turn the novel's (radical) counter-revolutionary sentiments towards undermining its conservative message, making the radical explicitly and subliminally present in opposing guises. And finally, Sibylle Erle shows how Blake's groundbreaking text-image compositions are crucially influenced by a secularizing shift of the inspirational source from divine to human, radicalizing the Enlightenment belief in limitless human potential, while promoting the non-rational, soon to be Romantic, force of inspiration.

Many of the points made in the individual essays about the intellectual, creative, and political developments, about the receptions and adaptations of cultural imports during the Revolutionary decade in the individual countries build on and confirm existing research. The innovative impetus of this collection, however, derives from its comparative approach – *within* individual essays and *between* the essays – which makes visible previously overlooked common ground and the diverse multiplicity of interpretations of the paradigm shifts experienced in the 1790s. At the same time the volume highlights the – often highly contingent – shifting of meaning in these processes of interpreting. In particular, the volume demonstrates the intellectual and political malleability of notions of radicalism and provides new insights into the emerging link between the political and the aesthetic – in its very different manifestations – during the 1790s. In this it hopes to stimulate more comparative and interdisciplinary research in this area, which will go on to highlight the influence of national demarcations *and* make the case for transnational viewpoints.

Versions of these essays were first given as papers at the conference *Breaking Boundaries – Revolution, Liberation and Excess: The 1790s in Britain, France and Germany*, which took place at the Institute of Germanic and Romance Studies in London, 22–24 April 2009, and was supported by the University of Nottingham and the British Comparative Literature Association.

'That war with softer cares may be united'

Harriet Lee, Georgiana Duchess of Devonshire, the Thirty Years' War, and the Politics of Adaptation

Imke Heuer

1.

In 1899, the journal *The Nineteenth Century* published an article which made a curious claim. According to Frederick Leveson Gower, Byron's tragedy *Werner* (1822) had been written not by Byron himself, but by Leveson Gower's own grandmother, Georgiana, Duchess of Devonshire (1757–1806).[1] His statement seemed particularly surprising because *Werner*, although hardly ever performed today, was one of the most popular plays on the Victorian stage, and Byron's most successful work at the box office. The Duchess, in contrast, then mainly famous as a Georgian 'society queen', was not known as a dramatist at all, and the two anonymous novels she had published at a young age had long been forgotten. However, the fact that Leveson Gower was taken seriously reflects the largely negative critical response to Byron's tragedy in the nineteenth century, which it owes both to its stage success and unique position in his oeuvre. While the plots of his other plays are either original, or dramatize historical or mythological events, *Werner* is Byron's only adaptation from a contemporary work of prose fiction – Harriet Lee's novella 'Kruitzner, or The German's Tale' (1801), published in the collection *The Canterbury Tales*, which she wrote with her sister Sophia.[2]

Although soon refuted by Byron's editor E. H. Coleridge,[3] Leveson Gower's claim turned out to be not altogether unfounded. As Devonshire's sister Harriet, Countess of Bessborough (1761–1821) reported to her lover Granville Leveson Gower (Frederick's father), in 1802 the two sisters indeed collaborated on an adaptation of Lee's novella:

1 Frederick Leveson Gower, 'Did Byron Write *Werner*?', *Nineteenth Century* 46 (1899) 243–250.
2 Harriet Lee, 'Kruitzner, or the German's Tale', in Harriet and Sophia Lee, *The Canterbury Tales*, 5 vols (London: Robinson, 1797–1805), IV (1801), pp. 1–368. The quotations in this essay are taken from this edition.
3 George Gordon, Lord Byron, *The Works of Lord Byron: Poetry*, ed. by Ernest Hartley Coleridge, 7 vols (London: John Murray, 1898–1904), V (1901), pp. 329–333.

I am very busy with our tragedy. I never intended you should know of this at all [...]
My sister work'd very hard at it [...] and it is almost done. But hers is the most considerable part. I suppose you will think it vanité d'auteur or sisterly partiality if I tell
you I really do not think it very bad. [...] You must never mention or hint at it to her
on any account. It is the story of Siegendorf in the Canterbury Tales.[4]

Considered lost for more than a century, in 2003 the manuscript play, entitled
The Hungarian. A Tragedy and crediting the Duchess of Devonshire alone, was
unearthed by Donald Bewley in the Kemble-Devonshire collection held at
the Huntington Library.[5] Whereas to my knowledge there are no other literary works by Bessborough (and, like the later family legend, she attributed the
'Kruitzner' adaptation mainly to her sister), the Duchess was a prolific writer,
author of two epistolary novels,[6] numerous poems, and at least six manuscript plays. As Linda Colley, Amanda Foreman and others have shown, Devonshire, a member of a prominent Whig family, was a major player in late
eighteenth-century politics.[7] Critical interest in her literary works, however, is
still fairly recent. While she is currently being revaluated as a novelist and poet,[8] my essay focuses on her dramatic ambitions and her complex involvement in the world of theatre.

In the opening part, I will introduce Harriet and Sophia Lee's *Canterbury
Tales* as a literary project, and briefly discuss how in 'Kruitzner' Harriet Lee
employs a politically charged historical background (the Thirty Years' War)
to comment on her own time. In the following section, I will focus on *The
Hungarian*, which I take to be primarily Devonshire's work, and explore the
dynamics between her appropriation of Lee's novella and her own Whig

---

4 Harriet, Countess of Bessborough, to Granville Leveson Gower, February 1802. Lord Granville Leveson Gower, *Private Correspondence, 1781–1821*, 2 vols, ed. by Castalia Countess Granville (London: John Murray, 1916), I, p. 332.
5 Huntington Library, Kemble-Devonshire Collection, MS K-D 571. I wish to thank the late
   Donald Bewley for letting me read his transcripts of Devonshire's plays. All citations from *The
   Hungarian* refer to this source. For a stylistic comparison between *Werner* and *The Hungarian* see
   Peter Cochran, 'Harriet Lee's *The German's Tale*, *The Hungarian* by Georgiana, Duchess of Devonshire, and Byron's *Werner*', *Keats-Shelley Journal* 18 (2004) 175–187.
6 The two epistolary novels, *Emma* (1773) and *The Sylph* (1778), were published anonymously,
   but are largely accepted as Devonshire's productions, and have been re-published under her
   name. See Georgiana, Duchess of Devonshire, *The Sylph*, ed. by Jonathan Gross (Evanston:
   Northwestern University Press, 2007); *Emma, or The Unfortunate Attachment*, ed. by Jonathan
   Gross (Albany: New York State University Press, 2004).
7 See Amanda Foreman, *Georgiana, Duchess of Devonshire* (London: HarperCollins, 1998); Linda
   Colley, *Britons. Forging the Nation 1707–1837* (London: Pimlico, 2003), pp. 242–250; Elaine
   Chalus, *Elite Women in English Political Life, c. 1754–1790* (Oxford: Clarendon Press, 2005),
   pp. 91–97.
8 See e. g. Jonathan Gross's critical editions of Devonshire's novels (n. 6). See also 'The Passage
   over the Mountain of St. Gothard', in *Romantic Women Poets. An Anthology*, ed. by Duncan Wu
   (Oxford: Blackwell, 1998), pp. 172–177.

politics.[9] Additionally, I will briefly look at the political dimension of her position as patron of the theatre. In particular, I will focus on an epilogue she provided for the first production of Joanna Baillie's tragedy *De Monfort* (1798), which is part of a complex strategy to purge the play from associations with foreignness and 'Jacobinism' and thus linked to her 'Kruitzner' adaptation. My discussion is informed by an ongoing 'rethinking of the political', and recent research in historiography and cultural studies, which emphasizes the crucial roles elite women, though they could hold no formal political office, occupied in public networks.[10] As will become evident, Devonshire's example illustrates the complex connections between political, theatrical, and pedagogical activities by such women.

2.

Now largely remembered as the source of Byron's *Werner*, Lee's 'Kruitzner' was very popular in its own time. Both Harriet and Sophia Lee were successful novelists and playwrights, whose works were translated into French and German. In recent years there has been a growing interest in the Lee sisters.[11] However, to my knowledge, hitherto there have been no detailed studies of *The Canterbury Tales*, arguably their most innovative work. Published in five volumes between 1797 and 1805, the *Tales* are an ambitious literary project. As the title suggests, the concept is derived from Geoffrey Chaucer's *Canterbury Tales*. The introduction (I, iii-xxiii) sets up a narrative frame in which a group of travellers gets stuck in an inn at Canterbury in a snow storm, and pass their time by telling stories. Like Chaucer's eponymous collection, the *Tales* explore different social classes and the range of human emotions. Set in diverse European countries and epochs, from the Middle Ages to the Lees' own time, their key themes are social hierarchies, family dynamics, class differences, and education, as well as war, exile, and displacement.

　　As the motto for the *Tales* the Lees employ a quote from Shakespeare's *Macbeth* (1606) describing 'A woman's story at a winter's fire/ Authoriz'd by her granddame'.[12] Thus, they align their project with the origins of modern

9　My essay applies the concept of cultural appropriation developed by Roger Chartier. See Roger Chartier, *Cultural History: Between Practices and Representations*, translated by Lydia G. Cochrane (Cambridge: Polity Press, 1988), especially p. 13.

10　See Amanda Vickery, 'Introduction', in *Women, Privilege and Power: British Politics, 1750 to the Present* , ed. by Amanda Vickery (Stanford, California: Stanford University Press, 2001), pp. 1–55, especially pp. 3–6; see also Elizabeth Eger et. al., eds, *Women, Writing and the Public Sphere 1700–1830* (Cambridge: Cambridge University Press, 2001).

11　See e. g. Jane Spencer, *The Rise of the Woman Novelist* (Oxford, New York: Basil Blackwell, 1986), pp. 123–127; Emma Juliet Clery, *Women's Gothic* (Horndon, Tavistock: Northcote, 2004), pp. 37–50.

12　William Shakespeare, *Macbeth*, ed. by Kenneth Muir (Walton-on-Thames: Arden Shakespeare, 1979), III, 4, ll. 64–65.

English literature, while also putting it into an older, female tradition of oral storytelling. Their use of the Chaucerian frame and title and the allusion to England's medieval literary tradition are also charged with political connotations. In 1803, the radical philosopher William Godwin published a *Life of Chaucer*, which represents the medieval poet as one of the architects of a genuinely 'English' literature and the first portraitist of a complex society not exclusively dominated by the nobility.[13] Like Godwin, the Lees were among the late eighteenth- and early nineteenth-century intellectuals who, associating Chaucer with the genesis of the 'English' nation and its liberal tradition, engaged in establishing his place within the literary canon.

Several stories focus on contemporary events. The Revolution and French *émigrés* feature both in 'The Frenchman's Tale – Constance' (I, 191–329) and 'The Scotsman's Tale – Claudine' (IV, 369–490). In allusion to the Revolutionary and Napoleonic Wars, the *Tales* form a prismatic, complex portrait of a Europe torn by war and social upheaval. Significantly, despite the series's anti-aristocratic dimension, the exiles in *The Canterbury Tales* have different political backgrounds and are exiled for a variety of reasons, both social and political. The collection expresses sympathy for victims of war, persecution, and oppression, irrespective of their political loyalties. Its mosaic structure and reference to oral storytelling reflect the Lees' approach to history and historiography, and to ideas about authorship and originality. They are interested in the ways in which stories are transmitted, becoming fragmented or changing their meaning along the way. The *Tales* are strongly informed by the eighteenth-century 'ballad revival' and contemporary discourses on oral literature reflected in works such as Thomas Percy's *Reliques of Ancient British Poetry* (1765) and James Macpherson's supposedly ancient Gaelic *Ossian* poems (1760–63). Eleven years before William Wordsworth and Samuel Taylor Coleridge published the *Lyrical Ballads* (1798), in her narrative poem *A Hermit's Tale* (1787),[14] Sophia Lee had already used the ballad stanza to emulate medieval poetry. By alluding to oral poetic traditions, *The Canterbury Tales* implicitly question the contrast between orally transmitted 'stories' and authoritative 'history',[15] emphasising that the representation of history is always incomplete, subjective and linked with power. The sisters' subversive approach to individual authorship is also mirrored in the collection's production history. In the original edition, the first volume was published under Harriet Lee's name alone. However, in the preface to the *Standard Novels* edition of the *Tales* (1832), Harriet, while claiming to be the

---

13 William Godwin, *Life of Geoffrey Chaucer, the Early English Poet*, 2 vols (London: Phillips, 1803), especially I, p. vii.

14 Sophia Lee, *A Hermit's Tale, Recorded by His Own Hand, and Found in His Cell* (London: T. Cadell, 1787).

15 See also Allen W. Grove, 'To make a long story short: Gothic Fragments and the Gender Politics of Incompleteness', *Studies in Short Fiction* 34 (1997) 1–10.

initiator of the series, mentions in passing that Sophia had contributed the introductory frame story.[16] Leaving the project's origins ambiguous, she thus hints at the collaborative nature of all literary production.

3.

Set in the Holy Roman Empire of German Nation, in Bohemia and Germany, during the Thirty Years' War, 'Kruitzner, or The German's Tale' engages with the Revolutionary and Napoleonic Wars through the lens of historical fiction. Originally named Frederick von Siegendorf, Lee's protagonist Frederick Kruitzner is a Bohemian nobleman in exile. Born as the heir to a county, Frederick is shown as an extraordinarily intelligent and sensitive youth, but also as a decidedly antisocial character who considers himself superior to ordinary humans, despite his personal failings. At the outbreak of the Bohemian Revolt against Hapsburg rule – the 'rejection of the Austrian yoke' ('Kruitzer', 63) – he is given the command of his father's troops, but proves irresponsible as a military commander and is discharged ('Kruitzer', 66–67). The Count purchases him a prestigious but less important position in the army, which Frederick also loses after missing a battle following a night of drinking and gambling ('Kruitzer', 68). Disinherited by his father ('Kruitzer', 73), he assumes the name of Kruitzner and lives as an embittered restless wanderer, until he falls in love with and marries Josephine, the daughter of a Florentine scholar in political exile in Hamburg ('Kruitzer', 76–89). After the birth of Conrad, the older of their two sons ('Kruitzer', 89), Frederick unsuccessfully tries to effect a reconciliation with his father. Instead, for a small allowance, the Count persuades him to let him adopt Conrad as his heir and raise him on the family estate. However, after the old count's death a distant relative of the Siegendorfs, Baron Stralenheim, attempts to claim the title, trying to have Conrad declared illegitimate ('Kruitzer', 131, 137). By chance, Frederick and Josephine meet both Stralenheim and Conrad at a small frontier town, where they have taken refuge from the war ('Kruitzer', 154, 179). Frederick uses this opportunity to steal Stralenheim's gold, hoping this will leave his enemy without the means to claim the title. Unknown to his parents, Conrad kills Stralenheim, and succeeds in convincing his parents that another stranger, only known as 'the Hungarian', is the murderer ('Kruitzer', 335–341). When Bohemia experiences a short period of peace Frederick returns to the Siegendorf estate, presents himself to the Bohemian Estates at Prague, where he is cheered 'like one arisen from the grave' ('Kruitzer', 274), and the family title is restored to him ('Kruitzer', 275). However, the family's happiness is destroyed by the arrival of the Hungarian, who discloses that Conrad

16 Harriet Lee, 'Preface', in Harriet and Sophia Lee, *The Canterbury Tales*, 2 vols (London: Henry Colburn and Richard Bentley, 1832), I, pp. v-vi.

is the killer of Stralenheim and a leader of a group of bandits, who have actually organised the cheering crowd and Frederick's welcome ('Kruitzer', 317–350). Preventing his arrest as a murderer, Conrad flees the estate and is soon killed by Austrian soldiers ('Kruitzer', 364–365), shortly before Frederick, sick and old before his years ('Kruitzer', 367), dies as well. It is left open whether Frederick's younger son Marcellin, still a small child, will succeed to the Siegendorf title.

With 'powerful features, a brow marked by sorrow', and eyes which, when 'kindled up by some sudden emotion, darted forward a fire that seemed like new-created light' ('Kruitzer', 13–14), Frederick foreshadows the Byronic hero, reflecting the impact Lee's novella was to have on the poet. However, in spite of his sensibility and intelligence, Lee's protagonist is pictured as a self-interested and self-pitying character, whose sense of superiority stands in sharp contrast to his personal limitations. Julie Shaffer has interpreted the Lees' *The Canterbury Tales* as an example of 'feminine Romanticism' – a community-oriented, evolutionary ideology opposed to 'masculine Romanticism' as the celebration of the exceptional individual.[17] Indeed, Frederick's moral decline during his time in the army is partly due to the corrupting influence of an all-male environment. Throughout the novella, his wife Josephine is represented as his counsellor, without whose balancing influence he repeatedly reverts to his former ways. However, Lee's interest here is not primarily in gender but in class differences and education. Stressing that an elite *habitus*[18] can easily hide personal failings, she poignantly has Josephine's father mistakenly attribute 'to the credit of nature [...] what was in fact the result of a highly cultivated education' ('Kruitzer', 81). In the same vein, Josephine herself, when she discovers her husband to be a disinherited aristocrat, is disappointed that rather than being 'a man gifted [...] beyond his fortunes', he has 'debased them' ('Kruitzer', 93–94). Characteristically, by contrast, Frederick himself fails to recognize his charisma as a result of his upbringing, believing instead his background has prevented him from realizing his true potential:

> [H]e had a loftiness of demeanour which seemed the expression of a noble soul. [...] [H]e was proud, not of his ancestors, but of himself. [...] The splendour, therefore, which the united efforts of education, fortune, rank, [...] threw around him, was early mistaken for a personal gift. [...] [A]s he believed, he was indebted to Nature, he resolved not to be accountable to man. [...] He never stopt to inquire what he could have made himself, had he been born any thing but what he was. ('Kruitzer', 59–61)

---

17 Julie Shaffer, 'Non-Canonical Women's Novels of the Romantic Era: Romantic Ideologies and the Problematics of Gender and Genre', *Studies in the Novel* 28 (1996) 469–492.

18 The term *habitus* is used in the sense established by Pierre Bourdieu. See Pierre Bourdieu, *Distinction: A Social Critique of the Judgement of Taste* (Cambridge MA: Harvard University Press, 1984).

An energetic, resourceful character quite different from his father, Frederick's son Conrad as a bandit captain acquires the reputation of someone 'super-human both as to strength and to beauty, [...] his influence [...] almost that of witchcraft.' ('Kruitzer', 329–330) However, as in Frederick's own case, his air of superiority is represented as a result of his social position. The Hungar-ian, when told about Conrad's fame, concludes that all this means is that 'he [is] rich' ('Kruitzer', 330), thus also hinting at the economic basis of an elite *habitus*. Conrad's image as a noble outlaw is completely destroyed when he is revealed a remorseless killer, who mockingly quotes Frederick's own excuse for his earlier theft: 'Remember *who* told me [...] that there were crimes ren-dered venial by the occasion: *who* painted the excesses of passion as the tres-passes of humanity: [...] is it so wonderful that *I* should dare to act what *you* dared to think?' ('Kruitzer', 354–355)

Significantly, Conrad's dynastic upbringing, deprived of female influence and the affections of his nuclear family, is employed to explain the lack of feelings that gives rise to his criminal career. Drawing on contemporary dis-courses on pedagogy, 'Kruitzner' is essentially a *Bildungsroman* about a failed elite education that is replicated in the subsequent generation, with disas-trous consequences. Like Jean-Jacques Rousseau's *Émile, ou sur l'Éducation* (1762), Stéphanie de Genlis's *Adèle et Théodore* (1782) or Johann Wolfgang Goethe's *Wilhelm Meisters Lehrjahre* (1795/96), Lee critiques an education that emphasizes fashionable accomplishments and pride in rank, arguing in-stead for the cultivation of inner qualities through learning and personal ex-periences.

Crucially, Lee also suggests that the notion of innate greatness is in itself class-bound and the 'loftiness of demeanour' of an apparently exceptional individual is merely a part of the *habitus* of a member of the social elite. Her critique of an inadequate elite education can be read as a political reflection on the legitimacy of aristocratic privilege. For her contemporary audience, however, her allusion to political radicalism would have been obvious by the novella's thematic parallels to Friedrich Schiller's *Die Räuber* (*The Robbers*, 1781), which, immensely popular in Britain throughout the 1790s and 1800s, was crucial in shaping the image of German literature.[19] While Lee rejects the idea of the 'noble outlaw', several plot elements in 'Kruitzner' draw on Schiller's play – a dynastic conflict, an estranged father, a disinher-ited heir, a wayward young aristocrat turned bandit captain, a war-torn country. By the time *The Canterbury Tales* were published, 'German' themes had already become a cliché, their association with 'Jacobin' tendencies well-established (see Barry Murnane's essay in this volume). Although reviews of 'Kruitzner' were largely favourable, *The Critical Review* dismissed it as 'con-

---

19 See Peter Mortensen, *British Romanticism and Continental Influences: Writing in an Age of Europhobia* (New York: Palgrave Macmillan, 2004), pp. 155–172.

structed on ideas which the modern German writers have so abundantly supplied', criticizing its 'gloomy, horrid, and unnatural picture'.[20] Labelling German or German-themed works as 'absurd' or 'unnatural' was a common strategy employed by anti-Jacobin writers, because the transcendence of class boundaries through sympathy displayed in many of them was perceived as politically subversive.[21]

The Thirty Years' War setting might equally be suggested by Schiller's writings. His recent *Wallenstein* trilogy on the imperial military commander was translated into English by Samuel Taylor Coleridge in 1800, when 'German themes' were at their height of popularity on the English stage.[22] A year earlier, William Blaquière published a very successful translation of Schiller's historiographical work on the period, *The History of the Thirty Years' War*.[23] The interest in this particular period of European history is by no means incidental. For the audience of the late 1790s and early 1800s, similarities between this turbulent epoch and the wars against Revolutionary and Napoleonic France were obvious, and the implicit association between Wallenstein himself and Napoleon meant that Thirty Years' War settings had a particular edge. Frederick's return to Prague, where he is cheered as a saviour symbolizing the return of feudal stability seems like a prophetic description of the coronation of Napoleon as Emperor of the French (1804), or the political Restoration in Europe at the Congress of Vienna (1814/15). For Lee's original readership, however, the association would have been with the return of French emigrants after the end of the Terror. Significantly, though, Frederick's position turns out to be based not on public acceptance, but on the criminal actions of Conrad's bandits, and his 'loyal' subjects are actually in his son's pay. The attempt at re-establishing pre-war order is represented as a chimera, or even a criminal act – a poignant comment against political restoration.

4.

Given the story's associations with 'Jacobin' radicalism, its adaptation by two members of the aristocratic political elite only a few months after its initial publication seems surprising at first sight. However, it is more than an inci-

---

20 *The Critical Review* 38 (1802) 331–332.
21 See e. g. Jane Moody, 'Suicide and Translation in the dramaturgy of Elizabeth Inchbald and Anne Plumptre', in *Women in British Romantic Theatre,* ed. by Catherine B. Burroughs (Cambridge: Cambridge University Press, 2000), pp. 257–284; Stephen Derry, 'Kotzebue Unbound: *Mansfield Park* and the 'Jacobinical'' *Trivium* 29–30 (1997) 257–263.
22 See e. g. Julie Carlson, *In the Theatre of Romanticism* (Cambridge: Cambridge University Press, 1994), pp. 63–93.
23 William Blaquière, *The History of the Thirty Years' War in Germany: Translated from the original German of Frederic Schiller*, 2 vols (London: Miller, 1799).

dental curiosity. For Devonshire in particular, like her other theatrical projects, the rewriting of Lee's novella is strongly informed by her political activities and agenda. Despite her presence in public life, the Duchess was so dis-
creet about her more ambitious literary productions that questions of
attribution have been major issues. In contrast to her two novels, her dramatic oeuvre is still virtually unknown. However, although none her plays were
ever performed in public, she had close connections to the theatrical world.
She was a patron of the playwright and politician Richard Brinsley Sheridan,
and of two of the most famous actresses of their times, Sarah Siddons and
Mary Robinson. The connection between her theatrical activities and her
Whig politics, central to her role as a patron, is particularly evident in an epilogue she wrote for the premiere of Joanna Baillie's tragedy *De Monfort* at
Drury Lane in April 1800. A day before the performance she announced to
her brother: 'I must now add a very nervous line, but I wish you to know the
confession from me: that I am guilty of having wrote the epilogue to 'de Montfort'
[sic] to be spoken by Mrs. Siddons tomorrow – I did not mean it should be
spoken but Mrs. Siddons has taken a liking to it – it is simple & that is all I can
say for it'.[24] Devonshire's shyness seems surprising, given her reputation as a
theatrical patron. The answer lies, perhaps, in the licentious image the theatre
still retained in the later eighteenth century. Actresses in particular, because of
their presence in a public space and their enacting of passions on stage, were
associated with 'unfeminine' conduct and sexual availability.[25] In the post-
Revolutionary era, acting itself was perceived as potentially subversive, both
politically and sexually, due to the opportunity it provided for experiments
with alternative identities, which suggested that social roles were in themselves flexible and unfixed.[26] Allusions to actresses were frequently invoked
in caricatures to chastise women who were perceived as crossing the boundaries of female domesticity.[27] Anxieties about her reputation probably also explain Devonshire's secrecy about her own plays and, although she made attempts to have them published,[28] why she ultimately decided against it. While
her theatrical activities were linked to her politics, had they been too open,

---

24 Letter from Georgiana, Duchess of Devonshire to her brother, the second Earl Spencer, 28
   April 1800, Althorp MSS (unfolded papers and correspondence of the Spencer family, British
   Library), G287; a shorter passage quoted in Foreman, *Georgiana*, 331.
25 See Laura J. Rosenthal, 'Entertaining women: the actress in eighteenth-century theatre and
   culture', in *The Cambridge Companion to British Theatre 1730- 1830*, ed. by Jane Moody and Daniel
   O'Quinn (Cambridge: Cambridge University Press, 2007), pp. 159–173.
26 Gillian Russell, 'Private Theatricals', in *Cambridge Companion to British Theatre*, pp. 191–203,
   200–203; Penny Gay, *Jane Austen and the Theatre* (Cambridge: Cambridge University Press,
   2002), p. 103.
27 Betsy Bolton, *Women, Nationalism, and the Romantic Stage* (Cambridge: Cambridge University
   Press, 2001), p. 38.
28 Devonshire to her mother, 1 September 1802, Chatsworth MSS, 5th Duke group, 1645.

they might have endangered her respectability as 'the Doyenne of the Whig Party'.[29]

Although the Duchess describes the epilogue as 'simple', the context of its performance suggests a very different interpretation. Both Devonshire's epilogue and the play's prologue, written by Francis North (1761–1817), are, in Gillian Russell's terminology, 'zones of mediation' between the audience, the performance, and the larger cultural and political context.[30] Transporting the viewers into the world of the play and back, such paratexts, often supplied by patrons, aimed to direct the audience's response to a performance. Devonshire and North, himself the author of a Gothic drama, *The Kentish Barons* (1791), and a member of an influential Whig family, were carefully selected collaborators, chosen by Baillie (who may have used Devonshire's protégée Siddons as a mediator) both for their contacts within the theatrical world and the political elite.

De Monfort tells the story of a haughty German aristocrat, whose near-pathological hatred leads him to murder his enemy Rezenfeldt, before he is himself killed by his own remorse and sense of guilt.[31] Set in early modern Germany, but calling its title character by the name of the famous 13th-century Anglo-Norman noble Simon de Montfort, the play can be interpreted as a portrait of an arrogant, self-destructive aristocracy incapable of reform. Baillie, who would later deny any influence of German plays on *De Monfort*,[32] strove to distance its first stage production from associations with 'German drama' and its supposed 'immorality' and 'Jacobinism'. North's and Devonshire's contributions are part of a strategy to promote Baillie as a female playwright and render *De Monfort* acceptable despite its politically charged theme and setting. The stage version differs from the original tragedy, published in 1798 before the height of 'anti-Jacobin' paranoia, in some significant details, the changes reflecting the play's anti-radical revision. In particular, de Monfort's fight with his enemy and his subsequent disarmament and disgrace are omitted.[33] Aware that a physical performance would enhance the poignancy of her aristocratic protagonist's public humiliation, Baillie avoids the political resonances such a scene would invoke. Crucially, North and Devonshire equally repudiate any radical and 'foreign' associations, emphasising instead the tragedy's 'British' quality. The prologue

---

29 Foreman, *Georgiana*, 362.

30 Russell, 'Private Theatricals', 197.

31 Joanna Baillie, *De Monfort*, in *Seven Gothic Dramas, 1789–1825*, ed. by Jeffrey N. Cox (Athens, Ohio: Ohio University Press, 1992), pp. 231–314. The prologue and epilogue are reprinted on pp. 233–234 and 313–314 respectively.

32 Catherine B. Burroughs, *Closet Stages: Joanna Baillie and the Theater Theory of British Romantic Women* (Philadelphia: University of Pennsylvania Press, 1997), p. 204, n. 10.

33 See Jeffrey N. Cox, 'Staging Baillie', in *Joanna Baillie, Romantic Dramatist*, ed. by Thomas C. Crochunis (London: Routledge, 2004), pp. 146–167, 158–159.

mourns the prominence of foreign 'Romance' (l. 2), stressing the superiority of native plays in a militant tone: 'O, Shame! – Why borrow from a foreign store/ As if the rich should pilfer from the poor. –/ We who have forc'd th' astonish'd world to yield; Led by immortal Shakspeare [sic] to the Field' (l. 5–8). After a list of English playwrights who 'boast eternal Fame', the first performance of *De Monfort* is celebrated as 'this auspicious day/ The British Drama reassumes her sway' (ll. 15–16).

Compared with North's straightforward claims, Devonshire's epilogue is subtler, and arguably more effective. Spoken by Siddons, it marks the transition from the world of the tragedy back to the audience's reality. During the first four lines she is still speaking as the character of the female main part, de Montfort's sister Jane de Monfort, who asks for sympathy for her 'sister's love' (l. 4). The following lines, in which the persona of Jane is left behind, emphasise the contrast between British civilization and the world depicted in the play: 'Dire is the passion that our scenes unfold/ And foreign to each heart of British mould/ For Britons Sons their generous code maintain/ Prompt to defend & slow in giving pain.' (l. 5–8). The epilogue expresses the hope that the play will 'wake the judgement & [...] calm the breast' and appeal to the audience's own civic virtues of 'Love & Kindness' (l. 40), friendship and temperance. The conclusion stresses the distance between the world of the tragedy and English domestic happiness: 'Thus let us bid the scene's dread horror cease / And hail the blessing of domestic peace' (ll. 45–46).

According to the epilogue, the play is meant to fulfil a cathartic function, cleanse the viewers from their own potentially dangerous passions and appeal to their sense of citizenship. Indeed, Devonshire here seems to emulate the Aristotelian concept of *katharsis* in classical Athenian theatre, a process 'effecting through pity and fear the purification of such emotions'.[34] However, the *katharsis* she invokes is a purge of 'foreign' passions and, by implication, political radicalism. Rather than rejecting 'German drama' in its entirety, her concept employs the passions expressed in it to cleanse her audience from such sentiments. With her epilogue in particular, the stage version of *De Monfort* becomes a decidedly anti-Jacobin rewriting of a play that, while not explicitly 'radical', might have been perceived as such in the politically heated atmosphere of 1800.

---

34 Aristotle, *Poetics*, 4.1 (section 1449b), in *Poetics. Translated with an Introduction and Notes by Malcolm Heath* (London: Penguin Classics, 1996), p. 10.

5.

Devonshire's involvement with *De Monfort* may well have inspired her own return to dramatic writing. Crucially, it introduced her to Joanna Baillie's concept of a drama of the 'closet', sketched in the famous 'Introductory Discourse' to the first volume of her *Plays on the Passions* (1798), which describes a genre not primarily interested in spectacle and action, but in the exploration of 'passions which conceal themselves from the observation of men' through the representation of scenes 'from a character's closet'.[35] A central element in Baillies's theory is the lack of an opposition between the 'closet' and the 'stage'. Focusing on a drama *about*, but by no means exclusively *for*, the 'closet', she is in no way opposed to theatrical performance.[36] However, she defines dramatic texts as *literary* works, to be measured by their conceptual and formal qualities, not by stage success, and indeed independent from physical performance. By implication, the position of the Baillean playwright is thus closer to the traditionally highly respectable role of the poet rather than that of the artisan – an attractive concept for Devonshire as a member of the social elite, for whom commercial writing was not socially acceptable.[37] Although never publicly performed (and probably not intended to be), *The Hungarian* would be perfectly stageable. Despite its focus on its characters' inner life, it has detailed stage directions, suggesting a lavish spectacle that could be staged physically, but equally in the reader's mind.

In July 1800, Bessborough wrote to Leveson-Gower about her experience of reading Schiller, whose *Wallenstein* and *History of the Thirty Years' War* apparently sparked the sisters' interest in the period: 'I have finished Schiller's 30 years' war [sic], which I like very much, and I am in love with Gustavus Adolphus. The plays of Wallenstein, which he wrote after his history, have ridiculous things in them like all German plays, but there are some very pretty also [sic] ...'[38] Like 'unnatural', 'ridiculous' was a term frequently applied to plays with 'Jacobin' associations, particularly if they were set in Germany. Bessborough's own reaction to *Wallenstein*, with its simultaneous expression of fascination with and repudiation of the plays' political connotations, illustrates what was at stake for elite readers in such works, as well as the desire to domesticate them. *The Hungarian* appropriates Lee's novella,

---

35 Joanna Baillie, 'Introductory Discourse' in Joanna Baillie, *Plays on the Passions* (1798 edition), ed. by Peter Duthie (Toronto: Broadview Press, 2001), pp. 67–113, 86.

36 Misty G. Anderson, 'Women playwrights', in *Cambridge Companion to British Theatre*, pp. 145–158, 155.

37 The publication of poetry under the author's name was acceptable for elite women. See Paula R. Feldman, 'Women Poets and Anonymity in the Romantic Era', in *Authorship, Commerce and the Public*, ed. by Emma J. Clery, Caroline Franklin, Peter Garside (Houndmills, Basingstoke: Palgrave Macmillan, 2002), pp. 44–53.

38 Bessborough to Granville Leveson Gower, 29 July 1800, in Leveson Gower, *Private Correspondence*, I, p. 281.

published only a year earlier, in exactly such a way by transforming its radical discourse into one of reform in accordance with Devonshire's Whig politics. A revisionist take on a 'Jacobin' text, it can be compared to more prominent rewritings such as the Drury Lane production of *De Monfort* discussed above, or an adaptation of *Die Räuber* by Elizabeth Craven, Margravine of Anspach, lavishly staged at her private theatre at Brandenburgh House (1799).[39] Additionally, if *The Hungarian* was indeed produced as a private theatrical, there would have been a significant analogy between the text's revisionist dimension and the context of its performance. The rejection of a public staging in favour of a private spectacle – a decidedly aristocratic form of entertainment – would have mirrored the appropriative domestication of political radicalism on the textual level.

Unsurprisingly, in *The Hungarian,* the anti-aristocratic sentiments in 'Kruitzner' are omitted. Instead, Devonshire updates the political allusions of the story's Thirty Years' War setting, implicitly referring to current affairs such as the Act of Union with Ireland (1800) and the Peace of Amiens (1802), which she also mentioned in the journal she kept at the time.[40] As only the last part of Lee's novella is dramatized, the entire action takes place after the Peace of Westphalia (1648), thus reflecting the play's focus on reconciliation. The main female character in Lee's novella, called 'Josephine' like Napoleon's wife, is renamed 'Leonora'. Alluding to the eponymous 1796 translation of Gottfried Bürger's ballad *Lenore*,[41] the name is suggestive of the 'Gothic', the sensationalist qualities of German literature, while avoiding obvious Napoleonic allusions. Mirroring Devonshire's own role as an advisor of political leaders, the adaptation turns Frederick into a high-ranking official, the Governor of post-war Prague, and significantly enhances the role of his wife. Throughout the play Leonora acts as his counsellor, often interacting with other nobles and officials in his place. Much of the action is set in public spaces, in the Governor's palace and during a ceremony celebrating the end of civil conflict. Frederick, whose transgressions are only narrated in retrospect, is transformed from an irresponsible to a sympathetic character, a man more sinned against than sinning. His bandit son Conrad becomes a clear-cut, self-proclaimed villain in the mould of Shakespeare's Richard III or Franz Moor from Schiller's *Die Räuber,* leaving aside both the subtleties of Lee's creation and any proto-sociological explanations. Instead, Devonshire adds two characters, Emma, daughter of Frederick's enemy Count Unna (equivalent of Lee's Stralenheim), and her be-

39 Moody, 'Suicide and Translation', 266.
40 Chatsworth MSS, V. 1611 C. For the reception of the Peace of Amiens see J. R. Watson, *Romanticism and War* (Houndmills, Basingstoke: Palgrave, 2003), pp. 84–95.
41 John Thomas Stanley, *Leonora, A Tale. Translated freely from the German of Gottfried August Bürger* (London: Miller, 1796). See also Mortensen, *British Romanticism*, 47–56.

trothed Herman, a kinsman of the Siegendorfs.[42] United at the end of the play, the couple embodies her ideal sensible heroine and hero.

Promoting an education in sympathy and politeness, *The Hungarian* assigns to women the task of teaching men to combine military with civilian virtues to 'blend/ Urbanity with courage'.[43] The 'sensible' Herman, brought up by Leonora, is courageous and willing to fight, but relieved that '[t]he wounds of thirty bloody years will close' (p. 22). In contrast, Conrad's villainy is evident in his rejection of female 'softer cares' in favour of 'military fame'. In a monologue echoing the opening speech of *Richard III* (I, 1, ll. 1–41), to which Franz Moor's self-nominating soliloquies are also indebted,[44] Conrad expresses his wish that the war may continue:

> Conrad [*alone*]:
> Peace! I disclaim thee, for thy reign returns […]
> Yet brings to me nor ease nor occupation.
> Peace may be cherish'd by the innocent
> […] but I crave
> Perpetual warfare strife and agitation […]
> […] There was a time when I had thought it likely
> That war with softer cares might be united –
> Down! down with retrospection […]
> For military fame alone dispenses
> Impunity to all – and yet I'd scorn
> To sell my life at some weak sovereign's nod.
> No! I'd command like Wallenstein and be
> Myself the fate of Empires and of Kings […], (*Hungarian* 23–24)

In Lee a local bandit captain, Conrad is here transformed into a warlord intent on emulating Wallenstein, his large-scale ambitions perhaps mirroring the authors' own position within the political elite. More importantly, in the context of the play, they pose a threat to the recent Peace of Westphalia. In analogy (and allusion) to the Peace of Amiens, the latter is thus presented as potentially unstable – a reflection of contemporary anxieties about Napoleon's ambitions and the fragility of the Treaty.

More than in Lee, the representation of Conrad illustrates an ambiguous approach towards the play's Ricardian villain-hero, which combines rejection with fascination. Like Bessborough's comments on Schiller, the adaptation displays both a pronounced interest in 'German' plays, and a desire to

---

42 Both names are from the anonymous translation of Benedikte Naubert's historical novel *Herman of Unna* (London: Robinson, 1794). Additionally, Herman's name may allude to Arminius, the German-born Roman officer whose betrayal of the Romans and victory over three legions in 9 AD made him famous as the 'liberator of Germania' (Tacitus), and who was rediscovered as a national German hero in the seventeenth century. The name characterizes Devonshire's Herman as a heroic defender of liberty rather than an aggressor.

43 Quotations taken from the transcript, cf. note 5, p. 41.

44 See particularly Franz's closing soliloquy in I, 1, which is also inspired by the villainous Edmund's monologues in Shakespeare's *King Lear* (I, 2, ll. 1–22).

'tame' them. The concluding lines, spoken by Herman, show the same ambivalence. Expressing the hope that Frederick's younger son, here named
Casimir, will learn a moral lesson from Frederick's and Conrad's failings,
they still attribute 'greatness' to both Siegendorfs, implicitly subverting the
play's argument for 'virtue' and moderation:

> [...] Bear witness Lords to noble Siegendorf's
> Expiring sentiments and manly virtue
> On Conrad's errors and his father's grief
> We'll draw a veil respectful – but we'll bear
> Due testimony to their parting greatness;
> And my young Casimir from their example
> Shall learn that virtue leads alone to honor. (*Hungarian*, 154)

The invocation of 'greatness', a concept implicitly repudiated by Lee, also reflects the play's revisionist politics. Although subtitled a 'tragedy', *The Hungarian* closes on a note of reconciliation, with the reference to Casimir (equivalent of Lee's Marcellin) emphasizing dynastic continuity. More importantly,
Devonshire, who translated three plays by the Italian librettist Metastasio
(1698–1782),[45] employs a device typical of his *opera seria* libretti: the introduction of a couple of young lovers, whose marriage provides the drama with an
optimistic ending – a *lieto fine*.[46] Sealing the peace between two aristocratic
houses, the union between Herman and Emma represents a renewal of traditional order mirroring the restoration after the Peace of Westphalia on a
smaller scale.

Showing a formerly warlike society turning into one based on 'urbanity'
and 'social feelings' (p. 42) after a long domestic conflict, *The Hungarian* can
be read as an appeal for future peace. Like Devonshire's *De Monfort* epilogue, which makes a similar statement, it is an example of the political appropriation of 'German drama', which illustrates the interaction between
the Duchess's literary and political activities. At the same time, the adaptation reflects her engagement with educational literature. Proclaiming a pedagogical purpose, implicitly assuming the position of a mother figure, was a
popular strategy for women to justify their literary ambitions. While she finally decided against publishing them, with her plays Devonshire attempted
to combine her role as a political advisor with that of a playwright without
offending the social codes of her class.

Despite the authors' very different political affiliations, there are striking
similarities between *The Hungarian* and Lee's 'Kruitzner'. Both works exemplify the ways in which the representation of the aristocrat as a literary character, especially in a 'German' setting, was charged with political connotations. In both, the attitude towards their aristocratic villain-heroes oscillates

---

45 Huntington Library, MS K-D 571.
46 See Patrick J. Smith, *Tenth Muse: A Historical Study of the Opera Libretto* (New York: Knopf,
    1970), pp. 8, 78.

between rejection and fascination, albeit for different political reasons. Both display a general sympathy for exiles and victims of war. Both advocate an education of sensibility, casting women in a crucial role as educators. Yet, far from propagating a common 'feminine' ideology, both works are deeply affected by their authors' respective social positions, and express an awareness of the inter-connections between the issues of gender, social position and politics. This short case study has shown how women writers used historical fiction to comment on current events and participate in contemporary debates. It illustrates the dynamics between private elite theatricals and the public domains of politics, the theatre and printed literature, and the ambiguities inherent in revisionist engagement with potentially 'radical' texts and in cross-cultural appropriation.

From Sentiment to Sexuality
English Werther-Stories, the French Revolution, and German Vampires

Susanne Kord

Goethe's novel *Die Leiden des jungen Werther* (1774) was not only a best-seller at home, but also reached a large audience abroad. In 1792 it even became the first work of German prose fiction ever to be published on the Indian sub-continent. Throughout Europe, literally hundreds of *Werther*-translations, imitations, adaptations, and parodies appeared over the next century, several of them in England during the 1790s.[1]

Both German and French ideas, 'erzählte Zeit' and 'Erzählzeit', figure prominently in these works, and their two main themes, German sentimentality and the French Revolution,[2] are also the subjects that fuelled the con-

---

1 For *Werther*'s reception history and *Werther*-inspired literature, cf. Stuart Atkins, *The Testament of Werther in Poetry and Drama* (Cambridge, Mass.: Harvard University Press, 1949); Ingeborg Bik-kelmann,'Goethe's *Werther* im Urteil des 19. Jahrhunderts: Romantik bis Naturalismus 1830–1180.' Doctoral thesis, University of Frankfurt/Main, 1937; Klaus Scherpe, *Werther und Wertherwirkung: Zum Syndrom bürgerlicher Gesellschaftsordnung im 18. Jahrhundert* (Bad Homburg: Athenäum, 1970); Ingrid Engel, *Werther und die Wertheriaden: Ein Beitrag zur Wirkungsgeschichte* (St. Ingbert: Röhrig, 1986); Ariane Martin, *Die kranke Jugend: J. M. R. Lenz und Goethes Werther in der Rezeption des Sturm und Drang bis zum Naturalismus* (Würzburg: Königshausen und Neumann, 2002); Bruce Duncan, *Goethe's Werther and the Critics* (Rochester: Camden House, 2005); Robyn L. Schiffman, '*Werther* and the epistolary novel' *European Romantic Review* 19.4 (2008) 421–438. A chronological bibliography of English editions of Goethe's works and their influence on English literature is provided by Jean Marie Carré in *Goethe en Angleterre: Étude de literature comparée. Bibliographie de Goethe en Angleterre* (Paris: Plon-Nourrit, 1920).

2 Whereas British responses to the events in France tended to be critical from the outset, there seem to have been two phases in Germany, the Age of Innocence until 1793, encapsulated by the watchwords *Freiheit, Gleichheit, Brüderlichkeit*, and the subsequent revulsion at the beheading of Louis XVI and the onset of the *Terreur*, deftly summed up in Schiller's 'Da werden Weiber zu Hyänen' in 'Das Lied von der Glocke' (*Werke in drei Bänden*, 3 vols, ed. by Herbert G. Göpfert and Gerhard Fricke (Munich: Hanser, 1984), II, pp. 810–821, 819). On German and British responses to the French Revolution, see Thomas P. Saine, *Black Bread, White Bread: German Intellectuals and the French Revolution* (Columbia, S.C.: Camden House, 1988); Matthew Orville Grenby, *The Anti-Jacobin Novel: British Conservatism and the French Revolution* (Cambridge: Cambridge University Press, 2001); Amanda Goodrich, *Debating England's Aristocracy in the 1790s: Pamphlets, Polemic, and Political Ideas* (Woodbridge, NY: Boydell Press, 2005); Thomas Philip Schofield, 'English Conservative Thought and Opinion in Response to the French Revolution 1789–1796.' PhD thesis, University College London, 1984; Lisa Plummer Crafton,

temporary gender debate. In Germany, Goethe's novel and its ideas on sentiment and reason, masculine compulsion and feminine virtue fell on fertile ground partly because of the huge success of Sophie von La Roche's *Geschichte des Fräuleins von Sternheim* (1771), which was already the focal point of a nationwide debate of the role of women in the family, education, and society when *Werther* appeared in 1774[3] and is still considered one of the foundational texts of German Sentimentality.[4]

Gender also played a major role in appraisals of the French Revolution. In the years immediately preceding the *Terreur*, three major authors in three different countries assessed the consequences of (male) liberté, egalité and fraternité for women: Theodor Gottlieb von Hippel in his *Über die bürgerliche Verbesserung der Weiber* (1792), Olympe de Gouges in her *Déclaration des droits de la femme et de la citoyenne* (1791), and Mary Wollstonecraft in her *Vindication of the Rights of Woman* (1792).[5] To demand that the Rights of Man be extended to women was no uncontroversial affair: Hippel and Wollstonecraft were vilified for their texts; de Gouges was beheaded for hers. All three respond to the same phenomenon – men's aspirations to full citizenship – and flag up the same problem, the exclusion of women from these aspirations. Wollstonecraft's argumentation, however, is rather distinct from Hip-

---

ed., *The French Revolution Debate in English Literature and Culture* (Westport, CT: Greenwood Press, 1997); Clive Emsley, *Britain and the French Revolution* (Harlow: Longman, 2000).

3   On La Roche and her novel, cf. Anja May, *Wilhelm Meisters Schwestern: Bildungsromane von Frauen im ausgehenden 18. Jahrhundert* (Königstein/Ts.: Helmer, 2006); Michaela Krug, *Auf der Suche nach dem eigenen Raum: Topographien des Weiblichen im Roman von Autorinnen um 1800* (Würzburg: Königshausen and Neumann, 2004); Thomas Pago, *Der empfindsame Roman der Aufklärung: Christian Fürchtegott Gellerts 'Leben der schwedischen Gräfin von G**** und Sophie von La Roches 'Geschichte des Fräuleins von Sternheim.' Eine vergleichende Untersuchung* (Munich: Meidenbauer, 2003); Hans-Joachim Maier, *Zwischen Bestimmung und Autonomie: Erziehung, Bildung und Liebe im Frauenroman des 18. Jahrhunderts* (Hildesheim: Olms-Weidmann, 2001).

4   Cf. Gerhard Sauder, *Theorie der Empfindsamkeit und des Sturm und Drang* (Stuttgart: Reclam, 2003). On the different forms of 'sentiment,' gender ideas of the period, and the scholarly view of the *Sturm und Drang* as a 'masculine' movement, see Susanne Kord, 'Discursive Dissociations: Women Playwrights as Observers of the Sturm und Drang', in *Literature of the Sturm und Drang*, ed. by David Hill (Rochester: Camden House, 2002), pp. 241–273; Irmgard Roebling, 'Sturm und Drang–weiblich: Eine Untersuchung zu Sophie Albrechts Schauspiel *Theresgen*' *Der Deutschunterricht* 1 (1996) 63–77.

5   On these texts and their political context, cf. Hamilton H. H. Beck, 'Hippel and the Eighteenth-Century Novel.' Doctoral thesis, Cornell University, 1980; Lesley Sharpe, 'Theodor Gottlieb von Hippel – argumentative strategies in the debate on the rights of women', in *Shifting the Boundaries: Transformation of the Languages of Public and Private in the Eighteenth Century*, ed. by Dario Castiglione and Lesley Sharpe (Exeter: University of Exeter Press, 1995), pp. 89–104; Joan Wallach Scott, *Only Paradoxes on Offer: French Feminists and the Rights of Man* (Cambridge, Mass: Harvard University Press, 1996); Sara E. Melzer and Leslie W. Rabine, eds, *Rebel Daughters: Women and the French Revolution* (New York: Oxford University Press, 1992); Claudia L. Johnson, *Equivocal Beings: Politics, Gender and Sentimentality in the 1790s: Wollstonecraft, Radcliffe, Burney, Austen* (Chicago: University of Chicago Press, 1995); Barbara Taylor, *Mary Wollstonecraft and the Feminist Imagination* (Cambridge: Cambridge University Press, 2003); Gary Kelly, *Revolutionary Feminism: Mind and Career of Mary Wollstonecraft* (London: Macmillan, 1996).

pel's or de Gouges'. Unlike de Gouges, who castigated male supremacy as a 'tyrannical empire' unprecedented in nature and divine creation,[6] and unlike Hippel, who compared women's oppression with slavery and defined men as slave-drivers,[7] Wollstonecraft places the blame for women's degradation, to a considerable degree, on women. She attributes it to women's excessive sentimentality, which she defines as simultaneously universally presumed, coercively produced in the process of women's education, and – this is the aspect that shall interest us here – modelled in sentimental literature.[8] Compared to that advanced by Hippel and de Gouges, Wollstonecraft's argument is astonishingly modern; it could easily be viewed as a precursor of the *Mittäterschaft*-model developed nearly 200 years later by Christina Thürmer-Rohr, which casts men as the perpetrators of oppression and women as their collaborators rather than merely their victims.[9]

Wollstonecraft's basic assumption is that the needs of the state are the same as the needs of the home. Both require rational inhabitants. Therefore, romantic love is dangerous to both. Her version of married bliss involves, first and foremost, the overcoming of sexual passion through that self-denial without which, Wollstonecraft claims, neither elevated emotions (love) nor elevated thoughts (reason) can exist. Husband and wife, having overcome their sexual appetites, are 'sufficient unto each other,'[10] both engaged in the great enterprise of family and society. To Wollstonecraft, there was a direct and irresolvable opposition between love, the emotion a woman inspires, and respect, the attitude a man inspires and also the attitude in which humans recognize the humanity of others:

> Love, in their [women's] bosoms, taking the place of every nobler passion, their sole ambition is to be fair, to raise emotion instead of inspiring respect; and this ignoble desire, like the servility in absolute monarchies, destroys all strength of character.

---

6   Olympe de Gouges, 'Les droits de la femme. A la Reine', in *Écrits Politiques* (Paris: côté-femmes éditions, 1993), pp. 204–215, 205–206: 'qui t'a donné le souverain empire d'opprimer mon sexe? ta force? tes talents? Observe le créateur dans sa sagesse; parcours la nature dans toute sa grandeur, dont tu sembles vouloir te rapprocher, et donne-moi, si tu l'oses, l'exemple de cet empire tyrannique.' 'Tell me, what gives you sovereign empire to oppress my sex? Your strength? Your talents? Observe the Creator in his wisdom; survey in all her grandeur that nature with whom you seem to want to be in harmony, and give me, if you dare, an example of this tyrannical empire.' (My own translation.)

7   Theodor Gottlieb von Hippel, *Über die bürgerliche Verbesserung der Weiber* (Berlin: bei G. Reimer, 1828), pp. 50–53.

8   On Wollstonecraft's campaign against sentimentality, cf. particularly Sydney McMillan Conger, *Mary Wollstonecraft and the Language of Sensibility* (Rutherford, N. J.: Fairleigh Dickinson University Press, 1994). An excellent introduction to the concept and its context is Janet Todd's *Sensibility: An Introduction* (London, New York: Methuen, 1986).

9   See Christina Thürmer-Rohr, Martina Emme, and Carola Wildt, *Mittäterschaft und Entdeckungslust*, 2nd edn (Berlin: Orlanda Frauenverlag, 1990).

10 Miriam Brody, 'Mary Wollstonecraft: Sexuality and Women's Rights', in *Feminist Theorists: Three Centuries of Women's Intellectual Traditions,* ed. by Dale Spender (London: The Women's Press, 1996), pp. 40–59, 46.

[…] Fragile in every sense of the word, they are obliged to look up to man for every comfort. In the most trifling dangers they cling to their support, with parasitical tenacity, piteously demanding succour; and their *natural* protector extends his arm, or lifts up his voice, to guard the lovely trembler–from what? Perhaps the frown of an old cow, or the jump of a mouse; a rat, would be a serious danger. In the name of reason, and even common sense, what can save such beings from contempt; even though they be soft and fair? Those fears, when not affected, may produce some pretty attitude; but they shew a degree of imbecility which degrades a rational creature in a way women are not aware of–for love and esteem are very distinct things.[11]

Wollstonecraft's word choice clearly encourages readers to understand this in both political and literary terms. She likens women's desire to inspire love to the subservience expected of the subject of an absolute monarch, which negatively implies the free citizen just as the simpering imbecile implies the intelligent, independent and self-sufficient woman she might be. Simultaneously, the fragile, servile female of this passage is obviously and profoundly indebted to the heroine of virtually every sentimental novel written in Wollstonecraft's century. Wollstonecraft presumed that such novels were predominantly read by women, who, 'unable to grasp any thing great, are necessarily dependent on the novelist for amusement. […] In fact the female mind has been so totally neglected, that knowledge was only to be acquired from this muddy source' (*Vindication*, 184–185). Wollstonecraft diagnoses a vicious cycle composed of societal prejudice, its expression in sentimental novels, and its assimilation and internalization by the female reader whose deliberately induced ignorance prevents her from seeking alternatives. In this way, Wollstonecraft claims, women are not respected, but 'deluded by hollow respect, till they are led to resign, or not assume, their natural prerogatives' (*Vindication*, 55–56).[12]

English *Werther*-literature of the 1790s, the decade of Wollstonecraft's text, seems to me to provide the ideal test cases for some of her theories. For one thing, these texts assume an added layer of meaning – as *Vindication* also does – when read in the context of the French Revolution. Secondly, many of them comment – as Wollstonecraft also did – on *Sturm-und-Drang*-type sentiment, with clearly outlined sub-topics, such as desperately unrequited love, literary sensibilities, and suicide. And finally, many of them adopt, as Wollstonecraft also did, a female perspective, by transferring either

---

11 Mary Wollstonecraft, *A Vindication of the Rights of Woman*, ed. by Carol H. Poston, 2nd edn (New York, London: W. W. Norton, 1988), pp. 37, 62.

12 Wollstonecraft was obviously not alone in arguing the dangers of sentimentality to individuals and society. But in her writing, the old hierarchy of reason over passion is employed in a new cause, that of women. Unlike other early feminist writers, her approach was not to take women out of the home. Rather, she moved the home, and the women in it, into the public sphere by aligning domestic concerns with those of the State (idea and interpretation in Brody, 'Mary Wollstonecraft'; see particularly her description of Wollstonecraft's idea of blending childcare with remunerated work on p. 52).

the story's thematic focus or narrative authority from Werther to Char-lotte.[13] Some examples of many are Sarah Farrell's gothic poem *Charlotte, or a Sequel to the Sorrows of Werter* (1792), Anne Francis's *Charlotte to Werter: A Poetical Epistle* (1790), Pierre Perrin's *The Female Werter, a novel* (1792), and William James's *Letters of Charlotte during her connexion with Werter* (1786, translated in the 1790s into both French and German).[14] Of these texts, several questions might be asked, inspired partly by their intertextual link with Goethe's novel and partly by the political and philosophical context in which they were written. For example: are these texts 'political', either in a direct sense – as commentaries on the French Revolution and the concomitant discussion of women's rights – or in Wollstonecraft's sense, as literary models for women's compulsory sentimentality which disqualifies them from full citizenship? Do they assign a new meaning to sentimental death: in the context of the suicide debate surrounding Goethe's novel; in the context of the French Revolution, during which the laws against suicide were relaxed in both Germany and France;[15] or in view of the fact that the main hero and narrative voice of these texts is now female rather than male? Which aesthetic or political consequences emerge in either English or German literary texts that follow Wollstonecraft's lead in linking female 'sentiment' and female sexuality?

Sentiment and Suicide: The Failure of Reason

Perhaps unsurprisingly, Werther's suicide for love emerges as one of the most prominent topics of *Werther*-adaptations. The anonymously published *Werter and Charlotte, A German Story, Containing Many Wonderful and Pathetic Incidents* (1790) makes some significant changes to Goethe's original. In this version, Albert, a soldier, is cast as an ardent, rather Werther-like lover, whose unmitigated passion has finally won the hand of the long-resisting Charlotte. Shortly after their marriage, Albert goes off to war again, and this is, predictably, when dashingly handsome Werter enters the scene. The narrative contains extensive descriptions of Werter's physical charms, and the love story – in which Charlotte is just as besotted with Werter as he is with her – proceeds apace, with ardent sighs, passionate declarations, secret meetings and numerous readings of highly sentimental poetry. The affair both culminates and terminates when Charlotte confesses to Werter that she is already married, after which both swoon dead away. Werter expressly asks Charlotte for permission

13 See Robert Withington, 'The Letters of Charlotte. An Antidote to *Die Leiden des Jungen Werthers*', *PMLA* 27.1 (1912) 26–46.
14 Many of these sources are discussed in Orie William Long, 'English and American Imitations of Goethe's *Werther*', *Modern Philology* 14.4 (1916) 193–216.
15 Georges Minois, *History of Suicide: Voluntary Death in Western Culture* (Baltimore: Johns Hopkins University Press, 1999), chapter 9.

to commit suicide: 'Give me but your leave, and I am gone directly,' in a note which he signs 'Distracted Werter.'[16] Post-suicide, most of the remaining narrative is taken up with Charlotte's lengthy announcements that she will soon join her dead lover, upon which she dies of consumption and is buried at his side.

While neither Werter's suicide nor Charlotte's adultery are explicitly judged in the text, the subject of sentiment emerges as one of the plot's main motivators, and it is Charlotte's sentiments, not Werter's, on which the text focuses. Charlotte, not Werter, is the sentimental and tragic heroine of the text, in her three intertwined roles as abandoned child, unhappy wife, and star-crossed lover. Passages foreshadowing the tragic ending inevitably emphasize one of these three roles: 'Poor Charlotte! the days of thy happiness are but few; sorrow and everlasting anguish will soon ensue. Mistaken Albert, thine is the enjoyment of the body, but her soul is indifferent to thee' (*Werter and Charlotte*, 15). The narrative opens with an extensive emotional scene showing us Charlotte at the bedside of her dying mother, uttering wild cries of distress and begging her mother not to desert her. '"My dear parent," cried the amiable maid, "leave me not in this affliction. Alas! I am not capable in this great charge..."' (*Werter and Charlotte*, 5). This continues for several pages, during which the mother, although dying, also finds sufficient breath for lengthy admonitions, benedictions and prayers before she finally 'sunk upon her pillow' and Charlotte, 'the afflicted fair,' emits her ultimate wail of despair: 'She is gone!' (*Werter and Charlotte*, 5–6).

Given that the text goes to such lengths to define Charlotte initially as a motherless child and subsequently as a helpless sentimental girl driven into an unhappy marriage by her own inability to cope with either her bereavement or Albert's passion, it is unreasonable to presume that she could withstand a third catastrophe. The text thus sets up Werter as responsible for Charlotte's death, because his suicide – in this text, a preventable act – furnishes this final catastrophe that leads to her demise. That Werter explicitly asks her permission for his suicide seems to acknowledge this responsibility. In pointing to Charlotte's lack of choices, Werter's choice is indirectly judged. Charlotte's death of consumption is as characteristic of the sentimental heroine as suicide is of the ardent and desperate lover. She does not act but is acted upon; she is abandoned by her mother, married by Albert, and finally killed by Werter.

In William James's *The Letters of Charlotte, during her Connexion with Werter* (2nd edn 1797), Charlotte is an entirely different character. In letters to her English friend Carolina, Charlotte describes her acquaintance with and the death of Werter. Since the novel follows Goethe's plot rather precisely, the

---

16 *Werter and Charlotte, A German Story, Containing Many Wonderful and Pathetic Incidents* (London: T. Sabine, [1790]), p. 24.

few changes stand out all the more. The text retains the original's description of the first meeting between the lovers, the dance, the thunderstorm ('Klopstock!'), Werter's unhappiness at court, the extensive reading of Ossian at their last private meeting, and their final encounter during which Charlotte, although filled with foreboding, gives Werter the pistols. One of the most significant omissions is the suicide debate between Albert and Werther, here replaced with a lengthy and rather less controversial discussion of the respective merits of Homer and Ossian. Among the most significant additions are Charlotte's frequent, lengthy and aloof criticisms of Werter's emotional distress. 'He has little command over himself; and whilst his natural temper thus overpowers him, how will he stem the torrent of passion?'[17] Elsewhere, she sums up Werter's distinguishing characteristics – his genius, his predictably short lifespan, and the danger emanating from him – in the following metaphor:

> There is a wild enthusiasm in the friendship and sentiments of Werter, that must subject him to perpetual extremes of happiness or misery. That spark of divinity which animates his frame, resembles one of those glaring meteors that sometimes cross the hemisphere, at once exciting dread and pleasure. I thank heaven, the soul of Albert more resembles a fixed star. (*Letters of Charlotte*, 57)

This Charlotte is hardly the kind of character who, after Werter's death, would find herself in danger of her life, as Goethe's Lotte does,[18] or even succumb to consumption, as does her namesake in *Werter and Charlotte*. That she survives Werter's death thus comes as no surprise; how she survives it is indicated in the book's frontispiece, entitled 'Charlotte at the Tomb of Werter' (*Letters of Charlotte*, fig. 1), which shows her gazing at Werter's urn, her face tear-streaked but serene, taking solace from reading, presumably the Bible. Most significantly, she is physically separated from Werter by a solid iron fence, a clear indication of the degree of her removal from his psychological predicament. In the work itself, she summons enough rational composure to describe to her friend the exact manner of Werter's death, adding pious ruminations that once more display her fondness for astronomic similes:

> Sure, 'tis a fearful, a tremendous act precipitately to rush before the awful throne of God! Not more dreadful would it be for men to behold at midnight, a rising sun shorn of his beams, spread horror on the earth, than it is for the angelic host to see an unsummoned spirit pass the everlasting portals of the heavens, and unprotected, stand before the great tribunal! (*Letters of Charlotte*, 239)

---

17 [William James,] *The Letters of Charlotte, during her Connexion with Werter*, 2 vols (New York: E. Duyckinck & Co., 1797), p. 52.
18 Johann Wolfgang Goethe, *Die Leiden des jungen Werther*, in *Goethes Werke: Hamburger Ausgabe in 14 Bänden*, ed. by Erich Trunz (Munich: Beck, 1981–), VI, pp. 7–124, 124: 'Man fürchtete für Lottens Leben.'

If suicide emerges as the main subject of the tale, condemnation of suicide is its object. Most of James's preface is taken up with a discussion of the hero's suicide in the original, which James considers

> a book which is not simply an apology for the horrible crime of suicide, but in which, as far as the author's abilities would go, it is justified and recommended! [...] the author, not satisfied with recommending a specific crime, has aimed a violent blow at all religion. (*Letters of Charlotte*, vi)

Citing a specific instance in which a young lady, having 'rashly ventured on the unknown shore' (*Letters of Charlotte*, viii), was found dead with Goethe's *Werther* under her pillow, James worries that particularly female readers of Goethe's novel would follow the author's 'recommendation' and kill themselves in droves. James's text, then, is explicitly defined as a response to this danger, or, in his words, a 'negative recommendation' (*Letters of Charlotte*, vi). Nowhere in this discussion does James distinguish between author, narrator and character, or between different levels of fictionality. Since his own text is an explicitly didactic project, he assumes the same for Goethe's novel; because his character's censure of suicide expresses his own convictions, he assumes the same relationship between Goethe and Werther.

> If the author gave his hero these sentiments, surely these are his own; and if they are erroneous, be whose they will, why are they published without their antidote? As a translator, the Editor tells us, that, to avoid giving offence, several exceptionable sentiments are omitted. Had the author been influenced by similar motives, the work would never have appeared; at least he might have indulged us with the efforts of his genius, without shocking us with the depravity of his principles. (*Letters of Charlotte*, x)

Defining both Goethe's 'recommendation' and his own 'negative recommendation' of suicide as didactic rather than literary projects, James even adopts the same fiction of authenticity: just as Goethe's fictitious editor does at the outset of his novel, James claims in his foreword to have found, rather than written, the letters of Charlotte, thus situating his work on the same level of authenticity as Goethe's novel. To him, it is this claim to authenticity that makes Goethe's text so dangerous.[19] True to his own conviction that 'exceptionable sentiments' had best be omitted, he states that Charlotte's letters are in no need of such censorship, since

> they abound with reflections which, if they do not display a brilliant understanding, discover a good heart, susceptible of the most tender impressions, and alive to all the feelings of refined sensibility. [...] It afforded me no small pleasure to find, that in the letters of Charlotte there was nothing to suppress. (*Letters of Charlotte*, xi)

In both *Werter and Charlotte* and James's text, it is sentiment that starts the plot, keeps it going, and brings it to its tragic conclusion. Both texts exemplify what

---

19 Martin Andree has recently published an account of the '*Werther*-effect' in light of modern ideas about the risks posed by violence in the media; see *Wenn Texte töten: Über Werther, Medienwirkung und Mediengewalt* (Munich: Fink, 2006).

I would call metonymic slippage: on the plot level, it is still the male hero who kills himself; on the didactic level, the problem that emerges is, paradoxically, *women's* sentimentality. *Werter and Charlotte* expresses this in the sheer lack of the heroine's viability; James in his assumption that reading Goethe's novel would drive women to suicide in inestimable numbers. But the problem of female sentimentality is also one that solves itself, as indicated in the final lines of *Werter and Charlotte:*

> Peace to their ashes, Fate can do no more,
> For this life's troubles now with them are o'er. (*Werter and Charlotte*, 28).

As this passage not so subtly implies, the trouble is over not only for the tale's hapless heroes, but also for its readers. Sentimental deaths, whether resulting from suicide or consumption, leave the world profoundly untouched. When Goethe made the point, it was an accusation; here, it is reduced to a heart-warming pious sentiment that divests the *Werther*-theme of every shred of controversy or social significance it once had.

In the age of Revolution, in the age of *Vindication,* it is this aspect, these texts' profound emptiness of any kind of social or political content, that is most surprising. They may be indirectly 'political' in the sense that they por-tray a sentimental hero/ine, here taken to mean someone who *needs* and whose needs go unfulfilled. But these needs are decontextualized to the point where they can no longer be understood as relating to anything other than a troubled psyche; whatever explosive potential the portrayal of the hero/ine at odds with the world might have contained is carefully counter-balanced in the painstaking excision of all 'exceptionable sentiment' from the text. Gone is not only the controversial suicide debate between Albert and Werther, but also the profound sense of alienation, injustice, and dis-placement that drove Goethe's *Werther* and possibly, for many of its partici-pants, also the French Revolution. Werther's rebellion against both bour-geois and courtly society is deleted entirely in one text and dismissed in the other as an example of his personal failure to adjust. In *Werter and Charlotte*, Charlotte dies not, as Goethe's Werther does, as a social misfit but as a sen-timental heroine, not as someone unable to find a place in family and soci-ety, but as someone unable to survive the loss of her lover. In James's text, Charlotte is presented as a reasonable heroine in Wollstonecraft's sense, but her manifest ability to overcome excessive sentiment does not result in greater control over her destiny, let alone in the attainment of Wollstone-craft's ultimate goal: woman's exercise of reason as evidence of her qualifi-cation for full citizenship. Charlotte's marriage with Albert, that 'fixed star' of her affections, can easily be read as the paradigmatic passionless Wollstonecraftian union, but it has no significance beyond the purely do-mestic realm. The respect Charlotte gains – her husband's, or the reader's –

remains without consequence, it is, as Wollstonecraft would have put it, 'hollow'.

The only passages in James's text that can be interpreted as directly political are Charlotte's and Werter's frequent invectives against French customs, language and culture. The fact that her friend Carolina is an Englishwoman gives Charlotte ample opportunity to express her boundless admiration for that nation and her equally boundless contempt for the French. 'I wonder you have the patience to learn the French;' she muses in one letter,

> for though it is easy enough, it has nothing to recommend it: neither the strength of the English, nor the delicacy of the Italian; and when one hears it spoken, one would imagine it was but a kind of half language, for there is a perpetual distortion of the body in gesticulation. (*Letters of Charlotte*, 58)

Or, in Werter's naturally less restrained formulation: 'if heaven was suddenly to endue baboons and monkies with the power of articulation, they would instantly jabber French' (*Letters of Charlotte*, 59). The text's sole 'political' statement, then, can be summed up in a smug chauvinism that does nothing but divest others of their humanity – in Charlotte's implied and Werter's expressed view of the French as baboons – but that simultaneously steers clear not only of direct commentary on political events in France, but also of Goethe's grandiose indictment of contemporary society. When Werther's story is turned into Charlotte's story, the switch from a hero to a heroine corresponds, despite (because of?) the revolutionary context, to a textual deletion of protest, rebellion, and all other themes of potential political and social significance. Above all, it means a return to that same sentimentality – in the sense of excessive sensibility – that Wollstonecraft had diagnosed as women's primary political problem.

Sentiments and Revenants: The Failure of Love

Nobody has depicted the dire consequences of suicide in more stringent terms than Sarah Farrell, the author of the gothic poem 'Charlotte, or a Sequel to the Sorrows of Werter' (1792). The poem begins after Werter's suicide and is set, almost in its entirety, at Werter's gravesite. The frontispiece, drawn by Sarah Farrell herself ('Charlotte', fig. 2), shows us a very different attitude, on Charlotte's part, toward Werter's death than the frontispiece to James's work. Werter is interred not in a graveyard, but in the wilderness, amongst the rocks and the trees. The text specifies that he is buried between two lime trees at 'a cross-road; according to the English custom in cases of premeditated self-murder.'[20] In Farrell's drawing, the edge of Werter's grave is already

---

20 Sarah Farrell, 'Charlotte, or a Sequel to the Sorrows of Werter', in *Charlotte and Other Poems by Mrs. Farrell* (Bath: Publish'd as the Act directs, for the Author, by Campbell & Gainsborough

partly overgrown by bushes, grass and flowers; Werter, having been outcast from society in both life and death, is in the process of being incorporated into nature. Rather unlike the frontispiece to James's work, in which Charlotte is distant and separated from the grave by a fence, Farrell places her heroine immediately adjacent to it. Charlotte's body position indicates that she was not kneeling by the grave, but lying next to it, the way one would lie next to a man in a bed. She is shown in an agonizingly contorted posture; half kneeling, half rising in an attempt to flee, she wards off whatever emanations may arise from the grave, her face averted and full of fear. Her hat on the ground, the ribbons on her dress untied, her left arm unclad hint simultaneously at an imminent state of undress and at a loss of control over the situation: Charlotte is literally coming apart. Her hair streaming loosely behind her adds to the dynamic movement of the entire figure, as if she were what she apparently wants to be, in full flight.

In case we missed the message of the frontispiece, the twenty-five page poem rather relentlessly spells it out. Werter, unable to find rest in the grave, calls for Charlotte to join him there. This is essentially the theme of Bürger's poem 'Lenore', which was published in the same year as *Werther* and to which Farrell's work owes as least as much as it does to its ostentatious source. Much of Farrell's poem is related in Charlotte's voice, which is also the principal carrier of the – by now rather familiar – main message:

> Attend ye infidels—unthinking race!
> Who bound your views within this narrow space,
> [...]
> Or else by arguments unjust, as vain,
> Maintain the right you have to end your pain:
> Unthinking man!—who wants religion's aid,
> And dares destroy what God supremely made,
> Bidding defiance to your Maker's will,
> Like cowards, plunge your bark in greater ill;
> Behold, example glares in Werter's grave,
> *No rest in sacred ground for passion's slave.* ('Charlotte', 6)

The final line is to be read quite literally: a corpse that cannot rest in peace becomes a restless corpse, a revenant. Being denied sacred ground, it is condemned to wander the earth, since unhallowed ground cannot hold the dead. At the time of Farrell's writing, this was not an uncommon thought. Throughout the eighteenth century, theologians and other writers, among them the Benedictine monk Augustine Calmet, argued in all seriousness that

---

at their Public Library, Burton Street Bath, May 12, 1792), p. 1. In folklore, crossroads were viewed as no man's land, a place between worlds, and thus a site where supernatural encounters could take place: the ideal place to conduct a ritual, cast a spell, create a makeshift altar, or sell one's soul to the Devil. It was also a place where gallows were frequently erected. On crossroads in folklore, see Martin Puhvel, *The Crossroads in Folklore and Myth* (New York: Peter Lang, 1989).

people excommunicated for suicide and buried in unhallowed ground returned as vampires to plague the living.[21] In Farrell's poem, it is not only Werter who finds no rest; Charlotte is continuously plagued by nightmares in
which she beholds 'Werter's mangled form' rising from the grave, beckoning
her, 'Each wound expressive of the love he bore,/ Which gaping they confess,
with reeking gore' ('Charlotte', 2). Despite her terror, Charlotte immediately
flies to Werter's graveside, where she first berates him for his suicide and then
admits her love for him, hastening to add, undoubtedly more for the reader's
benefit than Werter's, that she has never been unfaithful to Albert, to whom
she is bound in a loveless marriage. Charlotte ends as does Bürger's Lenore,
with her lover dragging her to her wedding bed six feet underground. In her
final lines, Charlotte calls out for help to her husband:

> Albert!–awake me from the horrid sights?
> What, Werter!–still appearing in my view!
> Hide! hide! that bleeding breast! nor still pursue,
> Leave me with Albert–he's my husband still!
> Why sounds thy voice with accents weak and shrill?
> [...]
> What!–seize my hand!–thou cold–thou pallid shade!
> Alas! he drags me to yon darksome glade;
> Oh! Albert! Albert! save your wife,' (she cried)
> Then sunk at once on Werter's grave–and DIED. ('Charlotte', 16–17)

This sounds like the traditional rousing finale of the gothic poem, requiring
nothing further but some admonitions against excessive sentiment and uplifting remarks about submission to God's will, such as provided by Bürger at
the end of 'Lenore'. Unlike Bürger, however, Farrell does not leave it at that.
Charlotte's death is followed by several pages of narratorial mourning, of the
'No more thy cheek out-vies the budding rose'-school of style ('Charlotte',
17). Then along comes her father Sickbert to pay his respects at Werter's
grave. Imagine his surprise when he finds his daughter's body lifeless upon it.
Imagine, too, his sorrow, and imagine it you must, since it cannot – according
to the narrator, who bids the Muse be struck dumb at this insurmountable
task – be expressed in words. Nevertheless, a further five pages are devoted
to Sickbert's wild grief and, gruesomely, his attempts at resuscitation ('Charlotte', 18–23).

Farrell's poem is a straightforward gothic tale, one that fails entirely to
convey a deeper cultural, metaphysical, or, for that matter, social and political meaning. It does, however, offer us a rather interesting explanation for
Charlotte's death. Farrell's Charlotte is, just like her English predecessors

---

21 Augustine Calmet, *Treatise on Vampires & Revenants: The Phantom World. Dissertation on those
    Persons who Return to Earth Bodily, the Excommunicated, the Oupires or Vampires, Vroucolacas, &c.
    by Dom Augustine Calmet*, translated by Rev. Henry Christmas, ed. by Dr Clive Leatherdale
    (Brighton: Desert Island, 1993).

(but unlike Bürger's Lenore), completely blameless. Nor is her death blamed on Werter, even though he is lengthily rebuked for his suicide and even though she cries out that she can feel him dragging her down into the grave. And yet, it is not Werter's uncontrollable passion that is ultimately blamed but Albert's *lack* of passion:

> Ah! misled Albert, had you still caress'd
> Your once-lov'd Charlotte, nor with doubt oppress'd
> Her gen'rous mind, distracted by neglect,
> Phrenzy had not produc'd this dire effect:
> No errors of the heart had caus'd this sight,
> 'Twas the keen horror of each lonely night. ('Charlotte', 23)

This is an astonishing about-face. Not only is it completely unmotivated in the rest of the poem, it also breaks radically with contemporary discourse on the dangers of sentiment. The problem here is not an excess of love but its absence, the horror is not that of ghosts arising from the grave, but that of loneliness and neglect. The poem can only arrive at this conclusion by obfuscating narrative levels: in the end, Charlotte's perspective becomes the narrator's, in his statement that she was the victim not of a passionate lover but of a dispassionate husband. Her fantasies, her temptations, and her pleas are turned into the poem's reality—she hears Werter cry out to her from the grave and follows; in her last moments, she cries out to Albert to save her, but he fails to appear.

Farrell's conclusion that it is lack of sentiment rather than its excess that kills brings us full circle, for this is also, we might suspect, what kills Werther in Goethe's novel. More concretely, what kills both Goethe's Werther and Farrell's Charlotte is the lack of a response, the constant experience of expending passion and enthusiasm on the world (on a person, a poem, an idea, two trees, a love story...) and finding this enthusiasm greeted with stony silence, ridicule or hostility. 'Passion's slave' cannot rest because there is an imbalance, an unresolved relationship between the individual and the world. In the gothic genre, this restlessness is expressed in its most literal form, in the image of the dead lover arising from the grave.

From Sentiment to Sexuality: German Vampires

Perhaps it is this aspect, the aspect of revenantism, that can help us re-think the connection between sentimentality and politics, as well as the two questions posed in the textual discussion, namely: to what extent these texts can be read as political, and to what extent they assign a new meaning to sentimental death. Revenantism points to a third philosophical category with which all of these texts, from Wollstonecraft's campaign against sentimentality to its idealization in English Werther-stories, are centrally concerned, namely, sexuality. Wollstonecraft already aligns sexuality with sentimentality in stating that women's full citizenship is contingent upon women's suppression not only of sentiment, but also of 'sexual appetites'. Werther-stories, as well, have much to say about sexuality, although the link between sex and sentiment in these texts is considerably more indirect than it is in Wollstonecraft's *Vindication*. When James's Charlotte, for instance, complains of Werter's uncontainable 'torrent of passion' (*Letters of Charlotte*, 52), she may well hint at considerably more than 'sentimentality' as expressed in tearful sighs, handkerchiefs pressed to bosoms, and ardent responses to Ossian. And yet, sex in this text is not merely sentiment taken to its logical conclusion. For example, Charlotte's comparison of the meteor Werter, a celestial phenomenon that quickly spends itself, and Albert, the 'fixed star' of her affections, clearly alludes to the difference between Werter's effeminate masculinity and Albert's reliable, even business-like, endurance.[22] The same logic applied to the reverse situation would indicate that the man's failure to take care of 'business' at home opens the door to destructive sentimentality. This is the solution suggested in Farrell's poem, which blames Albert's sexual deficiencies, not Werter's sentimental excesses, for the death of Charlotte, who, having succumbed to 'the keen horror of each lonely night', cannot be revived by the empty signifier of the sexual act (Sickbert's attempts at resuscitation).

These precise constellations linking suppressed political aspirations, sentimentality, sexuality, and death reappear obsessively in German literature of the 1790s and beyond, most particularly in vampire literature, which rests almost entirely on the idea, advanced by Farrell and others, that thwarted sexuality leads to 'restlessness' (read: revenantism).[23] Because vampire literature chiefly focuses on the erotic aspects of vampiric lore, the literary vampire retains very little of the mythological vampire's eeriness and power. In literature, the universal threat of the vampire myth is contained within the specificity of a sexual attack; literary vampires are no longer a threat to humanity but tend to focus their attentions on a single human, the either faithless, overly bashful, or lost lover. The link in this literature between vampirism and sexuality (or rather: the reduction of vampirism to an *aspect* of sexuality) practically mandates the protagonists' conformity with contemporary gender ideology.

In literature describing female vampires, this is even more pronounced, and it is this literature that most consistently revisits both Wollstonecraft's main point about excessive sentiment and the theme of unfulfilled sexuality that provides the subtext of English Werther-stories. Vampiric transformation here often coincides with central stages of female sexual initiation: it

---

22 I owe the idea to Barry Murnane, whom I'd like to thank here for our spirited discussion and his enthusiasm for this project.

23 For a brief history of mythological and literary vampires in Germany, see Susanne Kord, *Murderesses in German Writing, 1720–1860: Heroines of Horror* (Cambridge: Cambridge University Press, 2009), chapter 3.

occurs during the wedding night, as in Goethe's 'Die Braut von Korinth',[24] or, as is hinted in Hoffmann's 'Eine Vampirgeschichte' (from *Die Serapionsbrüder*, 1821), at the onset of pregnancy.[25] We might read these tales as textbook examples of Wollstonecraft's ideas on the compulsory formation of the 'feminine' gender through literary discourses on sentiment and sexuality. The 'virtuous vampires'[26] of these texts are not vampires but women in the most restrictive contemporary interpretation of 'femininity'; they are cast not only as blushing brides but also as obedient daughters. Mother plays a central part in both Goethe's ballad and Hoffmann's tale. Deference to feminine virtue coupled with the understanding of vampirism as awakening sexuality makes the usual means of transmitting the plague of vampirism, another vampire's bite, unworkable. Thus both authors hit upon an ingenious device: *Mother* causes the daughter's condition – either directly, through heredity (in Hoffmann's story), or indirectly, by forcing her daughter to renounce her love and languish in a convent, where she dies of a broken heart (in Goethe's poem). Both Goethe's and Hoffmann's vampires are thus victims in a twofold sense: first denied a life as a 'normal woman' by their mothers, they are later 'driven' (*getrieben*) by what masquerades as vampirism,[27] but can easily be deciphered as frustrated feminine sexuality.

If female vampirism in literature is a matter of thwarted sexual development, it comes as no surprise that the activities of female vampires are, as all female activity was expected to be, confined to home and hearth. Like

---

24 Johann Wolfgang Goethe, 'Die Braut von Korinth', in *Goethes Werke: Hamburger Ausgabe in 14 Bänden*, I, pp. 268–273. We might also think here of Kleist's Penthesilea, another domesticated vampire of contemporary literature, who, 'mistaking' bites ('Bisse') for kisses ('Küsse'), bites her lover Achill to death. Heinrich von Kleist, *Penthesilea. Sämtliche Werke und Briefe*, 2 vols, ed. by Helmut Sembdner, 8th edn (Munich: Hanser, 1984), I, pp. 321–428, 425.

25 Ernst Theodor Amadeus Hoffmann, 'Eine Vampir-Geschichte', in *E. T. A. Hoffmanns Sämtliche Werke. Historisch-Kritische Ausgabe*, ed. by Carl Georg von Maassen (Munich: Georg Müller, 1925), VIII, pp. 218–233. In the tale, a doctor explains Aurelie's extreme aversion to cooked food with her pregnancy and resulting strange appetites; this diagnosis is neither confirmed nor denied in the tale. One of the symptoms of pregnancy the doctor lists, the desire to bite, kill and eat their own husbands, is enacted by the Countess at the end of the tale. Cf. Silke Arnold-de Simine, 'Wiedergängerische Texte: Die intertextuelle Vernetzung des Vampirmotivs in E.T.A. Hoffmanns 'Vampirismus'-Geschichte (1821)', in *Poetische Wiedergänger: Deutschsprachige Vampirismus-Diskurse vom Mittelalter bis zur Gegenwart*, ed. by Julia Bertschik and Christa Agnes Tuczay (Tübingen: Franke, 2005), pp. 129–145, 133–134.

26 Silvia Volckmann, ' "Gierig saugt sie seines Mundes Flammen". Anmerkungen zum Funktionswandel des weiblichen Vampirs in der Literatur des 19. Jahrhunderts', in *Weiblichkeit und Tod in der Literatur*, ed. by Renate Berger and Inge Stephan (Cologne and Vienna: Böhlau, 1987), pp. 155–176, 157.

27 Cf. the different readings of the term 'getrieben' and its implications for female agency in Volckmann, 'Anmerkungen zum Funktionswandel', 162 and Clemens Ruthner, 'Untote Verzahnungen. Prolegomena zu einer Literaturgeschichte des Vampirismus', in *Poetische Wiedergänger*, 11–41, 39.

male literary vampires,[28] they attack only lovers, husbands, and bride-
grooms; unlike male vampires, they hardly appear threatening, even in the
already muted context of an individual attack. Hoffmann's Aurelie does not
drink the blood of the living but contents herself with eating the flesh of the
dead; her single vampiric attack on her husband, in the final sentences of
the story, is easily deflected:

> Doch sowie der Graf diese Worte ausstieß, stürzte die Gräfin laut heulend auf ihn zu
> und biß ihn mit der Wut der Hyäne in die Brust. Der Graf schleuderte die Rasende
> von sich zur Erde nieder, und sie gab den Geist auf unter grauenhaften Verzuckun-
> gen. ('Eine Vampirgeschichte', 233)[29]

Even in this scene, at her most menacing, the Countess is not granted full
vampiric status but remains what she has been throughout the tale, a hyaena,
a parasite feeding from dead bodies, easily flung aside the moment she attacks
something not entirely defenceless. In Goethe's ballad, there is a brief indication that the vampiric bride might pose a threat to others:

> Aus dem Grabe werd' ich ausgetrieben,
> Noch zu suchen das vermißte Gut,
> Noch den schon verlornen Mann zu lieben
> Und zu saugen seines Herzens Blut.
> Ist's um den geschehn,
> Muß nach andern gehn,
> Und das junge Volk erliegt der Wut. ('Braut von Korinth', 273)[30]

Here emerges, however fleetingly, the ancient understanding of vampirism as
a *plague*, as a threat that combines the universality of an epidemic with the
individuality of vengeance and evil intent. But since 'the woman in the vampire is always stronger than the vampire in the woman',[31] there is no real danger here. In what Ruthner has called 'pre-emptive obedience', the Bride in-
structs her mother (!) to burn her body along with that of her soon-to-be-
dead bridegroom, alluding simultaneously to the burial rites of antiquity, one
of the three means of killing a vampire, and the traditional execution method

---

28 Such as, for example, Ossenfelder's vampire, who, in a poem that is little more than a vicarious
    celebration of rape, overcomes the resistance of his 'Christianchen', cf. Heinrich August Os-
    senfelder, 'Der Vampir', *Der Naturforscher* 48 (25 May 1748) 380–381.
29 'But no sooner had the Count uttered these words than, wailing loudly, the Countess hurled
    herself at him, and with a hyaena's rage bit him in the chest. The Count flung the frenzied
    woman away from him, down to the ground, and she expired in gruesome death throes.' (My
    own translation.)
30 'From my grave to wander I am forc'd,/ Still to seek Desire's long-sever'd link,/ Still to love
    the bridegroom I have lost,/And the life-blood of his heart to drink;/ When his race is run,/ I
    must hasten on,/ And the young must 'neath my vengeance sink.' (My own translation).
31 The formulation is Gautier's, cited in Volckmann, 'Anmerkungen zum Funktionswandel', 164:
    'In der Vampirin ist allemal, wie Gautier es sehr treffend ausgedrückt hat, "die Frau stärker als
    der Vampir".'

for witches.[32] Given that Goethe's poem has often been read as representing the struggle between the sexual impulses of the individual and societal-ideological restrictions,[33] the role of the mother, the repressive element, is strangely validated. Initially the origin of the disease, she is finally charged to effect its cure; originally responsible for her daughter's death, she ultimately liberates her from an eternity of un-death. As Ruthner has pointed out, the daughter's own anticipation of continued vampirism/promiscuity might even be read as the text's confirmation of the mother's initial judgment that such unbridled sexuality might best be tamed in the convent.[34]

Of course there is more to Goethe's and Hoffmann's vampires than I have been able to convey in this brief discussion. They can be, and have been, productively interpreted in a number of ways – as metaphors for female sexuality and reproduction,[35] as allegories of an aesthetic debate,[36] as the personified struggle between individual desire and social control,[37] between Greek and Christian culture,[38] and most recently in the context of contemporary ideas on metaphysics and mesmerism.[39] Read in the literary and political context of the 1790s and beyond, these texts also offer some limited engagement with the question of women's public role posed during the French Revolution and, more obviously, with the question of women's sentimentality posed in Wollstonecraft's text. Vampire literature rather directly echoes Wollstonecraft in presenting female sentiment, love, and sexuality as a paramount problem. At the same time, however, these texts replace Wollstonecraft's shared emphasis on family and society with an exclusive focus on family relations and the excessive, thwarted, perverted or insufficient sentiments that govern them. In other words: just as post-Goethean Werther-stories eliminate the social and political aspects that are key to Werther's misery in Goethe's original, post-Wollstonecraftian vampire

32 On this scene, cf. Ruthner, 'Untote Verzahnungen', 35–39, the citation 39, and Volckmann, 'Anmerkungen zum Funktionswandel', 163.
33 For example in Volckmann, 'Anmerkungen zum Funktionswandel', 157.
34 Cf. Ruthner, 'Untote Verzahnungen', 39.
35 Volckmann on Goethe; on Hoffmann cf. Arnold-de Simine and Susan E. Gustafson, 'The Cadaverous Bodies of Vampiric Mothers and the Genealogy of Pathology in E.T.A. Hoffmann's Tales', *German Life and Letters* 52.2 (1999) 238–254.
36 Arnold-de Simine on Hoffmann, 'Cadaverous Bodies of Vampiric Mothers', particularly pp. 130–131.
37 Volckmann on Goethe.
38 This is one of the standard interpretations of Goethe's poem. See, among many others, Volckmann; Wolfgang Schemme, 'Goethe *Die Braut von Korinth*: Von der literarischen Dignität des Vampirs', *Wirkendes Wort* 36 (1986) 333–345; Stefan Hock, *Die Vampyrsagen und ihre Verwertung in der deutschen Litteratur* (Berlin: Alexander Duncker, 1900), p. 71.
39 Jürgen Barkhoff, 'Female Vampires, Victimhood and Vengeance in German Literature around 1800', in *Women and Death: Representations of Female Victims and Perpetrators in German Culture 1500–2000*, ed. by Anna Linton and Helen Fronius (Rochester: Camden House, 2008), pp. 128–143 (on Goethe and Hoffmann).

stories redefine as individual failure what Wollstonecraft diagnosed as a social problem. In so doing, these texts simultaneously misappropriate Wollstonecraft's question and withhold her answer.

In vampire literature, the erasure of the public realm, of Wollstonecraft's
revolutionary idea that the ability to suppress excessive sentiment might, in
the long run, lead to women's full humanity, citizenship and participation in
public life, is metaphorically accomplished in two ways. One is the presentation of female sexuality as perilously ungovernable; the second is – paradoxically – the domestication of the female vampire, whose activities, like
those of the woman she represents, have been excluded from the public
realm. Thus these texts' answer to Wollstonecraft's problem of female sentimentality is the very opposite of the answer she herself offered: the advocacy of family over community, of the personal over the political, and of a
concept of femininity so rigidly defined that any deviation can only be
understood as monstrous. The 'virtuous vampire' of literature is not a vampire but a woman; she is plagued by all-too-human sentiments rather than a
plague on humanity. Consequently, the task of the text becomes not to safeguard the community but to tend to the individual, either by returning the
virtuous vampire to true feminine virtue, or, failing that, to execute the
monster she has become.[40]

---

40 It has become standard in feminist criticism to see these aspects not as alternatives but ana-
    logies, understanding the death of the heroine as a metaphor for the ideal state of femininity
    and thus also as a powerful aesthetic symbol; see above all Elisabeth Bronfen's seminal *Over
    Her Dead Body: Death, Femininity and the Aesthetic* (Manchester: Manchester University Press,
    1992) as well as Elisabeth Bronfen and Sarah Webster Goodwin, ed., *Death and Representation*
    (Baltimore: Johns Hopkins University Press, 1994). But see also Barkhoff, who has taken a
    different stance in reading Goethe's and Hoffmann's texts 'as part of the literary imaginary that
    counters and destabilizes the dominant gender discourses of their time'. Barkhoff, 'Female
    Vampires', 141.

Fig. 1: 'Charlotte at the Tomb of Werter.' Frontispiece to: William James, *The Letters of Charlotte, during her Connexion with Werter* (2nd ed. 1797).

Fig. 2: Charlotte at the grave of Werter. Pencil drawing by Sarah Farrell. Frontispiece to: Sarah Farrell, 'Charlotte, or a Sequel to the Sorrows of Werter' (1792).

Radical Translations

Dubious Anglo-German Cultural Transfer in the 1790s

Barry Murnane

In the course of the eighteenth century a considerable network of translation and cultural interaction emerged across Europe which, by the end of the century, had become indispensable at all levels of late-Enlightenment culture. This is a reflection of the decline of Latin as lingua franca in the learned world, but it also points towards a surge in importance of national cultural identity at the close of the century as expressed in, and defined by, transporting intellectual discourse in respective national languages.[1] On the one hand, this twofold nature of the Enlightenment translation business adheres to cosmopolitan,[2] transnational processes of cultural transfer within the general terms of 'multiple ties and interactions linking people or institutions across the borders of nation-states':[3] different national cultures interact intellectually within the framework of enlightened cultural principles. This certainly holds true in the case of Anglo-German cultural transfer which first makes itself most visible on a large scale in German translations of British writing from the late 1760s onwards, only for the reciprocal British reception of German literature to begin in earnest – and almost explosively – towards the end of the 1780s.[4] The 1790s on the other hand seem to mark a change in how translation and transfer are to be viewed.

---

1   See Fania Oz-Salberger, 'The Enlightenment in translation: Regional and European aspects', *European Review of History/Revue europeene d'histoire* 13.3 (2006) 385–409 and Carla Hesse, 'Towards a new Topography of Enlightenment', *European Review of History/Revue europeene d'histoire* 13.3 (2006) 499–508. On the national tradition see Roy Porter, Mikulás Teich, eds, *The Enlightenment in National Context* (Cambridge: Cambridge University Press, 1981).

2   I am aware that I am employing the term 'cosmopolitan' in its contemporary, descriptive context here, in which it connotes mobility between cultures, cultural admixture and hybridity. The reasons for doing so – in a seemingly ahistorical manner – will become clear later my discussions. An initial helpful discussion of cosmopolitanism is Ulrich Beck, *Was ist Globalisierung? Irrtümer des Globalismus – Antworten auf Globalisierung* (Frankfurt a. M.: Suhrkamp, 1997); also H. J. Busch and Axel Horstmann, 'Kosmopolit, Kosmopolitismus', in *Historisches Wörterbuch der Philosophie*, ed. by Joachim Ritter (Darmstadt: Wissenschaftliche Buchgesellschaft, 1971-), IV, pp. 1155–1167.

3   Steven Vertovec, 'Conceiving and Researching Transnationalism', *Ethnic and Racial Studies* 22.2 (1999) 447–462, 448.

4   The classical studies on Anglo-German cultural transfer are Frank Woodyer Stokoe, *German Influence in the English Romantic Period 1788–1818* (Cambridge: University Press, 1926); Violet Stockley, *German Literature as known in England: 1750–1830* (London: Routledge, 1929).

   While recent studies on cultural transfer in Enlightenment studies have
focused in particular on the positive, cosmopolitan nature of translation, the
second wave of Anglo-German cultural transfer, with its most notorious
component of German Gothic writing, provides another perspective on the
transnational contexts in the 1790s, namely a seemingly contradictory narrative of national stereotypes which seek to mark German culture as the radical Other to British reason and order.[5] In the course of this exchange German literature becomes inseparable from images of radical politics,
revolution, violence and disorder. The methods of creating this image are
highly dubious and contradictory. In 1797 the *Anti-Jacobin Review* could print
a mock-German play, 'The Rovers', satirizing William Godwin as a supposed importer of German literature in order to fulfil their Conservative
British political aims; simultaneously the play points towards in-depth
knowledge of the German literature which the parody sets out to attack as
the radical Other to British taste. After firstly surveying the conditions of
Anglo-German relations in the period, I will return to 'The Rovers' in order
to focus in more depth on the political, social and cultural consequences of
dubious cultural transfer in the 1790s.

   Looking back on almost ten years of Anglo-German cultural transfer in
1799, the *Anti-Jacobin Review* could declare:

> It is with an equal portion of surprize and alarm, that we witness in this country, a
> glaring depravity of taste, as displayed in the extreme eagerness for foreign produc-
> tions, and a systematic design to extend such depravity by a regular importation of
> exotic poison from the envenomed crucibles of the literary and political alchymists
> of the new German School.[6]

The context of such vitriol is clear: if German literature is a poison destroying
the British national character, then this threat is inseparable from the cosmopolitan networks of writing and cultural transfer which emerged as a key
component of the European Enlightenment. Although Edmund Burke had
been highly critical of such processes of transnational networks of translation

---

5   See Daniel Hall, *French and German Gothic Fiction in the Late Eighteenth Century* (Oxford, Bern,
    Berlin: Peter Lang, 2005). Older are Michael Hadley, *The Undiscovered Genre: A Search for the
    German Gothic Novel* (Frankfurt a. M., Bern: Peter Lang, 1978) and Karl S. Guthke, *Englische
    Vorromantik und deutscher Sturm und Drang: M.G. Lewis' Stellung in der Geschichte der deutsch-englischen
    Literaturbeziehungen* (Göttingen: Vandenhoek and Ruprecht, 1958). Also my own essays 'Im-
    porting Home-grown Horrors? The English Reception of the *Schauerroman* and Schiller's *Der
    Geisterseher*', *Angermion* 1 (2008) 51–82 and 'Uncanny Translations, Uncanny Productivity: Wal-
    pole, Schiller and Kahlert', in *Translating the Enlightenment: The Circulation of Enlightened Thought in
    Europe by Means of Translation*, ed. by Stefanie Stockhorst (Amsterdam, New York: Rodopi,
    2010), pp. 141–165.
6   John Boening, ed., *The Reception of Classical German Literature in England, 1760–1860. A Docu-
    mentary History from Contemporary Periodicals,* 10 vols (New York, London: Garland Publishing,
    1977), I, p. 342.

and communication of learned discourse since the 1750s,[7] here in the *Anti-Jacobin Review* cultural transfer has another more dangerous context. In the images of 'envenomed crucibles' and the lack of difference between 'literary and political alchymists', the *Anti-Jacobin* suggests that cultural transfer is in fact the work of that most dastardly of 1790s paranoia-driven threats: Adam Weishaupt's *Illuminaten-Orden*, who – depending on the particular commentator – could be responsible for anything from poison to magic, from conjuring up ghosts to causing revolutions. The claim of a 'systematic design' to destroy the British national character is insane, if historically understandable. Nor is it the invention of the *Anti-Jacobin*. Since the translation of Frederick the Great's correspondence in 1790, the concept of a 'literary cabal' of intelligentsia networking between France and Germany was a potent image. Deane has shown how Burke's *Reflections on the Revolution in France* clearly links the atheism of Frederick's 'philosophe' of choice, Voltaire, with the Revolution and with German secret societies.[8]

Publication of the secret papers of the *Illuminaten* in 1786/87 had caused considerable commotion across Europe and the scandal surrounding Cagliostro's phantasmagorical confession before the Roman inquisition, in which he claimed to be a leading member, added fuel to the fire that the German secret society engaged in occult practices and were in league with revolutionary forces in France.[9] The claims of occult practices could not have been further from the truth of Weishaupt's radically rationalist, progressive social aims;[10] the charges of links to the Revolution were less easy to argue away. Owing to the hermetic communication structures of the *Illuminaten-Orden*, it was impossible to convince the public of the contrary. Furthermore, with Johann Christian Bode travelling to France at the dawn of the Revolution and German Jacobins such as Georg Forster in Mainz previously being members of the order, the Illuminati implicated themselves by

7   Seamus Deane's standard work *The French Revolution and Enlightenment in England* (Cambridge, Mass., London: Harvard University Press, 1988) covers this argument in quite some detail; regarding Burke's early writings – and of greater relevance to the discourse of the 1790s – his *Reflections on the Revolution in France* (1790) – see pp. 1–12.
8   Deane, *French Revolution*, 10–11.
9   See for example Walter Müller-Seidel, 'Cagliostro und die Vorgeschichte der deutschen Klassik', in Walter Müller-Seidel, *Die Geschichtlichkeit der deutschen Klassik: Literatur und Denkformen um 1800* (Stuttgart Metzler, 1983), pp. 49–65, and Johannes Rogalla von Bieberstein, *Die These von der Verschwörung 1776–1945: Philosophen, Freimaurer, Juden, Liberale und Sozialisten als Verschwörer gegen die Sozialordnung.* (Flensburg: Flensburger Hefte, 1992), pp. 60–63.
10 See the various studies on secret societies and the Illuminati by Müller-Seidel and Rogalla (note 9); Richard von Dülmen, *Der Geheimbund der Illuminaten: Darstellung, Analyse, Dokumentationen* (Stuttgart, Bad-Cannstatt: Frommann-Holzboog, 1975); W. Daniel Wilson, *Geheimräte gegen Geheimbünde: Ein unbekanntes Kapitel der klassisch-romantischen Geschichte Weimars* (Stuttgart: Metzler, 1991) and Hans-Jürgen Schings, *Die Brüder des Marquis Posa. Schiller und der Geheimbund der Illuminaten* (Tübingen: Niemeyer, 1996).

accident or directly in radical politics.[11] If one then reads those aspects of Weishaupt's writings which encouraged a utopian social order that would break radically with the tight structures of German enlightened absolutism,[12] it becomes understandable that writers such as Alois Hoffmann in Vienna, Ernst August von Göchhausen in Berlin, the Abbé de Barruel and John Robison could concoct conspiracy theories linking Weishaupt with the revolution in France.[13]

This is clearly the political context in which German literature is embroiled according to the *Anti-Jacobin*. The supposed vile plot to destroy the moral fabric of Europe becomes extended here not only to literature itself, but more importantly to the transnational networks of translation involved in importing German culture into Britain – despite the best efforts of William Taylor in Norwich, Thomas Beddoes and Coleridge in Bristol or German ex-patriots Peter Will, Constantin Geisweiler and Anton Willich in London (with their journal *German Museum*).[14] Such vitriol was not merely the domain of radically politicized literary criticism. When Jane Austen completed *Northanger Abbey* in 1798, her parody of the taste and narrative struc-

---

11 Bode was a central figure in the Illuminati and continued to be active long after the order had been officially disbanded; he – more than any other member – was the leading light of the Weimar-Gotha-Jena branches of Weißhaupt's society. On Bode's trip to Paris, see Rogalla, *Verschwörung*, 68–71, W. Daniel Wilson, *Unterirdische Gänge. Goethe, Freimaurerei und Politik* (Göttingen: Wallstein, 1999) and Johann Joachim Christoph Bode, *Journal von einer Reise von Weimar nach Frankreich: im Jahr 1787*, ed. by Hermann Schüttler (München: Ars una, 1994). On the connections between the revolutions in Paris and Mainz see Inge Stephan, *Jakobinismus in Deutschland* (Stuttgart: Metzler, 1976), pp. 79–82, and, more recently, and with reference to the Illuminati, see Schings, *Die Brüder des Marquis Posa*, 82–83, 154–156.

12 While Weißhaupt's 'Anrede an die neu aufzunehmenden Illuminatos dirigentos' and the so-called 'higher mysteries' did indeed include concepts such as revolution and upheaval, a direct link to France is highly unlikely. Firstly the 'higher mysteries' were not properly complete, nor were they known to more than a handful of high-ranking members of the order, lastly – and more importantly – the concept of revolution is more one of a moral philosophy and not conceived as political action. See Wilson, *Geheimräte*, 28–34.

13 [Ernst August von Göchhausen], *Enthüllung des Systems der Weltbürger-Republik. In Briefen aus der Verlassenschaft eines Freymaurers; Wahrscheinlich manchem Leser um zwantzig Jahre zu spät publizirt.* ([Leipzig: Göschen], 1786); Abbé Augustin de Barruel, *Memoires, Illustrating the History of Jacobinism* (London: Booker, 1797–1798); John Robison, *Proofs of a Conspiracy against all Religions and Governments of Europe, Carried on in the Secret Meetings of the Free Masons, Illuminati, and Reading Societies* (New York: Forgotten Books, 2004 [= reprint of 4th edn of 1797]). Hoffmann was responsible for various attacks on the Illuminati in the *Wiener Zeitschrift* between 1792 and 1793; another important source was the Berlin journal *Eudämonia* in 1795.

14 On these central figures in Anglo-German transfer see Stockley and Stokoe (note 3) and Horst Oppel, *Englisch-deutsche Literaturbeziehungen*, 2 vols (Berlin: Erich Schmidt Verlag, 1971), II: *Von der Romantik bis zur Gegenwart*. See also Graham Jefcoate, '"Hier ist nichts zu machen": Zum deutschen Buchhandel in London 1790–1806', in *Literatur und Erfahrungswandel 1789–1830*, ed. by Rainer Schöwerling et. al. (Munich: Fink, 1996), pp. 47–59; James Raven, 'Cheap and Cheerless. English Novels in German Translations and German Novels in English Translations 1770–1799', in *The Corvey Library and Anglo-German Cultural Exchanges, 1770–1837*, ed. by Werner Huber (Munich: Fink, 2004), pp. 1–33.

ture of the Gothic novel not only referred specifically to Karl Friedrich Kahlert's *The Necromancer* and Karl Grosse's *Horrid Mysteries*,[15] her list of 'horrid novels' extended to English works obviously hoping to profit from the German influx: Francis Lathom's supposed 'German story Founded on Incidents of Real Life', *The Midnight Bell*, Eliza Parson's 'German Story' *Castle of Wolfenbach* and her 'German Tale,' *The Mysterious Warning*.[16] A brief survey of German works appearing in translation on the British market in the 1790s does little to disperse this sentiment; if anything the contents of these novels seem to confirm British suspicions. Whether Schiller's *Geisterseher*, *Die Räuber* or *Kabale und Liebe*, Goethe's *Werther* or *Götz von Berlichingen* or Benedikte Naubert's *Herrmann von Unna*, the most prominent German imports deal with secret societies, social unrest and – at worst – revolution. While more considered analysis of these works points toward the critical portrayal of secret societies and related violence – as dangerous forms of radical enlightened philosophy in *Der Geisterseher*, the uncertain conditions of social communication in *Der Genius* or at least to the specifically antiquated contexts of social unrest in *Götz* and *Herrmann von Unna* as historically displaced critiques of degeneration in Goethe's and Naubert's contemporary society – it was relatively easy to bundle these works together to create an image of a 'German School' of horror revelling in the violence of the French Revolution. This German Gothic writing becomes synonymous with an irrational taste completely at odds with British sensibilities. *The British Critic* remarked: 'We should be sorry to see an English original so full of absurdities' as *The Necromancer*,[17] and the *Analytical Review* accuses Germans of 'giving unbounded licence to […] imagination' and of being 'extravagant'.[18] British or English is thus everything that German is not, and everything that is German is quite clearly an aesthetic form of unlicensed debauchery. As the *Anti-Jacobin* makes clear, this literature is inseparable from that other form of radical debauchery of the 1790s – namely revolutionary France.

If the albeit tenuous link between German secret societies and the Revolution in France gained in popular support throughout the 1790s, the displacement of such fears onto literary production is somewhat more complicated. Here the threat is twofold: not only are such literary works harmful to the general British public, the suggestion of a 'systematic design to extend such depravity by a regular importation', of which the *Anti-Jacobin* spoke

---

15 Karl Grosse, *Der Genius*, 1ˢᵗ 1791–95 (Frankfurt a. M.: zweitausendeins, 1982), translated by Joseph Trapp as *The Genius; or the Mysterious Adventures of Don Carlos de Grandez* (London: Allen and West, 1796) and Peter Will as *Horrid Mysteries. A Story* (London: Lane, 1796). Lawrence Flammenberg [Karl Friedrich Kahlert], *Der Geisterbanner* (1792), translated by Peter Teuthold as *The Necromancer*, 1ˢᵗ 1792 (London: Skoob Books, 1989).

16 See Jane Austen, *Northanger Abbey* (Ware: Wordsworth, 1993), p. 21 and *passim*.

17 Boening, *Reception of Classical German Literature*, I, p. 309.

18 Boening, *Reception of Classical German Literature*, I, p. 315.

above, points towards a threat to social order by the equally stealth 'import' activities of teams of translators, publishers and writers active in Britain and elsewhere. Indeed in the satirical play 'The Rovers', Canning lambasts the work of William Render in particular.[19] A pattern that is relevant for many forms of cultural transfer in the 1790s is becoming visible: translation is the radical work of conspiratorial forces and hence dastardly; the source culture is always the shady source of conspiratorial, cross-border conspiracy and hence tied into methods of radical cultural politics leading to revolution.

The most prominent example of such conspiratorial denunciations of the cosmopolitan networks behind German literature is John Robison's infamous *Proofs of a Conspiracy*. Robison's real interest lies in his criticism of Weißhaupt's *Illuminaten-Orden*, but this extends to discuss the publication and censure strategies of the order in critical terms. With their secret communication networks they are responsible for the worst 'blackguard productions of the German presses'.[20] If it is not bad enough that they do so in their home country, Robison then claims to 'know that the enemy is working among us', implying that the importation of German works amongst 'thousands of subscribing Brethren in London alone' is the work of a secret society.[21] If one pays close attention to the criticism of the 'German School' both here and in the *Anti-Jacobin* above, it becomes apparent that the figure of the cosmopolitan, as someone who shifts between and synthesizes cultures, is equally dangerous: Robison points to cosmopolitanism being a threat to 'normal' national patriotism.[22] To use the term 'cosmopolitan' in this context seems surprising, as the figure of the cosmopolitan 'Weltbürger' is generally considered as positive in accounts of the late-eighteenth century.[23] According to Andrea Albrecht, no one prioritized definition of cosmopolitanism exists around 1800;[24] instead the term seems to connote an

---

19 See for example the passage commenting on the 'ill-Rendered' translations of 'Mr. Render' in 'The Rovers' in Graeme Stones, ed., *Parodies of the Romantic Age*, 5 vols (London: Pickering & Chatto, 1999), I, pp. 216–242, 235–236.

20 John Robison, *Proofs of a Conspiracy*, 247. In total Robison uses the term on over twenty occasions, including links to the French Revolution (pp. 186–189) and as an import from French philosophy (p. 67). Peter Mortensen's study *British Romanticism and Continental Influences: Writing in an Age of Europhobia* (Houndsmills, New York: Palgrave Macmillan, 2004) alerted me to this material in the first instance. He does not discuss the wider terms of cosmopolitanism here, nor does he link the phrases in Robison's text to the German phrase and its use in German critical writings.

21 Robison, *Proofs of a Conspiracy*, 246.

22 Robison, *Proofs of a Conspiracy*, 68–69 and 230 respectively.

23 I thank Galin Tihanov for this reminder, which led me to re-read the texts in question. While I do not wish to overturn much of the important research carried out on the concept of the 'Weltbürger', it seems to me that this context is only beginning to be properly accounted for, cf. Andrea Albrecht, *Kosmopolitismus: Weltbürgerdiskurse in Literatur, Philosophie und Publizistik um 1800* (Berlin, New York: De Gruyter, 2005).

24 Albrecht, *Kosmopolitismus*, 56–57, 391–398.

ideal concept which was associated variously with bourgeois-liberal and rev-
olutionary-republican reform and a vague 'Kulturbewusstsein' of a *Weltliter-
atur*.[25] Besides these positive connotations, Albrecht also notes the critical,
conservative and patriotic anti-cosmopolitan discourses of Göchhausen and
the *Eudämonia* in Austria and Germany.[26] It is telling to look at what use
Robison makes of the phrase 'Weltbürger-Republik' which appeared in the
title of Göchhausen's original German publication.[27] Whereas Göchhausen
merely refers to the 'Weltbürger' as one of the widely-circulated names for
Weißhaupt's *Illuminaten-Orden*, Robison gives the phrase fear-inducing pro-
portions, announcing that the secret society 'sows the seeds of licentious
Cosmopolitism'.[28]

This recoding of 'cosmopolitan' to connote wholly negative cultural
practices raises the question as to how the actual practice of translating German literature is influenced by this critical framework. In other words, how
do actual German translations become linked firstly with bad taste and secondly with conspiracy theories surrounding secret societies, and thirdly how
do they contribute to creating national identities? One answer to this question is offered by Espagne and Werner's model of cultural transfer, which
identifies an inescapable change of semantic contextualisation that goes
hand in hand with translation: translation is always transformation,[29] as different cultural frames of reference de- and re-contextualize literary products. Benedikte Naubert's *Herrmann von Unna* helps in this regard. Naubert's
historical novel was incredibly popular in the 1790s, almost immediately
translated into French in 1791, into English in 1794, and even staged in
Covent Garden in 1795 as 'The Secret Tribunal'.[30] The novel's content provides suitable material for the conspiracy theories discussed thus far: Ida,
illegitimate daughter of a nobleman, but raised in a bourgeois family in

---

25 Albrecht, *Kosmopolitismus*, 308.
26 Albrecht, *Kosmopolitismus*, 97–99.
27 On Barruel see Rogalla, *Verschwörung*, 74–78. He also reconstructs the paths between Germa-
    ny, France and Britain in his account.
28 Robison, *Proofs of a Conspiracy*, 145.
29 For this essay I have drawn on Michel Espagne's 'Jenseits der Komparatistik. Zur Methode der
    Erforschung von Kulturtransfers', in *Europäische Kulturzeitschriften als Medien transnationaler und
    transdisziplinärer Wahrnehmung*, ed. by Ulrich Mölk (Göttingen: Vandenhoek and Ruprecht,
    2006), pp. 13–32, Espagne's *Von der Elbe bis an die Seine: Kulturtransfer zwischen Sachsen und
    Frankreich im 18. und 19. Jahrhundert* (Leipzig: Universitätsverlag, 1999), and Michel Espagne
    and Michael Werner, 'Deutsch-Französischer Kulturtransfer im 18. und 19. Jahrhundert', *Fran-
    cia* 13 (1985) 502–510.
30 [Benedikte Naubert]: *Herrmann von Unna. Eine Geschichte aus den Zeiten der Vehmgerichte*. (Leipzig:
    Weygand, 1788); *Herman d'Unna, ou Aventures arrivées au commencement du quinzieme siècle [Texte
    imprimé], dans le temps où le tribunal secret avoit sa plus grande influence;* translated by Baron de Bock.
    (Paris: Metz, 1791); *Hermann of Unna. A Series of Adventures of the Fifteenth Century, in which the
    Proceedings of the Secret Tribunal under the Emperors Winceslaus and Sigismond, are Delineated. In Three
    Volumes. Written in German by Professor Kramer* (London: G.G. and J. Robinson, 1794).

Nürnberg, appears at the court of King Wenceslas and instantly becomes the Empress's favourite. She falls in love with Herrmann von Unna, before becoming tied up in a series of conspiracies, which employ secret tribunals to separate her from Herrmann and imprison her falsely in various dungeons and convents. Naubert's novel was published in Germany in 1788; by the time of its translation in 1794, images of dungeons, violence and secret tribunals were no longer merely associated with the Middle Ages, but with the real violence of the Jacobin Terror in France.

The paths of transfer add to this association: the English text of 1794 seems to have been translated from the French of Baron de Bock (1791). De Bock was a well-known sympathizer with the Girondist faction of revolutionaries, a member of the General Assembly in France since 1789, and a Freemason who notoriously published a study on the *Vehmgericht* in Westphalia in order to illustrate the realistic nature of the text he translated. There are numerous amendments in the English text which seem to have their origin in Bock's historical studies, all of which increase the importance of the secret tribunals in the novel. Whereas the episodes before the *Vehmgericht* were merely one element of the two-volume German work, the English translation adds an entire middle volume which draws on Bock's study and emphasizes the conspiratorial elements of the plot.[31] With such dubious forms of translation in the 1790s it is easy to see how the transnational networks of cultural transfer themselves become inseparable from suspicions of radical conspiracy.

In many of the cases of cultural transfer mentioned thus far, one can talk of radical translation for numerous reasons. On the one hand, the paths of transfer involve radical politicians and literati; secondly the contents of the novels may focus on radical political goals, prefigure or portray the radical and secret cabals central to counter-revolutionary conspiracies, or the translations may finally amend the original works to make them appear more radical than the originals actually are. Simultaneously, however, the 'German School' becomes synonymous for all that is negative about home-grown British culture, as could be seen in Jane Austen's *Northanger Abbey*. The latter process is all the more insidious, as it leads to the construction of literary assumptions relating to the origins and nature of German Gothic writing which remained largely unchanged in English Studies until recent years. As Peter Mortensen has suggested, these reactions, ranging from scepticism to outright polemics, are borne out in British literary production of the period.[32] When T. J. Mathias declares: 'No Congress props our

---

31 See Hilary Brown, *Benedikte Naubert (1756–1819) and her Relations to English Culture* (Leeds: Maney Publishing, 2005). I thank Julia Ritter (Halle) for her assistance in surveying Baron de Bock's works in the French original.
32 Mortensen, *British Romanticism*, 25–42.

Drama's falling state,/The modern ultimatum is, 'Translate.'/Then sprout
the morals of the German school;/The Christian sinks, the Jacobin bears
rule' in his satirical poem 'The Shade of Alexander Pope' (1798),[33] German
literature replaces that which in his earlier 1797 poem 'The Pursuit of Literature' was called 'Frenchified', a form of British cultural shorthand for anything that is bad about modernity. This modernity is also inherently linked
to Barruel's and Robison's conspiracy theory: the translation activities of the
Minerva Press (mainly responsible for German imports) are linked by Mathias to the Illuminati.[34] One literary figure more than any other seems to
be responsible for inspiring this new direction of attack: Matthew G. Lewis
(author of the infamous *Monk*) is criticized repeatedly by Mathias. In referring to Germany and the 'Bleeding Nun' in the 'Advertisement' to *The
Monk*,[35] Lewis encouraged the German nametag for the 'homegrown' British Gothic; and the idea of a British aesthete staying in the home of a perceived Illuminati, the Headmaster, critic and cultural networker Karl-August
Böttiger,[36] during his stay in Weimar did nothing to help the reception of
Schiller's works either, as will later be seen.[37]

Mathias' poem – which Mortensen has only discussed in terms of its
inherent Europhobia – associates most of what is nowadays considered as
the first onset of modernity in the 1790s with the 'German School'. The
connection of mass-production and mass-readership of literature, transnational cultural connections, politics, and the formation of nationalism – all
that is boundary breaking in the 1790s – with 'the modern ultimatum' betrays the real uncertainty surrounding these dubious forms of Anglo-German cultural transfer in the 1790s. As Linda Colley has convincingly shown,
such connections point towards the fact that British society and British
identity were inherently insecure and unstable with or without the events in
France[38] to which Mathias' satirical poems critically refer. While Seamus
Deane and Linda Colley have focussed profitably on the home-grown so-

---

33 T. J. Mathias, 'The Shade of Alexander Pope on the Banks of the Thames at Twitnam. A Satire
    with Notes' in [T. J. Mathias], *Works of the Author of the Pursuits of Literature [...]*, 4 vols (Dublin:
    Millikan, 1799), III, pp. 56–60.
34 On these links see Mathias, *Works of the Author*, III, p. 52 and I, p. 280.
35 Matthew G. Lewis: *The Monk* (Harmondsworth: Penguin, 1998), p. 6.
36 On Böttiger's deep involvement in Weimar and German cultural life in the 1790s see Karl
    August Böttiger, *Literarische Zustände und Zeitgenossen. Begegnungen und Gespräche im klassischen Wei-
    mar*, ed. by Klaus Gerlach and René Sternke (Berlin: Aufbau, 1998). Böttiger had associated
    himself directly with the European conspiracy theories surrounding Bode's involvement in the
    Illuminati by writing a necrologue in his honour and defending him from charges of revolutio-
    nary activities. On this footnote in Böttiger's life in publishing, see Wilson, *Geheimräte*, 182–
    184.
37 On Lewis's stay in Weimar and his own – often highly over-exaggerated role – in the cultural
    life there see Louis F. Peck, *A Life of Matthew G. Lewis* (Cambridge, Mass.: Harvard University
    Press, 1961), pp. 11–14.
38 Linda Colley, *Britons. Forging the Nation 1707–1837* (London: Vintage, 1996).

cio-historical, economic and political instability in Britain in the 1790s, it is
no less profitable to limit the scope to literary considerations, although the
example of Jane Austen's *Northanger Abbey* unites both the aesthetic and social debates. Closer inspection of Austen's novel (and indeed Mathias' poetry) shows that what is troubling about modern reading habits is by no
means so clear cut as a simple critique of German literature. In highlighting
the shocking titles of the German works mentioned, Austen actually points
towards the role of *English expectations* of German literature. These expectations are clearly visible in the changes German works undergo in the
course of translation: the exorcist of Kahlert's *Der Geisterbanner* becomes the
more mysterious 'necromancer' in Peter Teuthold's translation for the Minerva Press in 1794.[39] On a micro-level these changes radicalize the horror
in the text: if in Kahlert's text one reads 'Furchtbar schwebte der Geist
meiner Mutter einher; – meine Sinne verließen mich'[40] Teuthold writes 'The
ghost of my mother hovered before my eyes with a grim, ghastly look; a
chilly sweat bedewed my face and my senses forsook me'.[41] The English
text is littered with such revisions.[42] It is clear that Teuthold considers this
to be in keeping with British taste and expectations, which points to a
home-grown taste for horror projected onto German sources. But what
precisely are these horrors?

Put bluntly, they are horrors caused by the processes of social modern-
ization mentioned in Mathias' poem above: consumerism, mass-readership
and cosmopolitanism. Social conditions and literary history re-combine in
Austen's novel, when Catherine Moreland must learn that the horrid mysteries of intrigue, conspiracy, and murder she has read of in such novels are
not transferable to British culture. Catherine may believe that Henry Tilney
and his father have killed her prospective mother-in-law and are out to imprison her, but she has to learn that the 'dreadful nature of the suspicions'
she has are the product of a 'riot in [her] own brain' brought on by her reading habits.[43] But the image that Tilney draws of contemporary Britain as
dominated by surveillance networks, political insecurity and radicalism
points to a less reassuring social situation at home. As Seamus Deane has
shown, the historical link between radicalism and histrionic reactionary politics – as is the case with the Treason Trials and the suspension of Habeas

---

39 [K.F. Kahlert], *Der Geisterbanner. Eine Wundergeschichte aus mündlichen und schriftlichen Traditionen*
    (Vienna: Wallishauser, 1792); [K. F. Kahlert], *The Necromancer, or the Tale of the Black Forest*,
    translated by Peter Teuthold (London: Minerva Press, 1794).
40 Kahlert, *Geisterbanner*, 34.
41 Kahlert, *Necromancer*, 15.
42 Alan Menhennet has looked at these changes in some detail, see his 'Schiller and the "Ger-
    manico-Terrific" Romance' *Publications of the English Goethe Society* 51 (1981) 27–47. Cf. also
    Hall, *French and German Gothic Fiction in the Late Eighteenth Century*.
43 Austen, *Northanger Abbey*, 128, 72.

Corpus from 1793 onwards – suggests that Catherine's fears could actually be justified.[44] The enemy 'working among us', of which John Robison so emphatically spoke in his conspiracy theory,[45] may not be an outsider contaminating the British soul at all, but rather home-grown, in the shape of radicals such as Wolfe Tone and his Irish rebellion of 1798, the various radical Dissenters placed under a gagging order by Pitt, such as Mary Wollstonecraft, William Godwin and many others. In a strange relay, however, conservative thinkers like Robison manage to disperse these home-grown uncertainties onto foreign sources. I call this a strange process because transnationalism in the form of translation and cultural transfer – although demonized – actually seems to be the necessary condition for this construction of 'healthy' British identity. Without intercultural contact, the *Anti-Jacobin*, the *British Critic* and Jane Austen could not construct their Pitt-friendly models of British nationalism. Crossing borders is bad, but it does allow one to define one's own borders and identities by identifying the Other of British identity in development. Cultural transfer seems to be a welcome element in the process of creating a stable political order and cultural identity in Britain.

In short, if by the mid-1790s German literature is – whether rightly or wrongly, and often indiscriminately – understood to be the epitome of all things radical, even revolutionary – and hence immoral, despicable and non-British, then this seems to be as much a displacement of British fears onto the continental Other. Nor is this recognition the work of postmodern cultural historians: Pitt the Younger recognized these dual dangers and opportunities of radical and dissenting culture in the construction of a national identity. In 1797, with support for his war on France at a dangerous low, radical intellectuals scoring popular successes and the French army lined up on the Normandy coast, the Prime Minister set up the now infamous *Anti-Jacobin, or Weekly Examiner* in order to win the 'cultural war' against both home-grown and continental radicals.[46] Contemporary and more recent observers have suggested that the difficulties suffered by advocates of German literature until well into the nineteenth century are solely traceable to the work of the *Anti-Jacobin*, both in its initial guise – featuring satirical literary spoofs by government members Canning, Gifford, Ellis and even Pitt him-

44 As an introduction see David Duff, 'From Revolution to Romanticism: The Historical Context to 1800', in *A Companion to Romanticism*, ed. by Duncan Wu, (London: Blackwell, 1999), pp. 23–34; on social unrest at home see Deane, *French Revolution*, 130–170. Linda Colley's excellent *Britons* is also indispensible in this regard.
45 Robison, *Proofs of a Conspiracy*, 126.
46 Cf. Emily Lorraine de Montluzin, *The Anti-Jacobins 1798–1800* (New York: Macmillan, 1988), pp. 1–52; Graeme Stones' 'Introduction to *The Anti-Jacobin*' in his *Parodies of the Romantic Age*, I, pp. xlv-lx. The following remarks on the production of the *Anti-Jacobin* are indebted to these two authors.

self – and in its later, less playful, more vitriolic version, the *Anti-Jacobin Review*, run by J. R. Greene from 1798, from which the 'political alchymist'-quote above is garnered.

The literary parodies of the first *Anti-Jacobin* mimicking the literary production of the radical intelligentsia are of interest for several reasons. In their subtle combination of politics with a canny eye for literary trends, the *Anti-Jacobin* points towards, and ultimately out-performs, the inherent politicization of literature amongst Britain's dissenting radicals with Godwin's, Wollstonecraft's and Southey's own methods. At the same time the speed with which their parodies were produced – appearing weekly during the parliamentary terms in 1797 and 1798 – was only possible because the contributors, the Tory MPs George Canning, George Ellis, John Hookham Frere and William Gifford, all engaged in a form of collective authorship, with written material left open on the table for others to alter, complete or delete, or with certain pieces being written by all four simultaneously. In an age in which political and intellectual excess dominates, Canning and company mimic this radical excess in probably the most renowned parody of the 1790s, a play published in volumes 30 and 31 of the *Anti-Jacobin*, supposedly written by a certain William Higgins of St. Mary's Axe going by the name of 'The Rovers. Or: The Double Arrangement.'[47]

I say that the play mimics the excesses of radical literature partly because it has *too* many sources, *too* many points of reference in contemporary culture. For example, it openly complicates the 'domestic bliss' (R, 216), which is mentioned in the introduction as the sign of healthy British life, as Matilda, the hero Rogero's love and mother of his children, has also borne children to Casimere, who in turn is married to another female character, Cecilia. The implications here are clear: healthy family life is not a priority in Germany and the social uncertainty featured in the play is a direct result of this decadent disregard for respecting the family as the most basic unit of social life. This is – so the reader should assume – one of the core components of a healthy British social order.

The *Anti-Jacobin*'s satire is more complex however, and points towards the employment of Germany as a field onto which internal British conflicts can be projected. This becomes clear when one identifies 'Higgins' as a barely disguised caricature of William Godwin and Samuel Taylor Coleridge. Higgins lives in St. Mary's Axe, a reference both to Godwin's wife Mary Wollstonecraft and to his condoning the assassination of Louis XVI in France; the images of debauched family life in the play are thus clearly linked with reactionary criticism of Wollstonecraft's efforts to gain equal

---

47 'The Rovers', in Stones, ed., *Parodies of the Romantic Age*, I, pp. 216–242. All further references are to this edition and will appear in the main body of the text with the abbreviation R and the respective page number.

rights for women. Furthermore Rogero's song at the close of Act I turns Coleridge's German University, Göttingen, into the object of satire: 'There first for thee my passion grew,/Sweet! sweet Matilda Pottingen!/Thou wast the daughter of my Tu-/-tor, Law Professor at the U-/-niversity of Gottingen/-niversity of Gottingen' (R, 228). Apart from this reference to Coleridge, it is also likely that Matilda refers to Wolfe Tone's young fiancé, Matilda Witherington, with whom he had eloped whilst studying at Trinity College, Dublin. The 'tutor' may also refer to the case of Robert Adair – a favourite target of Canning's – who was said to have fallen in love with his tutor's daughter in Göttingen.[48] In the following issues of the *Anti-Jacobin*, Coleridge attracted negative attention for having abandoned his family in order to travel to Germany to become a *philosophe*, thus linking British radicalism and Germany with familial unrest in his case too. These convoluted events are mirrored on the plot-level in the no less convoluted love-stories in 'The Rovers' itself.

This plot is quickly told – mainly because 'Higgins' does so in his introduction to the second instalment (R, 232–234). Rogero is in love with Matilda, the daughter of his college tutor, who in turn sends Matilda into hiding, where she meets Casimere. Casimere tires of Matilda and leaves her in order to marry Cecelia; having tired of her too, he invents a story of needing to go to Kamschatka on business, but moves to Weimar instead. Meanwhile the tyrannical Count Roderic has Rogero's father murdered in a political intrigue and his minister, Gaspar, ensures that Rogero is locked up in the mediaeval priory in Quedlinburgh by the evil Prior. The characters all descend on Weimar, where slowly Roderic's despotism is undone. Rogero having been freed, the Count, Gaspar, and the Friar are locked up in the priory dungeon. Leaving the ridiculousness of the plot aside, connections to the contemporary processes of cultural transfer I have focussed on here are clearly visible: the title, 'The Rovers', is an obvious reference to Schiller's *Die Räuber*; the 'double arrangement' of the title meanwhile refers to Goethe's *Stella*. In the introductory note to the second instalment in issue 31, and in the various footnotes provided throughout the play, the authors advertize their other main sources as *Kabale und Liebe*, Kotzebue's *Menschenhass und Reue* in Sheridan's translation, *The Stranger*, and *Graf Benyowsky*, as well as Matthew Lewis' adaptation of *Kabale und Liebe*, *The Minister*, and his own Gothic extravagance, *The Castle Spectre*, which draws heavily on Schiller.[49] While elements such as the dungeons point towards Lewis' novel *The Monk* and to Nau-

---

48 See Stones' notes to 'The Rovers', *Parodies of the Romantic Age*, I, pp. 287–240, 331.
49 Friedrich Schiller, *The Robbers*, translated by Alexander Fraser Tytler (London: J.J. and G.G. Robinson, 1792); Friedrich Schiller, *Cabal and Love* (London: T. Boosey, 1795); August Kotzebue, *The Stranger, or Reform'd Housekeeper*, translated by Richard B. Sheridan (London: W. Porter, 1798); August Kotzebue, *Count Benyowsky, or the Conspiracy of Kamschatka*, translated by William Render (Cambridge: University Press, 1798); Johann Wolfgang von Goethe, *Stella*,

bert's *Herrmann von Unna*, rattling chains and unmotivated ghosts draw attention to those stereotypes of German writing criticized by Jane Austen and others, yet are in fact inter-textual traces of Lewis' *Castle Spectre*, as Stones has identified in his extensive notes to the play.[50] This excessive form of inter-textual parody is also reflected at plot level. When Rogero narrates the story of his imprisonment, he does so in terms of quoting passages from Karl Grosse's *Der Genius*:

> Some demon whispered me that I should never see her more. – I stood gazing on the hated vehicle which was conveying her away for ever. – The tears were petrified under my eyelids. – My heart was crystallized with agony. Anon – I looked out along the road. – the diligence seemed to diminish every instant. – I felt my heart beat against its prison, as if anxious to leap out and overtake it. (R, 226)[51]

In the second instalment in particular, entire passages from Sheridan's *The Stranger* are quoted at length and finally ridiculed, but nevertheless belying thorough knowledge of the sources.

As the various footnotes and introductions make abundantly clear, all of the works mentioned in the play (whether Schiller or Naubert, Goethe or *Sturm und Drang* aesthetics departing from the Aristotle's three unities; R, 218) have been read in existing translations and thus do little to introduce German writing into a British setting. This is not to suggest that the play does not engage in any meaningful act of cultural transfer of its own, however. Indeed Canning and his cohorts seem to be *too* familiar with German culture for their own Conservative aims. A close reading of the play reveals far more knowledge of German literary precursors in *Sturm und Drang* and popular German drama than their footnotes let on. Apart from the obvious Schiller, Kotzebue and Goethe, there are traces of Lessing's domestic tragedies, novels of chivalry and most notably Lenz' *Die Soldaten* and Klinger's *Sturm und Drang*. Knowledge of German history and current affairs is also visible. Yet those elements of German culture singled out by the *Anti-Jacobin*'s editors all have one thing in common: they are inseparable from the conspiracy theories on the origins of, and supposed support for the French Revolution in Enlightenment Germany – and hence from the by now standard model of Anglo-German cultural relations seen thus far.

In Canning's astute introductory notes, Higgins claims to be imitating German drama and tells us that part of the play, 'the song of Rogero' is

translated by Miss T. Dalton (London: Hookham & Carpenter, 1798); Matthew Lewis, *The Castle Spectre* (London: J. Bell, 1798).

50 Stones, *Parodies of the Romantic Age*, I, p. 333.
51 Compare this for example with the expressions of fear and terror in the following passage from Grosse's original: 'Aber in dem Moment brachen sich zugleich ihre Augen, sie knirschte mit den Zähnen, sie beugte sich mit verzerrtem Munde und gräßlich starrenden Blicken zu mir hin, das eiskalte Gesicht einer Leiche fiel auf das meinige, ihre Hände ergriffen krampfhaft meine Arme mit einer zerfleischenden Heftigkeit. Entsetzt sprang ich auf.' (Grosse, *Der Genius*, 77)

'literally translated from the composition of a young German friend of mine, an *Illuminé*' (R, 219). The 'Almanac-maker at Gotha', from which the second song is supposed to derive, more than likely refers to Johann Christoph Bode, leading member of the Illuminati and publicist in Gotha and Weimar. Quedlinburgh, meanwhile, had – since a series of articles in the *Speculator* around 1790 – been associated with Klopstock, and it is likely that the evil Prior of Quedlinburgh is a parody of the theologian who had proclaimed the Revolution to be 'des Jahrhunderts edelste That' (the noblest deed of the century) and whose ode 'Der Freiheitskrieg' (War of Liberation)[52] had engaged critically with the same German-Austrian coalition forces who at one point walk across the stage seemingly unmotivated (R, 234 and 237). These soldiers are returning from the 'Seven Years' War', a strange case of politically motivated historical reference, as these German and Austrian soldiers had most recently been engaged in fighting back the threat of revolutionary France. In the course of the Anglo-German cultural transfer this truth is obviously less than helpful in creating an image of German debauchery. The subject of the anti-German sentiment is obvious: Sachsen-Weimar is conjured up as a nest of secret societies and conspiring revolutionaries. Thus, when by the end of the play a secret band of 'ten brave men', including Prussian grenadiers and a Knight Templar disguised as a waiter, march on Quedlinburgh to imprison Count Roderic and liberate Rogero (R, 240–2), the link between Germany, social degeneracy, secret society and revolution is complete.

The real target, however, are the enemies already within Britain, who are importing foreign ideas. Weimar as the site of Gothic tyranny and religious despotism seems to refer to Matthew Lewis's attempts to popularize German culture, a fact underlined by Matilda – the devilish *femme fatale* of his novel *The Monk* – turning up in Weimar of all places, where Lewis himself had stayed in 1792. This line of attack also extends to those cosmopolitans responsible for translating German writing and making it available to radical dissenters – notable victims are Mrs. Inchbald and Richard Sheridan. The translations of German plays on which the phantasmagorical Mr Higgins draws, therefore turn out to be equally phantasmagorical themselves – the product of radical British intelligentsia and literati such as Coleridge, Lewis and others. It is no surprise that the first act closes with a 'Laterna magica' conjuring up a student in Göttingen – where Coleridge was studying Kantian philosophy.

Does this mean that the *Anti-Jacobin* is not a genuine case of cultural transfer then? Even if the literary portrayals themselves are not, on closer

---

52 Friedrich Gottlieb Klopstock, *Sämmtliche Werke. Stereotyp-Ausgabe*, ed. by Augus Leberecht Back and Albert Richard Constantin Spindler, 18 vols (Leipzig: Göschen, 1839), IV, pp. 313, 323–324.

inspection, the sources of these images prove to be instances of Anglo-German cultural transfer. The *Anti-Jacobin* resorts to portrayals of Sachsen-Weimar and Sachsen-Gotha first mooted in conservative, anti-Enlightenment circles in Vienna and Berlin. It was from precisely these transnational networks of conspiracy theorists that writers such as John Robison drew their materials. Canning and his cohorts seem to be more canny than this, however, as they understand that the conspiracy theories of conservatives such as Göchhausen, Barruel, Edmund Burke, and John Robison in Edinburgh all rely in equal measure on similar transnational communication and translation networks for which they pillory radical dissenters and *philosophes*. When the *Anti-Jacobin* conjures up the phantasmagoric German conspiracy threat, it simultaneously reflects this act in the mode of parody – symbolized in the play with the self-referential 'Laterna magica'. On the one hand, this allows Canning and his cohorts to deploy conspiracy theories in order to strengthen Pitt's political course in Europe and reinforce British identity, *while at the same time* distancing themselves from the equally radical, and no less questionable, Gothic narratives in the writings of Barruel and Robison. The conspiracy theorists drew on the same symbolic valence of Gothic imagery (secret societies, dungeons, darkness) which British radicals such as William Godwin employed with astounding success in their critical novels such as *Caleb Williams*. The phantasmagorical 'German School' conjured up by the *Anti-Jacobin* does indeed reproduce the Gothic narratives of conspiracy and political turmoil, but it does so at a highly ironic remove almost reminiscent of Lawrence Sterne – including footnotes and introductions. Thus Canning, Frere, Ellis, and Gifford can highlight what they perceive as the *real* threat to traditional social and moral order without becoming fully paid-up members of the 'German School' themselves: namely those who threaten the British constitution from inside and outside.

Higgins' parody of the aesthetic affront in the *Sturm und Drang*'s attack on the three Aristotelian unities illustrates how this attempt to control political and cultural discourse functions. If the setting is anywhere between the twelfth century and the present, this also implies an inherent backwardness of German culture, which affords the monarchy too much despotic control. Britain, on the other hand, is held to have a superior constitution. This is underlined by the presence of Puddingfield and Beffington, two English noblemen 'exiled by the Tyranny of King John' but rescued by the signing of the Magna Carta. (R, 219) This is not quite the constitutional monarchy of which Britain was so proud in the 1790s, but the symbolic value of the Magna Carta compared to the medieval remnants in the German system in the 'present Century' is easily identifiable.[53] In opposition to the backward Ger-

---

53 On the importance of the constitutional monarchy as a sign of British superiority firstly over absolutist and then republican France, see Colley, *Britons*, 46–58, 91–96, 209–230.

man culture, which (according to Conservative conspiracy theories) produces secret societies, revolution and poisonous literature, Britain has a proper constitution with which to pursue tyrants. If the enemy is working among you, you must mimic the enemy's operations – then the excessive esoteric relays and haunting traces assumed to be related to secret societies and Republican ideology can be contained by virtue of the sacred constitution. And thus Pitt's politics are re-instated by virtue of a phantasmagorical trip through the magic lantern of German history.

Like the gothic novels mentioned in Austen's *Northanger Abbey*, 'The Rovers' is a counterfeit of a German play that lacks any real source and thereby enters into the rootlessness of transnational cultural transfer considered the domain of radical dissenters, secret societies and revolutionaries in the 1790s. Through the mode of parody 'The Rovers' can simultaneously criticize this very same rootlessness. The play transports a specific form of cultural knowledge – the image of Germany as a site of intrigue, conspiracy and violence – and is at the same time at one remove from these acts of cultural transfer, namely in commenting on and decentring cultural transfer as a motor of negative transnational border-crossing. Thus conservatives can engage in cultural transfer in order to create an image of healthy British identity as opposed to the German Other. If British identity emerges in the 1790s, then this seems to be the result of transnational paths of cultural transfer *even if precisely these* paths are simultaneously demonized. That the *Anti-Jacobin* does so with a phantasm of German culture need not be so surprising: after all, the image of German literature circulating around 1797 is that of a literature of ghosts and conspiracy. 'The Rovers' is a dubious, phantasmagorical form of translation and cultural transfer, – but no more phantasmagorical than the threats of the cosmopolitan it draws upon in order to re-assert a coherent sense of Britishness.

Goethe and Schiller, Peasants and Students
Weimar and the French Revolution

W. Daniel Wilson

The problem and the interest in dealing with the small duchy of Saxe-Weimar and Eisenach in the eighteenth century is that Goethe lived there. For beginning in 1776, Goethe was one of the most powerful men in the duchy, a member of the four-person Privy Council (Geheimes Consilium), which advised the Duke Carl August in all important matters of state. The problem is that Goethe is generally considered Germany's greatest writer, and of course that also summarizes the interest in dealing with the politics of Weimar in this period. Since the Second World War, Goethe has come to represent the better Germany, a world of beauty, culture and humanity that is set in stark opposition to the messy and traumatic sphere of politics: as such, Weimar has become something of a political alibi for Germany. This does not mean that politics has not entered interpretations of classical Weimar. Since the 1960s, it has, most prominently, become accepted wisdom that in many of his most important classical works, Goethe was reacting negatively to the French Revolution. But when it comes to the government in Weimar, in which Goethe participated, the image traditionally presented is that of a benign and benevolent regime in the mould of so-called enlightened absolutism, with Goethe and his Duke working tirelessly for the benefit of the Duke's subjects, in particular the non-privileged classes. In this interpretation, the population of the duchy was content and above all passive. This view, however, was achieved only because historians like Hans Tümmler, who was beholden to National Socialist notions of Weimar Duke Carl August as a would-be saviour of the old 'Reich', systematically excluded evidence of political conflict from their accounts and even from editions of documents.[1]

In a series of publications, I have been able to show that political conflict in Weimar between 1775 and about 1806 was much like that in other German territories – not a surprising conclusion for historians, but a scandalous one in the case of Weimar, which is supposed to be something very

---

1   Cf. W. Daniel Wilson, 'Tabuzonen um Goethe und seinen Herzog: Heutige Folgen national sozialistischer Absolutismuskonzeptionen', *Deutsche Vierteljahrsschrift für Literaturwissenschaft und Geistesgeschichte* 70 (1996) 394–442.

beyond the ordinary.[2] I was able to show, for example, that Weimar sold off inmates from local jails to the British as soldiers in the war against the Americans, and Goethe was even more involved in this activity than the other members of the Privy Council. Most important, peasant unrest and its suppression continued throughout this period. During the French Revolution, the situation heated up considerably, as elsewhere in German territories. Matters were most turbulent in two crucial years: 1792 and 1793.[3] This was of course the critical period of the First Coalition War, which led to the so-called second revolution in August 1792, the September massacres in the next month, the invasion of France and then retreat by the Prussian and Austrian forces between August and September, the French conquest of Mainz and Frankfurt in late October. In Mainz the first republic was established on German soil, only to come to an end nine months later when it was retaken by Prussian forces after a fierce siege. Meanwhile, in France the king was put on trial for treason and executed in January 1793. After the French forces were driven back, the Great Terror began in September 1793, with Marie Antoinette executed that autumn. These events caused tremendous dislocation in Saxe-Weimar and Eisenach, leading to protest and unrest – all of which was ignored or consciously suppressed by historians.

It should be stressed that the events in France and in occupied German territories met with a populace in Weimar and Eisenach that was in many ways susceptible to such influence. There had been unrest among peasants, in particular, throughout the centuries, and ultimately the grievances and demands of the peasants now were not different in substance from what had been voiced earlier. What was different was the forcefulness and self-confidence with which peasants expressed their demands now that the model of revolutionary France was in their minds. To be sure, they may not have grasped the Revolution in a very sophisticated way, but they certainly understood that feudal and monarchical authority had been challenged and overthrown in elemental forms that had hitherto been beyond the range of their experience – at most, it probably recalled for them the Peasants' War of the sixteenth century. And indeed, though most of their grievances were old, some were new. For example, with the advance of Prussian troops against France in the summer of 1792, the populace was required to provide accommodation for the soldiers and fodder for the horses, which led to severe shortages of grain, which in turn brought wild inflation and profiteering. There are reports of deep dissatisfaction among the populace at these

---

2   Cf. in particular W. Daniel Wilson, *Das Goethe-Tabu: Protest und Menschenrechte im klassischen Weimar* (Munich: Deuscher Taschenbuch Verlag, 1999), and the titles in the previous and next notes.

3   For the following, cf. W. Daniel Wilson, ed., *Goethes Weimar und die Französische Revolution: Dokumente der Krisenjahre* (Cologne and Weimar: Böhlau, 2004).

measures.[4] Some of the most important new grievances involved the peasants demanding the right to free speech and expression of their political grievances.[5] However, it is significant that these conflicts occurred mainly in Saxe-Eisenach. It was technically a separate duchy (geographically separate from Saxe-Weimar, far to the west), which had fallen to Saxe-Weimar in the 1740s; before that, it had had its own court, and the demise of the Eisenach court had meant considerable economic disadvantage for the populace – causing resentment that had not subsided half a century later. In addition, the authorities in Eisenach were more conservative and harsh than in Weimar, and were much hated. In October of 1792 Eisenach lay squarely in the path of the advancing French troops, and by early November everyone expected that it would be occupied – the rumours were that they were only hours away.

Despite various warnings, what happened next seems to have taken the authorities in Weimar by surprise. There was certainly a measure of 'Furcht und Schrecken' (fear and terror) of the French[6] in Eisenach, so that some citizens fled, but according to one very well-informed official, if the French had entered Eisenach, they would have been greeted 'mit vollem Jubel' (with great jubilation).[7] In fact, men, women and children had filled the marketplace and loudly proclaimed their joy at 'den nahen Einzug der FreyheitsBeschützer' (the imminent arrival of the guardians of freedom).[8] Children, especially in the poorer outer districts, sang rhymed verses saying that the French were coming to beat up the privileged ('es kommen die Franzosen, um zu prügeln die Großen!').[9] In short, a general revolt ('ein großer Umsturz') was expected in case of a French invasion.[10]

There is much more unrest that could be mentioned from the years 1792 and 1793, such as the disturbances by textile workers in the town of Apolda, and in particular the peasants' demands that went so far beyond pre-revolutionary claims that the ministers of state attributed their brashness to 'infection' by the 'poison' of French ideas of freedom and equality. The government responded to this unrest with mildly repressive measures, such as restricting freedom of speech, blocking the sale of revolutionary periodicals, and prohibiting the entry of French citizens who could not demonstrate that they had a legitimate reason for being in the duchy.[11] In most

---

4 Cf. Wilson, *Dokumente der Krisenjahre*, 32–33, and the documents cited there.
5 Cf. Wilson, *Das Goethe-Tabu*, 133–137 and 228–251.
6 Schnauß to Duke Carl August, 29 October 1792. Wilson, *Dokumente der Krisenjahre*, 403. All translations are my own, unless identified otherwise.
7 Thon's report, 27 Nov. 1792. Wilson, *Dokumente der Krisenjahre*, 436.
8 Wilson, *Dokumente der Krisenjahre*, 437.
9 Wilson, *Dokumente der Krisenjahre*, 437. 'The French are coming to beat up the privileged!'
10 Wilson, *Dokumente der Krisenjahre*, 437.
11 On all of this, cf. Wilson, *Dokumente der Krisenjahre*, 35–39, 50–52, and the documents cited there.

cases the government tried to keep such measures quiet in order to maintain their reputation for liberality and not to provoke more resistance. But the mood among the populace seems to have changed very quickly anyway. While most accounts stress the execution of the French king in January 1793 as a catalyst for a change of opinion in Germany, it is clear from the Weimar documents that public opinion began to turn against the French earlier than that. The reason was reports on abuse by the French occupying troops in other parts of Germany, or, as the document mentioned earlier puts it, 'das Betragen dieser FreyheitsPrediger in Deutschland' (the behaviour of these preachers of freedom in Germany).[12] To a certain extent, this reaction represents a limited understanding of what the revolution promised. For it was reported that the good citizens of Eisenach changed their minds about the French when they saw that the occupiers 'den Städten und Dörfern, die sie einnahmen, nichts mitbrachten' and 'daß sie ... auf Ordnung und öffentliche Sicherheit sähen'.[13] In other words, many seemed to have expected that the French would bring complete freedom to the point of anarchy. Others expected an immediate elimination of social inequality: 'Viele, die nichts oder wenig zu verlieren haben, bereicherten sich schon in Gedanken von Gleichheit und Rache.'[14] It is thus not surprising that such people were disappointed by reports from the occupied territories. However, for the more sophisticated, it seems to have been mainly military aggression and in particular the cynical tactics of the occupiers that contributed to soberness. For the French troops demanded very high so-called 'Contributionen' from occupied cities under threats of burning them (the tactic known as 'Brandschatzung'). These tactics were well known from many European wars, but the idealists imagined that the French would not stoop to behaviour previously exhibited by monarchs. The result was that opinion began to shift – not totally, but noticeably. By April 1793 an initiative had been launched by Weimar citizens to donate funds to the cause of war against the French.[15] As I said, the shift was not complete; many peasants, in particular, are reported to have continued to use the revolutionary ideals to lend force to their demands. But there does not seem to have been much more yearning for a French invasion.

2009 is a Schiller year, the 250th anniversary of his birth, and in fact Friedrich Schiller's experiences of the situation in Weimar were pivotal for the aesthetic and philosophical grounding of Weimar Classicism. Schiller had never been a friend of the French Revolution, though one can often

12 Wilson, *Dokumente der Krisenjahre*, 437.
13 Wilson, *Dokumente der Krisenjahre*, 437. 'brought with them nothing for the cities and villages that they took' and 'that they kept an eye on order and public security'.
14 Wilson, *Dokumente der Krisenjahre*, 436. 'Many who had nothing or little to lose already imagined themselves rich when they thought of equality and vengeance.'
15 Wilson, *Dokumente der Krisenjahre*, 48–49, and the documents cited there.

read that he was.[16] However, his early works gave the impression to many that he welcomed revolt, particularly the play *Die Räuber* (1781). The French certainly thought so; this play was performed in Paris in March 1792 to enthusiastic audiences – in fact, it has been called the greatest theatrical success of the revolutionary period.[17] This theatrical hit in the cauldron of revolution was only the first of three embarrassments to Schiller in 1792. The second was that students at the University of Jena adopted a song from this play, beginning with the line 'Ein freies Leben führen wir...' ('A free life we lead...') as their so-called 'Tumultlied' ('tumult song'), sung while they were demonstrating or even rioting.[18] These disturbances were essentially apolitical – the students were defending the existence of their secret societies – though they were fed somewhat by sentiments vaguely connected to the revolution, and the important point is that the ministers in Weimar most definitely associated the unrest among the students with the French Revolution – they often called them 'unsre Jacobiner zu Jena' (our Jacobins in Jena).[19] Again and again government reports mention this song, and on at least one report from the university a minister demonstratively underlined the word 'Räuberlied' (Robbers' Song).[20] Another minister, reporting on the singing of Schiller's song during student demonstrations, wrote: 'Schiller hätte auch etwas Besseres machen können.'[21] Even the Duke complained in a letter from the front, where he was commanding a Prussian regiment and received a steady stream of official and unofficial reports on the situation in Jena, that the thunder of cannons was 'das schlechteste Spectacle von der Welt [...] und [hat] jetzunder bei mir mit Schillers 'Räubern' einerlei Wert'.[22]

The third embarrassment for Schiller was more serious for the duchy, since news of it spread throughout Germany. In August 1792 Schiller was one of eighteen foreign notables to whom the National Assembly granted honorary citizenship in the French Republic because they had advanced the cause of freedom and the French Revolution in their writings. Others were

---

16 Most recently, a thorough airing of the issues is presented by Jeffrey L. High, *Schillers Rebellionskonzept und die Französische Revolution* (Lewiston, ME: Mellen, 2004).

17 Axel Kuhn, *Die Französische Revolution* (Stuttgart: Reclam, 1999), p. 175; see also Ehrhard Bahr, 'Der *Räuber*-Autor als Ehrenbürger der Französischen Republik', in *Ethik und Ästhetik: Festschrift für Wolfgang Wittkowski zum 70. Geburtstag*, ed. by Richard Fischer (Frankfurt a. M.: Lang, 1995), pp. 147–152.

18 Cf. Wilson, *Dokumente der Krisenjahre*, 41–42, and the documents cited there.

19 C. G. Voigt to Duke Carl August, 14 July 1792. Wilson, *Dokumente der Krisenjahre*, 218.

20 Prof. H. E. G. Paulus to Minister Voigt, 1 July 1792. Wilson, *Dokumente der Krisenjahre*, 196.

21 C. F. Schnauß to Duke Carl August, 6 July 1792. Wilson, *Dokumente der Krisenjahre*, 204. 'Schiller could have written something better.'

22 Duke Carl August to his mother, Anna Amalia, 12 October 1792. Wilson, *Dokumente der Krisenjahre*, 386. 'The worst spectacle in the world and has about the same value for me at the moment as Schiller's *The Robbers*.'

George Washington, James Madison, Thomas Paine, and in Germany Friedrich Gottlieb Klopstock, Joachim Heinrich Campe and Johann Heinrich Pestalozzi – the disparity of political viewpoints and the conservatism of some of these men is a clear indication of how fuzzy the notion of revolutionary partisanship was for the French delegates. The French decree was reported in newspapers, and contrary to what one can read in some accounts, Schiller and indeed all of Weimar knew about it from the papers – in Weimar the official revolutionary paper, the *Moniteur universel,* was widely read. The Duchess Louise wrote to her friend, the conservative writer Charlotte von Stein, reporting on Schiller's honorary French citizenship and expressing gingerly the 'hope' that he would refuse it.[23] On receiving this letter, Charlotte von Stein immediately wrote to Schiller's wife, saying that she had gotten a letter (without indicating from whom) expressing the 'belief' that Schiller would, of course, publicly refuse this honorary citizenship.[24] Schiller did not do so, since the report was only contained in the newspapers (and even there under the faulty name 'Gilleers'), and he had not received the decree itself[25] – it was to arrive in the mail only six years later, when the signatories had been long since guillotined. Presumably he did not respond because he did not want to draw more attention to the affair. The pressure from the Duchess, via Charlotte von Stein, was heavy enough, but it got worse. The most powerful minister, Voigt, reports in a letter to the Duke that Schiller had to put up with 'manchen scherzhaften Vorwurf' (many a joking reproach) because of the National Assembly's action.[26] It seems mainly to have been Charlotte von Stein who provided the humour. Like many contemporaries, she habitually called the revolutionaries 'Räuber' because they had seized property from nobility and church.[27] And in the context of Schiller's honorary citizenship, she wrote that 'vor jetz mag wohl das französische Bürgerrecht das Banditten recht seyn'.[28] So Schiller's robbers become French revolutionaries. And in the eyes of ministers, this was all associated with 'Jacobin' students singing songs about freedom while smashing windows in Jena.

All of this must have been deeply embarrassing to Schiller, who was a supernumerary professor of history at the University of Jena and thus directly in the pay – pitiful pay though it was – of the Duke. Previously to the

---

23 '…j'éspère qu'il le refusera.' Louise of Saxe-Weimar to Charlotte von Stein, 10 September 1792. Wilson, *Dokumente der Krisenjahre*, 363.

24 '…man glaube aber Schiller werde es natürlicherweise ausschlagen.' Charlotte von Stein to Charlotte Schiller, 14 September 1792. Wilson, *Dokumente der Krisenjahre*, 364.

25 Wilson, *Dokumente der Krisenjahre*, 391.

26 Voigt to Carl August, 12 November 1792. Wilson, *Dokumente der Krisenjahre*, 417.

27 Wilson, *Dokumente der Krisenjahre*, 391, note 32.

28 Charlotte von Stein to Charlotte Schiller, 15 October [1792]. Wilson, *Dokumente der Krisenjahre*, 391. 'The right to French citizenship presently seems to be the right of bandits.'

Goethe and Schiller, Peasants and Students 67

'heißer Herbst' of 1792, he had been relatively indifferent toward the revolution, if one can judge by the complete absence of any comments about it in his entire correspondence between October 1789 and October 1792. In this autumn, though, when the 'joking reproaches' about 'robbers' were flying fast and furious around Weimar, and when reports of the student disturbances and Schiller's honorary French citizenship had made their way into newspapers around Germany, Schiller suddenly conceived the project of writing a public defence of King Louis XVI, who was on trial.[29] I do not want to suggest that the pressure on Schiller was the only motivator behind this project; in fact, he seems to have been so idealistic that he thought of taking a professorship in France in order to gain influence on the revolutionaries and to convince them to take a more moderate path. I think, however, that the pressure on Schiller had a rather subtle, perhaps subconscious effect on him. With respect to the students and their use of his song from *Die Räuber* in their demonstrations, however, the impact on his thinking is more direct. His attitude toward student leaders was, in their eyes, surprisingly cool,[30] and then, in the middle of the worst anarchic crisis in Jena, we find him as one of nine university teachers who authored a letter to the government calling for forceful military measures against the students – the letter has never been noticed in Schiller scholarship.[31] The importance of this letter for an understanding of Schiller lies in the striking parallels between some of its passages and Schiller's letter from half a year later, 9 February 1793, that forms the core of his project leading to the central enunciation of classical aesthetics in Germany, the fifth of the tract *Über die ästhetische Erziehung des Menschen in einer Reihe von Briefen*. In these *'Aesthetic Letters'*, Schiller writes of 'der brutalen Gewalt der Thierheit' (brutal force of beastliness), 'Verwilderung' (savagery), 'Rohigkeit' (brutality), and 'rohe, gesetzlose Triebe' (savage, lawless drives) which are released after the bonds of civil society break down.[32] Strikingly, in the letter of the professors calling for military measures, we read, likewise, of 'Roheit und Verwilderung' (brutality and savagery), the 'roheste Sittenlosigkeit' (most brutal lack of proper behaviour), the 'Rohigkeit' (brutality) of the 'gesezlosen Haufen[s]' (lawless mob).[33] In the *Ästhetische Briefe* it is the French Revolution that has proven the unworthiness of a depraved mankind to be free unless it is morally en-

---

29 Cf. High, *Schillers Rebellionskonzept*, 65–84.
30 Wilson, *Dokumente der Krisenjahre*, 87.
31 8 July 1792. Wilson, *Dokumente der Krisenjahre*, 207–211 (Schiller is the next-to-last signatory).
32 Cf. the draft of the 5th letter in Schiller's letter to Prince Friedrich Christian of Schleswig-Holstein-Sonderburg-Augustenburg of 13 July 1793; both in *Theoretische Schriften*, ed. by Rolf-Peter Janz et al., *Werke und Briefe 8,* ed. by Otto Dann et al. (Frankfurt a. M.: Deutscher Klassiker Verlag, 1992), pp. 567–569 and 495–508; excerpts from the latter: Wilson, *Dokumente der Krisenjahre*, 631–634.
33 Wilson, *Dokumente der Krisenjahre*, 207–211.

nobled – and this ennoblement will be achieved only by art, by 'aesthetic education'. But it is not *only* the French Revolution that Schiller evokes in the *Ästhetische Briefe* as evidence of mankind's depravity – he speaks of a broader phenomenon, of 'gegenwärtige Menschheit' and in particular of conditions in 'den niedern und zahlreichern Klassen' (the lower and more numerous classes).[34] This phrase could easily have at its base Schiller's experience of students in Jena, who were known to be among the poorest in Germany.

It has always been recognized that the *Ästhetische Briefe* are an antipolitical project, at least in the ordinary sense of 'political': they outline a political *goal* – that is, freedom – but it is to be achieved by moral and aesthetic *means*. In turning away from politics so demonstratively, Schiller was following a model established by other professors in Jena under pressure from the government. In two cases, professors who had a liberal or even radical reputation were appointed in Jena despite the government's knowledge of their reputations, but only on the explicit stipulation that they abandon politics.[35] In another case, precisely in these months of the autumn of 1792, another professor and friend of Schiller's, Gottlieb Hufeland, got into hot water with the government when he gave lectures on the French Constitution. He eventually gave in, and soon we find him providing the government with information on suspicious students.[36] Such examples must have had an effect on Schiller. They suggest that his turn to the central theoretical project of Weimar Classicism, along with his project to defend the king of France, arose not only in response to the events in faraway France, but to the events on his doorstep in Jena, both the student disturbances and the intimidation of professors. These circumstances may suggest that Schiller actually had more sympathy for revolution than he indicated. However, we will never know if this was so, because he did not express it – even if he had been philosophically inclined to accept violent insurrection, his self-censorship under the pressure of Weimar repression effectively prevented him from saying so.

It was only a year and a half later, in the summer of 1794, that Goethe and Schiller formed the momentous friendship that was the key founding constellation of German classicism. Here, too, *local* politics in the face of the threat from France played a role. Naturally, it was not the only factor – the philosophies of the two men were converging and found expression in their views on natural science, as Goethe points out in his little essay *Glückliches Ereignis*. But in this essay Goethe gives a hint of the turbulent events of 1792 when he says that before his friendship with Schiller began, Schiller's

---

34 5th letter (cf. note 32 above).
35 Cf. Wilson, *Dokumente der Krisenjahre*, 40–41, and the documents cited there.
36 Cf. Wilson, *Dokumente der Krisenjahre*, 40, and the documents cited there.

play *Die Räuber* was particularly repulsive to him, and says that the play was much loved by 'wilden Studenten' (wild students) – a clear reference, never noted by Goethe scholars, to the events of 1792.[37] But Goethe had another reason to harbour suspicion of Schiller's politics, even if Schiller had in fact become very apolitical. Schiller invited Goethe to contribute to the new journal he was planning under the title *Die Horen*. The prospectus for the journal made clear Schiller's intention to exclude politics from it. But the list of prospective contributors contained the names of several writers who had appeared in the Weimar government files because they had raised political suspicions – two of them were Hufeland, mentioned above, and the philosopher Fichte, who was likewise appointed professor in Jena despite his democratic leanings, and was advised to leave politics at the border when he settled in Saxe-Weimar. Another contributor on Schiller's list was the minor writer Gottlieb Conrad Pfeffel, who had written poems about human rights, freedom and oppression under feudalism in a revolutionary newspaper that came to the attention of the Privy Council in Weimar, and was mentioned by name in the files.[38] As the then-director of the Goethe and Schiller archives in Weimar, Karl Heinz Hahn, pointed out in 1979 (but without reference to all of these cases), Goethe's response to Schiller's invitation to contribute to the journal – his very first letter to Schiller – went through several drafts which Goethe kept in a folder that apparently was meant to become a government file. Hahn's conclusion is that Goethe felt it his duty as a member of the Geheimes Consilium to keep an eye on Schiller's project.[39] There is no evidence that this sort of political suspicion later plagued the friendship between Goethe and Schiller. However, it certainly played a role in its inception.

As I said earlier, since at least the 1980s scholars have had no doubt that Weimar Classicism was partly conceived as a political alliance in the face of the French Revolution and its impact among German opinion-makers. For his part, Goethe went through a phase, in the years 1792–93, when he mobilized his talents more directly in the service of the anti-revolutionary cause. In fact, there is some evidence that he composed his anti-revolutionary comedy *The Der Bürgergeneral* in 1793 in direct response to a letter from Duke Carl August instructing him to help eradicate revolutionary sentiments among the elite in Weimar.[40] Caroline Herder, wife of Johann Gottfried Herder, one of the supporters of the revolution who was explicitly in the duke's sights, commented after seeing the play that it was directed partly

37 MA 12, p. 87; cf. Wilson, *Dokumente der Krisenjahre*, 42.
38 Wilson, *Das Goethe-Tabu*, 226–228.
39 Karl-Heinz Hahn, 'Im Schatten der Revolution – Goethe und Jena im letzten Jahrzehnt des 18. Jahrhunderts', *Jahrbuch des Wiener Goethe-Vereins* 81–83 (1977–79) 37–58.
40 Cf. Wilson, *Das Goethe-Tabu*, 266–270.

against her and her husband.[41] The period of Goethe's friendship with
Schiller, the decade from 1794 to Schiller's death in 1805, coincided roughly
with a period of peace for Saxe-Weimar (1796 to 1806), and in times of
peace the panic, fear and repression that break out among government officials in wartime are often relaxed. The historians Leopold von Ranke and
Hans Tümmler exaggerated the situation when referring to this period as
'Der Frieden des klassischen Weimar'.[42] In the first place, the Duke of Weimar desperately wanted peace because of the threat of inner disturbances
that would have been exacerbated if war were to continue, and which demanded that troops be available for the struggle against the enemy within.
But the peace treaty also did not guarantee domestic peace. While individual
intellectuals, including professors at the university, had been effectively si-
lenced through intimidation by 1793, organized institutional groups like students and peasants in their villages continued to create massive problems
during the supposedly peaceful decade, and in fact more insistently than before: firearms were used by students in one disturbance in 1795, and in
1800 a general revolt ('Aufstand') was feared when over a sixth of the population of Jena gathered in a protest, singing 'freedom songs' ('Freyheit-
sLieder').[43] The garrison commander did not dare to use force against
them, he wrote, because it would have given 'Studenten und Bürgern mehr
Muth zum Aufstand [...], als wozu ohnehin der grösere Theil der hiesigen
Einwohner sogar sehr geneigt ist'.[44]

It remains crucial, in our examination of the lofty world of intellectual
achievement, to pay close attention to political events that may have affected
the grand projects of privileged writers. We must not let the widespread attempts at repudiating recovery of these otherwise unheard voices deter us
from carrying out the task that progressive scholars in the 1960s and 1970s
prepared theoretically but did not consistently carry out in practice, in the
archives: writing an intellectual history 'from below'. In the case of Saxe-
Weimar, attention to previously neglected documents – and a critically scep-
tical attitude toward research that was founded on National Socialist interpretations of absolutism[45]– show clearly that the locus of Weimar Classicism was not a peaceful island of the blessed in a sea of political conflict.
Such a view was propagated in order to divorce Germany's almost univer-

41 2 June 1793. Wilson, *Dokumente der Krisenjahre*, 599; on the intimidation of Herder and his wife,
    see 43–47, and the documents cited there.
42 Hans Tümmler, 'Der Friede des klassischen Weimar', in *Goethe in Staat und Politik: Gesammelte
    Aufsätze by Hans Tümmler* (Köln: Böhlau, 1964), pp. 105–131 (and the essay by Ranke cited
    there).
43 Cf. Wilson, *Das Goethe-Tabu*, 288–289.
44 Major W. von Milckau to Duke Carl August, 2 January 1801. Wilson, *Das Goethe-Tabu*, 289. '…
    would have given students and citizens more courage to revolt to which the majority of the
    local residents are already very disposed.'
45 Cf. Wilson, 'Tabuzonen'.

sally recognized moment of ultimate cultural hegemony from any hint of political repression. The documents show that Weimar was not particularly repressive, but it was also not politically liberal. It suppressed liberal and revolutionary views just as effectively as Prussia or Saxony. It also partook in a pernicious game of upholding the façade of liberality while exerting behind-the-scenes pressure on intellectuals to exercise self-restraint and self-censorship in political matters. Only this game has allowed Weimar to maintain its reputation as the great exception to the abuses inherent in absolutism.

Revolution, Abolition, Aesthetic Sublimation
German Responses to News from France in the 1790s

Birgit Tautz

The French Revolution in German Lands: a Story and its Discontents

In the 1790s, German responses to the French Revolution were multifaceted and more nuanced than the predominant narrative about its influence suggests. According to the latter, public figures across the German-speaking territories were intrigued by, and even sympathetic to, revolutionary ideas until they learned of the second, bloody phase of the Revolution. And, while German thinkers endorsed the revolutionary actions taking place in France, they often rejected the same for their homelands: they staked their hopes on reform-willing princes who governed their respective provinces and who were supposed to embrace political change. The desired reform then became a cornerstone of a narrative of societal change that relied on the sublimation of politics into the aesthetic realm.

Many scholars have focused on delineating this narrative with respect to Weimar Classicism. Similarly, as recent criticism has challenged the nexus of aesthetic sublimation and benevolent rule by redirecting our attention to the political and economic motivations that shaped the life at the courts and of writers in their vicinity, it casts a more critical eye on classical Weimar's attitude towards revolutionary France.[1] An even more complicated picture emerges once we consider German responses to the French Revolution in a larger global context. Such considerations – especially of texts that probe attitudes towards slavery and abolitionism and their representation in fiction

1   The author thanks Maike Oergel and Dan Hall for convening the Breaking Boundaries conference in April 2009, with special thanks to Maike Oergel for wonderful suggestions about preparing this essay for publication. All translations are my own, with assistance by Steve Cerf, Ben Folkman, and Matthew Miller. Insights and interpretation first presented in this essay will be revised and further developed in a book manuscript in progress, provisionally entitled 'Translating the World: Remaking late eighteenth-century Literature between Hamburg and Weimar'. See W. Daniel Wilson, *Goethes Weimar und die Französische Revolution: Dokumente der Krisenjahre* (Köln: Böhlau, 2004); Jeffrey High, *Schillers Rebellionskonzept und die französische Revolution*, (Lewiston: Mellen Press, 2004).

in the 1790s – reveal striking gaps in the dominant narrative of aesthetic sublimation. Scholars have turned their attention to the ways in which Germans were politically and economically invested with maintaining a self-image of innocent, aesthetic bystanders in the French revolutionary process and global conquest, even if the reality did not match this ideal.[2] They have demonstrated how the positioning of female gender identity vis-à-vis global revolutions aided in the emancipation and formation of national bourgeois sentiment, even among aristocratic women at the time of the French Revolution.[3] They have delineated the massive intellectual, historical, and cultural shifts that occurred as the European, specifically German, intellectual tradition confronted a non-European reality that proved inextricably linked to France and was nevertheless exteriorized as Other.[4]

Further probing the German narrative of aesthetic sublimation, I argue that cultural production retained a political and economic side; the spectre of revolutionary France and anti-colonial uprisings was always present in the minds of German authors. It comes to the fore in our story of the 1790s in German lands, as we focus on accounts of the French Revolution – and of the Caribbean slave revolts – in journals and newspapers published in Northern German regions and Free Imperial cities, such as Hamburg.

Responding to news from revolutionary France, the political and aesthetic discourse of the 1790s calibrated a story which became central in the foundation of modern Germany and in which discussions of revolution, abolition, and aesthetic compensation intersected. This discourse was sustained in numerous journals, chiefly among them *Minerva*, which not only delivered the news from the neighbouring country, but also from its colonies. It soon evolved into a discussion of 'a revolution of friendship',[5] marking a shift from negotiating the national and socio-economic interests in political action to the public discussion of an intensely personal 'humanization.' The effort to educate individuals before advancing any political or social change was to be achieved with the help of a friend. I shall argue that this evolution took place, because interpersonal relations were haunted by the spectres of global uprisings and guilt and thus became inevitably entangled with abolitionist discourse or its contrarians. Friendship arose as a model of aesthetic compensation, complementing the paradigm of the fam-

---

2   Path-breaking in this respect was Susanne Zantop, *Colonial Fantasies. Conquest, Family, and Nation in Pre-Colonial Germany, 1770–1810* (Durham: Duke University Press, 1997).

3   Susanne Kord, 'The Pre-Colonial Imagination: Race and Revolution in Literature of the Napoleonic Period', in *Un-Civilizing Processes? Excess and Transgression in German Society and Culture. Perspectives Debating with Norbert Elias*, ed. by Mary Fulbrook (Amsterdam: Rodopi, 2007), pp. 85–115.

4   Susan Buck-Morss, 'Hegel and Haiti', *Critical Inquiry* 26.4 (2000) 821–865 continues to be an influential (and, in many ways, a stand-alone) contribution to this debate.

5   Wulf Segebrecht, 'Lyrik der Klassik', in *Europäische Romantik: Neues Handbuch der Literaturwissenschaft*, ed. by Klaus von See, vol. 14 (Wiesbaden: Athenaion, 1982), pp. 141–178, 158.

ily romance through which global news was most often narrated and dramatized around 1800.[6] Henceforth, friendships and communication among friends form discursive counterparts to the aforementioned act of aesthetic sublimation in philosophies of history. As I have shown elsewhere, philosophers like Hegel suppressed news of actual events and other remnants of 'empirical knowledge,' and forging a coherent story was part and parcel of narrating history.[7] In classical Weimar, too, one sublimated the news reported in journals like *Minerva*,[8] engaging in other aesthetic acts of sublimation, and at the end of my essay I will reconsider a well-known example of this trend: Schiller's correspondence with Prince Friedrich Christian von Schleswig-Holstein-Sonderburg-Augustenburg and Ernst von Schimmelmann. From simulating a nascent discourse of friendship it quickly turns into an exemplary piece of aesthetic discourse: this correspondence is the precursor to *Über die ästhetische Erziehung des Menschen in einer Reihe von Briefen*,[9] first published in 1795.

The Journal as a Modern Medium

Journals are of utmost importance in preparing this shift from authenticating political action to the cultivation of friendship and, ultimately, to aesthetic sublimation. They had started out as a medium of erudition and moral education and became the purveyor of actual news in the 1790s, anticipating the role of the daily newspaper in Germany. Engaging, even penning the currents of the times, the journal encodes a threshold of cultural relations: of translating facts and organizing information, of domesticating the world while keeping it at bay. For example, news about the French and British colonies, which made it into German newspapers and journals, was channelled through France and Great Britain. Often translated (or claiming to be translated) from foreign-language sources, news reports fashioned themselves as authentic documents. They simultaneously relied on the authority of the distant eyewitness whose observations had been recorded and made do without him or her. The published accounts were distinct in their targeting of the German reading public, instilling a sense of being an innocent, disinterested spectator

6   See Felicity Nussbaum, *The Limits of the Human: Fictions of Anomaly, Race, and Gender in the Long Eighteenth Century* (Cambridge: Cambridge University Press, 2003), p. 240; Birgit Tautz, *Reading and Seeing Ethnic Differences in the Enlightenment: From China to Africa* (New York: Palgrave, 2007), pp. 173–196; Zantop, *Colonial Fantasies*, 141–161.
7   Tautz, *Reading and Seeing*, 13–30.
8   Buck-Morss, 'Hegel', 852.
9   In English, the work is commonly referred to as *Aesthetic Education* or *Aesthetic Letters*.

in the global enterprise of colonialism.[10] Remaining ignorant of German entanglements in the economic realities of the slave trade, the news inadvertently exposed the inherent contradictions in the dominating narrative of aesthetic sublimation.

Thus today, eighteenth-century journals provide us with a glimpse into the manner in which authors – and, we must presume readers – filtered the news. The journals' task was to represent 'the reality' of events, which was forged by taking into account peculiarities of the location where the journal was published, and by preserving older, competing discourses that bestowed factuality upon the news and whose broad emotional spectrum appealed to diverse audiences. All of these aspects manifest themselves in a group of journals from the Northern German provinces, which I consulted to further discuss the nexus of revolution, abolition, and aesthetic compensation: *Minerva: Ein Journal historischen und politischen Inhalts, Beiträge zur Völker- und Länderkunde, Deutsches Magazin, Historisch-Politisches Magazin* and *Hannoverisches Magazin* offer valuable insights into how global events resonated with more local concerns.[11] Journals like these became influential cultural mediators, not just because of the factual, educational, and – last but not least – secular impetus they followed, but also because of the formidable role they played in imagining communities, groups of readers that 'bonded' as a result of the journals' reach beyond its place of publication. As different journals took great liberty in 'borrowing' from each other, information and news were truly spread across regions, and the medium emerged as the venue that separated fact from fiction.

The Ghost of Revolution:
News from France, News from the Caribbean

Minerva emerged as a main source of news from revolutionary France, not least because its publisher Johann Wilhelm von Archenholz had lived in Paris. He relocated to Hamburg in 1792 and established the journal.[12] The decade saw a steady stream of essays and reports devoted to France. In 1792, for example, *Minerva* published 67 articles about France, two of which reported about French colonies. A relative decrease in the next three years was fol-

---

10 Cf. Zantop, *Colonial Fantasies*, 141–145; Birgit Tautz, 'Cutting, Pasting, Fabricating: Eighteenth-Century German Travel Texts and their Translators between Legitimacy and Community', *German Quarterly* 79.2 (2006) 155–173.

11 On the role of the journal in Northern German cities, see Katharine B. Aaslestad, 'Old Visions and New Vices: Republicanism and Civic Virtue in Hamburg's Print Culture, 1790–1810', in *Patriotism, Cosmopolitanism, and National Culture*, ed. by Peter-Uwe Hohendahl (Amsterdam: Rodopi, 2003), pp. 143–165.

12 B. von Meerheim, 'Archenholz, Johann Wilhelm von', in *ADB* vol 1, pp. 511–512, http://www.deutsche-biographie.de/ (last access September 11, 2009, 9:32 EST).

lowed by (on average) 60 contributions per year about France between 1796 and 1798, before another sharp decline occurred. However, a fairly small number of essays were devoted to the French Revolution: in 1793, no more than sixteen contributions dealt explicitly and exclusively with revolutionary events; in the other years, ten to twelve per year were more common. Beginning with the 1798 installments, we see a sharp decline.[13] By the turn of the century, but especially with the 1802 installments and French expansionist movements across Europe, *Minerva* had 'gone global' and devoted the majority of its articles to wars in Egypt, trade relations with Asian countries, pseudo-scientific accounts of Africa and Asia, and travel reports from around the globe.

Minerva's 'authentic accounts' of events in France had an enormous impact, especially since the reporting commented on the international effects that French events had in Europe, Northern America, and on the Caribbean islands. Writing about the Caribbean, especially about St. Domingo, culminates in the publication of several series of articles devoted to the slave uprisings and published over a two-year period (1804 –1806). Accounts of the colonies appear interlaced with the 'domestic discourse' of the French Revolution, for they obscure – often already in their titles – the distinction between revolt ('Empörung') and revolution. Most articles invoke a stock repertoire of race and class attributes, transferring, for example, clichés associated with Africa onto the Caribbean world and mapping social differences along the lines of France's social outcasts.[14] But the reports also paint a more complex picture of non-homogeneous alterity which complicates the racialized/racist dichotomies that have been reconstructed for the European concepts of the Other at the time, especially when introducing multiple denominators of race and class, and heterogeneous descriptions of blackness and whiteness in one text, or proclaiming multiple perspectives on one event by printing several accounts.

The latter technique often proves misleading, nevertheless. Many pieces labelled 'neueste Nachrichten' barely conceal an old technique of text-production. They restate knowledge, observations, and news that are *en vogue* in sequels, in different genres, and in different publications, thus adopting a pattern typical of, among others, eighteenth-century scientific travel reports that presume to impart geographical or biological knowledge. Archenholz, for example, adapts this repetitive mode, while introducing new ways of engaging readers and producing narratives of local and national self-understanding. In one of his first essays about revolutionary France, 'Bemerkun-

---

13 The numbers are based on keyword searches of the digitized *Minerva*. in: *Retrospektive Digitalisierung wissenschaftlicher Rezensionsorgane und Literaturzeitschriften des 18. und 19. Jahrhunderts aus dem deutschen Sprachraum*, Universitätsbibliothek Bielefeld, http://www.ub.uni-bielefeld.de/diglib/aufklaerung/index.htm (last access September 11, 2009, 9:14 EST).

14 Zantop, *Colonial Fantasies*, 141–142; Buck-Morss, 'Hegel', 837–845.

gen über den Zustand Frankreichs am Ende des Jahres 1791',[15] he develops a style that has his readers interested in both the events and the journal *Minerva*, while engaging their thoughts on domestic and regional implications of the revolution. Charting detailed information – on economic conditions, social classes, and the interaction between Paris and the colonies – assists Archenholz in describing a context in which readers can imagine political alternatives, including aesthetic sublimation.

What matters to his readers is resonance with their daily experience, i.e. that of Hamburg merchants, businessmen, early industrialists; furthermore, readers are supposed to be interested in the events' utilitarian dimension and their intersection with domestic issues. Thus, in response to the severe financial crisis that crippled Europe in the 1790s, monetary and economic affairs constitute one pillar of Archenholz's reporting. He devotes a fairly large portion of his first article to discussing the ratio between coins and paper money in France, fully aware of and skilfully employing references to the perceived instability of paper money and the associated anxieties, suspicions, and fears that were rampant among the public.[16]

These larger economic interests are entwined with a discussion of the Revolution's impact on segments of the French population, in this case, the aristocrats. Archenholz chronicles their movements, which he delineates in both a physical and metaphorical sense. He predicts that the Revolution will trigger a wave of refugees, setting in motion a migration of aristocrats looking for asylum in adjacent European countries. But Archenholz also notes their inability to conceive of change and to move intellectually. He launches a spirited attack; criticizing aristocratic misconceptions and the stubborn unwillingness to understand both the popular roots and all-encompassing reach of the Revolution, he states cynically: 'In der That giebt es nur ein einziges unfehlbares Mittel alles wieder auf den vorigen Fuß zu bringen, und dies ist kein anders, als den größten Teil der Nation auszurotten'.[17]

Archenholz observes a phenomenon which travel texts depict as a symptom of the colonies. Talking about a 'general decay' in the streets of Paris, he laments the breakdown of administrative structures. He describes hopelessness among the inhabitants, which he sees manifest itself in indifference towards the Parisian mayoral elections and social compartmentalization in France, aspects that, in his opinion, pervade French society. What

---

15 Archenholz, 'Bemerkungen', *Minerva* 1 (1792) 8–46.
16 Richard Gray, *Money Matters: Economics and the German Cultural Imagination, 1770–1850* (Seattle: University of Washington Press, 2008), p. 54: Paper money 'produced value out of nothing', which aroused deep suspicion and formed one among many opposing opinions about the value of paper money. Cf. Gray, *Money Matters*, 29–30.
17 Archenholz, 'Bemerkungen', 22: 'Indeed, there is only one foolproof way to restore the status quo and that is to exterminate the biggest part of the nation.' Unless identified differently all translations are my own.

distinguishes Archenholz's account, I believe, is the assertion that all these undesirable tendencies are exported to – rather than imported from – the colonies. He praises the King's willingness to implement reform, interpreting his firm stand against the emigrants as a sign of trustworthiness and honesty, after doubts about the King's position had raised concern, more so than 'auswärtige Drohungen, Priesterränke und Empörungen der Neger'.[18] In sum, Archenholz's assessment remains modest: while he sympathizes with the Revolution – and correctly identifies a number of internal and external threats – he is most interested in preventing upheaval and instability, inevitably endorsing what would later come to pass as a German solution, namely to curtail aristocratic power by way of a benevolent ruler.

The somewhat resigned tone of various small pieces indicates that *Minerva*'s reporting from France had run its course around 1800. J.S. Ersch's essay, 'Betrachtungen eines unbefangenen Mannes, den Feinden der französischen Revolution vorgelegt, von einem Franzosen'[19] is but one example of this trend. Ersch endorses an evolutionary phase, emphasizing the necessity of civil process and behaviour to assure the legacy of the Revolution. What stands out in his reasoning are not so much the general recommendations for a consolidation of the Republic, but the insight that the development of humans, their adherence to reason and laws will parallel the development of the Revolution and vice versa. What Archenholz had merely alluded to in his depiction of the French situation – reasoned behaviour and benevolent modesty as alternatives to aristocratic and colonial excess – evolves in Ersch's text as a central rhetorical feature of the abolitionist, friendship, and aesthetic discourse of the 1790s; he ends with a tacit plea to build a community reliant on respectable individual action.

Another feature is the rhetoric that unfolds in commentaries on and analysis of the slave revolts in St. Domingo. News about the colonies – published already in the first volume of *Minerva* – are amalgamated rather than reported; they are 'aus verschiedenen Quellen gezogen' (compiled from various sources).[20] The anonymous author predicts that the colonies will be ruined because of the continuing violence, and he launches into an investigation of the roots of cruelty ('all die Grausamkeiten'). He locates one reason in the demographical situation, the dynamics among the four classes that make up the 'Volksmenge' (the people): 'weisse Colonisten, kleine

---

18 Archenholz, 'Historische Nachrichten vom neuern Frankreich', *Minerva* 1 (1792) 237–268, 237. 'threats from abroad, clerical agitation, and revolts by blacks'.
19 Ersch, 'Betrachtungen', *Minerva* 3 (1800) 303–318. 'Thoughts by a neutral party, presented to the enemies of the Revolution. By a Frenchman'.
20 Anonymous, 'Historische Nachrichten von den letzten Unruhen in Saint Domingo', *Minerva* 1 (1792) 296–319, 296.

Weisse, farbigte Menschen, und Sclaven (sic)'.[21] Among the plantation owners, good businessmen carry no debt and are loyal to France. They are also
friends of people of color whom they consider pillars of the colony. Another group of colonists is wasteful, loose in character and deep in the red, and
hence revolting against the new French laws that, at the beginning of the
Revolution, had suspended credit swaps, options trading, etc.[22] The hatred
of this group does not turn against their fellow white plantation owners, but
against the loyal and honest businessmen among the people of color, who
insist on the adherence to these new laws which had granted them rights
and legal protection. Not surprisingly, the author blames this group of white
colonists for the revolts, along with the 'kleinen Weissen, (die) das Unkraut
von Europa sind' (minor whites, who are the pest of Europe) and whose
survival and pride depended on the continuous suppression of the people
of color.[23]

Despite detailing such differences within racial groups, the piece lacks
reflection – or even a mention – of the issue of slavery. Slaves are not considered as grantees of rights; they are not perceived as human beings affected by the Revolution. Instead, they continue to be subjected to the shifting power dynamics among their enslavers. After upheavals, the author
claims, a period of appeasement began on the island, until a decree about
the future of the colony reached St. Domingo in the summer of 1791. The
French parliament was steadfast in its desire not to deal with the colony at
all, especially not with slaves and people of·color who were descendents of
slaves; at the same time it reaffirmed its endorsement of existing political
habits and decision-making procedures in the colonies. This decree led to
further unrest and rebellion, aggravated by a letter that circulated widely:
'So standen die Sachen, als ein Brief von einem Mitgliede der National-Ver-
sammlung bekannt wurde, worin er schrieb, daß in den Colonien die Sonne
bald keine andre als freie Menschen bescheinen würde. – Diese Nachricht
brachte die Weißen ausser aller Fassung'.[24] Years of revolt ensued.

The anecdote about this particular letter underscores the pervasive anti-
abolitionist stance among the colonists, while also pointing to sentiments
that had begun to pervade European culture. Though not outright aboli-
tionists, more and more writers became increasingly convinced that the end
of slavery was near. This trend is corroborated in essays about the West In-

---

21 Anonymous, 'Historische Nachrichten', 297. 'white colonists, minor whites, people of color,
   slaves'.
22 Attributes describing debt and monetary obligations ('schuldenfrei', 'tief in Schulden') characterize the moral uprightness of these groups. Cf. also Gray, *Money Matters*, 23–44.
23 Anonymous, 'Historische Nachrichten', 298.
24 Anonymous, 'Historische Nachrichten', 309. 'Such was the situation when a letter by a member of parliament became known. In it, he stated that soon in the colonies the sun would only
   shine on free people. -This piece of news enraged the whites tremendously'.

dies that were published in other magazines – often as early as the 1770s and 1780s – and that offer similarly detailed accounts of the social dynamics among the inhabitants of the colonies, along with reviews – and alleged corrections – of influential texts about the conditions of the Caribbean slaves.[25] The essays participated in the broader abolitionist discourse that prevailed around 1790 in Europe, and that was accounted for, in sober and analytical tone, in a lengthy article in *Deutsches Magazin*: 'Über die Vorbereitungen zur Aufhebung des Negerhandels und Abschaffung der Sklaverei auf den Englischen Westindischen Inseln'.[26] *Minerva* and *Politisch-Historisches Magazin* took an active part in this discourse, not least, perhaps, because the city of Hamburg had become a major centre for transatlantic trade in the second half of the eighteenth century. Taking advantage of the political conflicts among European merchant nations, especially during and after the Seven Years' War, Hamburg established a reputation as a safe port: sugar, cotton, and coffee reached Hamburg, were turned into riffles, liquor, or fabric, and exported across the ocean. And while the Hamburg merchant Caspar Voght bragged about his 'benevolent importation' of coffee, tobacco, and rubber from three continents, he and his contemporaries engaged in fierce competition. They knew about the slave trade's essential role in transatlantic import-export relations and were active participants.[27]

Humanists, Slave Traders, Benevolent Aristocrats: The Schimmelmann Family

The global and the local intersected in Hamburg in another, rather intimate way, namely in the Schimmelmann family. They counted among their prominent members a famous father-son-pair: Carl Heinrich von Schimmelmann (1724–1782), former Prussian war profiteer, elevated to the Danish aristocracy, sugar producer, Danish treasury secretary, and eventually 'one of the biggest slave traders in the world', and Ernst von Schimmelmann (1747–1831), himself in charge of the finance, commerce, and foreign departments of the Danish unitary state, a (secret) abolitionist, and well-known patron of Fried-

---

25 Examples, all of them anonymous, are: 'Anmerkungen über Ramseys Schrift von der Behandlung der Negersklaven in den Westindischen Zuckerinseln', *Beiträge zur Völker- und Länderkunde* 5 (1786) 267–292; 'Proclamation des Herrn Blanchelande an die freyen im Aufruhr begriffenen Leute zu St. Domingo', *Historisch-Politisches Magazin, nebst literarischen Nachrichten* 11.1(1792) 359–367; 'Concordat zwischen den weissen und farbigen Bürgern zu Port au Prince auf der Insel St. Domingo', *Historisch-Politisches Magazin* 9 (1791) 659–665.

26 *Deutsches Magazin* 1(1791) 580–613. 'On the preparations for the abolition of the trade in negroes and of the slave trade in the British West Indies'.

27 Cf. Klaus Weber, *Deutsche Kaufleute im Atlantikhandel 1680–1830: Unternehmen und Familien in Hamburg, Cadiz, Bourdeaux*, (Munich: Beck, 2004), p. 251; Franklin Kopitsch, *Grundzüge einer Sozialgeschichte der Aufklärung in Hamburg und Altona* (Hamburg: Christians, 1982), pp. 275–277.

rich Schiller.[28] Through marriage and government offices, the Schimmelmanns became involved in not only almost every influential cultural enterprise in mid- to late eighteenth-century Hamburg and Northern German
lands, but also in the administration of some West Indian colonies. The many
branches of the family – von Schimmelmann, von Reventlow, and von Bau-
dissin – put on soirees in Hamburg and at their rural mansions in Ahrens-
burg, Wandsbek, Lindenborg, and later, in Hellebek, and supported many artists as well as journalistic projects.[29]

But Ernst von Schimmelmann also took on an active, if secret role in
the abolitionist debate. He evidently began to utter first thoughts on necessary changes in the economic and legal status of the Danish slaves soon
after his father's death, proposing reform to the heirs of his estate. But his
plans for modest profit-sharing and for the slaves' conversion to Christianity as paths towards liberation met with resistance. In 1791, he began to
work towards changes in governmental policy, but – as a slave owner, trader, and politician – he chose to intervene publicly only via his surrogate
Ernst Philipp Kirstein. A long-time private secretary, Kirstein published
two treatises in favour of outlawing the slave trade – not slavery itself – and
thus advanced a debate that eventually resulted in Denmark's prohibition of
the trade. Based on Schimmelmann's handwritten 'Denkschrift' to a cabinet
secretary of June 1791, the first treatise was revised by Kirstein in December of the same year and published under the short, non-descriptive title
'Alleruntertänigste Vorstellung'.[30] The second treatise, a fully-fledged 60-
page essay was published in *Deutsches Magazin* around the same time, and
seems in many parts identical with the shorter piece as well as with Schimmelmann's 'Denkschrift'. Remarkably, it lists Schimmelmann as one of the
committee members preparing recommendations for the Danish Crown.[31]

Nevertheless, the reasons behind Schimmelmann's reformist, and seemingly humanitarian, impetus are complex and conflicting. Fuelled in part by
his deeply religious (i.e. Pietist) beliefs, his views on the slave trade are informed by his social, economic, and geographical threshold-position. Having become part of the aristocracy only a generation earlier, the Schimmelmanns believed in the enlightened and benevolent monarchy of the Danish

---

28 Christian Degn, *Die Schimmelmanns im atlantischen Dreieckshandel: Gewinn und Gewissen* (Neumün-
ster: Wachholtz, 2000).
29 See Degn, *Schimmelmanns*, 17; on Schimmelmann's role in Hamburg and Wandsbek: Birgit
Tautz, '"Das Hamburgische Parterre": Johann Christoph Bodes Westindier und die Verortung
des Globalen', *Zeitschrift für Germanistik* 1 (2009) 183–190, 186.
30 Cited in Degn, *Schimmelmanns*, 553; on a prior debate with Fritz von Reventlow, see pp. 256–
80. Degn claims that Kirstein published excerpts in April 1792 in *Minerva*; however, this publication could not be traced.
31 See Degn, *Schimmelmanns*, 256–295; E.P Kirstein, 'Auszug aus der Vorstellung an den König
wegen Abschaffung des Negerhandels für die Dänischen Staaten', *Deutsches Magazin* 3 (1792)
626–684.

Unitary State. Unlike their European counterparts who embraced democracy and experimented with republicanism, the Danes attempted to solve
the vexing questions surrounding slavery through decrees by the king, not
parliamentary debates. Their position in borderlands, with fluid territorial
markers and a steady stream and presence of Germans at the court – chief
among them the Schimmelmanns – solidified thinking in regional rather
than national terms. Nevertheless, Schimmelmann did not approach the
question of slavery and slave trade from a primarily humanitarian viewpoint.
He was first and foremost a shrewd businessman and driven by economic
calculations.[32]

These economic motivations notwithstanding, Schimmelmann had an
early, if short-lived infatuation with the French Revolution, after all, he was
a bourgeois at heart. He had sympathized with the revolutionary changes
that were enacted, with the help of the liberal aristocracy, in early August
1789. But ultimately, he wanted to avoid the fate of France in the 1790s: he
neither wanted to flee like the aristocrats who were forced to leave Paris,
nor did he want to become embroiled in violent conflicts like those among
the plantation owners in the French West Indies. Schimmelmann was certainly aware of the dangers of revolution. He knew that he could lose material possessions and influence if his ultimate advocacy for abolitionist causes
became known, which may very well be a reason for his insistence on anonymity in public word and action.[33]

The Schimmelmann-Kirstein writings display an awareness of these
practical implications. Criticizing the European powers for their overly national perspective, Schimmelmann proposed what he considered a global
solution, which had a two-pronged, and in his view, 'humanitarian' aim: to
protect profits and investments, while ending the slave trade. Yet key to the
success of this plan was a not very humanitarian strategy: slaves should pro-
create and, thus, slavery was to be perpetuated naturally, or as he states in
'Denkschrift':

> Wäre ein Plan, der auf diesen angegebenen Ideen beruhte, in Ausführung zu brin-
> gen, so daß nicht allein die jetzige Bevölkerung in den Kolonien erhalten, sondern
> nach gewissen Jahren so vermehrt würde, das künftig keine weitere Importation nö-
> tig wäre, so sollte ich dafür halten, daß die Vorschriften der Menschlichkeit nicht mit
> den politischen und ökonomischen Vorteilen des Staats in dieser Hinsicht in Wider-
> spruch sein könnten.[34]

---

32 See Degn, *Schimmelmanns*, 281–283.
33 Despite these precautions, Denmark and the Schimmelmann family suffered enormous losses
    through trade embargoes, inflation, and the take-over of ships by the British. See Degn, *Schim-
    melmanns*, 397–401.
34 Degn, *Schimmelmanns*, 286. 'If a plan based on these ideas could be realized, so that the current
    population in the colonies could not only be stabilized but increased to the point that, after a
    certain number of years, no further importation would be necessary, I would maintain that the
    principles of humanity would align with the political and economic advantages of the state'.

Kirstein detailed their motivation more bluntly, claiming that the importation of slaves was bad business, non-profitable to the core: 'ein eigentlicher Handelsgewinn ist niemals gewesen'.[35] Indeed, many slaves died on board of the ships or of diseases in the Caribbean; parts of the elaborate transatlantic trade operated at a loss and only the refineries and export of sugar products made the enterprise profitable. Hence they proposed to sustain slavery without trade. Other proposals, however, did not make it into the public sphere. Whereas 'Denkschrift' lays out a process for liberating and emancipating the slaves, Kirstein eliminates this final goal, refraining from advocating the liberation of Caribbean communities of slaves. He does retain the idea of an education leading to liberation: 'Ihre Erziehung muß ihrer Befreiung vorausgehen, sonst wird ihr eigenes Wohl und das Wohl ihrer Herren aufs Spiel gesetzt', writes Schimmelmann, detailing the impact that the Pietist missionaries could make[36] and anticipating what Schiller suggests for all human beings in *Aesthetic Education*.

In 1792 the Danes passed legislation on the slave trade, outlawing any trade outside of the West Indies after 1802 and bestowing high importation fees. Unlike in Hamburg, where he was much despised,[37] Schimmelmann gained a reputation in Europe as a humanist and promoter of abolition.[38] The secret abolitionist was no more. In keeping with his family's tradition, he mediated the utilitarian and edifying dimensions of Enlightenment and embarked on another 'secret' project: his support of Friedrich Schiller.

Sublimating the News: Friendship and Aesthetics

Schimmelmann secretly put up the money to pay a pension to Schiller and, along with the Prince von Augustenburg, 'befriended' the German poet.[39] Painfully aware of his dependency on wealthy, aristocratic benefactors, Schiller became a participant in 'the revolution of friendship', documented and

---

35 Kirstein, 'Auszug', 641. 'There never was an actual profit in the slave trade.'

36 Degn, *Schimmelmanns*, 287. 'Their education must precede their liberation, otherwise their own wellbeing and the wellbeing of their owners will be at risk.'

37 On the complicated relationship between the Senate and the aristocracy, see Aaslestad, 'Old Visions'; on the questionable reputation of the Schimmelmann family, Kopitsch, *Grundzüge*, 405.

38 Degn, *Schimmelmanns*, 291.

39 In his letter to Körner (1 January 1792), Schiller mentions that the identity of the prince and count were revealed; apparently Schimmelmann felt it would have been inappropriate to co-sign a letter with the prince. See *Schillers Werke. Nationalausgabe*, ed. for the Stiftung Weimarer Klassik and the Schiller-Nationalmuseums Marbach (Weimar: Böhlau und Nachfolger, 1943–), vol. 26: *Briefwechsel. Schillers Briefe 1.3.1790–17.5.1794*, ed. by Edith and Horst Nahler (1992), p. 135. All subsequent citations refer to the *Nationalausgabe* (= *SNA*). See also Klaus-Detlef Müller, 'Schiller und das Mäzenat: Zu den Entstehungsbedingungen der 'Briefe über die ästhetische Erziehung des Menschen', in *Unser Commercium: Goethes und Schillers Literaturpolitik*, ed. by Wilfried Barner (Stuttgart: Cotta, 1984), pp. 151–167.

recorded in his correspondence with Augustenburg and Schimmelmann. Offering a formidable account of the role of friendship in the formation of aesthetics, these letters are important precursors to the *Aesthetic Letters*. And while the latter respond to news from France and indict revolutionary terror, Schiller initially avoids any mentioning of revolution and revolt. Through carefully managed rhetorical moves, he secludes himself from global news reaching Weimar while putting forth a narrative that professed to offer a universal response. Often conflated with the *Aesthetic Letters*, the correspondence offers another model of aesthetic compensation for the events of the 1790s and mirrors the process of aesthetic sublimation against and despite the author's political and economic dependencies.[40]

The fewer than 20 preserved letters shed light on the gradual giving way of the revolutionary impulse and fascination with France to a narrative emphasizing the harmonious, and ultimately aesthetic, growth of individuals. Enlisting the rhetoric of friendship, this narrative projected a future born out of a culture of sociability.[41] Properly educated and sensitized to the beauty of life, friends were eventually capable to fulfil the promise of reasoned, measured behaviour that J.S. Ersch, who wrote about France in 1800 and whose essay I discussed earlier, had demanded. Friendship necessitated individually responsible actions, which in turn made possible a community.

The most famous letter of this exchange, written by Schimmelmann and Augustenburg on 27 November 1791 offering the three-year pension, begins with the words 'zwei Freunde, durch Weltbürgersinn mit einander verbunden'.[42] This opening line serves as a self-designation of the authors, describing the relationship they enjoy with each other; in addition, it identifies the type of friendship they hope to forge with Schiller. Hinting at the social inequality between Schimmelmann and the prince, the opening line smoothes the path towards an unthreatening acknowledgement of Schiller's lower social position, a fact that threatens to render the invocation of friendship meaningless. All too easily could 'friendship' deteriorate and become a hollow sentimental gesture; worse yet, it could set up a rhetoric of illegitimacy. But by tying 'friendship' to 'Weltbürgersinn' (cosmopolitanism), the letter creates a new basis for equality. A concept that carried multiple mean-

---

40 While it is unclear whether Schiller knew about Schimmelmann's involvement in the slave trade, he was aware of the Caribbean uprisings and probably of the abolitionist debate. For example, in 1791 Schiller received a letter from Reinhard reporting on the threats from the colonies; cf. *SNA* vol. 34.1: *Briefe an Schiller 1.3.1790–24.5.1794*, ed. by Ursula Naumann (1991), p. 105. In one of his letters to Augustenburg, dated 13 July 1793, Schiller writes about his disillusionment with the French Revolution and about his fear of a latent instability and domestic repression that came with the Caribbean revolts; cf. *SNA* vol. 26, pp. 262 and 264.
41 To include Jens Baggesen's letters in the interpretations of the friendship is crucial, because he was an important mediator. In any case, 'friendship' remains rhetorical, because by all accounts these were very much textual relationships.
42 *SNA* vol. 34.1, p. 113. 'Two friends united by a cosmopolitan sense.'

ings in late eighteenth-century culture, cosmopolitanism erases the manifestations of social and political inequality that existed between Schimmelmann and Augustenburg, while entrusting them with a more global task: to be interested in and supportive of an artist from a German province, whom they credited with a deep understanding of the historical process. They consider his works an affirmation of their friendship, which is rooted in the belief 'that all human beings are members of a single community and have obligations to all other human beings'.[43]

Fully aware of Schiller's fragile health, precarious economic situation and pride, they confront the situation head-on, urging him to accept their offer and regard them as nothing but equals: 'Nehmen Sie dieses Anerbieten an edler Mann! Der Anblick unsrer Titel bewege Sie nicht es abzulehnen. Wir wissen diese zu schätzen. Wir kennen keinen Stolz als nur den, Menschen zu seyn, Bürger in der grosen Republick, deren Grenzen mehr als das Leben einzelner Generationen, mehr als die Grenzen eines Erdbals umfassen. Sie haben hier nur Menschen, Ihre Brüder vor sich'.[44] The aristocrats know that their titles and station will prevent Schiller from feeling en par with them; but underscoring their unifying intent, they situate themselves firmly in the urban, modern context of Copenhagen. They praise the unity of economic, political, and cultural success the city affords and promise a political office, should Schiller be interested in relocating. In Copenhagen, the first stage of the French Revolution had concluded successfully: the prince had become an enlightened monarch, who championed trade and the stimulation of wealth; political and economic interests seemed perfectly aligned. The unity and equality of friendship cemented this success of Enlightenment. Conversely, the programme of aesthetic action that they had adopted from Schiller's earlier plays could be exported across the world.

Judging by his correspondence with Körner and Baggesen, Schiller's response was enthusiastic. He seemed re-energized, thankful, even emotional, especially when discussing the feelings of awe, numbness, even speechlessness that overcame him. In the letter to Baggesen, Schiller cites an inner obligation to produce his best work ever as the reason to accept the pension. Moreover, he sketches a path from friendship to aesthetic education. He begins by clearly differentiating between the friendships that exist between Weimar and Copenhagen and within the Danish aristocratic circle. He describes the joy that Baggesen must have felt when the two aristocrats came through and shared his wish to help Schiller; in turn, he states his

---

43 Pauline Kleingeld, 'Six Varieties of Cosmopolitanism in Late Eighteenth-Century Germany', *Journal of History of Ideas* 60 (1999) 505–24, 507.
44 *SNA* vol. 34.1, p. 114: 'Accept this offer, noble friend. Do not be moved to reject it in light of our titles. We value them, but our only pride rests in being human, citizens of the great republic, whose borders encompass more than the life of individual generations, more than the limits of the globe. You have before you only human beings, your brothers.'

hopes to boost the joy of his 'theurer und hochgeschätzter Freund' (dear and highly treasured friend) by accepting the gracious offer.[45] Friendship serves as a code that simultaneously acknowledges actual inequality and the manner in which it can be transcended, enshrining a rhetoric that veils social differences in favour of a higher, soon-to-be politicized idea of community. All together, Schiller's praise of Baggesen as a friend to both wealthy aristocrats and the impoverished poet is intended to bring personal satisfaction to the Dane, an affirmation that he already embodies the qualities of a member of the future community of friends.

Schiller's letter to Augustenburg and Schimmelmann strikes a decidedly humble, even submissive tone; the painful recognition of his position does not allow Schiller to call them his friends. Instead he opts for 'zwei schützende Genien' (two protective geniuses), and he considers himself the instrument of their noble intentions ('das Werkzeug Ihrer schönen Absicht').[46] He acknowledges the utilitarian purposelessness of their friendship for each other and lays out what reads like a threshold moment in the history of aesthetics when embracing their claim that Schiller's words have moved them to act. His economic (and thus poetic) freedom results from the aristocrats' beautiful action.[47] In what reads indeed like an inversion of Fiesko's statement on art and life, Schiller praises their action as a moral response to his aesthetic offering:

> Wie stolz machen sie mich, daß sie *meiner* in einem Bunde gedenken, den der edelste aller Zwecke heiligt, den der Enthusiasmus fürs Gute, fürs Große und Schöne geknüpft hat. Aber wie weit ist *die* Begeisterung, welche in Thaten sich äusert, über diejenige erhaben, die sich darauf einschränken muß, zu Thaten geweckt zu haben.[48]

To Schiller, Schimmelmann and Augustenburg are living proof that aesthetic education will work, forgotten seems the terror that rendered Schiller's planned defence of the French king mute. When he resurrects the allusion to revolutionary action for a moment, he knows that any threat of a violent outcome has already been sublimated – be it by the action of friends and, in the case of Schimmelmann, by the actions of a friend who is also a hesitant abolitionist.

Throughout the 1790s, several trends and attitudes emerge in German responses to the news from France and from its colonies in the Caribbean. Related in a manner that finds resonance in the bourgeois centres of Northern German provinces, this 'global news' is fashioned to fulfil the 'local

---

45 *SNA* vol. 26, p. 123.
46 *SNA* vol. 26, p. 124.
47 Letter to Jens Baggesen, 16 December 1791' in *SNA* vol. 26, p. 120.
48 *SNA* vol. 26, p. 125, emphasis in original: 'How proud you make me by making me part of your company, which is ennobled by the highest of all purposes, which enthusiasm for the good, for greatness and beauty has created. But how superior is the passion which expresses itself in action compared to the one that is restricted to merely having inspired action.'

needs' for facts, to sustain the dogma of religious pietism, and to mediate the possible adverse effects resulting from the economic entanglements with global trade. In all of this, slavery prevails as an uncontested discursive centre, with German involvement denied, remaining hidden or disguised in abolitionist texts. Not surprisingly then, in acts of admission and redemption, local interventions emerge: 'friendship' arises as an aesthetic gesture that levels differences in social rank and emphasizes the human dimension of cosmopolitanism. Subsequently, such actions among friends predict, even anticipate, the success of aesthetic education – a narrative that will proclaim its universal reach because it projects its success into the future and beyond the boundaries of the 1790s and, for that matter, the eighteenth-century world of discovery and revolution.

Print and Preserve

Periodicals in Late Eighteenth-Century Germany

Renata Schellenberg

In eighteenth-century Germany reading was a popular pastime. The explosion of print culture afforded unprecedented access to textual media and information, and the population indulged in this new solitary leisure activity with abandon. However, as the act of reading became both more mobile and more varied, it also became more complicated and there was open concern how best to understand and manage it. Discussions on the societal impact reading may have on the common mind dominated critical circles of the late eighteenth century, with many public figures questioning the aptitude of the general population to cope with such an extensive array of reading materials. Pejorative criticism consequently ensued with many branding the popularity of reading as *Lesesucht* or *Lesewut*, a type of mania, and condemning the quality of the activity to a sort of *Vielleserey*, an insubstantial dabbling with no real focus.[1] And while this highly contentious debate on what (and how) people should read is the cumulative product of many developments in the eighteenth century,[2] in the 1790s it takes a particularly interesting turn: for it is within this decade that certain types of print in Germany became increasingly self-referential with a wilful disregard for external political events.

The periodical was undoubtedly the publication in which this discussion was taking place. The simple fact of its availability, affordability, and poten-

---

1   For more on this please see, for example, Johann Georg Heinzmann, *Über die Pest der deutschen Literatur. Appell an meine Nation über Aufklärung und Aufklärer, über Gelehrsamkeit und Schriftsteller, über Büchermanufakturisten, Rezensenten, Buchhändler* (Bern: n. pub., 1795); Johann Gottfried Hokke, *Vertraute Briefe über die jetzige abentheurliche Lesesucht und über den Einfluss derselben auf die Verminderung des häuslichen und öffentlichen Glücks* (Hanover: n. pub., 1794); Johann Gottfired Pahl, 'Warum ist die deutsche Nation in unserem Zeitalter so reich an Schriftstellern und Büchern?', *Der Weltbürger* 3 (1790) 617–625.

2   The emergence of a distinct literary public sphere in German-speaking Europe in the late eighteenth century affected all aspects of reading culture and practice. To mention a few notable developments: the general literacy of the population increased, the notion of a commercial literary market evolved, new formats of publications appeared, critical reviews (i.e. books about books) began to be published, lending libraries were formed, reading societies were founded and an overall new sociability surrounding the act of reading was established. For a more detailed description of the socio-cultural ramifications reading had on the public sphere please see James van Horn Melton's excellent monograph *The Rise of the Public in Enlightenment Europe* (Cambridge: University Press, 2001), pp. 81–110.

tial range allowed for the quick exchange of ideas, a trait that had already secured the genre its place as a prime Enlightenment forum for polemical discussion. By the 1790s the periodical had, however, also evolved into a complex network of interactions that allowed for a sophisticated mode of communication. As a print form it appropriately addressed the needs of a growing reading public. Not only had it proven capable of bridging cultural and social divides, but it had diversified sufficiently to appropriate the most divergent intellectual issues. The market statistics pertaining to the number of publications are staggering. For example, in 1791, in the wake of the French Revolution and with the increased need for plentiful, quick, and diverse sources of information, there were more than a thousand documented journals in Germany, which was not only a record number of publications to be circulating on the market, but a true testimony to the vitality and importance of press culture.[3] The periodical combined intensive and extensive reading practices by including materials that were both informative and diverting for its readers, thereby demonstrating that it was able to adapt to the volume of the reading public and to its demand for constant change. The periodical's capacity to mediate was openly recognized as being much greater than the communicative potential of the book, leading contemporary scholars such as Johann Adam Bergk to conclude:

> Wer [daher] das Streben und die Meinungen der Zeitgenossen studieren will, muß periodische Schriften lesen, und wer in die dringendsten Angelegenheiten der Menschheit eingeweiht sein will, muß seine Zuflucht zur Lektüre von Journalen nehmen: hier hört man die Wünsche, sieht die Bedürfnisse, und vernimmt den Zustand unserer Mitmenschen [...]. Denn durch sie [die Lektüre von periodischen Schriften] kommen Sachen zu unserer Kenntnis, wovon wir vorher keine Ahnung haben.[4]

In eighteenth-century Germany, journals and other available press media also provided important cultural unity, connecting – through print – a disparate political entity. In these circumstances the reliance on reading and writing became closely intertwined with a sense of belonging for the thinking individual, which only augmented the weight of importance placed on what was published for a reading audience. Writers such as Christoph Martin Wieland were quick to grasp the inter-relationship that existed between print and the formation of cultural identity and looked to use the power of textual media to further German cultural presence. Wieland committed his journal *Der Teut-*

---

3   Michael Gross, *Ästhetik und Öffentlichkeit: Die Publizistik der Weimarer Klassik* (Hildesheim: Olms, 1994), p. 44.

4   Johann Adam Bergk, *Die Kunst, Bücher zu lesen. Nebst Bemerkungen über Schriften und Schriftsteller* (Jena: Hempelsche Buchhandlung, 1799), p. 386. 'Those who want to study the aspirations and the opinions of our contemporaries must read the periodical press, and those who want to immerse themselves in matters of humankind must take their refuge in the reading of journals, for one learns here the desires, sees the needs and comprehends the conditions of our fellow human beings [...]. Through such reading things come to our attention of which we had no previous knowledge.' All translations are my own.

sche Merkur (1773–1789, later renamed *Der Neue Teutsche Merkur* 1790–1810)
to the cause of creating precisely such a forum for greater socio-cultural communication. It was founded on the principle of collaboration, and Wieland, as
editor, openly solicited viable contributions. He stressed the fact that the journal was to be a venue for new thoughts and new talents, and encouraged un-
published and unknown authors to submit their work.[5] As the title of the
publication indicates, the journal was modelled rather obviously on the success of *Mercure de France,* a fact that would seem to contradict its aim of establishing an entirely autonomous national medium of communication. Wieland
was aware of the inevitability of the comparison, but claimed better critical
discernment for his publication, stating that by employing selective standards
Der Teutsche Merkur was a much better publication: 'Wir befinden uns, was
diesen Punkt betrifft, gar nicht in dem Falle des französischen Merkurs, dem
alles willkommen sein muß, was man ihm zuwirft, weil er jährlich sechzehn
Bände, es sei nun womit es wolle, anzufüllen hat'.[6] It must be noted that the
journal was also quite different from other publications at the time, as it had
no specific cultural or philosophical programme. Its overall intent was, quite
simply put, to stimulate the mental capacities of the German-speaking reader,
an engagement Wieland hoped would foster greater awareness of external
events, and which would then help counter regional and parochial thinking.

Wieland encouraged this sociable intellectual curiosity as a means to
cope with the increasing complexity of day-to-day life, and out of the genuine belief that publicity and the subsequent discussion of difficult issues facilitated their comprehension. This forum was, however, dependent upon a
larger social framework and a body of rules, protocols and procedures,
which allowed for this interaction to take place and which would permit the
exchange of opinions.[7] Wieland was aware of the ramifications such restric-

---

5   In the 'Vorrede' (preface) to the first edition of *Der Teutsche Merkur* Wieland wrote: 'Die Unter-
    nehmer wollen also Beiträge erhalten, und laden dazu nicht nur die Schriftsteller ein, welche
    bereits im Besitz der allgemeinen Hochachtung sind: sie sind gar nicht ungeneigt, auch für
    angehende Schriftsteller einen Schauplatz zu eröfnen, wo sie sich dem Publico zeigen können,
    und es würde ihnen sehr angenehm sein, wenn sie durch diese Unternehmung Gelegenheit
    erhielten, ein hier oder da noch schlummerndes Genie aufzuwecken, oder ein vielleicht noch
    unentschlossenes in die ihm angemessne Laufbahn einzuleiten.' Christoph Martin Wieland,
    'Vorrede', *Der Teutsche Merkur* 1 (Jan 1773) iii-xxii, iv. 'The editors would like to receive con-
    tributions, and invite to this cause not only authors who already command general respect.
    The editors want to give writers-to-be a space in which they can show themselves, and it would
    be pleasing to them indeed, if hereby an opportunity arose to awaken a sleeping genius, or to
    present an undecided one with an appropriate (literary) career.'
6   Wieland, 'Vorrede', p. v. 'We are not at all in the same circumstance as the French *Mercure*,
    which must accept everything that comes its way, because it has to fill its sixteen volumes a
    year, regardless of quality'.
7   This reference pertains to the overall development of a profession of letters in Germany and
    to the emergence of an independent literary market in which polemical discussion could flou-
    rish. For more on the social, cultural and economic ramifications of the expanding German

tions could have on the communication circuit he was attempting to establish and he argued, however subtly, against censorship and the curtailing of public thought. And so, in addition to negotiating a stirring range of editorial topics within *Der Teutsche Merkur*, Wieland also advocated the freedom of the press. He believed this freedom to be a human right, a criterion of civilized thought and conduct, and as early as 1785, he attempted to divorce its significance from political circumstance by comparing acts of writing to an expression of intelligence, and arguing therefore for both its protection and autonomy. In his short treatise 'Über die Rechte und Pflichten der Schriftsteller' (On the Rights and Duties of Authors) Wieland contemplated the status of the writer in society, noting that when deprived of information (which is contained in the work of the writer) a state of 'Unwissenheit' (ignorance) quickly deteriorates to a state of 'Dummheit' (stupidity), a degeneration that is not beneficial to the state, nor to humanity as a whole.[8]

It should be mentioned that Wieland was already an established author by 1773 and that he knowingly used this position within the public sphere to create a market that could sustain his writing ambitions. As Karin Stoll explains, by the time Wieland began working on *Der Teutsche Merkur* he was one of the most widely-read authors in Germany and thus well aware of both the conditions and the challenges facing the professional writer.[9] *Der Teutsche Merkur* was originally envisioned as a commercial enterprise and as Wieland's personal vehicle for publication as well as a means of protecting his materials from the growing problem of piracy that was rife on the literary markets of the eighteenth century. The uneasy question of the profitability of writing recurs at various points in his editorials and Wieland is never quite sure how to reconcile the profession of the writer with the everyday practicalities of the life of the writer. On the fifth anniversary of *Der Teutsche Merkur* he complained publicly about the conditions in which the educated writer '[muss] ums Brot schreiben' (has to write for money) and is thus unnecessarily distracted from more important intellectual pursuits by the demands of economic survival. He believed that the writer should achieve self-sufficiency on an independent literary market and not depend on patronage and affiliations that may compromise the integrity of his/her craft.

---

literary market in the eighteenth century, see Martha Woodmansee, 'The Genius and the Copyright: Economic and Legal Conditions of the Emergence of the "Author"', *Eighteenth-Century Studies* 17.4 (1984) 425–448.

8   Wieland, 'Ueber die Rechte und Pflichten der Schriftsteller in Absicht ihrer Nachrichten, Bemerkungen, und Urtheile über Nationen, Regierungen, und andre politische Gegenstände', *Der Teutsche Merkur* (Sept 1785) 193–207.

9   Karin Stoll, *Christoph Martin Wieland: Journalistik und Kritik. Bedingungen und Massstab politischen und ästhetischen Räsonnements im 'Teutschen Merkur' vor der Französischen Revolution* (Bonn: Bouvier, 1978), p. 30.

He saw the current conditions in Germany as a national disgrace and cited
historical precedent for this practice:

> Freilich soll kein wahrer Gelehrter ums Brodt schreiben. Indessen besorg' ich doch,
> schon mancher wahre Gelehrte hat in Teutschland ums Brodt schreiben müssen;
> und desto schlimmer für ihn und für das Land worin er das muß! – Wehe der Nation,
> die einen Kepler den Vorläufer Newtons, den Mann, ohne den vielleicht Newton nie
> geworden wäre, hungern, – aus Mangel, und Gram über das Unvermögen seinen
> nach Brot weinenden Kindern Brodt zu geben, verschmachten ließ![10]

Interestingly enough, by this time *Der Teutsche Merkur* was also subject to
criticism for precisely this reason.[11] Aware of Wieland's financial stake in the
literary market, people questioned the journal's commitment to critical commentary and Wieland's editorial ability to assess social circumstance. In other
words, they were questioning the purpose and effect the very publicity was
creating.

The issue of publicity was already under close scrutiny among political
thinkers. Bureaucrats like Friedrich Karl von Moser were actively investigating aspects of political *Publizität* and attempting to ascertain the effect it had
on the state and its public. In 1792 in *Neues Patriotisches Archiv für Deutschland*
Moser noted the variety of printed material available and remarked on the
urgent necessity for critical discernment among readers. Worried about the
levels of manipulation and subversion that could be achieved through the
proliferation of print among such a large audience, he bemoaned how difficult it was to read these materials and to differentiate their various intentions. In order to make the objectives of his own text unmistakably clear,
the title page carried an image of a lantern, under which one read: 'Zum
Leuchten, nicht zum Zünden' (to illuminate, not to ignite). In the text itself
he appealed to his readers to exercise caution and to read discriminately,
learning to separate true patriotic sentiment from mere babble and to at-

---

10 Wieland, 'Der Herausgeber an das Publikum', *Der Teutsche Merkur* (Oct 1777) 284. 'Surely no
    learned thinker should have to write for bread alone. Meanwhile I see that indeed many a true
    scholar in Germany has to write for bread: and this is as lamentable for him as it is for the
    country in which he resides. Pity the nation who allows someone like Kepler – Newton's
    precursor and a man without whom Newton may never have emerged – to starve and to pine
    with grief about his inability to provide his own weeping children with bread.'

11 Christian Gottfried Körner advised Schiller to publish his work in *Der Teutsche Merkur* precisely
    because of the profitability of such an endeavor, telling Schiller: 'Der Merkur, einige dramati-
    sche Arbeiten, Rezensionen in den Literaturzeitungen sind Mittel zum (ökonomischen) Zwek-
    ke, die Deine Kräfte nicht aufzehren und Deinen Geist nicht niederdrücken', cited in Gross,
    Ästhetik und Öffentlichkeit, 484. 'The *Merkur*, a few dramatic pieces, reviews in the literary jour-
    nals are means to an (economic) end, which will not use up your strength or depress your
    spirit.' However, because of its popularity and profitability, the *Merkur* also came under con-
    siderable – albeit later – critical attack. In his 1864 study of German literature Robert Eduard
    Prutz famously referred to *Der Teutsche Merkur* as 'der große Papierkorb der damaligen Lite-
    ratur' (the great waste paper bin of literature at the time), in *Neue Schriften; Zur deutschen Lite-
    ratur- und Kunstgeschichte* (Halle: Schwetschke, 1864), I, p. 59.

tempt to grasp the true intentions of the author. He wrote: 'Wie sehr unterscheidet sich der ganze Ton voll Würde von dem Gequacke pölitischer Frösche, von dem Geschnatter umherziehender in das Gewand von Patrioten sich verhüllender Marktschreier, deren Geschmier man mit Eckel liest und mit Unmuth wegwirft'.[12]

What is of interest here is that in both camps – the political and the literary/aesthetic – the concern was so similar. Although they approached the matter from very different vantage points and experiences, Wieland and Moser both recognized print culture as a new technology of communication and grappled essentially with the same questions: How does one manage the volume of information available? How does one steer the reading of information towards something beneficial? And, with so many choices available, how does one determine an authoritative text? Quite clearly, the realization on both sides was that the public sharing of information could not be stopped, and that the torrent of publicity was here to stay. Therefore the apparent consensus between the two camps was that print and publicity must be managed, and managed critically, for in doing so one could address the fixity and permanence of print culture,[13] while also imposing order and maintaining control over the ever-expanding discourse of public opinion. A conscious presence on all sides of this new circuit of communication was required.

Navigating the various domains of public discourse was a different matter. Many writers tried to 'read' public opinion and to write towards their taste. Friedrich Schiller had struggled for many years to communicate with contemporary readers and to address their needs and interests in his writings. Professional experience had brought him to the understanding that detachment must play a crucial role in the act of reading, but this same experience had also taught him how difficult it actually was to implement objective modes of reading and to have readers engage with texts in a critical way. In the past readers had rejected a number of Schiller's publications[14] and in the 1780s he had struggled quite publicly to survive as a writer. However, despite these setbacks and despite the odds stacked up

---

12 Friedrich Karl von Moser, *Neues Patriotisches Archiv für Deutschland* (Mannheim and Leipzig: Schwan und Götz, 1792), I, p. 523. 'How different the worthy tone of nobility is from the babble of political frogs, the chatter of wandering charlatans, disguised in the garb of patriots, whose scribbling one reads with disgust and throws away with ill humour.'

13 For a detailed discussion of the preserving qualities of printing, as well as of the impact print and book culture had on the formation and dissemination of knowledge, see Elizabeth Eisensten, *The Printing Revolution in Early Modern Europe* (Cambridge: University Press, 1983); Adrian John, *The Nature of the Book: Print and Knowledge in the Making* (Chicago: Chicago University Press, 1998).

14 Schiller published a number of journals that failed to find support among the reading public: *Das Wirtembergische Repertorium der Litteratur* (1782–83), *Rheinische Thalia* (1784–86), *Thalia* (1786–91), and *Neue Thalia* (1792–93).

against him, towards the end of the century Schiller was at it again, arguing strenuously for the primacy of criticism and searching for the proper means with which one can best implement and articulate an intellectual agenda. Unperturbed by the very public lack of success he had achieved with such ventures in the past, Schiller looked, yet again, to utilize print to this aim.

In the 1790s he approached the issue of critical engagement from a different angle and opted to instruct his readers in their aesthetic perception of the world by repudiating all external political reality in his writings. In his *Über die ästhetische Erziehung des Menschen in einer Reihe von Briefen* (translated as *Aesthetic Education* or *Aesthetic Letters*), he thus declared his critical and personal disappointment with the French Revolution, articulating a distinctive *Zeitkritik* that was directed against the historical objectification of these events. Schiller wanted his readers to retain their capacity for individual thought and to approach current circumstance with the clarity and empowerment that come with the individual's sense of personal freedom. In the second letter (and in reference to current external events) Schiller wrote:

> Daß ich dieser reizenden Versuchung widerstehe und die Schönheit der Freiheit voran gehe lasse, glaube ich nicht bloß mit meiner Neigung entschuldigen, sondern durch Grundsätze rechtfertigen zu können. Ich hoffe, Sie zu überzeugen, daß diese Materie weit weniger dem Bedürfniß als dem Geschmack des Zeitalters fremd ist; ja daß man, um jenes politische Problem in der Erfahrung zu lösen, durch das ästhetische den Weg nehmen muß, weil es die Schönheit ist, durch welche man zu der Freiheit wandert.[15]

In the letters he repeatedly argued for an intellectually heightened, but calm, approach when dealing with this tumultuous political event and appealed to his readers to retain this cogent personal poise.[16]

---

15 Friedrich Schiller, 'Über die ästhetische Erziehung des Menschen in einer Reihe von Briefen (Zweiter Brief)', *Die Horen: Eine Monatsschrift* 1 (1795) 7–48, 10–13, 12. 'Resisting this charming temptation and letting beauty precede freedom I think I can not only excuse through my inclination, but also justify through principles. I hope that I shall succeed in convincing you that this matter of art is less foreign to the needs than to the tastes of our age; and that to arrive at a solution for that political problem, the road of aesthetics must be pursued, because it is only through beauty that we arrive at freedom'.

16 In the ninth letter Schiller elaborated quite poignantly how art and aesthetic awareness shelter the individual. They help the individual grasp his/her own autonomy and achieve separateness from all external, including political, events. Schiller wrote: 'Vor allem was positiv ist und was menschliche Conventionen einführten, ist die Kunst sowie die Wissenschaften losgesprochen und beide erfreuen sich einer absoluten *Immunität* von der Willkür der Menschen. Der politische Gesetzgeber kann ihr Gebiet sperren, aber darin herrschen kann er nicht. Er kann den Wahrheitsfreund ächten, aber die Wahrheit besteht; er kann den Künstler erniedrigen, aber die Kunst kann er nicht verfälschen. Zwar ist nichts gewöhnlicher als daß beide, Wissenschaft und Kunst, dem Geist des Zeitalters huldigen, und der hervorbringende Geschmack von dem beurtheilenden das Gesetz empfängt. [...] Ganze Jahrhunderte lang zeigen sich die Philosophen wie die Künstler geschäftig, Wahrheit und Schönheit in die Tiefen gemeiner Menschheit hinabzutauchen; jene gehen darin unter, aber mit eigener unzerstörbarer Lebenskraft ringen sich diese siegend empor.' Schiller, 'Neunter Brief', *Die Horen* 1 (1795) 43–48, 43–44. 'Art, like

Schiller initially published his letters in *Die Horen*, the journal he founded and edited from 1795–1797. The *Horen* was dedicated to the purpose of cultivating disinterested contemplation among readers and it presented itself as a venue within which individual aesthetic discussion could flourish. The title of the journal clearly spoke to this aim. As he noted in the preface, the *Horen* – guided by goddesses Eunomia, Dice and Irene – was to serve the purpose of focusing attention of the distracted contemporary reader – 'den so zerstreuten Leser' – and to direct this attention to more ennobling causes than current circumstance could afford.[17] The objective was thus clearly to engage the reader through print, but to do so in an edifying manner that would not pander and not subject itself to the most immediate and base impulse.[18] Schiller furthermore considered his journal a public cultural platform and he opened up the publication to other writers of the era, soliciting help in accomplishing his aesthetic objectives. Much like Wieland, he appealed to the best minds in Germany to help actualize his literary plans and welcomed discerning collaboration as an essential component of the journal. The full title of the first volume, inserted into the preface of the journal, speaks to its collective nature: *Die Horen, eine Monatsschrift von einer Gesellschaft verfaßt und herausgegeben von* Schiller (a monthly periodical, written by a community and published by Schiller).

In the preface to *Die Horen* Schiller made it explicitly clear that the journal was to maintain a focus that was 'rein menschlich, und über allen Einfluß der Zeit erhaben'[19] and that in doing so, the journal and its authors would overcome the divisions political commentary creates.[20] With Schiller one can trace an uneasy, but distinct path towards such apolitical aspirations

---

science, is free from all that is positive, and all that is humanly conventional; both are independent from arbitrary human will. The political legislator may place its empire under an interdict, but he cannot reign there. He can proscribe the friend of truth, but truth subsists; he can degrade the artist, but he cannot falsify art. Nothing is more commonplace than to see science and art do homage to the spirit of the age, and creative taste to receive its law from critical taste. For ages philosophers as well as artists have debased truth and beauty to the depths of vulgar humanity. They themselves are swallowed up in it; but, thanks to their essential vigour and indestructible life, truth and beauty are victorious, and emerge triumphant from the abyss'.

17 Schiller, *Die Horen* 1 (1795) iii.

18 In the second letter Schiller warns his readers not to act on the basis of 'Bedürfniß' (need) and 'Nutzen' (utility): '[...] denn die Kunst ist eine Tochter der Freiheit, und von der Nothwendigkeit der Geister, nicht von der Nothdurft der Materie, will sie ihre Vorschrift erhalten. Jetzt aber herrscht das Bedürfniß und beugt die gesunkene Menschheit unter sein tyrannisches Joch.' Schiller, 'Zweiter Brief', 11. '[...] for art is a daughter of freedom, and she requires prescriptions and rules to be furnished by the necessity of the spirit and not by that of matter. But in our day it is necessity and need that prevail, as they bend a degraded humanity under their tyrannical yoke.'

19 'purely human and elevated above all influence of time'.

20 He hoped to unite the divisive political world 'unter der Fahne der Wahrheit und Schönheit', under the flag of truth and beauty. Schiller, *Die Horen* 1 (1795) iv.

from earlier work on other publications. His desire for cultural and intellectual autonomy and an existence apart from political interference had been
evident already in his work in *Rheinische Thalia*, the failed journal which he
had edited and published throughout the 1780s. While announcing the journal in 1784, in an editorial intended to state the aims and objectives of the
publication, he identified himself assertively as a 'Weltbürger', an independent cosmopolitan entity who self-consciously and deliberately opted not to
be subject to external political influence ('der keinem Fürsten dient'[21]). Later, in 1795, in the second *Aesthetic Letter* he appealed to the responsibility of
the individual to act both as *Zeitbürger* and *Staatsbürger* (citizen of one's time
and as a citizen of the state)[22] in society, maintaining the simultaneous coexistence of both identities as the ideal state of being. The term *Bürger*
appeared to be entirely depoliticized by the juxtaposition of *Zeit* versus
Staat in this statement. Needless to say, the majority of the public did not
share these aesthetic aspirations and therefore rejected Schiller's texts and
editorials. The *Rheinische Thalia* attempted to reinvent itself several times in
the 1780s, but it finally and definitively folded in 1793. Having experienced
commercial failure in these earlier endeavours, and knowing the difficulty of
sustaining himself as a writer first-hand, Schiller was well aware of the relative impossibility of marketing idealism alone to a mass audience. To do so
again would seem a particularly odd decision so late in the 1790s when political events carried obvious currency and marketability and were the real bait
to attract readers. It is common knowledge that Cotta – Schiller's publisher
– agreed to publish *Die Horen* only after Schiller had agreed to consider
overseeing a separate publication entitled *Allgemeine Europäische Staatenzeitung*.
The publication of the *Horen* was indulged on the part of the publishing
house for the sake of the predicted profitability of the politically tuned *Staatenzeitung*. In his negotiations with Cotta, Schiller voiced his intellectual aversion to political writing,[23] and he stalled the project at various points until
he finally withdrew altogether, claiming that, all in all, the *Staatenzeitung* did
not hold enough 'charm' for him to continue ('hat nicht soviel Reiz').[24] He
did, however, continue to publish *Die Horen* until it folded in 1797.

Within the close-knit community of Weimar Classicism it is impossible
not to mention Goethe and his *Propyläen*, the journal he published between

21 Friedrich Schiller, 'Ankündigung der Rheinischen Thalia', *Deutsches Museum* 2 (1784) 569.
22 Schiller, 'Zweiter Brief', *Die Horen* 1 (1795) 10.
23 In a letter dated 19 May 1794 Schiller admitted to Cotta: 'Was mich selbst betrifft, so gestehe
     ich aufrichtig, daß ich die politische Schriftstellerei nicht aus Neigung, sondern aus Spekulation
     erwählen würde.' Friedrich Schiller, *Briefe I: 1772–1795*, in *Werke und Briefe in zwölf Bänden*
     (Frankfurt: Deutscher Klassiker Verlag, 2002), XI, p. 682. 'As far as I am concerned, I must
     admit openly that I would not elect political writing out of inclination, but rather out of spe-
     culation.'
24 Cited in Gross, *Ästhetik und Öffentlichkeit*, 179.

1798–1800. It also sought to establish an autonomous aesthetic platform and, in doing so, distanced itself from all matters political. Goethe's intentions for the periodical were clear. In the first few lines of the introduction he took a strong stance against contemporaneity, arguing for a reflection that stretches beyond the immediate and the obvious. As Goethe noted, the passage of time was vital for quality of thought to germinate and he distinguished sharply between the intellectual ambitions of the impetuous youth ('*Jüngling*') and the moderate considerations of the mature mind ('*Mann*'), siding with the latter as the proper mode of judgement. Goethe's predilection for a measured, informed and contemplative point of view was reinforced by the journal's symbolic title. *Propyläen,* was intended to remind readers of the infinite state of knowledge and to humble them in their approach:

> Der Jüngling, wenn Natur und Kunst ihn anziehen, glaubt, mit einem lebhaften Streben, bald in das innerste Heiligthum zu dringen; der Mann bemerkt, nach langem Umherwandeln, daß er sich noch immer in den Vorhöfen befinde. Eine solche Betrachtung hat unsern Titel veranlaßt. Stufe, Thor, Eingang, Vorhalle, der Raum zwischen dem Innern und Äußern, zwischen dem Heiligen und Gemeinen kann nur die Stelle sein, auf der wir uns mit unsern Freunden gewöhnlich aufhalten werden.[25]

The language and tone of the introduction indicate that Goethe is writing with a sober sense of self-knowledge and that he sees the agenda of the periodical as a matter of personal necessity as well as the expression of his own professional experience. The material presented in the *Propyläen* was therefore not subject to ongoing formulation, but was rather the result of an already formulated and finalized mature thought, published for the purpose of setting an appropriate standard to understanding art.

Unlike Schiller, Goethe did not presume immediate or easy collaboration. He knowingly worked against popular trends and was aware of the censure the journal would encounter. He did not share Schiller's editorial *Bildungsoptimismus* and adopted an openly defensive position vis-à-vis his readers. In fact, in the *Propyläen* he pointedly questioned their overall intellectual capacity, openly doubting whether they were equipped to grasp the purity of the journal's aesthetic objectives: 'Allein, wer bescheidet sich nicht gern, daß reine Bemerkungen seltner sind, als man glaubt?'[26] Goethe realized that the periodical had to be distributed among like-minded friends;

---

25 Johann Wolfgang Goethe, 'Einleitung in die *Propyläen*', in *Sämtliche Werke. Briefe, Tagebücher und Gespräche. Vierzig Bände* (Frankfurt: Deutscher Klassiker Verlag, 1998), XVIII, p. 457. 'The young man, when nature and art attract him, thinks that with a vigorous effort he can penetrate into the innermost sanctuary; the man recognizes, after long wanderings, that he is still in the outer court. Such an observation has influenced our title. It is only on the step, in the gateway, the entrance, the vestibule, the space between the outside and the inner chamber, between the sacred and the common, that we will ordinarily commune with our friends.'

26 Goethe, *Propyläen*, 458. 'Who has not experienced the humility of realizing that pure commentary is much rarer than one would like to admit'.

friends who, like him, were capable of thinking, but also capable of taking sides, advocating the necessity of artistic and intellectual autonomy and therefore not afraid to voice dissatisfaction with the current (and sagging) intellectual status quo. He wrote: 'Wem um die Sache zu thun ist, der muß Partei zu nehmen wissen, sonst verdient er nirgends zu wirken'.[27] However justified he may have perceived his approach to be, Goethe's belligerent stance had its obvious negative effects, for within the journal it elevated the notion of discussion to the point of dispute, and he alienated many of his readers in the process.

The adherence to aesthetic principle became the trademark of Weimar Classicism and the focus of the idealism it tried to disseminate. It was also the primary cause for the commercial failure of its publications. Without consensus with and communication from the general public Weimar Classicism became its own best audience, perpetuating a deep isolation that precluded all possibility for a wider dialogue. There is an inherent and obvious impracticality in publishing materials in journal form, for which one anticipates, regularly and repeatedly, only disapproval as a response. Without the slightest expectation of a positive reaction from a broad or interested audience, Weimar Classicism was damning itself, and it was thus bound to fail on a commercial level, because it had no other choice than to dissolve into its own self-referentiality. Some critics have interpreted the financial failure of Weimar Classicism periodicals as the ultimate manifestation of its objective. Their failure to succeed – to publish for profit – only highlighted the idealistic aesthetic position they tried to assume. Michael Gross explains:

> Dieses Scheitern war programmatisch präfiguriert und wurde durch redaktionelle-editorische Defizite in der Umsetzung konkret. Jedoch erhält die Weimarer Publizistik ihre vielfältige Bedeutung und epochale Relevanz gerade, weil sie ihre Ziele verfehlte und gegenteilige Effekte zu ihren Intentionen auslöste. Das Scheitern ist insofern 'produktiv' – ein Phänomen, das auch für die Weimarer Ideale gilt: Die ausgebliebene sozialhistorische Wirkungskompetenz erhöht das unendliche Wirkungspotential autonom-ästhetischer Intentionen.[28]

It should be noted that although they lacked some of the combative energy Goethe exhibited, editors of smaller journals were also advocating a contemplative remove as the purpose of their publications. Less lofty in aspiration than the model provided by Schiller or Goethe, they too were preoccupied with the definition and the manifestation of the aesthetic. Journals like *Der*

---

27 Goethe, *Propyläen*, 461. 'Those who are dedicated to a cause, must take sides, for otherwise they do not deserve to be effective'.
28 Gross, *Ästhetik und Öffentlichkeit*, 458. 'This failure was programmatically predetermined and was realized through editorial deficits. Yet, Weimar journal culture achieves its manifold importance and its epochal relevance precisely because it missed its intended target and produced such an opposite effect. The failure is 'productive' in this sense, a phenomenon that also applies to the ideals of Weimar Classicism in general: the failed socio-historical effect only increases the infinite potential of its autonomous aesthetic intentions'.

Torso, eine Zeitschrift der alten und neuen Kunst gewidmet (1796–1798) were adopting titles that revealed a cultural aesthetic platform and that clearly pointed
backwards in time as the proper direction to take for achieving cultural clarity.
Der Torso itself is an interesting publication because it was designed for the
aspiring artist/reader, so in addition to endorsing antiquity as the paradigm
of aesthetic perfection, it imparted to the reader the skills with which to reach
it. At the beginning of each issue it taught the reader how to sketch, drawing
everything from a perfect line to the head of Laokoon himself. Once this was
accomplished, the reader could engage with the theory of its neo-classical
agenda. The editors of the journal deliberately integrated the practical aspect
with the theoretical, because they deemed both to be essential for a proper
evaluation and a proper understanding of art: 'Ohne Zeichnen können keine
Werke der Kunst entstehen, und ohne theoretische Kenntnisse nicht beur-
theilt werden'.[29] According to the editors of the journal, Carl Daniel Bach
and Karl Friedrich Benkowitz, the two seemingly opposite skill sets were necessarily intertwined and therefore led to a 'proper' reading of authoritative
classical culture.

Neo-classicism was of course experienced on a greater social scale
through the reading of Winckelmann and through the popularity of the
Grand Tour. Journals documenting the journey to Italy were popular and
numerous *Kunstzeitschriften* were published to this aim. Such periodicals were
important because they brought the aesthetic domain to the attention of the
reader and encouraged the consideration of the artifact as part of everyday
life. In the late eighteenth century there is a surge in magazines and periodicals that seek to discuss collecting and the importance of material culture
among a wide readership. For example, in 1790 Heinrich Sebastian Hüsgen
gathered information on collectors in the Frankfurt area and published *Artistisches Magazin* as a document to the existence of this collecting culture.[30]
Proof that collecting was indeed a preoccupation of the aesthetic elite can
be found by reading Goethe's *Propyläen* in which he too joined the discussion on collecting and preserving the aesthetic object. In 1799 he dedicated
an entire novella to the topic, entitled *Der Sammler und die Seinigen*.

Other journals were perhaps less erudite in their intentions, but they
spoke directly to the day-to-day concerns of their readers. The one that
comes most readily to mind in this regard is Georg Melchior Kraus' and
Friedrich Justin Bertuch's *Journal des Luxus und der Moden* which aimed un-
apologetically at the new consumer culture. Published between 1786 and

---

29 Cited in Heide Hollmer and Albert Meier, 'Kunstzeitschriften', in *Von Almanach bis Zeitung: Ein
    Handbuch der Medien in Deutschland 1700 -1800,* ed. by Ernst Fischer, Wilhelm Haefs and York
    Gotthard Mix (Munich: Beck, 1999), p. 153. 'Without drawing, no work of art can emerge,
    without theoretical expertise, it cannot be evaluated.'
30 Heinrich Sebastian Hüsgen, *Artistisches Magazin: enthaltend das Leben und die Verzeichnisse der Wer-
    ke hiesiger und anderer Künstler* (Frankfurt: Bayerdorffer, 1790).

1827 Bertuch's journal included advice on contemporary living and offered
a deliberate distraction from contemporary political and philosophical discussions. In his journal he presented fashion as a necessity for the new German bourgeois existence and provided comparative examples from French
and English contexts. Bertuch continuously updated the scope of the journal's interests by expanding its title to reflect change.[31] (Cf. also Christian
Deuling's essay in this volume.) In order to persuade readers to participate
in the new consumer culture, he also taught them how to read past the textual surface of the journal. Bertuch included illustrative fashion plates as
part of the publication, combining word with image and introducing visual
literacy as an integral part of the publication. The efficacy of this tactic is
evident. The journal, despite its considerable cost, had a circulation of over
1500 copies. The irony of this is, of course, that this publication was published in Weimar concurrently with Goethe's journal *Die Propyläen*, which
was such a clear, if anticipated, financial failure.

   While Bertuch was clearly deviating from the course of educating the
reading public in a traditional textual sense, he was helping establish the
public as an independent cultural entity. He recognized the potential of print
to form a new bourgeois identity and consciously utilized the journal for
this cause. The journal contained an *Intelligenzblatt* – an advert supplement
that was directed towards its readers' consumer needs, a strong indication
that the journal was closely tied to the lifestyle and point of view of its readers. Rather than inciting or stifling debates, this publication merely validated the realm of private experience by accentuating its needs and endorsing its existence. The colourful publication also satiated the pervasive
taste for novelty and taught the German bourgeois mind how to see itself in
comparison with other European nations. It sanctioned the differentiation
of taste and the need for private individuation, but did so by encouraging
consumer behaviour and by promoting the enjoyment of material culture.
The focus on consumerism, the concrete acquisition of material goods,
countered, in a very perceptible way, the unachievable aims of the idealism
of Weimar Classicism and proved to be popular with the reading public.
This type of reading allowed for a new cognitive experience, which mediated
the notion of taste to a broad audience, but did so inclusively, by keeping
that audience perpetually in mind.

   In closing, it is helpful to return to Wieland and his activities, for he indeed was an exemplary figure in the world of printing and publishing in the
late eighteenth century. In 1773, with his *Der Teutsche Merkur*, he opened up

---

31 In 1786 the title of the journal was *Journal der Moden,* from 1787–1812 it was *Journal des Luxus
    und der Moden,* in 1813 the title changed to *Journal für Luxus, Mode und Gegenstände der Kunst,* from
    1814–1826 it was *Journal für Literatur, Kunst, Luxus und Mode* and in 1827 it changed to *Journal
    für Literatur, Kunst und geselliges Leben.*

the communicative process of the public sphere, relying on public reception and public interaction to create a journal that would correspond to the needs of contemporary reading audiences. However, by the 1790s it seems as if he too was reconsidering his publishing activity and the role of print in the public sphere. In 1796 he began to publish *Attisches Museum*, a side project to the ongoing *Der Neue Teutsche Merkur*, which was a journal dedicated to the study of antiquity. As a publication, it side-stepped contemporary issues entirely by bringing apolitical classical texts to the attention of the reader, texts that Wieland himself had carefully compiled and retranslated for this purpose. The *Museum* was envisioned as a rediscovery of the classical literary tradition, and initial reviews for this publication were very favourable. The *Allgemeine Literatur-Zeitung*, reviewing the journal in 1798, fêted its objective, stating that the publication contained material for readers 'welche [Sinn] für etwas besseres und gehaltvolleres haben',[32] a comment that clearly noted the merit of such classical texts when compared to what was otherwise available in print through popular literature. Rather than perpetuating discussion for the sake of discussion, in the end Wieland appeared ready to acquiesce, at least momentarily, creating an archive of sorts for a tradition that he seemed interested in both protecting and preserving.

---

32 Anon., 'Vermischte Schriften', *Allgemeine Literatur-Zeitung* 93 (1798) 737. 'who have the sensibility for something better and more substantial'.

Aesthetics and Politics in the Journal *London und Paris* (1798–1815)

Christian Deuling

In the 1790s, the fascination that Germans felt for the big cities of London and Paris reached a new level. This increased fascination related above all to the new aesthetic experiences these places seemed to offer – their aesthetics of (luxury) goods that found expression in illuminated shop windows, shop signs and early forms of advertisements. Equally interesting to the German public, whose own nation within the loosely knitted Holy Roman Empire of the German Nation lacked a comparable metropolis, were the manners of these cities' inhabitants. The increasing number of publications on this topic, describing the daily life, manners and morals of people living in the two political centres of (Western) Europe, stressed the need for first-hand reports authentic enough to satisfy the curiosity of the German readership. Due to growing competition among publishers, only publications with a highly original profile had even the smallest chance of attracting the attention of their readership and, in the case of periodical publications, of having a future beyond the first few issues. The aim of this essay is to determine what was original about the political and entertainment-based journal *London und Paris*, published by the Weimar editor Friedrich Justin Bertuch (1747–1822) between 1798 and 1815, analyzing some of its aesthetic implications as well as political tendencies.[1] Although the journal was able to catch the attention of its German readership especially with the help of the 'mixed genre' caricature, which comprises both text and image, *London und Paris* is not a purely satirical magazine relying on caricatures; as Rolf Reichardt has pointed out, it is also a magazine that compares London and Paris from a broad perspective, integrating and discussing caricatures as a satirical element.[2]

---

1   Research into *London und Paris* has increased since the 250th anniversary of Bertuch's birth in 1997, when the wide scope of his activities and enterprises came into focus, cf. especially Gerhard R. Kaiser, 'Jede große Stadt ist eine Moral in Beispielen. Bertuchs Zeitschrift *London und Paris*', in *Friedrich Justin Bertuch (1747–1822): Schriftsteller, Verleger und Unternehmer im klassischen Weimar*, ed. by Gerhard R. Kaiser and Siegfried Seifert (Tübingen: Niemeyer, 2000), pp. 547–578.

2   *London und Paris* was 'keine Karikaturzeitschrift, auch wenn Karikaturen und ihre Erklärung in jedem Heft einen zentralen Platz einnehmen und insgesamt gut die Hälfte aller 350 Graphiken des Journals ausmachen, sondern eine Zeitschrift mit und über Karikaturen. Insofern hat das Journal keine eigentlichen Vorläufer, auch nicht hinsichtlich seiner aufwendigen Ausstattung

The Journal's Profile

The journal appeared eight times a year *in octavo* and comprised between 80 and 100 pages. Its price was comparatively high at six *Reichsthaler* and eight *Groschen* or eleven *Gulden Reichsgeld*, even higher than that of the famous fashion magazine that Bertuch had been publishing since 1786.[3] Each issue of *London und Paris* consisted of three parts: it opened with articles from London, went on to those from Paris, and concluded with the third, satirical, part comprising English and French political (and occasionally social) caricatures, which were commented upon by Carl August Böttiger.[4] The articles from the two big cities drew a lively picture of what Germany lacked at that time: an urban centre. Even cities like Berlin, Hamburg, Leipzig and Frankfurt did not equal the English and the French capitals in their political importance and vitality. The correspondents tried to evoke the atmosphere of these fast-growing cities and sent early forms of 'news reports' to the German principality of Weimar, then a duchy of only several thousand inhabitants. The German readership rewarded Bertuch's and Böttiger's efforts with good sales: in 1804, 1325 copies were printed and almost all (1289) sold. In 1808, the number of copies of *London und Paris* even exceeded that of the fashion magazine by 50 (1250 vs. 1200 copies), with 70 copies more sold (1190 vs. 1120).[5] Today these figures seem modest, but at the time they were remarkable. Although no subscription lists have survived, we can assume that *London und Paris* had an area of distribution similar to that of the fashion magazine, which is known to have been circulated far beyond the borders of the German states, to France, Britain, Austria, Denmark, even as far afield as Russia, although the main emphasis for its distribution lay, of course, on the German territories.[6]

---

sowie der engen Verbindung von Karikatur und Textkommentar.' Rolf Reichardt and Wolfgang Cilleßen, 'Nachgestochene Karikaturen. Ein Journal und sein bildgeschichtlicher Hintergrund', in *Napoleons neue Kleider. Pariser und Londoner Karikaturen im klassischen Weimar*, ed. by Rolf Reichardt, Wolfgang Cilleßen, Christian Deuling (Berlin: G+H, 2006), pp. 7–35, 12. '… was no journal of caricatures, even if caricatures and their explications have a central place in each issue and make up about half of the journal's 350 graphics. In this sense the journal has no real precursors, neither in regard of its expensive format nor the close connection between caricature and textual commentary.' Unless indicated otherwise, all translations are my own.

3   Bertuch's fashion journal started as *Journal der Moden* in 1786 and was published by him and the artist Georg Melchior Kraus, who had been taught by Johann Heinrich Tischbein the Elder (1722–1789) and Johann Georg Wille (1715–1808) in Paris. The bookseller and publisher Carl Wilhelm Ettinger (1741–1804) from Gotha was first in charge of the distribution of the journal but was bought out only one year later. In 1787 the journal was renamed *Journal des Luxus und der Moden* and continued under different names in 42 volumes until 1827.

4   Böttiger, from Guben in Saxony, was headmaster of the Weimar grammar school, and an acquaintance of Bertuch's.

5   Cf. Goethe- and Schiller Archives, Weimar (GSA), Bertuch papers, manuscripts concerning the editing of the fashion journal 06/5209 and 06/5186.

6   For the distribution of the *Journal des Luxus und der Moden*, cf. Rainer Flik: 'Kultur-Merkantilismus? Friedrich Justin Bertuchs *Journal des Luxus und der Moden* (1786–1827)', in *Das Journal*

From 1798 on, Johann Christian Hüttner from Saxony, Bertuch's correspondent in London, became a frequent customer in Hannah Humphrey's
print shop at 27 St. James Street. She had extensive, if not exclusive, rights
to sell the caricatures of James Gillray (1757–1815), by far the most successful and important satirical artist since William Hogarth (1697–1764). It was
actually Hüttner who had first called on Bertuch (via Böttiger, Hüttner's former headmaster at school in the Saxon town of Guben) and suggested to
him the publication of a new journal called *London* that should be based on
first-hand information.[7] Hüttner was preaching to the converted, Bertuch
was already preparing to launch several new journals at that very time. So
Bertuch took up Hüttner's idea, but modified it to a dual concept, focusing
the new journal on *two* urban centres, introducing a comparative perspective. Bertuch and Böttiger wanted Hüttner and other correspondents to
supply them with topical caricatures, which could then be explained and
commented upon for the German readership. Apart from the prospect of
increasing sales due to the entertaining function of the caricatures, the editors hoped to convey an authentic image of what they called 'Volksgeist'
(national spirit) and 'nationale Volkslaune' (national mood), for example the
specific British humor that came to the fore in the work of individual artists
like Gillray. Although these two German terms specify British humor as a
collective phenomenon, the editors of *London und Paris* were the first to emphasize Gillray's achievements as an individual artist, obviously a paradox
that they appear not to have reflected on.[8]

The Functions of Caricatures in *London und Paris*: Politics and Entertainment

From the beginning, *London und Paris* published anti-French caricatures,
though Böttiger still tried to exercise caution in his commentaries. Nelson's
offshore victory at Abukir was welcomed by the English caricaturists: Gillray
published a print showing French 'Revolutionary Crocodiles' severely beaten
by Admiral Nelson, who is depicted in heroic pose (cf. Fig. 1).[9] Another car-

---

des Luxus und der Moden: Kultur um 1800, ed. by Angela Borchert and Ralf Dressel (Heidelberg:
    Winter, 2004), pp. 21–55, 40–46.
7   Cf. Hüttner's letter to F.J. Bertuch, 25 January 1798 (Sächsische Landes- und Universitätsbi-
    bliothek [SLUB] Dresden, Böttiger papers, h37, Bd. 4[2°], no. 44). Hüttner suggested that the
    new journal should start as a supplement to the fashion magazine before becoming a new and
    independent journal.
8   Cf. for example Böttiger's extensive footnote on Gillray's life in his discussion of the caricature
    'Search-Night; – or – State-Watchmen, mistaking Honest-Men for Conspirators', *London und
    Paris*. 1 (1798) 195–204, plate IV.
9   James Gillray, 'Extirpation of the Plagues of Egypt; – Destruction of Revolutionary Croco-
    diles; – or – The British Hero cleansing the Mouth of the Nile', published 6 October 1798 by
    H. Humphrey, 27 St. James Street. Cf. Mary Dorothy George, ed., *Catalogue of Political and*

Fig 1: Carl Starcke after James Gillray: Extirpation of the Plagues of Egypt; – Destruction of Revolutionary Crocodiles; – or – The British Hero cleansing the Mouth of the Nile. In: *London und Paris* 2.7 (1798) no. XXIV.

icature by Gillray shows John Bull prodigiously devouring French ships (cf. Fig. 2).[10] A third caricature by the same artist shows British politicians of the opposition in the utmost despair when faced with Nelson's victory.[11] Many English caricatures use revolutionary symbols, such as the cocard or the tricolore colours of the national flag in order to discredit British politicians of the Whig party as traitors. After no openly anti-French caricature had been published in *London und Paris* for almost two years, an increasing politicization is evident in the journal's last two issues of 1801. Gillray reacts to the peace of Amiens by suggesting a shift of perspective: he depicts an apocalyptic political nightmare experienced by the Minister of War, William Wyndham, Lord

---

Personal Satires Preserved in the Department of Prints and Drawings in the British Museum, vol 7 (1942), no. 9250. Copied by Carl Starcke, *London und Paris* 2.7 (1798), no. XXIII. The *Catalogue* will in the following be referred to as BM.

10 James Gillray, 'John Bull taking a Luncheon: – or – British Cooks, cramming Old Grumble – Gizzard with Bonne Chére', published 24 October 1798 by H. Humphrey, 27 St. James Street. BM, VII (1942), no. 9257. Copied by Carl Starcke, *London und Paris* 2.7 (1798) no. XXIV.

11 James Gillray, 'Nelson's Victory: – or – Good-News operating upon Loyal-Feelings', published 3 October 1798 by H. Humphrey, 27 St. James Street. BM, VII (1942) no. 9248. Copied by Carl Starcke, *London und Paris* 2. 7 (1798) no. XXV.

Fig. 2: Carl Starcke after James Gillray: John Bull taking a Luncheon: – or – British Cooks,
cramming Old Grumble – Gizzard with Bonne Chére.
In: *London und Paris* 2.7 (1798) no. XXIV.

Grenville (1759–1834) who does not trust the peace.[12] In 'The first Kiss this
Ten Years! – or – the meeting of Britannia & Citizen François', he satirizes
the deceptive peace between the two powers.[13] With increasing aggression,
Gillray attacks the peace of Amiens through a travesty of Shakespeare's *Macbeth*: the skeleton of Britannia escapes from a huge cauldron of magic potion
prepared by the 'three weird sisters', alias Prime Minister Addington, Hawkesbury and Fox.[14] Addington supplies ingredients, throwing in taxpayers'

---

12 James Gillray, 'Political Dreamings! – Visions of Peace! – Perspective Horrors!', published 9
   November 1801 by H. Humphrey, 27 St. James Street. BM, VIII (1947), no. 9735. Original
   caricature served as a model for copy. Cf. Kunstbibliothek Berlin, Sammlung Lipperheide,
   Lipp Xd4, no. 41. Copied by Carl Starcke, *London und Paris* 8.8 (1801), nos. XXII-XXIII.
13 James Gillray, 'The first Kiss this Ten Years! – or – the meeting of Britannia & Citizen François', published 1 January 1803 by H. Humphrey, 27 St. James Street. BM, VIII (1947), no.
   9960. Cf. Kunstbibliothek Berlin, Sammlung Lipperheide, Lipp Xd4, no. 55. Copied by Carl
   Starcke, *London und Paris* 10.8 (1802), no. XXII.
14 James Gillray, 'A Phantasmagoria; – Scene – Conjuring-up an Armed Skeleton', published 5
   January 1803 by the artist, cf. BM, VIII (1947), no. 9962. Original caricature cf. Kunstbibliothek Berlin, Sammlung Lipperheide, Lipp Xd4, no. 56. Copied by Carl Starcke, *London und Paris*
   11.1 (1803), no. I.

money, while Hawkesbury, who had signed the peace treaty of Amiens for Britain, kindles the fire using written guarantees towards France and sacrifices British possessions. Charles Fox is discredited as a traitor by a French cocard on his hat as he extols peace. Böttiger differentiates between Gillray's political statement, with which he cannot agree, and his talent for composition: 'Auch wird jeder, wer für Composition und Gruppirung Auge hat, den ruchlosen Politiker und Kriegstrommler gern über dem geistreichen Zeichner und Anordner seiner Figuren vergessen.'[15] Commenting on the French and English caricatures, Böttiger saw himself in the tradition of Georg Christoph Lichtenberg (1742–1799), who had commented on Hogarth's prints in the *Göttinger Taschenkalender* (pocket calendar) in the 1780s and later on the larger prints copied by Riepenhausen in the *Ausführliche Erklärungen* (detailed explanations) from 1794 onwards. Böttiger might almost have succeeded Lichtenberg as the commentator on Hogarth. At that time, however, August Wilhelm Schlegel had warned Böttiger in his polemical *Notizen* (in the *Athenaeum*), not to 'roll empty barrels in front of him', alluding to the meaning of Böttiger's name in German, which is barrelmaker.[16] It is also a reference to 'Plan und Ankündigung' (plan and announcement) in *London und Paris*, in which Bertuch and Böttiger had promised not to deliver empty barrels to their readership.[17] Böttiger gave up his plan of succeeding Lichtenberg as commentator of Hogarth's prints on the advice of the classical philologist Christian Gottlob Heyne (1729–1812) from Göttingen. Heyne received complimentary copies of *London und Paris* for several years: not exclusively for himself, but also for his wife, who would write to Böttiger and ask impatiently when she would receive her favorite journal, an indication that parts of *London und Paris* tended to appeal especially to a female readership.[18] So Böttiger continued to explain the intricate allusions of the French and English caricatures, and thus participated in a unique process of cultural transfer: the caricatures came to be seen as examples of French and English national character and the popular humour of those two nations respectively.

15　Carl August Böttiger, 'III. Englische Caricaturen. Die Geisterbeschwörung. Szene: Ein bewaffnetes Skelet wird hervorgezaubert', *London und Paris* 11.1 (1803) 75–89, 89. 'Anyone having an eye for composition and grouping will readily forget the heinous politician and warmonger in favour of the inspired artist and talented arranger of his characters.'

16　August Wilhelm Schlegel, 'IV. Notizen', *Athenaeum* 2.2 (1799) 285–327, 310.

17　[F.J. Bertuch, Carl August Böttiger], 'Plan und Ankündigung', *London und Paris* 1.1 (1798) 3–11, 4.

18　Cf. the letters of Georgine Heyne to Böttiger, in Sächsische Landes- und Universitätsbibliothek Dresden, h 37, vol 84, nos. 74, 76 and 79.

Ideological Tendencies

The journal's ideological tendencies, which exhibit a generally pro-British stance and a mild condescension towards educated classicism, may be summarized as follows: an assumed inferiority of French taste, as compared to its English counterpart, becomes evident in the caricatures, which must question the journal's claim to political neutrality. Positive statements concerning Paris only serve the editors to conceal their partiality. Böttiger's commentaries on the caricatures can be seen as semi-serious statements concerning the classicism of the time, which was dominated by the aesthetics of Johann Joachim Winckelmann (1717–1768).

French caricatures, which are generally considered rude and primitive, lacking subtlety and taste, are represented as inferior to the English ones, which are regarded as the products of political liberty and freedom of the press. However, the French caricatures, as they appear in the journal, do not reflect the full range of caricatures on offer in Paris. The editors omit almost all French political caricatures, even though some were sent to Weimar or at least mentioned by the Paris correspondent Friedrich Theophil Winckler (1772–1807). Out of the 349 pictures in *London und Paris* 176 are caricatures, 132 are English and only 44 are French. In addition to this, there are large numbers of traditional prints, such as non-satirical portraits, landscapes, architecture, maps and outlines of paintings.

The critical view of the French caricatures corresponds to the editors' criticism of French censorship and the lack of liberty and freedom of the press during and after the *Directoire*. Winckler, an Alsacian who had studied at Jena where he became acquainted with Bertuch's son Carl (1777–1815), who later became co-editor of *London und Paris*, hated the five French directors and commented upon their regime in a cynical way. For that reason, he initially welcomed the rise of Bonaparte. But his relatively positive view of Napoleon gradually changed, reaching a low-point when the French leader had himself crowned emperor in 1804.

After the *Coup d'Etat* of the 18th Brumaire, an anonymous French artist utilized the tradition of the graphic representation of the 'Cris de Paris', the shouting of newspaper sellers and street traders, in pictorial broadsheets, in order to satirize this latest political development (cf. Fig.3).[19] The print does not disclose its explosive nature at first glance. The servant and the carrier on the left are relieved that they no longer have to carry the 750 official robes of the representatives. In his commentary on this caricature in *London und Paris*, Böttiger quotes a letter from Winckler, who gives background information regarding how he had bought the original print:

---

19 Anonymous artist, 'Les nouveaux Cris de Paris', *London und Paris*, 5.1 (1800), no. II.

Fig. 3: Carl Starcke (?) after an anonymous artist: Les nouveaux Cris de Paris.
In: *London und Paris* 5.1 (1800) no. II.

[Als ich] sie kaufen wollte, sagte mir der Kupferstichhändler, das Centralbureau habe nicht nur alle Abdrücke saisirt, sondern auch die Kupferplatten weggenommen und zerschlagen, so daß man keine mehr haben könne. Ich wurde nun um so begieriger mir dieselben zu verschaffen, und es gelang mir […].[20]

Was the story of the confiscation just a trick by the print trader to increase the demand for such prints? Had Böttiger simply manipulated the alleged letter of his correspondent from Paris in order to convey his political convictions? The original letter that Böttiger quotes has not survived. Did it ever exist at all? There are certainly cases in which Böttiger freely manipulated his material when this served his publicistic purposes. But in the present case, Winckler's (and Böttiger's) stories appear to be true, as of the two prints in question only the copies in *London und Paris* were listed in French print collections, not the

---

20 *London und Paris* 5.1 (1800) 86. 'When I wanted to buy the prints [the originals being two separate prints, etched together on one plate in the *London und Paris* copy, C.D.], the print trader told me that the Central Bureau had not only seized all copies but also the copper plates, which were then destroyed, so that no additional copies could be made. I became even keener to get hold of them and, finally, I succeeded in doing so.'

Fig. 4: Carl Starcke after James Gillray: Integrity retiring from Office!
In: *London und Paris* 7.4 (1801) no. X.

originals.[21] In this specific case, the journal became the only safe haven for
confiscated prints, which otherwise would not have been preserved at all.
Impartiality was an important value for a late-Enlightenment journal that had
declared in its first issue that it would be on its guard *against* politics. Despite
this statement, political content was envisaged from the beginning. But Bertuch and Böttiger had to make sure that their journal would not lose its *appearance* of neutrality, if they did not want to risk censorship in their own Duchy
of Saxe-Weimar. So they introduced yet another construct that could at least
partially even out the all too critical view of the French caricatures: Winckler
was an admirer of the French satirical *vaudeville* theatre of the day, a form of
highly popular music theatre characterized by its topicality and its catchy mel-
odies. The *vaudevilles* were praised in the journal, whereas English songs that
had been sent by Hüttner and by Nina d'Aubigny, a music teacher who
worked for *London und Paris* between 1804 and 1807, were criticized as being
inferior. The French national character, so it seemed, did not lack a sense of

21 Cf. *Collection De Vinck*. Bibliothèque Nationale de France, Département des Estampes. Un
    Siècle d'Histoire de France par l'estampe, 1770–1871. Inventaire analytique par François-Louis
    Bruel et al., 9 vols (Paris: Bibliothèque Nationale 1909–1968), nos. 7397–7398.

satire – it merely realized itself in a different genre: in the vaudeville, and not in caricature.

Böttiger's commentaries can be regarded as a semi-serious contribution to the classicism of his time. His constant use of the ancient world as a frame of reference had two effects: first, contrasting antiquity with the present served his programme of education that consisted in his attempt to sketch a lively and colourful picture of the ancient world. Secondly, on the basis of Johann Joachim Winckelmann's programme of classicism, the caricatures were, somewhat ironically, elevated to the same level as the art of the ancients. Thus, Gillray appears as the modern Aristophanes. It is remarkable that, in this respect, graphic satire, which was at that time considered as 'low art', here seems to take over the function of ancient satirical literature.

Böttiger's Commentaries

Böttiger's method may be exemplified with reference to Gillray's caricature entitled 'Integrity Retiring from Office' which appeared in *London und Paris* in 1801, after Gillray's publication on 24 February 1801 (Fig. 4). The print refers to the resignation of William Pitt the Younger, who was succeeded by Addington, and his ministers. The reason for his resignation was his refusal to agree to the uncompromising policy of King George III towards the Irish and their demand for autonomy. We see Pitt and his ministers leaving the Treasury and being insulted by a loutish group of opposition politicians.

> Es kann manchem nasenrümpfenden Kunstrichter ein großes Aergerniß geben, wenn bei einer bloßen Caricatur von Composition und Haltung der Figuren die Rede seyn sollte. Die Gilrayschen Caricaturen halten indeß wirklich auch die höheren Kunstforderungen aus. So wird niemand in Abrede seyn können, der die vorliegende Caricatur mit unbefangenem Blicke betrachtet, daß sowohl die stille ruhige Größe, mit der Pitt und seine treuen Gehilfen hier aus dem Reiche ihrer Herrlichkeit ausgehn, als auch die übersprudelnde, tobende und schäumende Heftigkeit des anstürmenden Haufens sowohl gegen einander als in sich selbst sehr gut zusammengestellt sind.[22]

Böttiger's commentaries are characterized by an ambiguity of tone. Does he want to seriously convince the readership of the possibility of reading the caricatures in terms of high art based on Winckelmann's classicism? In that

---

22 Böttiger commenting on Gillray's 'Integrity retiring from Office!', *London und Paris* 7.4 (1801) 333–348, no. X, here pp. 387–388. 'Many art critics turn up their noses and become annoyed when people talk about the composition or the poses of the figures in a mere caricature. Gillray's caricatures, however, genuinely fulfil the demands of high art. Looking at this caricature with an objective eye, no-one can deny that the calm, quiet grandeur with which Pitt and his faithful companions leave their realm of glory is superbly composed and set against the overflowing, frenzied, raging violence of the attacking mob.'

case, he would have stressed the fact that the caricature can be seen as a whole before dissecting it into its many details during his analysis. The chaotic details would then be regarded as less important than the overall effect of the caricature on the observer. Or does he merely echo the ironic attitude towards the theory of classical art which Gillray manifests when he attributes the gesture of Apollo Belvedere to Pitt and sets the groups of people in the tradition of the mock-heroic, mocking a triumphal procession? In the first volume of his work *Ideen zur Kunst-Mythologie* (Ideas for a Mythology of Art),[23] Böttiger reflects on his role as co-editor and commentator of *London und Paris*, hinting at the semi-serious, partly ironic quality of his commentaries:

> In den Erklärungen der politischen Spottbilder im Journal London und Paris knüpfte ich stets das Neueste an die Witzspiele und Gestaltungen des Alterthums an, und mein Liebling Aristophanes mußte sich oft bequemen, ein Vorläufer Gillray's, Hogarth's Geisteserben, zu seyn.[24]

And in his review of the continuation of the commentaries on Hogarth by the artist Johann Peter Lyser (1803–1870) in the penultimate issue, Böttiger reminisces, three years before his death in 1835, on his role as commentator on caricatures in *London und Paris*:

> Ich hatte seit 1797 in Weimar das Journal London und Paris herausgegeben und Gilray's unerschöpflichen Stachelwitz gegen die damalige britische Opposition für Pitt gegen Bounaparte [sic], mit seltenen Hilfsmitteln ausgerüstet, meine Feder geliehen. Fand ich doch da meinen Aristophanes wieder, der schon auf der Schule in Pforte mein Lieblingsdichter gewesen war.[25]

Böttiger had asked Lyser if he wanted to contribute the etchings for a new edition of Gillray's best caricatures. Evidently, Böttiger planned a new separate edition of his commentaries from *London und Paris* together with the copies of Gillray's prints. Lyser suggested the participation of Ernst Ludwig Riepenhausen (1765–1840), who had provided high-quality copies of Hogarth for Lichtenberg's *Ausführliche Erklärungen* (detailed explications) of 1794. Lyser informed Böttiger that, impoverished in his old age, Riepenhausen had to etch horses to print sheets for children. In any case, the plan of a new edition of Gillray's caricatures and Böttiger's commentaries was not realized.

---

23 Carl August Böttiger, *Ideen zur Kunst-Mythologie*, 3 vols (Dresden: Arnold, 1826).
24 Böttiger, 'Vorrede', *Ideen zur Kunst-Mythologie*, I, pp. X-XI. 'In my explanations of the political caricatures in the journal *London and Paris*, I have always associated the latest news with the puns and satires of the ancient world, and Aristophanes, my favorite, often had to put up with being called a predecessor of Gillray's, Hogarth's spiritual heir.'
25 B. [i.e. Böttiger], 'II. Erklärung der Hogarth'schen Spottbilder, fortgesetzt von J. Pierre Lyser', *Artistisches Notizenblatt* (22 November 1832), pp. 85–87 (a supplement, edited by Böttiger, for the *Abendzeitung* in Dresden): 'I had edited the Journal London and Paris in Weimar since 1797 and equipped Gillray's inexhaustible spiky satire against the British opposition for Pitt against Buonaparte with rare instruments of help, lent it my pen. For I found here my Aristophanes again, who had already been my favourite writer at school in Schulpforta [an elite school near Naumburg].'

Böttiger's commentaries did not just relate ancient culture and philology to the present, he constantly referred to the English satirical tradition. From Sterne, he borrowed the technique of digression, from Sterne and Addison the irritatingly unstable status of utterances, oscillating between serious point and joke. Often he took up the allusions and quotations the caricaturists had made concerning Shakespeare, Milton or the Bible, and elaborated on their work. Frequently, he wove in references to German literature, quoting Wieland, Goethe, Herder and Schiller, as well as writers less well known today. Böttiger was blending the ancient world with the contemporary, sometimes even crossing the borders between the timeless and the ephemeral, the platitudinal and the sublime.

Despite his extensive knowledge of the most recent publications in England and France, as well as in the German-speaking world, Böttiger's commentaries did not succeed in retaining his readers' attention for long. In one respect Lichtenberg's commentaries on Hogarth were superior to Böttiger's efforts: the sensitive modulation of their tone. Böttiger's commentaries, however, are characterized by high levels of expressivity and rhetorical intensity, which run the risk of tiring their readers in the long run. Böttiger displayed an awareness of his stylistic limitations when he wrote to Bertuch, lamenting that he could not adapt his way of writing to the topic at hand, so that his authorship would always be easily identifiable. The only thing he could do, he promised, was to restrict the number of footnotes, but even that he did not achieve. Therefore, the possibility that Böttiger could fabricate an *alter ego*, a commentator in the tradition of the satire of the learned man, seems doubtful. The links between the stylistic limitations of the commentator with his overflowing footnotes and Böttiger the philologist would be too obvious. The exaggerations in the commentaries were intentional, of course, but this fact alone does not constitute excellent satirical writing. The total lack of self-irony is another important distinguishing feature of his style and further illustrates his limitations as a satirist. Over the years, Böttiger's style perpetuated itself and may well have had an exhausting effect on his readers, if the decreasing sales figures of the journal are anything to go by. Indeed, it was not so much for reasons of style that Böttiger's commentaries attracted the attention of readers, and continue to engage critics in our own time, but rather for their historical content, especially the information on now often forgotten publications of the day. Böttiger might have gained an enduring profile as a satirist, writing his antiquity-laden commentaries against Bonaparte's instrumentalization of ancient symbols and gestures during his reign, especially in the wake of his self-coronation as emperor, if his method, the juxtaposition of ancient culture and philology with contemporary culture, had not become an end in itself, lacking satirical sharpness and direction.

The Originality of *London und Paris*

The journal *London und Paris* broke boundaries in two respects: politically, it introduced a new style of active political participation and debate to a German public that was not used to political graphic satire of such high quality and such large quantity. Aesthetically, it called into question the normative role of classical art theory in Winckelmann's classicism through the anti-classical, chaotic and reflexive tendencies of the caricatures it published. Böttiger's commentaries opened up a field of discussion, providing serious, semi-serious and jocular statements of an experimental character, which challenged the basis of classicism's normative celebration of fine simplicity and silent grandeur, replacing it with a lively and sensual image of the ancient world.

London und Paris was the first periodical to choose as its rationale the international transfer of images from London and Paris to the Dutchy of Saxe-Weimar. The originality of its profile has never been equalled since. *London und Paris* served later caricaturists as a stock cupboard of prints and visual ideas, when the production of anti-Napoleonic propaganda prints reached a high during the Napoleonic wars between 1812 and 1815, and beyond. However, it is not possible to prove empirically the decisiveness of this function, as parallel to the dissemination of prints through the journal, a transfer of images by travellers, print traders, and collectors was taking place: one cannot tell for certain from which precise source a visual idea found its way into Central Europe, unless explicit written evidence can be traced in the estates of the artists.

The Reception of and Reactions to *London und Paris*

The adaption of professional prints by anonymous amateurs is exemplified by Gillray's caricature entitled 'Scientific Researches! – New Discoveries in Pneumaticks! – or – an Experimental Lecture on the Powers of Air', published 29 May 1802, which shows the performance of a public experiment at the London Royal Institute under the supervision of the Professor of Chemistry Dr. Thomas Young and his assistant Humphry Davy (cf. Fig. 5).[26] Sir John Hippesley, according to Hüttner's information a very famous servant at St. James's Palace, breathes in a mixture of oxygen and hydrogen while Dr. Young holds his nose. On this occasion, Hippesley proves responsible for the escape of air of another kind. Having written additional explanations on the back of the original caricature, Hüttner mentions that this accident really happened to Hippesley. During the Napoleonic wars, a German amateur

---

26 James Gillray, 'Scientific Researches! – New Discoveries in Pneumaticks! – or – an Experimental Lecture on the Powers of Air', June/July 1802. Copied by Carl Starcke, *London und Paris* 10.5 (1802), no. XIII.

Fig. 5: Carl Starcke after James Gillray: Scientific Researches! – New Discoveries in
Pneumaticks! – or – an Experiment Lecture on the Powers of Air.
In: *London und Paris*, 10. 5 (1802) no. XIII.

adapted Gillray's caricature and replaced Dr. Young with Napoleon. The subtitle identifies the experimenter as Lavoisier – an anachronism, for Lavoisier
had been guillotined in 1794 (cf. Fig. 6).[27] It is characteristic of popular adaptations like this one that the complexity of the original caricature is reduced
by the amateur artist, who left out large parts of the original print and hid his
identity behind the signature of James Gillray.

London und Paris could easily have become a transitory phenomenon in
the field of journalism, only paving the way for Bertuch's later liberal political journals and newspapers, especially for the political journal *Nemesis*,
which he edited together with the historian Heinrich Luden (1778–1847)
between 1814 and 1818, and for one of the first political daily newspapers,
the *Oppositionsblatt oder Weimarische Zeitung*, published between 1817 and

27 Anonymous artist, 'Napoleon eilt bey Annäherung der Alliirten zu dem grossen Chemiker
Lavoisier in Paris um sein flüchtig gewordenes Genie aufs neue wieder herstellen zu lassen'
(1814). 'Upon the approach of the Allies Napoleon hurries to Lavoisier, the great chemist, in
Paris, to have his escaping genius restored'. Universitätsbibliothek Eichstätt, print collection
(without classmark). Cf. Sabine and Ernst Scheffler, eds, *So zerstieben getraeumte Weltreiche. Napoleon I. in der deutschen Karikatur* (Hannover, Stuttgart: Wilhelm-Busch-Gesellschaft, 1995),
p. 295.

Fig. 6: Anonymous artist: [Napoleon eilt zu Lavoisier/(Napoleon hurries to Lavoisier],
(1814) no. 7; (courtesy of the University Library of Eichstätt).

1821. The prevailing political outlook changed, however, not long after the
introduction of the comparatively liberal constitution of Weimar in 1816.
The political climate in Germany turned conservative with increasing censorship and pressure from Metternich's Austria in the wake of the Carlsbad
decrees in 1821, which followed the assassination of August von Kotzebue
(1761–1819) by the student fanatic Carl Ludwig Sand (1795–1820). Bertuch's liberal press came to a sudden end, which must have been a bitter
disappointment for the veteran editor at the end of his life. *London und Paris*
was soon forgotten, except for some negative publicity from Karl Rosenkranz (1805–1879) in his *Aesthetik des Hässlichen* (Aesthetics of the Ugly) in
1837, a Hegelian study that tried to find the beautiful 'ex negativo', analyzing the different phenomena of the ugly not without being fascinated by
them. The caricatures in *London und Paris* inevitably provoked Rosenkranz's
particular distaste because he regarded caricatures in general as the epitome
of the ugly. And he declares in the final chapter, entitled 'Caricatur', that it
was even less acceptable that caricatures should serve as a model for copy-
ing, as, thus, the ugly would repeat itself and deteriorate even further.

   London und Paris made a pioneering contribution to a fledgling public
sphere in Germany, and it is worth stressing the historical constraints placed

on the journal, especially in the form of political pressure and censorship. In light of this, it is all the more astonishing how long *London und Paris* continued to exist, although it lost most of its satirical impact after the French took control of the press in 1806. The intended re-launch of the journal in 1815 did not proceed beyond the first issue. Carl Bertuch, the publisher's son, who had been responsible for *London und Paris* since 1804, decided to close down the journal in the explosive political situation at the end of 1814. He attended the Congress of Vienna, together with the editor Johann Friedrich Cotta (1764–1832), with the aim of fighting for the rights of the book trade, the copyright of authors, and against illegal printing. But when Bonaparte had escaped from Elba, Carl Bertuch decided to abandon the journal as he could not find anyone in Vienna ready to take the risk of writing about politics.[28]

    One last question might be this: what did James Gillray think of the German journal? There is evidence in the journal itself as well as in the letters of people involved with *London und Paris* that the journal was sold in both cities. We find *London und Paris* in Remnant's bookstore as well as in the club of Sir Joseph Banks (1743–1820) in London. We also find it in the circle of Aubin-Louis Millin (1759–1818), the director of the Musée des Medailles at the Bibliothèque Nationale in Paris, whose assistant was Friedrich Theophil Winckler. Hüttner, who had been frustrated by Gillray's repeated refusal to give any information about the details of his caricatures, wrote contentedly to Böttiger that the artist had declared great pleasure in the journal that a German friend had (probably orally) translated for him.[29] This is indeed a compliment for the copies of Gillray's caricatures in *London*

---

28 Cf. Carl Bertuch's letter to his father of 26 April 1815 (GSA 06/151, no. 59): 'Den Artikel Wien betreffend, so habe ich mich hier überzeugt, wie schwer es ist, zuverläßige Correspondenten in Wien zu erhalten. Alle Schriftsteller von Text sind Staatsbeamte, die aus Rücksichten keine Beiträge liefern, auch nicht den umsichtigsten Forschungsgeist für ein solches Journal haben. Die Fremden sind zu unbestimmt hier, u. man kann sich nicht darauf einlaßen, zumal da Alles jetzt in Krieg zieht, und Wien sehr öde werden wird. – Nach diesen Ansichten würde das Journal mit meinem besten Betreiben sehr mittelmäßig ausfallen, u. wir thun beßer, es jetzt gleich mit einer paßenden Erklärung mit dem 1n Stücke zu schließen, [...]. – Das Debit der Zeitschriften wird von Neuem jetzt wieder sinken, u. man kann schwerlich in diesem Jahr viel hoffen'. – 'Concerning the Vienna article, I could convince myself here how difficult it is to have reliable correspondents in Vienna. All writers (of text) are civil servants who, taking precautions, do not provide any articles, they also lack any gift for the research required for such a journal. The foreigners are too uncertain here, and you cannot count on them, even less as everybody is now going to war and Vienna will become deserted. – According to those prospects, the journal would turn out to be quite mediocre, and we had better close it down with a suitable explanation in the first number [...]. – Journal sales will certainly decrease again, and there is not much to hope for this year.'
29 Hüttner to Böttiger, 30 October 1800. Böttigers papers, vol 4 (2°), no 71, SLUB Dresden, h37. This German friend was a certain A.F. Thoellden, who is mentioned in the journal several times. We learn about him only that he had considerable knowledge of chemistry and that he was rich enough to live in London, together with his wife, on independent means.

und Paris (all copied by the engraver Carl Starcke) as well as for Böttiger's commentaries: this positive feedback by the London artist himself could be considered a final endorsement of this Weimar project of cultural transfer.

Changing Authorities on HMS *Bounty*

The Public Images of William Bligh and Fletcher Christian in the Context of Late Eighteenth-Century Political and Intellectual Conditions

Maike Oergel

This essay investigates how the contemporary intellectual and political conditions relate to the dramatic reversal which the images of the two opponents in the 'Mutiny on the *Bounty*' undergo in the course of the 1790s. By tracing how the changing and fluid political and intellectual conditions of this decade directly impacted on the public understanding and interpretation of this contemporary event, I shall be able to show how these conditions shaped this reversal to such an extent that it becomes a reflection of them. To be specific, I will show how the occurrence and initial outcomes of the revolution in France and the fundamental changes in intellectual paradigms effect a transformation in the public image of William Bligh from courageous British seafaring hero engaged in advancing knowledge and Britain's imperial interests into the epitome of an unjust tyrant, while, by the same token, Fletcher Christian turns in the public imagination from villainous mutineer into a heroic 'soul in agony'. These specifics represent general trends: as the *Bounty* story, and its protagonists, become public property, not just in Britain, but in the entire sphere of European influence, the interpretation of this news story becomes a barometer of political and intellectual preferences. In this respect, the *Bounty*-story provides a case-study of how, through public appropriation, a contemporary event is given meaning, or different meanings, and begins to exhibit features of a modern myth.[1]

---

1 I use the term *myth* here – along the lines of Hans Blumenberg's, Manfred Frank's, and Kurt Hübner's interpretaions – to denote a narrative that through symbolic content visualizes the currently inexplicable or simply disparate in human experience, and aims to provide some kind of ordering or meaning, without a binding reference to the particular or overtly historical. The origins of this understanding of myth lie themselves in the context of secularization during the later eighteenth century, in the classical and Hebrew philology of that period, and the reinterpretation of sacred texts, such as the Bible, which was linked to these philological studies. Cf. Maike Oergel, *The Return of King Arthur and the Nibelungen: National Myth in 19th-century English and German Literature* (Berlin: de Gruyter, 1998), pp. 1–13; Hans Blumenberg, *Arbeit am Mythos* (Frankfurt a. M.: Suhrkamp, 1979); Manfred Frank, *Der kommende Gott* (Frankfurt a. M.: Suhrkamp, 1982); Kurt Hübner, *Die Wahrheit des Mythos* (Munich: Beck, 1985).

The literature dealing with the *Bounty*-story is vast, and its production shows no sign of abating.[2] It divides into two main areas: historical and fictional treatments. Historical treatments have aimed to investigate what 'really happened', before, during, and after the mutiny. They largely focus on the causes of the rebellion and Bligh's character and actions. Or, in the shape of autobiographies and biographies, historical treatments seek to position their subjects favourably within the developing events. Like all historical fiction, the fictional treatments of the *Bounty*-story aim, more openly than their historical counterparts, to provide disparate historical facts with a contextual narrative that invests them with meaning. While most historical treatments originate from academic quarters, the fictional treatments belong to the realm of popular culture and have not engaged much critical or academic interest. It is surprising that the reception history of the historical and fictional treatments is largely unwritten: no intellectual historian has yet asked (or answered) at any length questions regarding *what* has accrued to the bare bones of the historical facts, *at which times* and *why*.[3] This essay treats the very beginning of such interpretations.

Issues of general, rather than individual, reception tend to revolve around some form of public sphere. The growth of the modern public sphere during the eighteenth century, and its configuration on print media, mass literacy, and widening political participation, is well known.[4] The public images under discussion here owe their existence and their power to exactly these historical conditions. Public images occupy the shifting territory between facts and the creation of a meaningful context for these facts: a public image represents the way in which the 'public' makes sense of them. To what extent this understanding is directed or spontaneous is always a

---

2   Cf. Donald A. Maxton, *The Mutiny on HMS Bounty: A Guide to Non-Fiction, Fiction, Poetry, Film, Articles, and Music* (Jefferson NC, London: McFarland, 2008). After declining interest during the nineteenth century, there is a noticeable resurgence during the twentieth: in Britain, America, Australia, Germany, and France new *Bounty* fiction appears regularly. The story of the mutiny returned to the public arena in the 1930s, with numerous historical and fictional treatments, and experienced a predictable peak in historical descriptions around 1989, the bi-centenary of its key event. The most recent fictional treatment in English is John Boyne's *Mutiny on the Bounty* (2008), the most recent historical work is Anna Salmond's *Bligh: William Bligh in the South Seas* (Berkeley, Los Angeles, London: University of California Press, 2011).

3   Johannes Paulmann's short article 'Macht-Raum: Die Geschichte(n) von der Meuterei auf der Bounty', in *Ritual-Macht-Raum: Europäisch-ozeanische Beziehungswelten in der Neuzeit*, ed. by Johannes Paulmann et al. (Bremen: Überseemuseum Bremen, 2005), pp. 57–76 gives a broad outline of this history. Caroline Alexander's highly readable *The Bounty: The true story of the Mutiny on the Bounty* (London: Harper Collins, 2003), which retells the story relying predominantly on original sources, does make an effort to contextualize the events intellectually, but does not aim at anything beyond a very general picture.

4   Cf. Jürgen Habermas' seminal work *Strukturwandel der Öffentlichkeit: Untersuchungen zu einer Kategorie der bürgerlichen Gesellschaft* (Neuwied: Luchterhand, 1962) and the research and discussions it spawned.

debatable matter. Images are created for specific reasons, but only if an image is widely accepted can it function as 'public'. Such acceptance is predicated on fitting the historical context and the *Zeitgeist*, it always points to a consensus based on probability and credibility. This in turn allows conclusions to be drawn about the context in question. Context, creation, and acceptance stand in direct relation to each other.

Bearing this in mind, it cannot come as a surprise that in the 1790s the *Bounty-story* evolved as a mix of facts, appropriation, and contemporary myth: a significant current affairs story, which attracted extensive media coverage, turned into an event of contemporary history, which in turn intrigued and interested large numbers of people and inspired intellectuals. I shall argue that the longevity of the *Bounty*-material as a story is not only rooted in its content, being a gripping tale of adventure, but also in the interaction between 'real event' and its meaning-generating interpretation(s). It is in the protagonists' public images, and their shifts, that this generation of meaning originated.

The *Bounty*-story was highly topical, pulling together key issues of its time, which produced the very reciprocity between (unfolding) events and their interpretation, re-interpretation, and reception. In order to demonstrate this reciprocity of events, image- and story-making, and intellectual and political context, I will focus on three areas: the economic, political and intellectual contexts of the expedition and the mutiny, the public images of Bligh and Christian and how they changed in response to political and intellectual developments, and the literary appropriation of the material in the 1790s, i.e. how it fitted (into) the literary and intellectual scene of the time. Before I proceed, however, it is necessary to give a brief summary of the 'historical' events – the 'facts'.

In late 1787 HMAV *Bounty*[5] was sent to Tahiti, under the command of Lieutenant William Bligh, to collect breadfruit plants and transport them to the West Indies. After a six-month stay on Tahiti, longer than anticipated, the *Bounty*, laden with breadfruit saplings, duly left for the West Indies. A few weeks later, on 28 April 1789, just over half the crew mutinied under the leadership of Fletcher Christian, the ship's acting second lieutenant, who took the ship, and set its captain along with loyal members of the crew (and officers they did not trust) adrift in the *Bounty's* open launch. The seamen in the launch survived – with one exception – a voyage of 46 days to the Dutch colony on Timor, from where all who survived the after-effects of their ordeal returned to England in the course of 1790, William Bligh among the first in mid-March. The mutineers, on the other hand, returned to Tahiti twice, and about half of them decided to stay on the island and

---

5   The vessel is commonly referred to as HMS, but her official naval rating was His Majesty's Armed Vessel.

wait for the next British ship. Some of those staying had simply not fitted into the launch, others had subsequently decided they were not mutineers after all. With a small group of committed rebels, their Tahitian women, and some Tahitian men, Fletcher Christian set off in the *Bounty* in search of a place beyond the reach of British naval law, which he found in the shape of the incompletely charted Pitcairn Island. There the ship was burnt and sunk. The mutineers set up a community, which was however dogged by violence, apparently caused by racial discrimination and sexual envy. When the island was finally (re-)discovered by an American ship in 1808, only one – white – man, along with a number of women, and over twenty children, had survived. Following Lieutenant Bligh's report to the Admiralty upon his return in March 1790, the frigate HMS *Pandora* was despatched to the Pacific to hunt down the mutineers, finding only those on Tahiti. Although the *Pandora* was shipwrecked on its return journey, many onboard survived and returned to England in 1792, which meant that the inevitable court-martials of the surviving mutineers could take place. Meanwhile the newly promoted *Captain* Bligh had embarked (in 1791) on his second, and successful, breadfruit voyage.

In most treatments, historical and fictional, the conflict on board the *Bounty* is seen as a confrontation between Lieutenant William Bligh, commander of the vessel, and Fletcher Christian, the vessel's Master's mate, who in the early stages of the voyage had been promoted to acting lieutenant, i.e. became the second-highest ranking officer. These two figures have come to represent conflicting ideas and concepts. On one level it is a conflict about *authority*, its uses, range, and legitimacy, and the rights and needs of the individual. But it was also a confrontation between two competing visions of human existence: between the natural and the modern, i.e. between an (imagined) harmonious existence based on natural conditions, and the striving, conquering, 'civilized' (and 'civilizing') world of European modernity driven by science, discovery, and commerce. In this opposition Bligh comes to represent late eighteenth-century modern civilization with its achievements and its (at the time and now) much debated defects, such as oppressive hierarchical structures, the dominance of alienated de-naturalized reason, and grasping exploitative materialism. Christian, due to his close association with Tahitian culture, becomes associated with recapturing the natural by throwing off the oppressive structures of modern society. This is the naturalness which the same eighteenth-century modernity was projecting not just onto Tahiti, but onto much of the exotic utopia known as the 'South Seas'. In the contemporary imagination Tahiti was conceived as an island paradise, populated by unrepressed noble savages, who due to nature's plentiful supplies did not need to toil, but enjoyed a simple life of ease, and considerable sexual licence.[6] This constellation, straddling questions of authority and the purpose of human existence, explains the *Bounty*-story's capacity to engage with key philosophical, political and intellectual concerns not just of the 1790s, but of the entire 'Sattelzeit' (Koselleck). In order to substantiate the claim that the images of Bligh and Christian represented contemporary dichotomies, it is necessary to look at the historical individuals.

William Bligh, a well-educated and articulate descendant of Cornish gentry, was a career officer in the Royal Navy. Intellectually he was rooted in Enlightenment traditions and ideas. He was keenly interested in science and technology. Bligh had a particular aptitude for charting, and a number of coastlines in the southern hemisphere were first committed to paper by his hand. The recording of topography was a crucial part of achieving mastery over the physical world. Eradicating white areas from the map of the globe was a contemporary undertaking similar in status and importance to the more recent charting of the human genome. It, too, promised vast practical applications: improved navigation would bring rich benefits in the form of trade and colonies and a clearer understanding of the world humanity inhabited. Bligh was fully up-to-date on the very latest navigation technology, which was making ground-breaking progress at the time. For much of the century research had focused on finding a reliable and practicable way of determining longitude at sea, which in the 1770s had finally been achieved through John Harrison's marine timekeeper. With Bligh on the *Bounty* travelled a chronometer (later) named Kendall 2, which was an exact copy of Harrison's definitive prototype and the most cutting edge technology available. That Bligh was able to take, and use, such technology on a small-scale and somewhat quirky expedition as the *Bounty's*[7] testifies to his scientific and technological nous, and his connections. Bligh was equally interested in scientific empirical enquiry in the shape of anthropological, botanical, and zoological observations, as the meticulous and lengthy records he kept of the plants, animals, and human cultures he encountered make plain, which he intended to publish, in the name of advancing knowledge. He also took an

---

6   The early visitors of the mid-eighteenth-century were fairly unanimous on this point, whether Louis-Antoine de Bougainville, who named Tahiti 'New Cythera', or characters as different in political and intellectual outlook as Joseph Banks, James Cook, or Reinhold Forster. The latter three all praised the idyllic quality of the island in their journals. Cf. J.C. Beaglehole's editions of *The Journals of Captain James Cook on his Voyage of Discovery*, 3 vols (Cambridge: Cambridge University Press, 1955), I: *The Voyage of the 'Endeavour' 1769–1771* and of *The 'Endeavour' Journal of Joseph Banks 1768–1771*, 2 vols (Sydney: Angus and Robertson, 1962) and Johann Reinhold Forster, *The 'Resolution' Journal of Johann Reinhold Forster 1772–1775*, 4 vols, ed. by Michael Hoare (London: The Hakluyt Society, 1982).

7   The *Bounty* was a tiny ship by anyone's standards, with a small complement, without marines to enforce the commander's authority, who – another cost-cutting measure – was an officer of the rank of lieutenant rather than captain.

enlightened scientific approach to health, diet, and hygiene on board, and implemented measures accordingly, foisting them on his crews with all the conviction of an enlightened absolutist ruler. And as all commanding officers in the Royal Navy, he was wedded to the notion of inviolate hierarchical structures.

Bligh's interests and pursuits represent the eighteenth-century outlook of the Enlightenment: scientific exploration of the world, with the intention of mastering and conquering it, a desire to bring improvement, achieve perfectibility even, sustained by a belief in progress. It is also an outlook that prioritized European achievements and wished to export these for humanitarian as well as power- and profit-driven ideological reasons. In fact in Bligh one has an exponent of the unity of intellectual and scientific enquiry, professionalism, and imperialistic politics, which characterised the eighteenth-century British approach to the world. In most respects Bligh modelled himself on his famous teacher, James Cook, whose voyages can equally be described in terms of this unity.[8] Cook travelled with naval and governmental funding as well as scientists and intellectuals, and his efforts were seen as benefiting navigation, science, Britain, and mankind. This was scientifically and politically cutting edge (then as now), as there was considered to be a clear link between using public funds for scientific research and achieving economic and political impact. Bligh's association with Cook's, and Joseph Bank's (see below), circle situates him at the forefront of navigational, scientific and imperial developments in the 1770s and early 1780s. On the one hand, his close association with late Enlightenment outlooks in science and politics places him squarely amid a contemporary power-base, but on the other hand these outlooks associate him with intellectual paradigms that are beginning to be questioned. The most obvious of the latter is the absolutism Bligh – and any other commander in the Royal Navy – practised on board their ships. But concepts of exploration were also changing. While the eighteenth-century approach of scientific and empirical exploration and discovery did not go away – Darwin's voyage on the Beagle was still conceived in the image of Cook's – these eighteenth-century concepts of discovery were being challenged by notions of exploration relying on empathy rather than empirical-scientific or political conquest. The concept of exoticism mentioned above is an example of this. But this is part of a general intellectual and cultural trend: interest in the primitive, the original, and the natural also found expression closer to the European home, in the growing intellectual and artistic interest in folklore and popular culture, which char-

---

8   The young Bligh sailed with Cook as sailing master on the *Resolution* on the latter's third – and fatal – voyage (1776–80), when Cook was at the height of his fame and influence. On board the *Resolution* Bligh would have gleaned much regarding health management at sea and navigational technology from Cook. One of Harrison's prototypes had accompanied Cook on his second voyage, who in the course of this trip became an advocate of marine timekeepers.

acterized the contemporary engagement with ballads, medieval epics, customs and culture.

Bligh's return from Cook's third voyage alive – unlike Cook – had granted him some measure of fame in naval and governmental as well as intellectual circles.[9] Bligh became very well connected: he was highly regarded by Sir Joseph Banks, the late eighteenth-century intellectual-scientist politician *par excellence*, who himself had travelled with Cook on the latter's first voyage. Through his wife Elizabeth Betham, whom he married shortly after his return from Cook's last voyage, he acquired connections to the Scottish Enlightenment as well as to the top-level merchant class. His father-in-law, Dr Richard Betham, had studied at Edinburgh, and her maternal grandfather, Dr Neil Campbell had been Principal of Glasgow University and in the orbit of such leading intellectuals as David Hume, Adam Smith, and William Robertson. Dr Campbell's son, Mrs Bligh's uncle, Duncan Campbell was an influential transatlantic merchant and owner of plantations in the West Indies, with excellent government connections, who together with the ubiquitous Joseph Banks pushed for the breadfruit expedition. Campbell very much represents the international British businessman of his time who worked hand in hand with the government in the interest of capitalism and imperialistic globalization, to create new wealth and to expand the British sphere of influence.[10] It is clear that William Bligh's interests, talents, and connections associated him with a particular kind of late eighteenth-century thinking and politics.[11]

There is considerably less detail regarding Fletcher Christian's life, which of course invites imaginative gap-filling. Christian was of gentlemanly but impoverished Manx descent. His family had more recently settled in the North West of England, where he attended the Free Grammar School at Cockermouth, together with the young William Wordsworth. He was a professional seaman of the officer-class, and well-known to Bligh: Christian

---

9 It also granted him some – potentially career-destroying – notoriety: his outspoken disapproval of the conduct of senior officers at the time leading up to and following Cook's death on Hawaii halted his career. Cf. Salmond, *Bligh*, 42–44.

10 Another in-law relative was the by then elderly vice-admiral of the white and former governor of Newfoundland John Campbell, a highly esteemed Navy commander with a lifelong interest in navigation technology, who was a much respected member of the Board of Longitude. Campbell may have been another influence on Bligh's excellent understanding of navigational technology.

11 It is worth pointing out, though, that this is an *association* with ideas which were defined with such definite clarity as my statement suggests only once 'intellectual history' had become an academic subject. The fewest individuals are so one-dimensional, and Bligh, as well as Cook, were not only aware, but appreciated the 'other' outlook and type of existence, and its advantages and benefits. Cf. e.g. Bligh's log of the *Bounty* and its intermittent positive comments on Polynesian culture. In this both were the children of their (changing) times. Bligh's one-sided positioning in this particular corner of eighteenth-century thinking is again evidence of the image-making his personality and story underwent.

had sailed under Bligh on (Duncan Campbell's) merchant ships on West Indies trading routes in the early 1780s. Bligh and Christian belonged to that stratum of middle-class gentry who had to get an education and make it in a profession to live comfortably and be respected: while Bligh and Christian chose the Navy, Fletcher's brother Edward chose the academic route, and became a professor of law at Cambridge.[12]

The *Bounty's* mission had its own specific contemporary context. The expedition's purpose was to make breadfruit readily available as cheap food for the slaves working on the West Indian plantations. In today's value system this makes it an unpalatable venture, linked with exploitative colonialism and slavery, both aspects of morally bankrupt (ancien) regimes. And indeed the very nature of the *Bounty's* mission, moving goods or materials halfway round the globe for the utilitarian purpose of economic profit and efficiency, was, and was going to be, a common imperial(ist) practice in an Empire whose sphere of influence covered the world. Yet in the contemporary context, there may have also appertained to this enterprise a humanitarian (scientific-enlightened) aim: to broaden and simplify the provision of food in the West Indies, in the same modernizing and enlightened manner in which potatoes were introduced as mass fodder in Europe in the eighteenth century, or sugar beet was mass-produced in Prussia to replace the expensive cane sugar and make sugar cheaply available.[13] This complexity highlights the fluid political, economic and intellectual situation of this historical moment, which let political and social conservatism co-exist in close proximity to cutting-edge global commercial-capitalist interests and modern humanitarian considerations, and illustrates once more the dialectic of Empire and Imperialism, which has been the subject of much post-colonial discourse.[14] And it was exactly the sort of commercial venture the Admiralty and the government would support at the time, through the figures of Joseph Banks and Duncan Campbell.

With the above scene-setting in mind, I now turn to the public images. When Bligh returned to England in March 1790, the story of the mutiny

12 Fletcher Christian was cousin to John Fletcher Curwen, a prominent radical Whig politician, who in conservative circles was linked with revolutionary French ideas. To what extent this connection was known or influenced his public image requires further research.
13 When reporting on the fate of the *Bounty*, *The Gentleman's Magazine*, for example, foregrounds this humanitarian aspect by referring to the mission as a means to provide food to everybody 'in times of scarcity'. Cf. *Gentleman's Magazine and Historical Chronicle* (May 1790) 463.
14 Cf. e.g. Ian Baucom, *Out of Place: Englishness, Empire and the Locations of Identity* (Princeton NJ: Princeton University Press, 1999) for the dialectics of imperial identity, and Bernard Porter, *The Absent-Minded Imperialists: Empire, Society and Culture in Britain* (Oxford: Oxford University Press, 2004), which discusses the involvement in and support for the Empire at home, as well as, of course, Edward Said's seminal *Culture and Imperialism* (London: Chatto and Windus, 1993). Outside the Academy, the complexity of these issues were clearly reflected in Jeremy Paxman's BBC1 documentary series *Empire*, first broadcast in March 2012.

and, most of all, the astonishing voyage in the open launch was spreading rapidly, and he was celebrated. In May *The Gentleman's Magazine* urged for Bligh's promotion:

> His seamanship appears matchless, as his undertaking seems beyond the verge of probability. [...] He only holds the rank of lieutenant in our navy. His merit pointed him out to the Admiralty as highly qualified for this expedition. [...] [one hopes] that in the present Admiralty Board there exists a disposition to foster and protect suffering merit.[15]

Bligh was duly promoted twice in the following six months and received a gratuity of 500 guineas from the Jamaican assembly for his troubles, even though he had not brought the plantation owners any breadfruit plants yet. The story attracted great attention: only weeks after Bligh's return to England, the Royalty Theatre was putting on *The Pirates or the Calamities of Captain Bligh* as part of a variety show, which included scenes of his reception at Tahiti, 'his seizure in his cabin,' 'the attachment of the Otahaitean women to, and the distress at parting from the British sailors', 'their distress at sea', and an 'Otaheitian Dance', 'rehearsed under the immediate instruction of a person who was onboard the *Bounty*' (!).[16] Bligh passed into popular culture, and became affectionately known as Breadfruit Bligh. However, when Bligh returned from his successful breadfruit expedition in 1793 with, if contemporary evidence is to be believed, a happy crew,[17] he experienced a very different reception. The very fact that we know such details, i.e. that his return was keenly watched and publicly recorded, illustrates the extent of public interest: Bligh, his behaviour, and his leadership were eminently noteworthy. The Admiralty was rather frosty, refusing to give him an appointment and, most significantly in this context, he found he was no longer nick-named Breadfruit Bligh, but the Bounty Bastard.

What had happened? The court-martials of the retrieved *Bounty* crew members had taken place. Bligh himself had been court-martialled following his return in 1790 (22 Oct), which was routine Admiralty procedure for any captain who lost his ship.[18] He was honourably acquitted, which established that the events of 28 April 1789 constituted mutiny, which in turn spelt an automatic death-sentence for any mutineer. So the purpose of the trials in the late summer of 1792 was to determine *who* had mutinied, *not* whether

---

15 *Gentleman's Magazine* (May 1790) 464.
16 Play-bill facsimile printed in George Mackaness, *The Life of Vice-Admiral William Bligh* (Sydney: Angus and Robertson, 1961) as plate between pp. 176/177.
17 Cf. *Gentleman's Magazine* (August 1793).
18 This procedure suggests that the notion of a captain's accountability – for Admiralty property in his care, at any rate – existed. Whether it suggests that there may be legal grounds for removing a captain from his position, rather than initiating disciplinary proceedings against him on the ship's return, is less clear, as in practice all mutinies were illegal and a captain's authority on board represented a microcosm of absolutism: he is ruler, judge, and priest in one.

removing Bligh was justified. In line with the findings of Bligh's court-martial, those who could be identified as having taken part in the mutiny were found guilty and sentenced to death, but only some of them, the 'men', were executed, while the higher ranking members of the crew, Peter Heywood and James Morrison, the 'officers', were recommended to the King's pardon, which they duly received. This was largely the result of the activities of interested parties on the behalf two people: Peter Heywood and Fletcher Christian. Heywood, a teenage midshipman, who had sided with Christian in April 1789, but decided to stay behind on Tahiti, was very well connected within the Admiralty. Fletcher Christian, who himself was of course not present, had been identified as the leader of the mutiny, which inevitably blackened his and his family's name, and galvanized his lawyer-brother Edward Christian into action. Although largely due to good connections, and hence reinforcing the difference social class made before the law, the pardoning of Heywood and Morrison could also be utilized to engender suggestions of doubt in the public imagination regarding the (il)legitimacy of the mutiny. It is this circumstance to which Edward Christian contributes and on which he could eventually capitalize in terms of salvaging some of his brother's damaged reputation.

Edward Christian had a transcript of the mutineers' court-martial published in 1794 to which he added his own 'Appendix', which is based on statements by returned crew members and programmatically subtitled 'a full account of the real causes and circumstances of that unhappy transaction [the mutiny], the most material of which has been withheld from the public'.[19] The Appendix purported the view that William Bligh was not fit to command HM's ships because he was an unjust tyrant, unfit for leadership on account of his cruel and sadistic nature. By this unfit commander Fletcher Christian had been driven to mutiny – against his better nature – out of despair over conditions on the ship and his own situation. Edward Christian presents his findings as a corrective to wrong public perceptions:

> Every friend to truth and strict justice must feel his attention awakened to the true causes and circumstances which have hitherto been concealed or misrepresented of one of the most remarkable events in the annals of the navy. ('Appendix', 133)

His publication is intended 'to reduce to its just measure the infamy which this dreadful act has brought upon them [families, friends and mutineers]' ('Appendix', 133). Careful not to come across as a revolutionary trouble-maker, he stakes his hopes on evoking empathy when he concludes:

---

19 I quote from the Penguin Classics edition, William Bligh and Edward Christian, *The Bounty Mutiny, with an introduction by* R. D. Madison (London: Penguin, 2001), which reprints *Minutes of the Proceedings of the Court-Martial held at Portsmouth, August 12, 1792. On ten Persons charged with mutiny on Board His Majesty's Ship The Bounty, with an Appendix containing A full Account of the real Causes and Circumstances of that unhappy Transaction, the most material of which has been withheld from the Public* (London: J. Deighton, 1794) on pp. 67–152; the 'Appendix' covers pp. 129–152.

The sufferings of Captain Bligh and his companions in the boat [originally the celebrated feat! MO], however severe they may have been, are perhaps but a small portion of the torments occasioned by this dreadful event; and whilst these prove the
melancholy and extensive consequences of the crime of mutiny, the crime itself in
this instance may afford an awful lesson to the navy, and to mankind, that there is a
degree of pressure beyond which the best formed and principled mind must either
break or recoil. And though public justice and the public safety can allow no vindication of any species of mutiny, yet reason and humanity will distinguish the sudden
unpremeditated act of desperation and frenzy from the foul, deliberate contempt of
every religious duty and honourable sentiment. [...] when they reflect that a young
man is condemned to perpetual infamy, who, if he had served on board any other
ship [...] might still have been an honour to his country and a glory and comfort to
his friends. ('Appendix', 152)

These paragraphs contain the basis for all subsequent favourable interpretations of Fletcher Christian, ranging from tormented soul to the notion of
Christian's actions as a trigger for reform in the Navy, or by another leap of
the imagination (which will not be taken until the mid-19th century) as a defender of British liberty. The text subtly shifts the focus from law-breaking
onto the nature of legitimacy: it is no longer primarily a question whether sub-
ordinates mutinied against their commanding officer – which is an act of treason and intolerable -, but whether the conditions of authority were unacceptable, and hence illegitimate. Taking this to its full conclusion would make the
mutiny a more fundamental upheaval than insubordination, it would question
the foundations of the hierarchical and political system in the same way the
French Revolution questioned the *ancien régime*. However, no-one hoping for
a continuing career in the Law in 1794 Britain would want to be associated
with the Revolution in France, and Edward Christian does enough to cover
himself in this respect: he does not suggest that the mutiny was legitimate, he
explains rather than *excuses* his brother's behaviour, but does not shrink from
providing his readers with damaging inferences.[20]

So, on his return from his second, successful, breadfruit mission, Bligh
not surprisingly felt the need to respond to the changed assessment of his
achievement and engaged in a public spat over his reputation and leadership
qualities.[21] Once the dust had settled on this story as a current affairs item,
the Admiralty did not take the accusations against Bligh seriously, as he con-

---

20 This was also the line of argument that John Barrow perpetuated in 1831 with this influential
    The Eventful History of the Mutiny and Piratical Seizure of HMS Bounty: Its Causes and Consequences,
    which has never been out of print since its first publication. The most recent edition is *Mutiny!:
    The real History of HMS Bounty*, with an introduction by Edward E. Leslie (New York: Cooper
    Square Press, 2003).
21 Answer and counter-answer go back and forth in 1794 and 1795; cf. *The Bounty Mutiny*, 153–
    194: William Bligh, *An Answer to Certain Assertions contained in the Appendix to a Pamphlet [...]*
    (originally published in late 1794) and Edward Christian, *A Short Reply to Capt. William Bligh's
    Answer* (originally published in 1795).

tinued his naval career successfully,[22] but his reputation never recovered. And there are three reasons for this. The first, and least significant, was the fact that Bligh did not handle his responses as cleverly as Edward Christian did his attacks. Far more crucial are the following two: from 1794 towards the end of the decade there was, fanned by the political climate, unprecedented unrest and discontent in the Navy. This discontent found a focus in the image of the capricious, unaccountable, unjust – and hence possibly illegitimate – captain. This coincided, to Bligh's disadvantage, with a growing public and intellectual interest in figures such as Fletcher Christian now came to represent, which are best characterised as 'Romantic souls in agony'.

    After the opening of war with the Revolutionary French Republic in 1793, unrest among British naval crews steadily increased and culminated in 1797 in two (onshore) mutinies: first at Spithead and then at the Nore, when seamen went on strike over conditions and pay. The same year saw the mutiny on HMS *Hermione*, reportedly occasioned by the captain's routine brutality, during which the officers were killed by the crew and the ship was surrendered to the Spanish. While the Spithead mutiny was resolved peacefully, the Nore uprising resulted in court-martials, and the hanging of the rebel leader Richard Parker. Both at Spithead and the Nore, the strikers had elected republican-style delegates to represent them in the negotiations with their employers; Richard Parker had been the elected president of the Nore delegation. While in the conservative press these activities were presented, not just as treasonous, but as the result of conspiratorial infiltration by French republican agents, there is clear evidence that conditions in the Royal Navy were very bad indeed. While any number of historical persons might have served as the image of the brutal unjust tyrant of a captain,[23] it is likely that in the collective imagination Bligh became the name for the conflation of these figures into a stereotype that established itself from this point onwards,[24] despite the fact that Bligh, who was personally involved in the events at the Nore, and as commander of the ship of the line *Director* han-

---

22 Bligh commanded ships of the line under Admiral Nelson, was personally commended by this naval superhero in 1801, became vice-admiral of the blue, and eventually governor of New South Wales.

23 Apart from HMS Hermione's commander Captain Pigot, who was in the habit of having the 'last man off the yardarms' flogged to increase efficiency, there are numerous other examples of brutalized authority, e.g. the infamous Lieutenant Irwin, who punished a sailor for 'silent contempt' with 36 lashes (cf. Mackaness, *William Bligh*, 306), or indeed Captain Edward Edwards of the Pandora, who kept all *Bounty* crew he found on Tahiti, even those who Bligh had already exonerated during his court-martial, in irons below deck, which increased the number of casualties in the shipwreck as some 'prisoners' were not freed in time.

24 One nineteenth-century example of this naval myth is Alfred Tennyson's poem 'The Captain' of 1865, which presents a brave and gallant crew of English freemen under the tyranny of a harsh disciplinarian commander.

dling part of the proceedings on the Admiralty's side, was not listed among those commanders whom the mutineers considered intolerable and asked to be removed.

The image of Fletcher Christian as 'soul in agony' fitted the *Zeitgeist*, particularly the intellectual and cultural conditions, and fashions, of the time: his brother Edward paved the way for Fletcher as the Romantic hero. The key characteristics of the Romantic hero are so well known that even popular online encyclopaedias are reliably accurate on this point.

> The Romantic hero is a literary archetype referring to a character that rejects established norms and conventions, has been rejected by society, and has the self as the center of his or her own existence. [...] Northrop Frye noted that the Romantic hero is often 'placed outside the structure of civilization and therefore represents the force of physical nature, amoral or ruthless, yet with a sense of power, and often leadership, that society has impoverished itself by rejecting'.[25]

His mutiny places Christian outside the structure of society, his readiness to mutiny can be seen as breaking free from moral and social restraints. As a force of nature he disempowers an individual whose power was invested in him by (a decadent authoritarian) society. This force of nature in him is strengthened by his contact with the natural, non-decadent, native culture of Tahiti. Thus his actions, and the stimulus for them, engage with the prevalent contemporary critique of modernity. *Wikipedia* continues that '[...] another common trait of the Romantic hero is regret for his actions, and self-criticism.'[26] Christian also fits this bill, to which self-centered, brooding introspection may be added, shifting much of the interest from the 'traditional' hero's actions towards the Romantic hero's psyche. There is plenty of evidence that, when Bligh was finally ordered into the launch, the historical Christian exclaimed 'I am in hell'. Bligh himself reported the following in his own account of the events, the *Narrative of the Mutiny*, published only months after his return to Britain: 'He [Christian] appeared disturbed by my question, and answered with much emotion, "That, Captain Bligh, – that is the thing; I am in hell – I am in hell"'.[27] This section was not altered when it was incorporated into the longer account entitled *A Voyage to the South Sea*, published in 1792.[28] Bligh was not the only one to report this outcry; Edward Christian's version runs 'I have been in hell for weeks past with you',[29] and its veracity is corroborated by a number of other eye-witnesses, as Edward Christian re-

25　http://en.wikipedia.org/wiki/Romantic_hero. Last accessed on 2 July 2011.
26　Cf. note 25.
27　William Bligh, *A Narrative of the Mutiny, on Board his Majesty's Ship Bounty; and the Subsequent Voyage of Part of the Crew, in the Ship's Boat, from Tofoa, one of the Friendly Islands, to Timor, a Dutch Settlement in the East Indies* (London: George Nichol, 1790), repr. *The Bounty Mutiny*, 1–66, 10.
28　William Bligh, *A Voyage to the South Sea, undertaken by Command of his Majesty, for the purpose of Conveying the Breadfruit Tree to the West Indies etc* (London: George Nichol, 1792) repr. in *The Book of the Bounty* (London: Dent, 1938), pp. 1–188, 115.
29　Christian, 'Appendix', 142.

ports.[30] Bligh's rendition, however, has the greatest potential to work as evidence for a tormented mind, not least because he describes the way in which the utterance was made. I am inclined to credit the specifics of Bligh's report. His testimony is the one closest in time to the actual event, and, perhaps more significantly, Bligh had little reason to create a sympathetic picture of Christian, which the emotionality he describes, in terms of its mitigating or extenuating circumstances, does. Bligh was clearly unaware of the almost redemptive quality of this outburst for Christian's character and reputation. They are the key piece of evidence for the 'soul in agony', and writers and critics from Byron to Hough have picked up on them.[31] In this respect Fletcher Christian fits very well what Lilian Furst has described as the ambiguous hybridity of the Romantic hero, who is half-way between traditional hero and twentieth-century anti-hero:[32] he is still committed to ideals but unable to realise them, still committed to actions, but bringing destruction rather than constructive solutions, i.e. he is marked by the period of transition that brought his type to the fore.

Fletcher Christian's romantic potential increased when rumours of his survival started circulating in the mid-1790s, fanned by the publication in 1796 – hard on the heels of the Bligh-Edward Christian exchange – of post-mutiny letters allegedly written by him on his return to Europe. The letters were quickly turned into a travelogue, which, if the holdings of British university libraries are anything to go by, were fairly widely disseminated.[33] Labelled 'spurious' in most library catalogues, which no doubt they are, these letters are curiously pro-Bligh:

> It is but justice that I should acquit Captain Bligh, in the most unequivocal manner, of having contributed, in the smallest degree, to the promotion of our conspiracy by any harsh and ungentleman-like conduct on his part. So far from it, that few officers in the service, I am persuaded, can in this respect be found superior to him, or produce stronger claims on the gratitude or attachment of the men they are appointed to command.[34]

---

30 Christian, 'Appendix', 141–142.
31 Richard Hough makes the quote the title of the opening chapter of his *Captain Bligh and Mr Christian: The Men and the Mutiny* (London: Hutchison, 1972), which has been reprinted numerous times. For Byron see below. John L. Lowes already pointed out in 1927, in the context of Coleridge's Notebooks, how fertile this sentence must be for the creative imagination as well as for any philosophical speculation about the state of the self uttering it. Cf. Lowes, *The Road to Xanadu. A Study in the Ways of the Imagination* (Boston MA: Houghton & Mifflin, 1927), pp. 27–28.
32 Lilian Furst, 'The Romantic Hero, or is he an anti-hero?', *Studies in the Literary Imagination* 9.1 (1976) 53–67.
33 *Letters from Mr Fletcher Christian, Containing a narrative of the transactions on board His Majesty's Ship Bounty, before and after the mutiny, with his subsequent voyages and travels in South America* (London: H. D. Symonds, 1796) and *Voyages and Travels of Fletcher Christian, and a narrative of the mutiny, on board his Majesty's Ship Bounty at Othaheite etc* (London: H. Lemoine, 1798).
34 *Voyages and Travels of Fletcher Christian*, 29.

One wonders how ironic, or self-protective, this is. The mutiny is presented as the result of a 'predilection' for life on Tahiti,[35] an argument Bligh had also put forward in his publications, and which is based on the contemporary idea of the 'Island Paradise'. While Christian's actions are presented as a lapse, induced by a temptation, they should nevertheless be understandable. If they are not openly condoned, they are explained as the result of overpowering urges:

> I shall not weary your patience with needless repetitions of my regret [...], neither shall I attempt to palliate my guilt. I was tempted, and I fell; and most probably [...] in spite of all the remorse I have since experienced in consequence of my crime, I should, notwithstanding, be induced to repeat my offence.[36]

Attractively renegade, he would do it again. The letters, which for the first time take Christian's 'story' into the realm of fictionalization proper, go on to relate an exciting tale of exoticism and exploration. The flawed hero, not quite soul in agony, although '[he] suffered more than words can express from the conflict of contending passions',[37] is in touch with his emotions and desires, but not without knowledge of right and wrong. This presentation taps right into contemporary notions of 'sensibility'. While engaging with current notions of emotionality, regarding their approach to authority, *Voyages and Travels* shows no sign of wishing to shatter the current political and naval power structures.

Not surprisingly Christian's soul in agony-potential is taken up with relish by the English Romantic poets. Although chronologically later than Coleridge's *Rime of the Ancient Mariner*, I will deal with Byron's *Bounty*-poem first: *The Island or Fletcher Christian and his Comrades* (1823) stays close to the available historical versions:

> When Bligh in stern reproach demanded
> Where was now his grateful sense of former care?
> Where all his hopes to see his name aspire,
> And blazon Britain's thousand glories higher?
> His feverish lips thus broke their gloomy spell,
> 'Tis that! 'tis that! I am in hell! In hell!'[38]

---

35 'Our mutiny is wholly to be ascribed to the strong predilection we had contracted for living in Otaheite; where, exclusive of the happy disposition of the inhabitants, the mildness of the climate, and the fertility of the soil, we had formed certain tender connexions, which banished the remembrance of Old England entirely from our hearts.' (*Voyages and Travels of Fletcher Christian*, 30)
36 *Voyages and Travels of Fletcher Christian*, 33.
37 *Voyages and Travels of Fletcher Christian*, 32.
38 George Gordon Lord Byron, 'The Island or Christian and his Comrades', in *Byron. Poetical Works*, ed. by Frederic Page, new edn, revised by John Jump (Oxford: Oxford University Press, 1970, repr. 1991), pp. 349–366, Canto 1, ll. 156–163.

He goes on to imagine an agonizing and gory end for Christian:

> Christian died last – twice wounded; and once more
> Mercy was offered when they saw his gore; [...]
> He tore the topmost button from his vest,
> Down the tube dashed it, levell'd, fired, and smiled
> As his foe fell; then, like a serpent, coiled
> His wounded, weary form, to where the steep
> Looked desperate as himself along the deep;
> Cast one glance back, and clench'd his hand, and shook
> His last rage 'gainst the earth which he forsook;
> Then plunged: the rock below received like glass
> His body crushed into one gory mass.[39]

This is a grim description of the self-destructive side of the new (Byronic) hero-type: almost demented with disgust for, rejection of, and inability to constructively negotiate the world around him.

There are suggestions that the story of Fletcher Christian inspired Samuel Taylor Coleridge's *Rime of the Ancient Mariner* (1799). The Mariner is of course the original 'soul in agony'. Although the Mariner cannot be identified directly as Christian, Coleridge clearly intended to do *something* with this story, as his Notebooks of 1795–98, the time leading up to the genesis of the *Rime*, prove.[40] It is extremely likely that Wordsworth took a personal interest in this current affairs story, as he had known Christian as a boy, and considering the close contact between Wordsworth and Coleridge at the time, he may well have discussed it with Coleridge. Critics have debated at length the possibility of Christian functioning as an inspiration, or even model for Coleridge.[41] Crucial in my context is the reciprocity between the public image of Fletcher Christian and Coleridge's mariner-figure: the seminal importance accorded to the figure of the Mariner in literary and intellectual history underlines the readiness of the *Zeitgeist* for such a figure, no matter whether it helped to establish Christian around 1800 as a Romantic hero or whether his story inspired the mariner-figure and shaped the definition of the new hero-type. In this respect it is worth remembering that the 'Romantic hero' as defined above was only in the process of 'becoming' in the

---

39 Bryon, 'The Island', canto 4, ll. 323–343.
40 'Topic 22: "Adventures of Christian, the Mutineer" (Folio 25b, Archive, p. 354). Interestingly, this entry was made shortly after the public spat between Bligh and Edward Christian.
41 Cf. Neil B. Houston, 'Fletcher Christian and the "Rime of the Ancient Mariner"', *Dalhousie Review* 45 (1966) 13–25, who argues that Christian served as model and inspiration for Coleridge, an idea which is rejected by Robert C. Leitz in the same journal four years later, cf. 'Fletcher Christian and the Ancient Mariner: A Refutation', *Dalhousie Review* 50 (1970) 62–70. C.S. Wilkinson's earlier monograph *The Wake of the Bounty* (London: Cassell, 1953), which also proposes a close link between Coleridge's poem and the figure of Christian, even declares on its concluding pages that 'somewhere in the year of 1795, Christian and Wordsworth must have met' (p. 160), suggesting that Christian returned to England and that via Wordsworth Coleridge had first-hand knowledge of Christian's experiences.

1790s. So, clearly, Christian's public image was not so much shaped in the image of the Romantic hero, as it coincided with it.

There is, however, one literary ancestor of the Romantic hero who may well have influenced Christian's post-1793/94 image: Goethe's Werther, another soul in agony who breaks under the unbearable pressure of social, moral, and intellectual constraints, *or* who valiantly frees himself from them through a desperate act of self-destruction. The phenomenal extent of the Werther-reception in England is well documented, and it reached a particular peak in the 1790s.[42] Edward Christian could be sure of his readers' recognition of this fashionable type. An association with the Werther-figure, and other sentimental heroes, had another advantage that would serve Edward Christian's purpose well: Werther's evident inability to pro-actively change an unjust world avoids any *open* link to the regime-changing ideals of the Revolution, a consideration for anyone interested in creating a positive image of Fletcher Christian in the mid-1790s. Especially after 1797, with the naval mutinies and the fate of Richard Parker fresh in everybody's mind, links to revolutionary ideas would have prevented the successful creation of an acceptable image of Christian in Britain.[43] That the emerging and powerful fascination of the rebel individual whose greatness is linked to wrongdoing and a fall easily crosses political persuasions is demonstrated by David McCallam's essay on Xavier de Maistre in this volume.

So it would appear that the development of Bligh's image towards the '*Bounty* Bastard' was driven as much by the successfully created image of Christian as tormented soul whose virtues are destroyed by intolerable con-

---

42 Cf. Susanne Kord's essay in this volume.

43 His image as the revolutionary freedom fighter who reinstates down-trodden English liberties will come to the fore in the later nineteenth and twentieth centuries, when the (self-)destructive element, which is clearly present in the image of Fletcher around 1800, and still in Byron in 1823 and Barrow in 1831, has faded and been replaced by activism. There was a resurgence of interest in the *Bounty* story in 1930s, largely triggered by the best-selling trilogy of *Bounty*-novels penned by Charles Nordhoff and James Norman Hall, the first part of which, *Mutiny on the Bounty*, appeared in 1932, soon to be followed by *Men against the Sea* and *Pitcairn Island* in 1933/34. The first novel is the basis for the enormously successful 1935 film of the same title, which was one of the first Hollywood block-busters. At the same time authoritative biographies of Bligh appeared, in 1931 (George Mackaness', *Life of Vice-Admiral William Bligh*) and 1936 (Owen Rutter's *Turbulent Journey: A Life of William Bligh, Vice-Admiral of the Blue*). There is little trace of a Wertheresque hero in Hall-Nordhoff's *Mutiny on the Bounty*, and the 1935 film. Mutiny is still wrong-doing, but Christian is cast as the heroic freedom fighter who opposes the unjust tyranny of the captain. This interpretation is indebted to the nineteenth-century view of the British/English role in world history, with love of freedom and liberty as innate English qualities; Christian is a good Englishman, in spirit, if not by law. The film makes extensive use of *Rule Britannia* in its soundtrack. Clearly this interpretation is inspired by the contemporary (Western) unease about the early twentieth-century European dictatorships under Hitler and Stalin, which calls upon Britannia to guard liberty. A first instance of this change from the tortured 'soul in hell' to the mutineers as upholders of English liberties can be found in Alfred Tennyson's poem 'The Captain. Legend of the Navy' of 1865, cf. note 24.

ditions as by Bligh's own behaviour on board the *Bounty*. It is evident that
William Bligh's and Fletcher Christian's images developed in a specific political and intellectual context. The political aspects of this context are specifically British. The *Bounty*-story was, however, discussed beyond British borders. Would different national or political contexts produce variant images?
For a snapshot of this I will take a look at the 1790s German reception.
This reception was largely directed by two individuals, the writer, scientist
and political activist Georg Forster and his father Reinhold, which neatly
limits my field of investigation and which, due to the decided political stance
of the younger Forster, guarantees the inclusion of political aspects.

As in other countries, in Germany the initial reception of the *Bounty*
story beyond newspaper reports occurs through the translation of the early
key *Bounty* texts, especially Bligh's two accounts. As in Britain, they too appeared in the context of great public demand for travel literature during the
heyday of travelogues and reports from far-flung corners of the globe. Accounts of trips to the Pacific had particular appeal, spurred, in the context
of contemporary exoticism, by a fascination with the South Seas and Oce-
ania as well as the scientific priorities of geographical discoveries, their mapping, recording, and investigation. Bligh's earlier *Mutiny* (1790) responded to
the public's interest in the dramatic adventure aspect of the aborted breadfruit mission, focusing on the mutiny and voyage in the launch, while the
second, *Voyage to the South Sea* (1792), conformed more to the notion of a
classical travelogue, describing the whole journey.[44] German interest was
immediate: the *Mutiny* appeared within months in German translation
(1791) and was swiftly followed in 1792/93 by the translation of the *Voyage*.[45] The translation of the *Voyage* was re-published in 1794 in *Die neusten*

---

44 Interest in the mutiny and its consequences inspired a wave of 'authentic' accounts. Almost
    everybody connected to this story and capable of holding a pen produced their version: John
    Fryer and James Morrison of the *Bounty*, both accounts were made available to the reading
    public in the 1930s through the efforts of the historian and Bligh-biographer Owen Rutter.
    Almost all the officers on the *Pandora* set about writing accounts of their voyage as well. Most
    famous of those is the account by George Hamilton, *Voyage around the World in His Majesty's
    Frigate Pandora* (1793). This underlines both the topicality of the story and the size of the
    market for such materials. Bligh also intended to publish an account of his second (and suc-
    cessful) breadfruit voyage, with charts and illustrations, but *he* was unable to secure any fun-
    ding for this venture. He still entertained hopes of achieving this as late as 1803 (Mackaness,
    Life of Vice-Admiral William Bligh, 303). It was finally published as William Bligh, *The Log of
    HMS Providence 1791–1793* (Surrey: Genesis Press, 1976), and with editorial content as *Return
    to Tahiti: Bligh's Second Breadfruit Voyage*, ed. by Oliver Douglas (Honolulu: University of Hawaii
    Press, 1988); as was Lt. George Tobin's journal of the same voyage, as *Bligh's Second Chance. An
    Eyewitness Account of his Return to the South Seas*, ed. by Roy Schreiber (London: Chatham, 2007).
45 Both translations appeared in the *Magazin von merkwürdigen neuen Reisebeschreibungen* published in
    Berlin by Voss, in vols 5 (1791) and 9 (1793) respectively, as William Bligh's *Bericht von dem
    Aufruhr an Bord des Schiffes Bounty und seiner Reise nach Tofoa* (*Narrative of the Mutiny*) and *Reise nach
    der Südsee* (*Voyage to the South Sea*).

Reisen nach Botany Bay und Port Jackson together with George Hamilton's account of the ill-fated voyage of the mutineer-hunting *Pandora* 1790–02. Georg Forster was the translator of the *Voyage*, his father Reinhold oversaw the publication of the volume combining the *Bounty* and the *Pandora* accounts. The Forsters clearly made it their business to publicize the *Bounty*-story in Germany.[46] They were eminently suited for translating this type of text, Georg was bilingual, having spent his formative years in Britain, and both had accompanied James Cook on his second voyage in 1772–75, which gave them a genuine affinity with and first-hand understanding of the topic covered.

By 1792 the *Bounty*-story was already so well known that the *Allgemeine Literaturzeitung* reviewed the original publication of Bligh's *Voyage* and gave a kind of preview of the forthcoming translation by Georg Forster at the same time.[47] The actual translation was reviewed in 1793, beginning with the words 'es ist weltbekannt, dass das große Unternehmen durch die Meuterei auf dem Schiffe unausgeführt blieb'.[48] The review relates the story of mutiny and open launch, the latter as exciting and amazing, focusing on Bligh's navigational feat and his contribution to mapping and describing unknown territories, i.e. to ethnology, geography, and botany.[49] The review's neutral tone differs markedly from that of Georg Forster's 'Vorrede' to his translation of the *Voyage*, which takes a decidedly moral stance.[50] The mutiny is a 'ruchloser Aufruhr' (heinous revolt), the mutineers 'Seeräuber, die mit Kapitän Bligh's Schiffe durchgingen' (pirates who ran off with Captain Bligh's ship, *Reise*, v) and 'Spießgesellen' (criminals, *Reise*, vi) whose violence and pillage set the natives of the first island they tried to settle against them (*Reise*, viii). Fletcher Christian is 'der Anführer dieser zügellosen Bande' (ringleader of this lawless gang, *Reise*, xii) who should be caught and punished. Bligh on the other hand is the paragon of the competent captain, whose unsurpassable seamanship, courage, and moral rectitude have en-

---

46 To some extent the Forsters may have been making up for lost money after Reinhold had been unable to cash in on their participation in James Cook's second voyage in the mid-1770s.

47 *Allgemeine Literaturzeitung,* Jahrgang 1792, vol. 4, no. 307, 389–393.

48 *Allgemeine Literaturzeitung,* Jahrgang 1793, vol. 2, no. 97, 35. 'It is known the world over that this great enterprise was not accomplished due to the mutiny on board ship.' All translations from Forster's preface are my own.

49 Significantly, the *Voyage* is reviewed under *Erdbeschreibung*, a literal German translation of the Greek 'geography'. But the review also makes clear that the events on the *Bounty* are still the subject of an ongoing criminal investigation: 'die Vorrede giebt Nachrichten von den [...] Bemühungen des zur Aufsuchung der Aufrührer ausgeschickten Kapitän Edwards [...], die dem deutschen Publicum angenehm seyn werden' (*Allgemeine Literaturzeitung* (1792) 4, 392). 'The preface bears news of the efforts made by Captain Edwards sent out to find the ringleaders, which will please our German readers.'

50 *Magazin von merkwürdigen neuen Reisebeschreibungen* vol. 9 (1793): William Bligh's *Reise nach der Südsee (Voyage to the South Sea)*.

deared him to the British public.[51] Forster is equally fulsome in his praise of Bligh's intellectual and mental qualities:

> So […] zeigt uns [die gegenwärtige Reisebeschreibung] den Mann […] von lehrbegierigem Forschungsgeiste, von richtiger Urteilskraft, von milden Sitten [und einer seinen Stand in England so ehrenden feineren Bildung]. Mit Vergnügen werden wir gewahr, dass er nicht nur ungewöhnlich scharfsinnig beobachtet, sondern auch mit einer ungeschmückten, aber gleichwohl anmuthiger und reiner Einfalt erzählt.[52]

In fact he 'erzählt mit einem eindringenden, überzeugenden Tone der Wahrheit' and the reader profits from the 'stehts begleitende Belehrung eines festen und dabei so einfach und edelguten Charakters wie der des Erzählers'.[53] This is praise indeed for Bligh, the intellectual and scientist, because when Forster chooses to highlight Bligh's style, and praise the way in which Bligh conveys his information on the new discoveries, he refers to an on-going contemporary debate about how such empirical information is best handled when written up for dissemination.[54]

While it is perfectly obvious why Forster was so interested in Bligh's scientific observations of the South Seas, it is less clear why he engages in such a crusade on Bligh's behalf. From his vehement condemnation of the mutineers one can conclude that he may have been aware of the (very recent) turn in public opinion against Bligh. It is evident that he followed the developing story keenly: he was well informed about the voyage of the *Pandora*, must have followed the 1792 court-martials (cf. notes 49 and 55) and, intriguingly, he had an amazing knowledge of ultimately insignificant events on the second breadfruit voyage, such as Bligh's illness, while the voyage was

---

51 'Diese Nachricht (Bligh's *Mutiny*), die er gleichsam zu seiner Beglaubigung und zur Befriedigung der Wissbegierde des englischen Publikums […] herausgab, gewann ihm die Theilnehmung aller empfindenden Menschen, und weckte das Gefühl von Achtung und Liebe, welches die Rechtschaffenheit, der Edelmuth, die Standhaftigkeit und der Muth allemal gleichsam zu erzwingen pflegen.' (*Reise*, iii) 'This account, which he published […] to account for himself and to satisfy the thirst for information of the British public, won him the sympathy of all individuals of sentiment, and awakened those feelings of love and respect, which moral rectitude, nobility of spirit, steadfastness and courage produce without fail.'

52 *Reise*, iv. 'Thus [this travelogue] shows us a man […] gifted with a thirst for knowledge and the spirit of research, with true judgment, with mild manners and the superior education which characterizes the members of his class in England. With pleasure we realize that his observations are not only highly acute and clever, but are related to us with unadorned, graceful and pure simplicity.'

53 *Reise*, iv, v. In fact 'he narrates in the deeply affecting, convincing tone of truth.' The reader profits from the 'instructions given by a constant and, at the same time, simple and noble character, such as the narrator possesses.'

54 This debate was of course occasioned by the growing wealth of such information over the last decades. Cf. Wolfgang Griep, 'Über Reisen und Auflärung in der zweiten Hälfte des 18. Jahrhunderts', in *Georg Forster in interdisziplinärer Perspektive*, ed. by Claus-Volker Klenke (Berlin: Akademie Verlag, 1994), pp. 103–112, where Griep discusses the debate about the 'kritische Prüfung der Kriterien, wie empirische Beobachtungen zu verarbeiten und vermitteln seien' (p. 112).

still ongoing. At the same time, 1792–93, Forster was also engaged in his
most revolutionary political activities in Mainz, which by conservatives and
many moderates were considered as subversive and threatening to public
and political order as the revolution in France, or any naval rebellions. And
yet Forster, the avowed hater of 'tyranny' and champion of new forms of
government, will have no truck with the mutineers. In fact he quite deliberately detracts from any notion that Christian and his comrades are engaged
in setting up a legitimate democratic system in the wake of throwing off
Bligh's yoke. 'Christian verlohr alle Authorität über seine Gefährten, und
hielt es für das Beste, sich mit ihnen zu beratschlagen [...], wobei er sich zugleich erbötig war, alles auszuführen, was die Mehrheit beschließen
würde.'[55] Nascent egalitarian democratic structures of discussion and consensus are not praised. For Forster these men are a bunch of violent pillag-
ing criminals. This is in some contrast to his father's views. Reinhold Forster
seemed to have a more lenient understanding of the effect the Island Paradise might have on ordinary sailors, a notion that was of course rapidly becoming a contemporary commonplace.[56]

One possible explanation for Georg Forster's pro-Bligh stance could be
a personal acquaintance between the two young men in 1776. After the Forsters had returned from their voyage with Cook they remained in close contact with the Admiralty, while Bligh was preparing with Cook to set off on
the next expedition.[57] Both Cook and Joseph Banks would have had ample
opportunity to introduce the two young men, not least because they had
similar interests and were of similar age. Such a (vaguely romantic) explanation is currently still conjecture on my part, as I have not yet found any record of an acquaintance between the two. Another reason, and a more interesting one in this context, could be that Forster regarded the mutiny as
anarchy, not democracy, and that he either genuinely abhorred this state of
affairs or that he wished to make clear to the public that he was no anar-

55 *Reise*, viii. 'Christian lost all authority over his companions, and judged it best to consult with
   them [...]; he was willing to execute what(ever) the majority would decide.' It would appear that
   Forster's information is based on what the men who returned on the *Pandora* had to say.
56 'If we fairly consider the different situations of a common sailor on board the Resolution, and
   of a Tahitian on his island, we cannot blame the former if he attempts to rid himself of the
   numberless discomforts of a voyage round the world, and prefers an easy life, free from cares,
   in the happiest climate of the world, to the frequent vicissitudes which are entailed upon the
   mariner.' This is quoted by Barrow (*Eventful History*, 92–93) without reference, and the origi-
   nator is only identified as 'Forster (who accompanied Cook)', which would of course fit both
   father and son who travelled with Cook on his second voyage of circumnavigation. I assume it
   is Reinhold Forster, because after the rather long full quotation describing the blissful conditions on Tahiti, Barrow characterizes the writer as a 'cold, philosophical German *doctor*' (*Eventful History*, 94, my italics).
57 Bligh was appointed to the Resolution on 20 March 1776 and from then on involved in super-
   vising the refitting of Cook's ship, which was to be used again, before he departed on the third
   voyage in July 1776.

chist. It would appear that Georg Forster's interpretation of the 'mutiny on the *Bounty*' provides another example of the abiding difficulties of Forster criticism: the uncertainty regarding the nature of his Jacobinism, his changing concepts of revolution, and his views of the uncontrollable aspect of the people, the mob, which surface particularly between 1792 and his death in 1794.[58]

Another possibility is that Forster's view is an illustration of the image of William Bligh as the heroic British seaman, before the interpretation of Fletcher Christian as 'soul in agony' gathered momentum; the 'Vorrede' was written before Edward Christian's 'Appendix' appeared. But it was also written at exactly the time – the autumn of 1792 – when the efforts on behalf of Peter Heywood and Fletcher Christian were bearing some fruit in the shape of the court's recommendations to the King's mercy for Heywood and James Morrison.

Whatever the reason, the interpretation of the mutiny that is introduced into 1790s Germany is staunchly pro-Bligh and supportive of naval order. That this interpretation is put forward by a democratic-minded German with republican ideals suggests that even Georg Forster, who, however dialectically, espoused the ideals of the French Revolution, was, in late 1792 on the eve of the execution of Louis XVI (21 January 1793) and only months from the Terror, not ready for a revolution that replaced governmental authority with *Basisdemokratie*.

Fletcher Christian's impact on the German reading public of the 1790s appears to have been negligible. There are no poems by heavy-weight Romantic poets about him. While the spurious 'Letters' that make up the *Voyages and Travels* were translated into German in 1802 as *Fletcher Christian's Reisen und Schicksale*, they were not reviewed in any of the major journals. And we have already seen that, while these letters tried to set up an attractively 'interesting' image of Christian as a man of (over-indulgent) sensibilities, they were at pains to leave Bligh's reputation intact. This lack of a Fletcher Christian-myth further supports the view that the *Bounty*-story was not received in a Romantic or covertly revolutionary way in Germany.

To conclude: I have read the public presentation of the Bligh-Christian conflict in the course of the 1790s in connection with, on the one hand, its very specific historical background, and on the other in connection with larger paradigm changes, such as challenges to established authority or authorities, and Enlightenment values. I have linked the gradual increase in sympathy for Christian to the sentimental and Romantic notions that unbearable oppression will lead to liberation and destruction. And I have

---

58 For a review of critics grappling with how to claim Forster's revolutionary legacy in general, cf. Helmut Peitsch, *Georg Forster: A History of his critical Reception* (New York: Peter Lang, 2001), pp. 163–210; for the final years, pp. 275–280.

shown the contemporary political and intellectual resonance of this conflict, which is responsible for the extensive public interest in this story and for the shift in public sympathy from Bligh to Christian, following Edward Christian's successful intervention in the image-making process. Edward Christian's redesign of his brother's public image was so successful precisely because it was so suited to the intellectual *Zeitgeist*. Despite the popularity, at least in England, of the image of Fletcher Christian as a tormented soul in the vein of a proto-Romantic hero, it has become clear that the challenges to *actual* political and legal authority only went so far: in the materials relating to Christian there is no praise for direct action in the name of individual or communal liberation or any *open* association with the aims of the French Revolution. The negative association of the naval mutineers of 1797 with (treacherous) French agitation makes such a link undesirable.[59] In Germany, at least in the reception directed by the Forsters, not even the Romantic hero image appears for Fletcher Christian, let alone that of a political freedom-fighter, which suggests that regional, and personal, political contexts played a key part in the reception and interpretation of politically sensitive materials. Nevertheless, Bligh's and Christian's images *did* change in public opinion in the 1790s, at least in Britain, which indicates that (considerable sections of) the public sympathized with such a change. It illustrates equally clearly the shifting ground on which authority now rested: the notions of *legitimate* authority were becoming blurred in the wake of fundamental revisions to the notions of individual freedom and personal responsibility. Bligh had acted within the law, but it had become possible to consider that the law was no longer right. Christian had acted illegitimately, but it had become possible to consider that he had a right as a moral individual to free himself from an intolerable law, the intolerability of which somewhere further down the line signalled its injustice. As these questions surfaced into the public sphere and the creative imagination with great force during the 1790s, the *Bounty*-story was a narrative in which they crystallized.

---

59 Although it must be noted that far from being spontaneous expressions of 'British public opinion' *per se*, these associations were largely created and exploited by the conservative forces in the political arena aiming at preventing a destabilisation of the political status quo.

A Fictional Response to the Categorical Imperative

Women Refugees, Servants and Slaves in Charrière's *Trois femmes*[1]

Judith Still

> La raison du plus fort est toujours la meilleure
> Nous l'allons montrer tout à l'heure.[2]

Introduction: Critiques of 'le droit du plus fort'

One of the last books by the great Enlightenment questioner Jacques Derrida begins with this epigraph from La Fontaine's 'Le loup et l'agneau'. The book's title in English, *Rogues: Two Essays on Reason*, with its reference to rogue states, alerts us to the present-day ramifications of the reasoning or the law of the strongest, but the subtitle reminds us that the Enlightenment is implicated. Derrida opens the Preface with two possible interpretations of La Fontaine's 'moral'. The wolf's line would be that might is always right. The second interpretation, which he relates to Kant, neither quite wolf nor quite lamb, is that the very concept of *droit* (*right*, law), of *raison juridique*, includes *a priori* the possible recourse to constraint, coercion, even violence. One of the critical insights I would take from Derrida is the interpenetration of ethics and politics, however much we need to keep them apart. Another and related point is the question of 'who?' or 'for whom?' This is a very important question in reading Kant, and one which is raised sharply in Isabelle de Charrière's *Trois femmes*.

1   This research was largely done during my Major Research Fellowship funded by the Leverhulme Trust to whom I should like to express my thanks. See my *Enlightenment Hospitality: Cannibals, Harems and Adoption* (Oxford: The Voltaire Foundation, 2011) and *Derrida and Hospitality: Theory and Practice* (Edinburgh: Edinburgh University Press, 2010). As well as presenting this paper at the 1790s conference in London, I gave earlier versions in Nottingham and Oxford, and I should like to thank all the audiences for their contributions.
2   Jean de La Fontaine, *Fables* (1668), cited as an epigraph in Jacques Derrida, *Voyous: Deux essais sur la raison* (Paris: Galilée, 2003). 'The strong are always best at proving they're right./ Witness the case we're now going to cite' ('The Wolf and the Lamb'), in *Rogues: Two Essays on Reason*, translated by Pascale-Anne Brault and Michael Naas (Stanford: Stanford University Press, 2005), p. x.

Reading the Enlightenment has become particularly polarised in recent decades – there are those who still wish to claim the Enlightenment legacy, and others who maintain that it is largely an inheritance of guilt. One strong line of argument particularly prevalent in the Anglophone world (but not unique to it) is that (a) Early Modern thought is imbued with racism just as Early Modern culture is founded on racial slavery in the first wave of modern colonialism which established settlements in the 'New World'; and (b) our readings of Enlightenment thinkers today perpetuate the racist scandal (which smoothed the path for the second wave of modern colonialism) by ignoring it. Thus the Enlightenment privileging of freedom as quintessentially human, and the demand for 'liberté, égalité et fraternité' in the face of tyranny, should be met by the response today but for whom? Who gets to be free? The wolf's desire for freedom (as an outlaw in La Fontaine's 'Le loup et le chien') can coincide with his sovereign imposition of arbitrary *droit* on lambs. An essay by Susan Buck Morss runs through Dutch, English and French examples of apparent blindness to the ultimately exclusive nature of the claims to liberty:

> Slavery had become the root metaphor of Western political philosophy, connoting everything that was evil about power relations. Freedom, its conceptual antithesis, was considered by Enlightenment thinkers as the highest and universal political value. Yet this political metaphor began to take root at precisely the time that the economic practice of slavery – the systematic, highly sophisticated capitalist enslavement of *non*-Europeans as a labor force in the colonies – was increasing quantitatively and qualitatively to the point that by the mid-eighteenth century it came to underwrite the entire economic system of the West [....]. If this paradox did not seem to trouble the logical consciousness of contemporaries, it is perhaps more surprising that present-day writers, while fully cognizant of the facts, are still capable of constructing Western histories as coherent narratives of human freedom.[3]

Buck Morss ends with Hegel where she takes a different path; she does not regard the absence of references to *real* masters and slaves in the Americas as such a problem in the *Phänomenologie*. The metaphorical master and slave would, she asserts, have a clear reference point in the Caribbean for Hegel, devoted reader of the political periodical *Minerva* which had very regular articles on the slave revolution in Haiti (the largest producer of cane sugar at the time) during the 1790s and early 1800s when he was writing. Equally his readers would have known what he was talking about. I find this quite convincing; and certainly today the reference to 'rogue states', for example, does not necessarily require any dotting of 'i's for readers although in a couple of centuries an author may be castigated for a failure to spell out her or his horror of American policy in the Gulf. Subtending this article will be Buck Morss's question: what about slaves, but *also* what about women and servants?

---

3 Susan Buck-Morss, 'Hegel and Haiti', *Critical Inquiry* 26.4 (2000) 821–65, 821, 822.

Kant and Charrière

The main part of this article will be an analysis of the *Suite* (sequel) to Charrière's novel *Three Women*, first published as *Drei Weiber*, translated by Ludwig Ferdinand Huber, in Leipzig in 1795, with the original published as *Trois femmes* in London in 1796.[4] Charrière (1740–1805) embodies cosmopolitanism; she can be claimed as Dutch or Swiss as much as French.[5] *Trois femmes* is an engagement with Kant's moral theory, in particular with his essay 'Über den Gemeinspruch: Das mag in der Theorie richtig sein, taugt aber nicht für die Praxis', published in 1793.[6] While Charrière was writing the novel in Neuchâtel, her neighbour and translator Huber was working on Kant; offering a translation of 'Über den Gemeinspruch' to the revolutionary French government (the *Convention nationale*), in the person of Abbé Henri Grégoire, eager to promote morally uplifting philosophy.[7] In this article Kant responds to the critics of his theory of duty or right by giving examples of three 'consequentialist' male philosophers who have misunderstood the necessity of praxis and theory following the same absolute and universal maxims of the categorical imperative.[8] They cover the spheres of (i) the ethical interactions of the individual in society (Christian Garves), (ii) the political contract that founds civil

---

4   Both the *Suite* and *Trois Femmes* in vol 9 of Isabelle de Charrière, *Oeuvres complètes*, 10 vols, ed. by Jean-Daniel Candaux, Cecil P. Courtney, Pierre H. Dubois, Simone Dubois-DeBruyn et al. (Amsterdam: G.A. Van Oorschot, 1981). This is the first time that the *Suite* has been published in full. All quotations are taken from this edition.

5   I shall refer to her as 'Charrière' rather than Mme de Charrière as is still common practice in critical works on women writers from early periods – particularly in France. I believe that the use of titles reinforces a sense of the marginality of women authors since eighteenth-century forms of address are rarely used when referring to male authors.

6   Immanuel Kant, *Abhandlungen nach 1781*, vol 8 of *Werke*, ed. by the Königlich Preußische Akademie der Wissenschaften (Berlin and Leipzig: Walter de Gruyter, 1923), pp. 273–313. 'On the Common Saying: That may be Correct in Theory, But it is of no Use in Practice' in *Practical Philosophy*, translated and ed. by Mary J. Gregor (1996), vol 4 of the *Cambridge Edition of the Works of Immanuel Kant*, ed. by Paul Guyer and Allen W. Wood (Cambridge: Cambridge University Press, 1992–), pp. 273–309. Kant's supreme principle of morality is explicated in the 'General Introduction', pp. xxiii-iv.

7   Kant, with his cool rationality, was considered appropriate to help revive (virile) republican and patriotic virtues after the demoralization caused by the Terror; this was part of plans for national education, state-sponsored literature, teacher training and so on. For analysis of Charrière and Kant, and the interest in Kant in France under the Thermidorean regime, see especially Carla Hesse, 'Kant, Foucault and *Three Women*', in *Foucault and the Writing of History*, ed. by Jan Goldstein (Oxford: Blackwell, 1994), pp. 81–98. See also Jacqueline Letzer, *Intellectual Takking: Questions of Education in the Works of Isabelle de Charrière* (Amsterdam: Rodopi, 1998), pp. 123ff, and Emma Rooksby, 'Moral Theory in the Fiction of Isabelle de Charrière: The Case of *Three Women*', *Hypatia* 20.1 (2005) 1–20. Charrière herself is much exercised by the question of education; Hesse sees a parallel between Charrière's depiction of Théobald's educational reforms in Altendorf (see *Trois femmes*, e.g. pp. 101ff.) and French national plans.

8   Consequentialists argue that you should take into account the consequences of your actions rather than simply considering whether an action is right or wrong in itself. For example Kant claims that lying is always wrong; Benjamin Constant responds that sometimes the end justifies

society (Thomas Hobbes), and (iii) the cosmopolitan sphere of relations between nations (Moses Mendelssohn). Kant is frustrated that many of his
readers accept his ethics in principle, but find that there are numerous per-
missible exceptions to his rules in practice – he can accept no such division.
The French narrator of *Trois femmes* (the Abbé de la Tour) claims to his
would-be reader, the Baronne de Berghen, a young German woman with
whom he has been discussing Kant and his doctrine of *devoir*, that it *might* shed
some light on this. In the face of the horrors of warfare, the Baronness would
be 'extremely grateful' to a man who could take her mind off the fate of her
country. This is an interestingly worldly 'frame' or set-up to an investigation
of ethics provided by the subtle novelist Charrière who might provoke us to
ask: what is in it for the writer? Who profits, whether from philosophy or
fiction? In any event, the susceptible clergyman proposes that he might shed
light on the question of duty by relating the fortunes of three Francophone
women in Germany, two of whom (the young aristocrat Emilie and her servant Joséphine), who are refugees from the French Revolution, marry German
men in the course of the novel. The third, Constance, a wealthy cosmopolitan
widow, also features in the unfinished sequel to the novel in which she tells
the tale of a *fourth* woman, a black slave in Martinique.

Emilie, the first of the women to be introduced, begins with a strong
ethical attachment to abstract duty and virtue. When faced with what she
sees as Joséphine's sexual misconduct (*Trois Femmes*, 45ff) she cannot bring
herself to punish her beloved and good-hearted maid. Her principles are
tested again when Constance, like Joséphine a benefactor and mother-fig-
ure, acknowledges that her wealth is the result of (others') financial misconduct (*Trois Femmes*, 63–64), yet that she will *not* renounce it for she intends
to spend it all on good works. Finally Emilie herself is drawn into deceit
both to help the pregnant but unmarried Joséphine, and in her own elope-
ment with the man she loves, Théobald Altendorf.[9] The eponymous three
women all practice a beneficence which hovers between a specifically
evoked Kantian sense of absolute duty, *Devoir*,[10] and a more pragmatic accommodation with the circumstances of life.

The novel is first published in the same year as Kant's *Zum ewigen Frieden*
(*On Perpetual Peace*), his work on cosmopolitan hospitality, and the role of

---

the means, say, if enemy soldiers have come to kill a friend who has taken refuge in your home
you might deny that he is there.

9 I analyse Emilie's relationship with Joséphine, as a response to Kant, in more detail in 'Isabelle
de Charrière's *Three Women* – Adopting and Adapting Hospitality after Kant', in *Sex and Politics.
In Honour of Elizabeth Boa*, ed. by Margaret Littler, Franziska Meyer and Rachel Palfreyman,
German Life and Letters 64.1 (2011) 19–30.

10 See Introduction, pp. 41–42 and the Frontispiece, p. 39. Apart from Kant, a number of references are made to Rousseau and Voltaire (e.g. pp. 50, 57, and Part II, Letters V, VI, VII and
IX).

hospitality (and adoption) is crucial in the novel. Charrière had friends amongst the asylum-seekers from France, many of whom were dependent on degrees of public and private hospitality, and had indeed intended this novel to profit one woman, an impoverished aristocrat in London.[11] However, hospitality (including the specific long-term form of adoption) is not always easy nor straightforwardly to the benefit of the guest or adopted child, particularly where the context is one of extreme political, social or economic inequality. Even Charrière's would-be act of beneficence to support a female friend, who is a refugee, fails. With its representation of relative female autonomy, the tale was deemed shocking and was mutilated by censorious editors in early editions forcing Charrière to have it republished. But the failure of hospitality as adoption is most clear with the little-known example of the shadowy 'fourth woman' in a Caribbean section of the sequel (*Suite des Trois femmes*), a marginal and fragmentary text published only after the author's death. Morally right behaviour, as Charrière, Kant, and the Revolutionary government in France all agree, is encouraged by a good education. However, the critical matters of the defining and control of education, *who* is to be educated, and the relative roles of philosophy and fiction, are less easy to agree upon.

A key analysis of *Trois femmes* is an article by Carla Hesse, 'Kant, Foucault, and *Three Women*'.[12] Hesse suggests that most of Charrière's readers assume that she is simply and derivatively another consequentialist – responding to Kant that devotion to duty in the abstract in fact needs to take account of circumstances and consequences. Hesse claims that there are far more significant differences between Kant's position and what Charrière sets in motion in *Trois femmes*, most notably as regards sexual difference – and, I would add, class and race.

Kant's *depositum*, or safekeeping, example in the section on personal morality of 'Über den Gemeinspruch' is, according to Hesse, rewritten by Charrière in Constance's first confession regarding her inheritance.[13] Hesse does not consider the sequel and thus Constance's longer confession. I would add that Charrière reworks the terrain even more subtly. In so far as Charrière rewrites the case of a *dépôt*, I would suggest that she is less interested in material possessions and more concerned with a kind of deposit

---

11 Charrière's aim of giving the profits to Angélique-Marie Darlus Dutaillis, comtesse de Montrond, who was in serious financial difficulties, was thwarted by the incompetence (or moralism) of her English publisher; see Cecil P. Courtney, *Isabelle de Charrière (Belle de Zuylen): A Biography* (Oxford: Voltaire Foundation, 1993), pp. 649–650 or Letzer, *Intellectual Tacking*, 123–124.

12 See also Hesse, *The Other Enlightenment: How French Women Became Modern* (Princeton: Princeton University Press, 2001).

13 Yet Constance has quite legally inherited her large fortune (even if her family acquired it by ethically dubious means of which she knows little or nothing), and thus the force of the law would in fact be on her side, a key element in Kant's analysis of right (*droit*).

seemingly far from Kant (and yet one which hovers near some classical texts on this question), that of a child, with her examples of maternal adoption as both successful and failed safekeeping. The successful or potentially successful examples are to be found in the novel itself – and revolve around the maternal maid Joséphine. She makes possible, and *human*, a typical Enlightenment experiment in relation to class. When Joséphine's son is born he is accidentally confused at birth with the son of the Comtesse de Horst so that neither can tell which child belongs to whom. While the noblewoman more or less abandons maternity until she can be sure she has the right (well-born) child, Joséphine loves and happily breast-feeds both together equally. This rewrites the opposition between virtuous maternal breast-feeding (much celebrated in the Revolution under the aegis of Rousseau) and the unworthy practice of the wet nurse. While historically much 'baby farming' was indeed a dangerous and pernicious phenomenon, Joséphine, as good biological and adoptive mother indiscriminately, suggests something rather different – the focus is less on the unworthy noblewoman and more on Joséphine's loving generosity. Constance is interested in this as an experiment to show whether or not class traits are inherited, and will be revealed in spite of two children having the same upbringing; she conducts other experiments to show the role of upbringing on gender characteristics, for example. Where a child is concerned the ethical responsibility to return the deposit to the original holders (which is universal for Kant) is far more complex, and the question of what they will do with the child is critical. Charrière humanizes the enlightened experiment (rational and scientific) by her portrait of Joséphine. In 'Histoire de Constance' she goes further, focusing not on a maidservant, with all the limitations on autonomy even that supposes, but a female black slave – at the time the tale is set, by law, a *thing* not a person. Before passing on to this tale, where the slave is both made a human subject, striving towards moral autonomy, and also shown to be radically constrained however kindly she is treated, I shall briefly examine an earlier Kant essay, often seen to encapsulate 'Enlightenment'. *Beantwortung der Frage: Was ist Aufklärung?* (1784) begins:

> Aufklärung ist der Ausgang des Menschen aus seiner selbstverschuldeten Unmündigkeit. Unmündigkeit ist das Unvermögen, sich seines Verstandes ohne Leitung eines anderen zu bedienen.[14]

---

14 *Werke*, VIII, pp. 33–42, 35. 'Enlightenment is man's emergence from his self-imposed immaturity. Immaturity is the inability to use one's understanding without guidance from another.' *An Answer to the Question: What is Enlightenment?*, in Kant, *Perpetual Peace and Other Essays*, ed. and translated by Ted Humphrey (Indianapolis and Cambridge: Hackett, 1983), p. 41. There is a question of translation: Mary J. Gregor gives 'Enlightenment is the human being's emergence from his self-incurred minority. Minority is inability to make use of one's understanding without direction from another.' (*Cambridge Edition of the Works of Immanuel Kant*, p. 17). Translation

Kant chides us for our laziness – thinking we can pay others (pastors, physicians, even authors of books) to guide us – thus making it easy for some to establish themselves as guardians:

> Daß der bei weitem größte Teil der Menschen (darunter das ganze schöne Geschlecht) den Schritt zu Mündigkeit, außer dem daß er beschwerlich ist, auch für sehr gefährlich halte: dafür sorgen schon jene Vormünder, die die Oberaufsicht über sie gütigst auf sich genommen haben. Nachdem sie ihr Hausvieh zuerst dumm gemacht haben und sorgfältig verhüteten, daß sie diese ruhigen Geschöpfe ja keinen Schritt außer dem Gängelwagen, darin sie sie einsperrten, wagen durften, so zeigen sie ihnen nachher die Gefahr, die ihnen drohet, wenn sie es versuchen, allein zu gehen. (*Was ist Aufklärung*, 35)[15]

Kant's *Gängelwagen* is rendered as 'walking cart' by Gregor, not much better than Humphrey's 'go-cart', in fact this is a baby walker – used to support children learning to walk. It is a slightly perverse choice of term since the point of using a baby walker is to teach toddlers to walk not the opposite. And the translations are perversely unclear to an English ear. Kant's mixed metaphor, which may be troubling translators if only unconsciously, rolls together domestic animals and toddlers. I shall suggest later the differences between those naturally unfit for citizenship – here animals and children. While animals may stay unfit, *male* children can, though they may not, grow up to be citizens – what about the fair sex? They are seemingly included in *Menschen* and yet can they grow up to humanity? Not according to 'Über den Gemeinspruch'. And are servants and slaves assimilated to domesticated animals or to children? Kant writes: 'Zu dieser Aufklärung aber wird nichts erfordert als *Freiheit*; und zwar die unschädlichste unter allem, was nur Freiheit heißen mag, nämlich die: von seiner Vernunft in allen Stücken *öffentlich Gebrauch* zu machen' (*Was ist Aufklärung*, 36).[16] Obey laws, Kant says, but argue. He notes that it is easier to have a political revolution than to reform a manner of thinking – feminists might well agree.

In a significant part of the 'Histoire de Constance', in the sequel to *Trois femmes*, Constance tells of Bianca, a slave who belonged to Constance's great-aunt Madame Delfonté, and of the fate of Bianca's daughter.[17] This is

---

decisions here not only include 'man' and 'his' but the natural sounding 'immaturity' *or* legal 'minority' (more accurate to the letter perhaps).

15 'The guardians who have so benevolently taken over the supervision of men have carefully seen to it that the far greatest part of them (including the entire fair sex) regard taking the step to maturity as very dangerous, not to mention difficult. Having first made their domestic livestock dumb, and having carefully made sure that these docile creatures will not take a single step without the go-cart to which they are harnessed, these guardians then show them the danger that threatens them, should they attempt to walk alone.' (*What is Enlightenment?*, 41)

16 'Nothing is required for this enlightenment, however, except *freedom*; and the freedom in question is the least harmful of all, namely the freedom to use reason *publicly* in all matters.' (*What is Enlightenment?*, 42)

17 This is not the only slave to appear in Charrière's fiction; more critical attention has been devoted to the dying male slave helped by Cécile in *Lettres écrites de Lausanne*. It is sometimes

written a few years after the Haitian revolution (1791), and in a time when pro- and anti-abolition arguments are raging in Europe.[18] Madame Delfonté is a generous woman, but her generosity is not tempered by justice. She gives without measuring the consequences and hence her kindness can often have unjust results – as eighteenth-century discussions of beneficence would tell us.[19] The primary recipient of her generosity is her sole heir Victor, her nephew and the narrator's uncle, to whom she can refuse nothing. Although he has a good nature, such an indulgent 'education' is harmful to his character. The second most important person in her world is: 'son esclave favorite, la plus belle et la mieux faite de celles de sa nation qu'on eût vu jamais à la Martinique. Noire comme de l'ébène par plaisanterie on l'avait nommée *Bianca* et le nom lui était resté' (*Suite*, 147).[20]

We can note the significant *naming* which is characteristic of course of slave-owners in general, who dehumanise by removing cultural, genealogical or personal given names, and reinforce their property rights by naming anew, as well as of adoption and 'second birth'. The naming of Bianca by inversion, as this is presented, is interesting: Bianca's name does not represent her person but the inverse of her skin. Even affectionate owners reveal their power in joking about such matters, their legal power to give privileges and also to take them away. Likewise an animal (even a lamb) may be given a human name, but will be whimsically treated as a family member only while it suits the owners. Yet we should not over-exaggerate the one-sided dimension of power since owners may of course love, or become utterly dependent upon, their pet humans or animals. Bianca's daughter, a beautiful mulatto we are told, is named Biondina. We are further told: 'le nom de Nerina lui aurait fort convenu mais elle ne laissait pas d'être une charmante enfant' (*Suite*, 148).[21] We might note the narrator's ambiguous hint that lacti-

---

suggested that slavery and racial marginalisation are simply metaphors for women's condition in this text as in others by eighteenth-century women writers; see for example Madeleine Dobie, 'Romantic Psychology and Kantian Ethics in the Novels of Isabelle de Charrière', *Eighteenth-Century Fiction* 10.3 (1998) 303–324. Dobie is of the view (against some readers who see Romanticism as almost inevitably misogynistic) that Charrière's feminism increases over time with her espousal of a more Romantic narrative. This would fit with 'Histoire de Constance' in which deaths resulting from melancholia or misery abound, and yet the importance of material and social circumstances for women's lives is not ignored. However, a feminist sensitivity need not preclude awareness of the situation of slaves.

18 Slavery and the slave trade are abolished by the Convention in 1794, but the war of words continues (with Grégoire a key protagonist arguing for racial equality) and, shamefully, Napoleon will restore slavery in 1802.

19 See my *Justice and Difference in the Works of Rousseau* (Cambridge: Cambridge University Press, 1993), e.g. p. 20.

20 'Her favourite slave, the most beautiful, with the best-looking body, of any woman of her nation that had ever been seen on Martinique. Black as ebony, she had been named Bianca as a joke and the name had stuck to her'. Unless referenced, all translations are my own.

21 'The name Nerina would have been highly appropriate for her but she was still a lovely child'.

fication, a key issue in the Caribbean, might have been desirable – and yet the authorial choice is to have beautiful and admirable women with notably black skin. Nerina, another Italian name like Bianca and Biondina, in referring no doubt to the blackness of her skin, echoes with the apparent naming by opposition of her mother. Yet this 'highly appropriate' name also suggests by its Greek etymology (*neros*) an association with water – a sea nymph, daughter of Nereus. I shall leave that hanging; we shall see later the role of water in the tale, and indeed black water insofar as water reflects the colour around it, and we shall encounter a black bath.

Madame Delfonté keeps her almost adopted daughter hidden away from her nephew and his guests whose pastimes can be, and are, easily left to our imagination. When they are at her plantation she keeps Bianca protected, happily incarcerated in a strange womb-like space – a white marble room where all the furnishings are stone so that water can flow through and over them and it can become a bath. The door to it is invisible and the window a kind of cupola, but history and literature tell us that no prison or refuge, however well-hidden, is utterly secure. It is then no surprise to the reader that one day the aunt will leave the key in the door after her daily bath together with her favourite slave, and her nephew will discover Bianca, water up to her waist, arranging roses whose petals she gaily strews on the water to protect her modesty from this interloper into the innermost sanctum. The nephew may seem less of a 'guest' in his aunt's house in the everyday sense of the word, and more of an adopted son in the full sense who should be at home in her house. However, the aunt maintains separation, building him his own dwelling in her grounds rather than giving him the run of her house. This is both a mark of true hospitality, enabling him to be not her guest but a host himself, *and* it is a sign that she wishes to be mistress in her own abode. His entrance into the locked room thus seems transgressive, echoing classic tales such as David's observation of Bathsheba or Actaeon catching Diana at her ablutions (with its unhappily appropriate end as he, translated into a stag, is torn apart by his own hunting dogs). Victor will eventually be mentally torn apart by his guilt.

Love blooms, and, since Delfonté can refuse Victor nothing, in spite of all her misgivings about the likely outcome she *gives* Bianca to him (or at least leaves her free to go) and he takes her away, saying that she will be the mistress in his home (or of his home): 'elle sera la maîtresse chez moi' (*Suite*, 148). For a few years Bianca's beauty, love and devoted service, as well as the birth of their daughter, make Victor so happy that he writes to his aunt that he is considering marrying her and legitimising the child, but, as the reader knows it will, tragedy strikes. This is in the shape of two actresses who arrive in St. Pierre, and take advantage of Victor's fatal flaw, his weakness, to invade his life. The rest of the troupe of actors have stayed in St. Domingue (Haiti), a noteworthy location. Victor constructs a theatre in his garden in which he and other young men play music and act with the two professionals. Bianca has to support this mistaken hospitable enterprise with her labour – adding lighting, costumes and refreshments to all the household tasks she previously excelled at. Charrière is unusual amongst eighteenth-century writers in her references to the reality of (women's) work. Bianca had been seen by Victor's friends as an excellent 'mistress', this word's ambiguity in a patriarchal society thus highlighted.

Victor will not allow the exhausted Bianca (worked almost to death) to return to his aunt's distant plantation, and she knows that if she goes without permission she could meet someone, be brought back and treated as a runaway slave: 'elle pouvait être rencontrée, ramenée et traitée en esclave fugitive' (*Suite*, 149). She now sees him as a tyrant rather than a lover, husband or the father of her child. Is she then a slave-mistress rather than the mistress of the house? Even if she were the latter then she would be vulnerable in receiving guests, as many classic tales (of Penelope, Helen or Lucretia for instance) relate. These famous instances relate to male intruders, obvious threats, but the eighteenth century is also interested in the role of women as intermediaries of male violence or sexual predation – apart from Sade, one might cite Rousseau's 'Emile et Sophie ou Les Solitaires' or Laclos's *Les Liaisons dangereuses*. In this case, when the master of the house is absent to deal with a neglected plantation (both terms, 'neglected' and 'plantation' troubling in different ways), the theatre enters his house. The two actresses pretend to have received a letter from him (this second, imaginary letter from Victor destroying all the good intentions of the first real one we hear about) inviting them to treat Bianca effectively *as a slave* to wait on them. The final insult is their use of the marble bathroom Victor had constructed for her in imitation of his aunt's sanctuary, where they order Bianca to bring food, wine and liqueurs. Bathing, like eating and drinking, is an intimate part of hospitality, an integral part of the ritual in the *Odyssey* for example. But in this story the doubled transgression of the bath, first by Victor bursting in upon Bianca, then by the actresses *demanding* the use of what should be *offered*, sets in motion a lethal chain of events. Bianca had asked her lover to make this imitation refuge in black marble instead of white – we can speculate that this detail relates to her position as the mistress of the house (rather than as one of Victor's mistresses) and assume that her reinvention of the bathroom, as a room of her own, means perhaps that for a while she is happy in her self (including the beautiful colour of her skin and that of her daughter), not needing to be bleached or lactified, and visibly respected. The dark water could mirror her and her daughter in a happy and healthy Narcissism. But the sanctuary is defiled when the returning Victor cannot bring himself to end the odious spectacle, and we should note the theatrical tropes: 'jouer le rôle insolent', 'cette odieuse scène' (*Suite*, 150). Culpable in his typical weakness, he delays both any explanation to Bianca and the expulsion of the intruders. 'Rape', as the meaning of sexual encounter in the story, is deferred; Victor's 'rapt' or seizure of Bianca in the first instance *could* have been reinvented as hymen. It is decided as abuse after the event by his silent permission to the actresses who are cruelly mimicking by inversion the first bath scene, their white skins (we presume) against the black, returning Bianca to the slavery that therefore perhaps she never left. The question whether sexual relations between (white) master and (black) slave, even if she is named Bianca, can ever be anything other than rape is a delicate one, since the question of consent is in the hands of the master. The only definitive refusal may seem to be suicide.[22]

In a fit of rage and despair that night Bianca stands over the sleeping Victor with a knife; he wakes and unfortunately cries out. That inadvertent cry is enough for those who run to his aid, and so in spite of all he says and invents she is bound, imprisoned and executed – as she appears to wish. This death is presented less as an indictment of colonial justice than as a kind of slave suicide (a resort to the only real equality of bleached white bones), a suicide which makes Victor her murderer whether he likes it or not.[23] Her lethal gesture proves contagious: Madame Delfonté dies of guilt and grief first, then Victor who has fled with Biondina to France where his sister (Constance's mother) is infected with Victor's depression and dies with him. Constance, for her part, vows (and is typically constant in keeping her vow) never to fall in love; she is forced to marry but is eventually able to live without legal or biological bonds – only adoptive ones. Charrière shows in much of her fiction how women work at constructing whatever autonomy they can, granted their *situation*.[24] When her mother and uncle die, the sixteen-year old Constance watches over their bodies until they begin to decay – shocking convention both in that, her own gift to the dead, and in her dismissal of the formal funeral rites. She asks her adoptive

---

22 This is clear in the case of a slave; however, in terms of the analogy sometimes made with women's position in general, we might note the celebrated case of Lucretia, a free noblewoman who nevertheless is trapped thanks to the conventions regarding women's culpability in cases of sexual transgression and can only defeat her rapist by public suicide.

23 While much could be said about the historical practice of suicide by slaves in the Americas and the Caribbean, in the French eighteenth-century context I could also mention Roxane at the end of Montesquieu's *Lettres Persanes* who has been seen as finding freedom from a tyrannical master in this way.

24 This summary of an exotic episode in Charrière's fiction – which is typically seen as rooted in everyday life in provincial towns such as Neuchâtel or Lausanne (or a village in Westphalia in *Trois femmes*) – is interesting in the way in which it echoes the *same* feminine concerns. Bianca's position as a slave is an extreme one, and yet her situation as a woman who loves a man who is not her husband, and who is not reliable however much he loves her, is the same as Caliste (another case of adoption and sexual predation) in the novel of that name. The plight of the unmarried mother occurs earlier in *Trois femmes*, and in *Lettres Neuchâteloises*, and the fate of the illegitimate child is always a consideration in Charrière in fiction and in life (in the case of Charrière's maid, for example) – it *must* be provided for.

daughters to do the same for her. This invention of rituals of mourning and remembrance, and the holding of the dead one as a guest within oneself, is an important constancy for daughters, lovers or friends. Constancy and haunting of lives and texts is a topos throughout the tale. The adoptive story becomes a little happier eventually with the next generation. Attempts to disinherit Biondina and strip her of all her possessions fail, and she is adopted by a kindly 'tuteur' in Martinique provided in her father's or his relatives' will. She is educated and secure as her mother was not. The saddest element then is that she is separated from her cousin, the older sister and becoming a surrogate maternal-figure, Constance, who is sent off to a different colony. Young unmarried women are not slaves, but neither are they easily mistresses of their own destiny. Constance will, however, be the one who tells Bianca's, the blood mother's story, and, unusually for Charrière, the first part of *Trois femmes* has the fiction of male narrator and author, thus the shift to this female voice feels particularly significant.

The absence of parents in 'Histoire de Constance' – Bianca *is* an orphan as far as we are concerned although we are told nothing of her parents who might indeed be alive – can be related to the particular devastation of family life caused by slavery, an institution that *deliberately*, as well as contingently, breaks up family life in order to weaken bonds between slaves. 'Histoire de Constance' is also a warning about 'adoption' without proper maternal care. The context in the colonies is one where temptations to abuse are many; indeed abuse of power is legal and normal. Madame Delfonté should have educated her heir, Victor, in virtue, self-discipline and moral strength rather than self-indulgence; and she should have protected Bianca as a daughter from sexual predators; she should have regarded her as a *depositum* to be kept safe. Victor indeed blames her almost as much as himself (rightly, even as this blaming of another is another sign of his self-indulgence). While all these characters are good-hearted, in this context of extreme legal inequality adoption still *becomes* sexual predation, and indeed lethal. There is no overt suggestion that the aunt is a sexual predator herself, although a reader may wonder at their daily baths together or indeed her practice of locking up a naked young woman in a bathroom on a regular basis even if it is to keep her safe. In any case Delfonté does leave Bianca exposed, and, once exposed, allows her nephew to have her for his pleasure, which Delfonté is convinced will not last. She has not educated the girl to have any intellectual or cultural resources, we are told. Bianca, who provides the material grounds for Victor's misdirected hospitality to the point of exhaustion, is eaten up. The giving aunt is thus the unwitting author of much misfortune – including the double loss of Constance's beloved mother, first through depression and then through death, making Constance seem, and feel, like an orphan herself until she is eventually reunited with her corrupt father in the colonies.

Female Autonomy

Hesse's determination, and my own, to read Kant and Charrière *politically* is in fact far from a betrayal of the spirit of Kant's article. He sets out to prove, against his critics, that theory and praxis should be one whatever sphere you are operating in, the ethical interactions of the individual in society, the political contract that founds civil society, or the cosmopolitan sphere of relations between nations. The issue of suffrage, and thus the natural exclusion of women and servants, never mind slaves, from citizenship, is raised by Kant in 'Über den Gemeinspruch' as a critical application of the categorical imperative of justice.

For Hesse, what Charrière most importantly adds to the consequentialist critique of Kant's absolute principle is the feminist question of autonomy. In the second section of his article, devoted to the social contract, Kant explicitly excludes, Hesse notes, two categories from full participation in the originating contract between citizens which is a precondition for the functioning of the categorical imperative. Hesse suggests that, for Kant, *women and servants by nature* do not have the capacity for maturity, that is to say autonomous self-determination. She writes:

> The Kantian model, Charrière revealed, left the problem of female moral autonomy *categorically* contingent on women's relationship to men and their laws. Moral contingency, in the case of women, was a symptom of their being categorically denied the right of autonomous self-constitution. Her critique of Kant's examples, then, was not from the consequentialist perspective, but from the perspective of those remained categorically outside the law.[25]

I should like to add a few observations to this analysis. Kant indeed excludes from citizenship (and suffrage) two or three categories of person. He says that there are two qualities requisite for the right to vote; the first is the natural one of *not being a child or woman*.[26] That is a crucially split category, however, since, of course, all of us pass through childhood (and democracies still exclude those defined as children from the vote). Kant does not gloss this at all, deeming 'not being a woman' perhaps as obvious a requisite (negative) quality as 'not being a child'. The second quality is the positive one of *being one's own master (sui iuris)* – this is much more difficult to determine as Kant admits, an unusual near-admission of defeat in this amazingly clearly assertive text. It is difficult to determine since it is a property qualification, but in his liberal fashion he wishes property to include any art, craft, fine art or science. This does, however, exclude servants (who to the modern reader here seem to approximate to slaves as those who have no mastery over themselves) so a barber is not a citizen while a wig-maker is; a shop clerk does not get the vote but a tailor does. Kant admits that this may seem odd – yet it is part of the triumph

25 Hesse, 'Kant, Foucault and *Trois Femmes*', 94.
26 Kant, 'Über den Gemeinspruch', 295; 'On the Common Saying', 295.

of morally practical reason as he sees it. Servants might be considered part of the *familia* of their masters, and, like wives, would have to vote as instructed by the *pater familias*. I assume then that, just as male children may pass from the position of naturally ineligible to be citizens to the position of eligibility, so servants might pass in time from being barbers to being wig-makers. The issue that is not clear is whether some are born naturally incapable of being their own masters (as some are born women) as Hesse's gloss would suggest. However, since a legal property qualification would not exclude those who eventually inherit property from their erstwhile masters, this seems unlikely. In Charrière's novel Constance sets up a series of experiments to test this very question of nature versus nurture – crucial for women, servants and slaves – the reader is not given the results of these of course since perhaps s/he needs to conduct at least a thought-experiment herself in order to learn.[27] Kant's position here seems strangely dependent on *circumstances* for an essay which in its entirety wishes to focus on abstract reason and prevent readers fastening short-sightedly on matters of their own experience.

Conclusion

Through philosophical fiction Charrière raises a whole range of issues *cutting across* the personal, the political and the cosmopolitical and across each other: truth, ownership of property, safekeeping, citizenship, sexual relations. For example, what is the truth for Bianca about her sexual relations with Victor when she is his property? In a less extreme form, Jacqueline's history of sexual abuse by male masters is the background to her trading of sexual favours to help the destitute Emilie. Neither woman could be a citizen because of their class as well as sex. As a woman writing about female subjects – including female servants and slaves who act as autonomously as possible in dire circumstances – Charrière is self-consciously in a very different position from the academic philosopher whose interest lies in the man who is master of

---

27 In *Trois femmes* Constance tests the relative role of nature and nurture in the cases of class and sex, while supporting the son of the local feudal lord Théobald d'Altendorf in his attempts (beset with problems) to begin to offer a general education to children on his lands. Hesse sees a distinction between Constance's re-enacted experiments (more radical) and Théobald's pedagogical projects which she likens to those of Grégoire or Kant. However, each gives some support to the other, and importantly, while Théobald's first choice is to educate boys, where a family has no boy of a suitable age he will happily encourage the most suitable daughter to attend school – this might imply that girls too could achieve enlightenment. Equally no boys or girls of the right age are excluded from schooling even if only one per family is actively encouraged. Constance's experiments meanwhile take little account of the possible consequences for the individuals concerned – the boy brought up as a girl or the girl treated exactly as a boy who will one day realise what has happened to them; the son of the aristocrat and the son of the servant brought up with strict equality in an unequal world. Constance is not Charrière, and the author is only too aware of the imperfections and complexities at play.

himself. My initial questions were: 'who is to be free?' or 'for whom?' is the writer writing. Kant urges *Menschen* to break free of the *Gängelwagen* and walk unaided, by which he means, above all, think and speak as your own master. His virile model of the moral subject as an end in himself coincides with his picture of the citizen as an independent man, free from the obligation to sell his labour. Yet even independently wealthy widows, such as Constance or her aunt, do not get the vote according to his 'universal' precepts. The debates amongst Europeans and Americans over slavery in the 1790s raise the question whether Africans are men or beasts (whether pro-slavery voices truly believe what they claim or simply find it economically expedient). Women's suffrage is not agreed in France until after the Second World War. Charrière's characters aspire to move beyond pragmatism yet their choices would be limited not only by their fictional circumstances but by philosophers arguing for 'freedom'. Kant's universal principles are thus not only too universal, as the consequentialist would have it, but *not universal enough*.

Appropriately the defining of paranoia throughout the history of psychiatry and psychoanalysis has involved much shifting between a greater and a lesser territory of mental imbalance – the Greeks used the term in the widest possible sense. In the twentieth century it becomes a specific chronic psychosis; Freud relates it particularly to the defence against homosexuality. Melanie Klein develops the term 'projective identification' to describe a paranoid-schizoid defence against the persecutory anxiety common in all of us, and post-Kleinians have taken this up to explore the projection of disowned aspects of the self into the opposite sex. While Kant is hardly clinically paranoid, the work of any systematic thinker with a mania for interpretation can typically be shown to have a paranoid structure.[28] In highly anxious political times such as the 1790s it could be claimed that Kant (like many other Enlightenment and Revolutionary thinkers) wishes to establish *some* bounds to freedom when so many bonds have been untied – hence women cannot be fully free. However, when reflecting on paranoia, we should at least consider the opposite perspective – that Kant defensively projects onto the weaker sex and slaves an inability to be free which he finds an unacceptable impulse in himself (or in men of his class more generally). The symptomatic 'ungrammatical' articulations I have noted in his writing could certainly be read as the insistence on a 'not-me' in order to deny identification. It would then be literature which, with its ambiguity and refusal to decide, is the more rigorously political as well as personal formulation.[29]

---

28 See my 'The Disfigured Savage: Rousseau and De Man', *Nottingham French Studies* 25 (1985) 1–14 for an analysis of the role of the passion of fear in Enlightenment anthropology and politics, and for the paranoid structure of interpretation.

29 See Paul de Man, *Allegories of Reading* (New Haven: Yale University Press, 1979), p. 157.

Sade, Revolution, and the Boundaries of Freedom

Melissa Deininger

Few authors have broken more boundaries than the Marquis de Sade. Notorious for his libertine writings, he was also a politically charged author, urging society to reach for evermore freedoms. Throughout his long career, he continuously pushed the limits of socially acceptable writing and behaviour, by mingling sexual deviations with radical political beliefs. It was Sade's hope that the French Revolution would not only allow, but would encourage criticism of societal failings under the Ancien Régime. Sade saw the Revolution as a moment of potential for absolute freedom, an idea which is clearly exploited in his seminal *La Philosophie dans le boudoir* (1795). In this late eighteenth-century novella, power, pleasure, and sexual domination are all intimately intertwined and presented as tools to be mastered in order to prosper during these chaotic times. Sade deftly juxtaposes Revolutionary rhetoric with libertine philosophy, demonstrating the necessity for yet more freedom. By appropriating contemporary political ideals, Sade hoped to push his fellow Frenchmen into that 'encore un effort' needed to see the fulfilment of the Revolution's promise.

The Marquis de Sade became heavily involved in Revolutionary politics, primarily as a means to safeguard his own freedom, but also because the idea of expanded liberties appealed to his desire for a society not based on communal laws. Persecuted for years for pursuing his own unique vision of personal happiness, Sade truly believed that the fall of the Ancien Régime could signify the beginning of a new era of individual liberty. Issues he had struggled with his entire life, such as personal liberty, abuse of power, and freedom of speech now took centre stage in newspapers and political speeches. Sade felt that there could be no limits to true freedom, for as Sadean scholar Annie Le Brun so adeptly observes, 'liberty is that which knows no limit, otherwise it isn't liberty at all.'[1] The apparent absence of power following the end of the monarchy represented for Sade an unlimited opportunity to overcome old mentalities and to create a new society, free of old prejudices and judgements. Maurice Blanchot describes this moment for Sade as:

---

1   Annie Le Brun, *A Sudden Abyss*, translated by Camille Naish (San Francisco: City Lights Books, 1990), p. 173.

le temps pur où l'histoire suspendue fait époque, ce temps de l'entre-temps où entre anciennes lois et les lois nouvelles règne le silence de l'absence des lois, cet intervalle qui correspond précisément à l'entre-dire où tout cesse et tout s'arrête, y compris l'éternelle pulsion parlante, parce qu'il n'est plus alors d'interdit.[2]

This 'suspended' time is exactly the moment when the Revolution can fulfil its promise and deliver real freedom unrestricted by laws based on an outdated system of morality.

Sade spent much of his time justifying his devotion to the Revolution, mostly as a course of self-protection from the new political powers. A prisoner in the Bastille shortly before its fall, Sade never ceased claiming that he was one of the primary catalysts for its destruction. He recalls his crucial role in inciting the crowds in a 1790 letter: 'J'échauffais, disait-on, par ma fenêtre l'esprit du peuple [...] je l'exhortais à venir jeter bas ce monument d'horreur.'[3] Just one year after supposedly rousing the Parisian mobs to tear down the edifice that symbolized the old régime's abuses of power, Sade became involved with the Section des Piques, one of the city's most radical neighbourhoods. In 1793, he rose to prominence with popular speeches, including a well-received eulogy for Marat and Le Peletier, two martyrs of the Revolution. With the sound of the guillotine operating in the background, Sade delivered his fervently republican speech, in which he referred to the Revolutionaries as 'l'heureux modèle de toutes les vertus' (the happy model of all virtues).[4] He was undoubtedly somewhat tongue-in-cheek with this tribute to men who were responsible for considerable violence and suffering, but his praise played to the Revolutionary crowd. Although he detested societal concepts of virtue, this idea was one of the key terms bandied about by politicians on a daily basis, and as such, a necessary component in a eulogy for the Revolution's latest martyrs.

Well aware of the importance of pleasing both the crowds and the radicals now in charge, Sade devoted considerable effort to his political writings. Critics have long tried to explain and define Sade's role in writing the Revolution, both in his political and fictional output. According to Georges Bataille and Simone de Beauvoir, Sadean violence is rationalized, most likely stemming from the complexities of Sade's own life. Bataille sees Sade as a

---

2   Maurice Blanchot, *L'Inconvenance majeure* (Paris: Pauvert, 1965), p. 39. 'The pure moment when suspended history makes the epoch, this moment of the meantime where, between ancient and new laws, the silence of the absence of laws reigns, this interval that corresponds precisely to the forbidden where everything ceases, including the eternal speaking compulsion, because there is no longer a forbidden.' Unless indicated otherwise, all translations are my own.

3   Sade's letter to Gaufridy, May 1790, quoted in Alice M. Laborde, *Correspondances du Marquis de Sade et de ses proches enrichies de documents, notes et commentaires*, 27 vols (Genève: Éditions Slatkine, 1996), VIII, p. 229. 'They say I inflamed the people from my window [...] I exhorted them to tear down this monument of horror.'

4   Quoted in Maurice Lever, *Donatien Alphonse François, marquis de Sade* (Paris: Librairie Arthème Fayard, 1991), p. 506.

frustrated nobleman, who lashed out at the Ancien Régime through his writings. For him, Sade's criticism of the past was based on two lines of attack:

> In the one, he sided with the Revolution and criticized the monarchy, but in the other he exploited the infinite possibilities of literature and propounded to his readers the concept of a sovereign type of humanity whose privileges would not have to be agreed upon by the masses.[5]

It is this negation of the right of the masses that is at the heart of so many of Sade's fictional works, which he would, contrary to the rhetoric of the Republican ideals, espouse in his public life. Indeed, the plot of Sade's *La Philosophie dans le boudoir* is the indoctrination of a privileged young girl into the world of libertinage, where masters dominate and the space around them is dedicated to their pleasure, negating the very idea of fraternal equality.

For Simone de Beauvoir, Sadean violence is a parody. According to her, when confronted with the events surrounding the Revolution and its subsequent Terror, Sade 'did not try to set up a new universe. He contented himself with ridiculing, by the manner in which he imitated it, the one imposed upon him.'[6] The only escape Sade offers is to be found in his libertine world of power and sexual fantasies. Forced to deal with tough political and social realities, Sade immersed himself and his readers in topsy-turvy worlds that value vices over virtues. Beauvoir believes this attempt to deal with the world created by the Revolution was a common reaction among Sade's peers. She sees the libertine movement among young aristocrats as an attempt to recapture the power that should have been theirs, noting that:

> Scions of a declining class which had once possessed concrete power, but which no longer retained any real hold on the world, they tried to revive symbolically, in the privacy of the bedchamber, the status for which they were nostalgic: that of the lone and sovereign despot.[7]

Because their previous world of privilege had been completely destroyed, young noblemen like Sade struggled to create a new society in which they could regain control over themselves and their milieus. According to Beauvoir, it is this illusion of power that Sade is trying to recover, even though the status he seeks would never be restored to him. While Sade tried to restore his real-life status through involvement in Revolutionary politics, most of his need for power had to be fulfilled in the fictional libertine worlds he created. In literary works like *Philosophie*, he could once again rule his world, abolishing

---

5   Georges Bataille, *Eroticism*, translated by Mary Dalwood (London: Marion Boyars Publishers, 1987), p. 166.
6   Simone de Beauvoir, 'Must We Burn Sade?', translated by Annette Michelson, in *Marquis de Sade: The 120 Days of Sodom and Other Writings*, ed. by Austryn Wainhouse and Richard Seaver (New York: Grove Press, 1966), pp. 3–64, 35.
7   de Beauvoir, 'Must We Burn Sade?', 8.

societal norms of acceptable behaviours and creating a safe space for libertine freedom.

Although he struggled to adjust to the new societal norms, Sade's fictional concepts often collided with accepted Revolutionary ideals and language. Like other Revolutionaries, the Marquis de Sade was a forceful proponent of liberty, but its meaning for him was very different. Sadean freedom is based on individual power and control, but never on the group. Maurice Blanchot defines Sadean equality as the right to use others equally, while freedom is the power to bend others to your will.[8] In contrast, Revolutionary freedom could only be achieved through connections of equality and fraternity between fellow citizens. For Sade, it is through the power one holds, and how it is yielded, that individuals will succeed. The best way to counter threats to one's sovereignty is to acquire yet more power. According to Blanchot, Sadean power is based in negation – of God, of societal laws, and, eventually, of nature.[9] For Sade, it was only by moving beyond established and accepted barriers that society would be able to attain true freedom.

While waiting for society to catch up to this new limitless freedom, Sade recognized that both he and his characters would need to stage their voluptuous expressions of freedom far removed from the public. Throughout his works, Sade privileges small private groups of libertines who seek their pleasure and power in sexual domination. He attached great importance to private versus public spaces, while the Revolution subjected most aspects of daily life to public consideration and regulation, an idea that Sade found abhorrent. For him, complete freedom necessarily meant being excluded from the public gaze. He notes:

> On n'image pas comme la volupté est servie par ces sûretés-là et ce que l'on entreprend quand on peut se dire : 'Je suis seul ici, j'y suis au bout du monde, soustrait à tous les yeux et sans qu'il puisse devenir possible à aucune créature d'arriver à moi ; plus de freins, plus de barriers.'[10]

By pushing against the limits of society, he is able to break through the barriers that force him into socially-defined behaviours. Absolute freedom, a cherished goal for Sade, is only possible in a secluded and protected space that allows libertine natures to flourish.

8   Maurice Blanchot, *Lautréamont et Sade* (Paris: Editions de Minuit, 1949), p. 222.
9   Blanchot, *Lautréamont et Sade*, 255.
10 Donatien Alphonse François de Sade, *Les cent vingt journées de sodome* (Paris: Société Nouvelle des Editions Pauvert, 1986), p. 225. 'Ah, it is not readily to be imagined how much voluptuousness, lust, fierce joy are flattered by those sureties, or what is meant when one is able to say to oneself: "I am here, I am at the world's end, withheld from every gaze, here no one can reach me, there is no creature that can come nigh where I am; no limits, hence, no barriers; I am free."' English translation from Wainhouse and Seavers, *The 120 Days of Sodom and Other Writings*, 412.

The Revolution intrudes on this ideal libertine seclusion in the middle of *La Philosophie dans le boudoir*, when a pamphlet entitled *Français, encore un effort si vous voulez être républicains* (*Frenchmen, one more effort if you wish to be republicans*) is introduced. While some critics, such as John Phillips, tend to reduce the novel's impact to mere 'sexual pedagogy',[11] the arrival of the political treatise establishes it firmly in the political and social sphere. The pamphlet has supposedly been purchased in the Palais de l'Égalité, a location which echoes the former Palais Royal, site of gambling, prostitution, and pornographic pamphlets under the Ancien Régime. According to Caroline Weber, the pamphlet thus 'manifests not only a rapprochement between the democratically minded rabble of the Palais de l'Égalité and the decadent elite of Saint-Ange's boudoir, but also a confusion in the political origins and alliance of "republican" doctrine itself.'[12] Sade thus uses both public and private practices to set the stage for his coming arguments about what the Revolution must do next in order to prosper.

Sade's *Philosophie* is a carefully constructed layering of philosophical teachings interspersed with scenes of sexual deviancy. The novella serves in many ways as a mirror of the chaotic times in which it was written. The story is based on Sade's *Eugénie de Franval* (1788), but *Philosophie* itself was only finished in 1795, with the writing process thus spanning the Revolution and subsequent Terror. Carefully explained philosophical concepts, coupled with ruthless physical indoctrination are redolent of contemporary political speeches and decrees, but the juxtaposition of sex and philosophy are quintessential Sade.

Once again, Caroline Weber's research is invaluable for situating Sade's writing within a contemporary context. She illustrates how Sade responded to the new Republic's contradictory actions and broken promises by comparing the libertine's works to Revolutionary staples such as Rousseau's *The Social Contract* and Robespierre's 'Fête de l'Etre Suprême.' Rousseau's duality of man and citizen serves as the basis for many of Sade's arguments for a lessening of legal restrictions, while the idea of a Supreme Being is dismissed as false idolatry that limits citizens' minds and bodies. Weber is also careful to remind us that, along with Sade's various literary strategies, there is an 'almost constant vacillation between Terrorist collusion and anti-Terrorist critique'[13] in his post-revolutionary output that must be taken into account.[14] An earlier critic of Sade, Maurice Lever, had noted Sade's tendency to mock current political discourse, noting that his *Français, encore un effort*

---

11 John Phillips, *The Libertine Novels* (London: Pluto Press, 2001), p. 86.
12 Caroline Weber, *Terror and its Discontents: Suspect Words in Revolutionary France* (Minneapolis: University of Minnesota, 2003), p. 193.
13 Weber, *Terror and its Discontents*, 177.
14 The term 'Terrorist' here refers specifically to the group of radicals who engineered the Terror of 1793–1794.

's'agit de la *reductio ad absurdum* de la théorie révolutionnaire et de la dérision la plus radicale de la philosophie jacobine.'[15] Through the clarifying lens of such in-depth analysis, Sade's political theories and objectives become perceptible, despite the author's frequent attempts to hide his message behind sarcasm and political distortions. The extreme lengths to which the libertine master pushes his students in *Philosophie* frequently seem absurd, but the violence within the boudoir is an echo of the everyday violence taking place outside the pleasure palace's walls.

The story describes the indoctrination of a young girl, both in the ways of libertine behaviour and in the failings of the Revolution. Political and moral rhetoric dealing with notions of freedom are inserted between scenes of increasingly frenetic sexual activity. The philosophical dialogues blur the lines between lustful bodies and thoughtful minds, seducing the reader into considering Sade's beliefs without consciously stopping to consider their validity.[16] The abrupt dousing of the reader's ardour with cool philosophical discussions forces him to focus on Sadean logic, all the while awaiting the next promised bout of debauchery.

Despite the licentious scenes that advance *Philosophie*'s narrative, it is ultimately through logical argument and cool discussion that the main character is persuaded to adopt a truly libertine lifestyle. As her body is indoctrinated into physical pleasures, Eugénie, the young libertine protégée, begins to understand libertine values by being exposed to Sade's political philosophies. The two indoctrinations necessarily go hand in hand for Sade. Conveyed through a political pamphlet read during a break in the sexual activities, Sadean concepts of liberty and civic duty seduce the girl more surely than anything she had experienced up to this point. Lynn Hunt describes the force of this moment by pointing to the power of rhetoric:

> Eugénie can be corrupted by the sheer force of language. Words have this power in the new order because people are discovering that society is its own source of power, that society itself has an imagined base in social convention rather than in otherworldly truths.[17]

Like thousands of her compatriots, Eugénie has been seduced by powerful language and skilful rhetoric. While both the nation and the girl have come to accept the importance of freedom, Sade pushes his character to evince a desire for virtually limitless freedom, based solely on libertine values.

15 Maurice Lever, *Que suis-je à présent?* (Paris: Éditions Bartillat, 1998), p. 234. '[…] deals with the *reductio ad absurdum* of revolutionary theory and the most radical derision of Jacobin philosophy'.
16 See Jean Goulemot, 'Sadean Novels and Pornographic Novels: Narration, Its Objectives and Its Effects', *Paragraph* 23.1 (2000) 63–75.
17 Lynn Hunt, *The Family Romance of the French Revolution* (Berkeley: University of California Press, 1992), p. 133.

As can be seen in the evolution from Sade's earlier works to *Philosophie*, the events of the French Revolution and the Terror had a profound effect on Sade as a man and as a writer. In the beginning, Sade militated for and encouraged the Revolution as a means of fulfilling his lifelong desire for personal liberty, free from societal judgements. For him, it was a moment apart, a chance for true freedom in the interregnum of two regimes. However, as he became disenchanted with the Revolution's results, he began to mock the work and ideals of the Terrorist leaders. Throughout *Philosophie*'s political pamphlet, we find numerous examples of Sade appropriating and twisting Revolutionary rhetoric to suit his vision of a truly free society.

Maurice Blanchot devotes great effort to comparing Sade's ideas and terminologies to those of the Revolutionaries. He observes how reasoned Sade's writing tends to be: his style is encyclopedic, with its lists and descriptions of sexual positions and implements; the didactic nature of many of his works serves as a primer for future libertines; and Sade frequently uses a syllogistic style to draw his readers into his beliefs. This Enlightenment style of writing then turns current political and moral doctrines on their heads. For example, Sade advocated communal homes, in order to facilitate debauchery; children were to be removed from their families, so that they could be educated as libertines; and true fraternity would necessarily lead to incest, as the natural expression of man's fondness for his fellows. Ideals of freedom were espoused by Revolutionary philosophers, but their goal, of course, was to promote national unity and the education and formation of good citizens, rather than Sade's desired goal of creating decadent and empowered libertines.

For the most part parodies of Revolutionary values, Sade's interpretations of contemporary ideas served to mock the political rhetoric of the time. While much of his discourse is couched in libertine terms, Sade occasionally takes advantage of the increased freedom to criticize the realities of the Revolution under the Terrorist regime. For example, he attacks the Terrorists for betraying the main motto of the Revolution, *liberté, égalité, fraternité*. In a 1793 letter to fellow libertine Cardinal de Bernis, he observes: 'Liberté ? Personne n'a jamais été moins libre, on dirait un fleuve de somnambules. Égalité ? Il n'y a d'égalité que des têtes tranchées. Fraternité ? La délation n'a jamais été plus active. [...] Chacun veut la mort de chacun.'[18] Sade also points to glaring discrepancies between the Revolutionary rhetoric about freedom of speech and Terrorist practices, such as the de facto cen-

---

18 Quoted in Philippe Sollers, *Sade contre l'Être Suprême* (Paris: Quai Voltaire, 1992), p. 22. English translation from Deepak Narang Sawhney, ed., *Must We Burn Sade ?* (Amherst and New York: Humanity Books, 1999), pp. 133–158, 139. 'Liberty? People have never been less free, they're like a crowd of sleepwalkers. Equality? The only equality is among guilliotined heads. Fraternity? Informing on one's neighbors has never been more active. [...] Everyone wants everyone else's death.'

sorship under the Law of Suspects, as problems that must be solved in order for the Revolution to flourish.

Although he had frequently experienced the dangers of challenging authority, both in real life and in his writing, Sade felt increasingly freed by the Revolution to communicate with what he believed would be a more receptive audience. The continuous shifts in political power raised Sade's expectations for further freedoms; indeed, he urges true Republicans to yet more immoral behaviour as a means of supporting their government. After describing the great republics of history as realms in continuous insurrection, Sade states that: 'L'état *moral* d'un homme est un état de paix et de tranquillité, au lieu que son état *immoral* est un état de mouvement perpétuel qui le rapproche de l'insurrection nécessaire, dans laquelle il faut que le républicain tienne toujours le gouvernement dont il est membre.'[19] A Sadean republic is not a stable state; rather it is in constant movement, forever on guard against both internal and external threats.[20] This need for constant action is at odds with man's moral state, and, therefore, traditional morality must be jettisoned in order to save the Republic. Unfortunately for Sade, his fellow Frenchmen were only able to maintain this state of insurrection for a few years.

Anxious about the Republic's future, the unidentified pamphleteer in *Philosophie* begins his political treatise with concerns about the current state of affairs: 'Je ne le cache point, c'est avec peine que je vois la lenteur avec laquelle nous tâchons d'arriver au but; c'est avec inquiétude que je sens que nous sommes à la veille de le manquer encore une fois.' (*Philosophie*, 490)[21] While the identity of the fictional pamphlet's author is unknown, Sade's *porte-parole* in the work all but admits he is the author, making it clear that Sade's greatest fear is that the Revolution will fall short of its potential of true freedom for all.

Although the idea for the novella comes from an earlier short story, the pamphlet stands out as a post-Revolutionary addition. The story itself offers very few clues to the exact time period in which it is set. It is only with the insertion of the pamphlet that the reader is able to unmistakably situate the

---

19 Donatien Alphonse François de Sade, *La Philosophie dans le boudoir* (Paris: Société Nouvelle des Éditions Pauvert, 1986), p. 510. 'The state of a *moral* man is one of tranquility and peace, the state of an *immoral* man is one of perpetual unrest that pushes him to, and identifies him with, the necessary insurrection in which the republican must always keep the government of which he is a member.' English translation from *Justine, Philosophy in the Bedroom and Other Writings*, ed. by Richard Seaver and Austryn Wainhouse (New York: Grove Press, 1965), pp. 177–367, 314. All further translations of *Philosophie* are taken from this edition, referred to as *Philosophy*.

20 Blanchot, *L'Inconvenance majeure*, 26. This theory of instability and insurrection as necessary components for a successful revolution will enjoy a long life in revolutionary theory, including the Maoist 'continuous revolution.'

21 'We near our goal, but haltingly; I confess that I am disturbed by the presentiment that we are on the eve of failing once again to arrive there.' (*Philosophy*, 296)

events as taking place during the Terror. Sade's allusions to the place of its purchase, contemporary arguments against religion and monarchical despotism, and the use of terms like *citoyen* all serve to situate the pamphlet. Of course, the discourse itself leaves no doubt as to when it was written, as when Sade compares the current Revolution to Christianity's overthrow of pagan idols.

> Me dira-t-on que nous ne sommes pas assez mûrs pour consolider encore notre révolution d'une manière aussi éclatante ? Ah ! mes concitoyens, le chemin que nous avons fait depuis 89 était bien autrement difficile que celui qui nous reste à faire, et nous avons bien moins à travailler l'opinion, dans ce que je vous propose, que nous ne l'avons tourmenté en tout sens depuis l'époque du renversement de la Bastille. (*Philosophie*, 497)[22]

The original moment of revolution may have passed, but there is still work to be done in order completely to overthrow old prejudices. By playing to his reader's civic pride and sense of duty, Sade implores him to continue the fight for total liberty.

In keeping with the title of his pamphlet, Sade reassures the people that the recent past has presented far more difficulties than their attainable future. In case they have doubts about their power, he provides concrete evidence of what they have already brought to fruition:

> Croyons qu'un peuple assez sage, assez courageux pour conduire un monarque impudent du faîte des grandeurs aux pieds de l'échafaud ; qui dans ce peu d'années sut vaincre autant de préjugés, sut briser tant de freins ridicules, le sera suffisamment pour immoler au bien de la chose, à la prospérité de la république, un fantôme bien plus illusoire encore que ne pouvait l'être celui d'un roi. (*Philosophie*, 497–498)[23]

The 'phantom' the people are encouraged to abolish is, of course, Christianity, but the real goal of this section is to convince Frenchmen that they can accomplish whatever they wish, having already overcome so many obstacles. Sade appeals to their vanity by vaunting their bravery and sagacity, while he diminishes the 'ridiculous impediments' that stood in their way. If Frenchmen would only continue to push, they could overcome any and all remaining obstacles to attaining the cherished goal of complete freedom.

Sade raises many points in the pamphlet that were debated in the drafting of the new Constitution and other political documents of the day. For

---

22 'Will someone tell me that we are not yet mature enough to consolidate our revolution in so brilliant a manner? Ah, my fellow citizens, the road we took in '89 has been much more difficult than the one still ahead of us, and we have little yet to do to conquer the opinion we have been harrying since the time of the overwhelming of the Bastille.' (*Philosophy*, 303)
23 'Let us firmly believe that a people wise enough and brave enough to drag an impudent monarch from the heights of grandeur to the foot of the scaffold, a people that, in these last few years, has been able to vanquish so many prejudices and sweep away so many ridiculous impediments, will be sufficiently wise and brave to terminate the affair and in the interests of the republic's well-being, abolish a mere phantom after having successfully beheaded a real king.' (*Philosophy*, 303)

example, his calls for a civic religion to replace Christianity echo the speeches made by Robespierre for a cult of reason. Sade points out the necessity of such a cult, as the basis for future laws:

> Il nous faut un culte, et un culte fait pour le caractère d'un républicain, bien éloigné de jamais pouvoir reprendre celui de Rome. Dans un siècle où nous sommes assez convaincus que la religion doit être appuyée sur la morale, et non pas la morale sur la religion, il faut une religion qui aille aux mœurs, [...] et qui puisse, en élevant l'âme, la tenir perpétuellement à la hauteur de cette liberté précieuse dont elle fait aujourd'hui son unique idole. (*Philosophie*, 490)[24]

Although Sade abhorred the idea of organized religion, he is willing to advocate a system of beliefs based on man's true nature. Playing to the idea of republican pride, Sade ties his new religion to a new morality, something far removed from Christian ideals. By obeying natural impulses, Frenchmen would necessarily arrive at a cult dedicated to liberty, because everyone should be devoted to promoting and protecting their own personal freedoms.

According to Sade, the protection and adoration of liberty must serve as the ultimate goal of a civic creed. At the beginning of the pamphlet, Sade states that religion teaches us to 'rendre à César ce qui appartient à César,' but he quickly notes that 'nous avons détrôné César et nous ne voulons plus rien lui rendre.' (*Philosophie*, 490)[25] For Sade, it is only through continued devotion to liberty that Frenchmen can escape the domination of Rome and the tyrants who have ruled them for centuries.

With *Philosophie*, Sade presents an inverted world, in which crimes are depicted as right and morally correct acts. He believes that society must rid itself of the absurd notion that laws can be applied wholesale to all. The author of the pamphlet claims that it would be 'une absurdité palpable que de vouloir prescrire des lois universelles ; [...] c'est une injustice effrayante que d'exiger que des hommes de caractères inégaux se plient à des lois égales.' (*Philosophie*, 505)[26] Of course, once again, Sade has turned Revolutionary terms on their heads. Article VI of the *Declaration of the Rights of Man and of the Citizen* insists on the supremacy of the populace over the rights of the individual, stating:

---

24 'We must have a cult, a cult befitting the republican character, something far removed from ever being able to resume the worship of Rome. In this age, when we are convinced that morals must be the basis of religion, and not religion of morals, we need a body of beliefs in keeping with our customs and habits, something [...] that could, by uplifting the spirit, maintain it perpetually at the high level of this precious liberty, which today the spirit has made its unique idol.' (*Philosophy*, 296)

25 'render unto Caesar that which is Caesar's [...] we have dethroned Caesar, we are no longer disposed to render him anything.' (*Philosophy*, 296–297)

26 'to seek to impose universal laws would be a palpable absurdity [...] it is a terrible injustice to require that men of unlike character all be ruled by the same law.' (*Philosophy*, 310)

La loi est l'expression de la volonté générale. [...] Elle doit être la même pour tous, soit qu'elle protège, soit qu'elle punisse. Tous les citoyens, étant égaux à ses yeux, sont également admissibles à toutes dignités, places et emplois publics, selon leur capacité et sans autre distinction que celle de leurs vertus et de leurs talents.[27]

Because law derives from the desires of the group, the majority is able to dictate rules to all members of society. The only differences the law is willing to admit are those of talents and virtues, meaning that everyone must obey basic tenets, only showing individuality in their skills. In every other way, all citizens are created and remain perfectly equal, facilitating the introduction and implementation of collective laws.

It is exactly this sort of 'group fit' that Sade is railing against in his work. He believes that one law cannot possibly apply to so many different people, since nature has constituted them in such different ways. Sade exhorts his fellow citizens to see the obvious error in such thinking: 'Français, vous êtes trop éclairés pour ne pas sentir qu'un nouveau gouvernement va nécessiter de nouvelles mœurs ; il est impossible que le citoyen d'un Etat libre se conduise comme l'esclave d'un roi despote [...].' (*Philosophie*, 501–502)[28] Once again, Sade plays to his audience's vanity in urging them to break through existing societal and moral barriers. Comparing adherence to old morals to a form of slavery is a calculated means to appeal to Republican freedom, although Sade himself continued to desire the personal benefits of a hierarchical society. He then points out that the obvious differences between free men necessarily demand a new comportment, between men and within the law.

Sade goes on to demonstrate how Frenchmen have already broken old societal and legal barriers, by committing courageous acts that were widely regarded as illegal before the Revolution:

Une foule de petites erreurs, de petits délits sociaux, considérés comme très essentiels sous le gouvernement des rois [...] vont devenir nuls ici ; d'autres forfaits, connus sous les noms de régicide ou de sacrilège, sous un gouvernement qui ne connaît plus ni rois ni religion, doivent s'anéantir de même dans un Etat républicain. (*Philosophie*, 501–502)[29]

---

27 'Law is the expression of the general will. [...] It must be the same for all, whether it protects or punishes. All citizens, being equal in the eyes of the law, are equally eligible for all dignities, public positions, and occupations, according to their abilities and without any distinction except that of their virtues and talents.'

28 'Frenchmen, you are too intelligent to fail to sense that new government will require new manners. That the citizens of a free state conduct themselves like a despotic king's slaves is unthinkable [...].' (*Philosophy*, 307)

29 'A crowd of minor faults and of little social indelicacies, thought of as very fundamental indeed under the rule of kings [...] are due to become as nothing with us; other crimes with which we are acquainted under the names of regicide and sacrilege, in a system where kings and religion will be unknown, in the same way must be annihilated in a republican State.' (*Philosophy*, 307)

Sade here reminds his audience that they are already guilty of crimes under the old regime, and as such, can only recognize the need for new laws and morals. A republic, free from religious and legislative tyrants, must accord substantial freedoms to its citizens. A Sadean republic requires a version of fraternity, but no universal laws,[30] concepts which were irreducibly joined for the Revolution's theorists. Sadean political theory inscribes exclusion, since men must be allowed the freedom to operate outside of socially accepted boundaries.

The world created in *Philosophie dans le boudoir*, and the rules for a new society laid out in its *Français, encore un effort* represent Sade's attempt to tempt his audience into accepting and expanding the freedoms presented by the Revolution, by crossing and destroying many of the barriers established by old morals. Once students were indoctrinated, both physically and logically, in the new libertine-inspired fashion to accept ultimate freedom, they would go on to become ideal citizens, defending and upholding personal liberty at all costs. Libertine education would provide a solid basis for future societal interaction, eliminating the need for laws and ensuring that everyone could fulfil his or her potential. This concept of educating the individual for the betterment of society reaches back to Rousseau and is taken up by German Idealism; it is in itself is not a new idea. However, for Sade, the individual could only attain his full potential in complete independence, from the law as well as from those around him. As Sade frequently noted, 'la philosophie doit tout dire' (philosophy must say everything),[31] but he felt that truth is only possible in absolute freedom. In order to achieve the freedom to say everything, it might be necessary to crush those who would cling to traditional codes and beliefs. For instance, as a final exam of sorts, Eugénie, *Philosophie*'s libertine protégée, is encouraged to destroy her mother, the one person who tries to interfere with her new-found freedoms. This symbolic destruction of the old ways is Sade's not-so-subtle message to his readers that only through the suffering of the mother can the child truly be free. Extending this metaphor to the nation, for Sade, France could only experience real freedom once all traces of the past have been wiped clean. While the idea of 'la patrie' is frequently associated with the father, in France the nation is frequently portrayed as a female character. In addition to this common trope, there is a libertine rationale behind the decision to torture the mother. Sade begins Eugénie's tale by telling the reader that the father has already granted permission both for the daughter's education and the mother's punishment, showing that both females are ultimately answerable to

---

30 Hunt, *Family Romance*, 136.
31 Donatien Alphonse François de Sade, *Œuvres complètes*, ed. by Gilbert Lely, 16 vols (Paris: Au Cercle du livre précieux, 1967), IX, p. 586; *Histoire de Juliette ou les Prosperités du vice*.

male authority. In none of Sade's works is a female ever granted absolute authority, meaning that the women remain ultimately subject to male power.

The Marquis de Sade sought to shock and seduce the reader through alternating scenes of sex and philosophy, thus luring the audience into accepting his political beliefs. The use of explicit descriptions removes the reader from his comfort zone, leaving him open to a new and perhaps more visceral way of thinking about politics. Sade felt that if his fellow countrymen would only make a bit more effort, they would be able to break through old boundaries and arrive at a new, freer society. For Sade, the Revolution was an essential Event, a moment to push for promised freedoms, and he believed that the potential existed to create a new Utopia, in which citizens would have almost limitless freedom. Sade the politician militated for expanding the promised liberty of the Revolution, while Sade the writer realized that society would probably never achieve the complete freedom he required. As a result, he chose to ridicule and break down barriers in the only way available to him, by writing tongue-in-cheek representations of the Revolutionary ideals.

La Philosophie dans le boudoir was composed during a time of uncertainty, but unlike the years of the Terror, 1795 offered some hope for the future. Robespierre and his cohorts had been, for the most part, executed and France was moving to a new form of government, which seemed willing to respect the freedoms gained by the Revolution, but without the violence and extreme chaos of the past two years. For Sade, this critical time would represent the Revolution's ultimate testing ground. It was the moment to decide the future of France, and Sade saw it as the last barrier to be crossed on the way to absolute freedom. He was unwilling to return to the abuses of the Ancien Régime, but he proved unable to adapt to the coming Empire. Sade needed to remain in some sort of revolution and felt that the country could only benefit from continued, and yet limited, chaos.

Impossible Crossings

Friedrich Hölderlin's *Hyperion* and the Aesthetic Foundation of Democracy

Jakob Ladegaard

In *De l'Allemagne* (1810) Madame de Staël helped establish what Frederick C. Beiser has since termed 'the myth of the apolitical German',[1] when she claimed that the flowering of German art and philosophy in the last years of the eighteenth century happened at the expense of the German intellectuals' practical engagement with the socio-economically backward and politically instable conglomeration of small states in the Holy Roman Empire of the German Nation. While French writers were involved in political struggles in the years following the revolution of 1789, she believed, their German neighbours were content to pursue freedom in the ephemeral realm of speculations and poetical dreams.[2]

If this myth has continued to live on into the present, this might not least be due to the prominent place of autonomous art in the works of many of the most important German philosophers and writers of the 1790s inspired by Kantian aesthetics, such as Friedrich Schiller, and the founders of the *Frühromantik* (the brothers Schlegel, Novalis and others) and associated writers like the young Hegel and Friedrich Hölderlin. For it has repeatedly been claimed that this concept of art, accompanied by the invention of the solitary genius and the institutionalisation of the private consumption of art works, provoked a split between the realms of aesthetics and progressive politics.[3]

The durability of this view could be one of the reasons why the question of politics was generally treated as a secondary matter in Hölderlin's writings

---

1   Frederick C. Beiser, *Enlightenment, Revolution, and Romanticism: The Genesis of Modern German Political Thought, 1790–1800* (Cambridge and London: Harvard University Press, 1992), pp. 7–10.
2   Germaine de Staël, *De l'Allemagne*, 2 vols (Paris: Flammerion, 1968), I, pp. 55–57.
3   This claim has been central to critics related to the Frankfurt School, such as Georg Lukács, in his 'Hölderlins *Hyperion*' (1st edn 1934), in *Goethe und seine Zeit* (Bern: A. Francke Verlag, 1947), pp. 110–127, Herbert Marcuse, in his 'Über den affirmativen Charakter der Kultur' (1st edn 1937), in *Kultur und Gesellschaft*, vol. 1. (Frankfurt a. M.: Suhrkamp Verlag, 1965), pp. 56–101, and Peter Bürger in his *Theorie der Avantgarde* (Frankfurt a. M.: Suhrkamp Verlag, 1974), pp. 49–63.

until the 1960s.[4] Only in 1969 did the appearance of Pierre Bertaux' controversial *Hölderlin und die Französische Revolution* spark a broader interest in the politics of Hölderlin's writings resulting in important work by Bernhard Böschenstein, Manfred Frank, Gerhard Kurz and others. Surprisingly, even though Hölderlin's epistolary novel *Hyperion oder der Eremit in Griechenland* (1797–99) is not only one of his most overtly political works, but also subtly dramatizes many of the key political issues of German aesthetic thinking of the 1790s, it has not played a prominent part in these attempts at re-interpreting Hölderlin, which have instead mainly focused on his late poetry (1800–6).[5] Thus, two of the most influential interpretations of the novel – Georg Lukács' 1934 essay 'Hölderlins *Hyperion*' and Lawrence Ryan's *Hölderlins 'Hyperion': Exzentrische Bahn und Dichterberuf* (1965) – rely heavily on the 'myth of the apolitical German'.

In Lukács' view, the story of the young Hyperion, who leaves the Greek island of his childhood to revive the democratic ideals of antiquity, only to see his hopes shattered in the unsuccessful uprising against the Ottoman occupation in 1770, reflects Hölderlin's commitment to both the republican values of the French Revolution and the impossibility of imagining a 'bourgeois revolution' in the Germany of his time.[6] After the failed uprising, Hyperion is abandoned by his fellow freedom-fighter, Alabanda, and his beloved Diotima, who dies in his absence. He finds some consolation in nature and in the letters he writes to a certain Bellarmin recounting his adventures. These letters make up the entire novel except for a few letters written by the young Hyperion and Diotima during the insurrection. But according to Lukács, this only amounts to a 'despairing mysticism' that affirms the fundamental irreconcilability of 'the iron hand of economic and social development' and the secluded life in harmony with nature's beauty.[7]

Lawrence Ryan reverses Lukács' evaluation of the two poles in the dichotomy between political action and poetic withdrawal. He seeks to demonstrate that the hero's reflections on his past through the process of narration to Bellarmin lead to a gradual acceptance of his former actions. For Ryan, this reconciliation, mediated by the retrospective letters, spells the coming of age of Hyperion as a poet. What for Lukács is the necessary de-

---

4   Heidegger's influential post-war interpretation of Hölderlin as the poet of 'Being' also contributed to this tendency. See e.g. Martin Heidegger, "'… Dichterisch wohnet der Mensch…'", in *Vorträge und Aufsätze* (Pfullingen: Verlag Günther Neske, 1954), pp. 187–206.
5   This relative neglect testifies to a continuing marginalisation of Hölderlin's only novel in the reception of his work. There are some exceptions, especially noteworthy is a recent anthology edited by Hansjörg Bay, *Hyperion – Terra Incognita – Expeditionen in Hölderlins Roman* (Wiesbaden: Westdeutscher Verlag, 1998).
6   Lukács, 'Hölderlins *Hyperion*', 116. The translations of Lukács from the German are mine.
7   Lukács, 'Hölderlins *Hyperion*', 116, 123. For a similar interpretation of the novel, see Günther Mieth, *Friedrich Hölderlin: Dichter der bürgerlich-demokratischen Revolution* (Berlin: Rütten & Loening, 1978), pp. 54–63.

feat of the isolated revolutionary, for Ryan becomes the triumph of the solitary genius mediating action and thought, nature and idea through literature.[8]

Even though both critics recognise the political theme in *Hyperion*, thereby partly puncturing the 'myth of the apolitical German', they reinstall it on another level by claiming that Hyperion's withdrawal into a world of natural and artistic beauty spells a farewell to politics. This, in my view, is an over-simplification of Hölderlin's meditation on art and – particularly democratic – politics. I will argue that his novel does not neatly separate the two realms. Rather, it both unites and separates them in a paradoxical knot which writing does not untie, but rather strengthens. This knot, I will further argue, also ties Hölderlin's novel into German aesthetic thinking of the 1790s, in particular to one of its main aesthetic-political works, Friedrich Schiller's *Über die ästhetische Erziehung des Menschen in einer Reihe von Briefen* (1795). My interpretation of this central paradox in Hölderlin's novel is inspired by the recent work on aesthetics and politics by the French philosopher Jacques Rancière. Since this work might be unfamiliar for some readers, I will begin by briefly outlining its main points of interest for a discussion of democratic politics in 1790s German aesthetics.

Rancière and the Politics of Art

Rancière started his philosophical career as a student of Louis Althusser, to whose *Lire le capital* (1965) he contributed. But since the 1970s Rancière has developed an independent theory of radical democracy comparable to the ones advanced by Alain Badiou, Étienne Balibar and Claude Lefort. For Rancière the term democracy does not denote a specific form of government. In order to understand this we might evoke Aristotle's definition of man as a political animal endowed with rational speech enabling him to address matters of justice and injustice, good and evil, in a common world. This ability, according to Aristotle, sets him apart from other animals whose voices only express private pain or pleasure.[9]

The Aristotelian definition is for Rancière not just an anthropological truism. It addresses, more profoundly, the logic of division working *within* any social order between those included in the common world of rational political discourse, and those whose speech can only be heard as the expression of particular and private interests. This fundamental division in every

8   Lawrence Ryan, *Hölderlins 'Hyperion': Exzentrische Bahn und Dichterberuf* (Stuttgart: J. B. Metzler, 1965), pp. 229–236. Ryan's argument is the main inspiration for M.H. Abrams' reading of *Hyperion* in his influential *Natural Supernaturalism: Tradition and Revolution in Romantic Literature* (New York: W.W. Norton, 1971), pp. 237–244.

9   Aristotle, *The Politics and The Constitution of Athens*, ed. by Stephen Everson (Cambridge: Cambridge University Press, 1996), repr. 2008, p. 13.

social order Rancière has termed 'le partage du sensible': the distribution of social occupations based on 'natural' links between ways of being, speaking, and acting that divide political man from the men and women destined to be ruled.[10]

Democracy, in Rancière's sense, is the name of the historical moments in which this fundamental inequality is addressed and altered through emancipatory actions by subdued groups seeking to demonstrate that their speech is rational discourse addressing a common world, and that they are therefore entitled to the same rights as the ones in power. Democracy is a conflictual and fundamentally creative practice that makes visible the democratic axiom of radical equality on the political stage and momentarily disrupts the dominating logic and unquestioned presuppositions of the social order in an act that reveals its fundamental contingency.[11]

For Rancière, art is political insofar as it is involved in the struggle over this fundamental *partage*. The basic characteristics and possibilities of this involvement are, according to Rancière, shaped by the logics of three historical *art regimes* – the ethic, the representative, and the aesthetic – dominating the history of Western art. A regime of art is a discursive logic that identifies art as a specific object with its own way of being, its own functions and history, while at the same time regulating the conditions of art's relation to the surrounding social order.[12] Since the three regimes of art rest on incompatible axioms, Rancière's history of art is one of ruptures.[13]

One of the deciding breaks in this history takes place in the second half of the eighteenth century, when the aesthetic regime replaces the representative regime that dominated the classical era and whose arche-text is the *Poetics* of Aristotle. This text defines the art of writing as a specific *techné* calculated to obtain a certain effect. The point of departure of this procedure is the separation between the high or low nature of the subject matter to be represented, each of which has its appropriate genres and a possible range of characters that must speak and act according to their noble or base nature.[14] This defining hierarchy establishes an analogy with a hierarchical so-

---

10 Jacques Rancière, *Disagreement: Politics and Philosophy* (1995), translated by Julie Rose (Minneapolis and London: University of Minnesota Press, 1999), pp. 1–12.

11 Rancière, *Disagreement*, 99–101.

12 Jacques Rancière, *Le partage du sensible: Esthétique et politique* (Paris: La Fabrique, 2000), p. 30.

13 Although Rancière himself has pointed out that his artistic regimes resemble what Michel Foucault in the field of epistemology has termed an *episteme*, it is important to note that Rancière's regimes, although dominating in different historical epochs, are never exclusively tied to a certain space and time, but can lend themselves to forms of re-articulations and re-inventions and therefore clash in certain epochs. Cf. Rancière, *Le partage du sensible*, 13 and 'Literature, Politics, Aesthetics – Approaches to Democratic Disagreement', *SubStance* 92 (2000) 3–24, 13.

14 Aristotle, *Poetics*, translated by George Whalley (Montreal and Buffalo: McGill-Queen's University Press, 1997), pp. 51–57.

cial order where those possessing noble virtues and performing heroic actions must govern those who are merely born to reproduce their material existence.[15]

When it comes to defining the relation between art and politics in the aesthetic regime, Rancière returns repeatedly to German aesthetics of the 1790s, where, he claims, aesthetic art is founded on a series of paradoxes between singularity and universality, autonomy and heteronomy. Even though he rarely discusses the founding philosophical work of this era, Kant's *Kritik der Urteilskraft* (1790), it serves to illustrate his line of thinking. Kant asserts the freedom of the artist. This creative autonomy dismisses any hierarchy of high and low subject matters and any proper ways of treating them in specific styles and genres, and thereby undermines the very foundations of classicist poetics. In Rancière's view, this implicates the breakdown of any objective, pragmatic criterion for separating art and non-art.[16] From now on art can be anything, and everything can become art. In principle, it follows that the creation and reception of art works are open to everyone: no knowledge of pre-established norms any longer separates those who have the skill to make and appreciate art from those who do not. This does not mean that everything *is* art or that the art world is in practice equally open to anyone, but only that there are no necessary objective preconditions for creating art and that it is impossible to determine in advance what objects might give rise to an aesthetic experience.

At the same time, however, Kant both defends the idea of the artist as an individual genius and defines the aesthetic experience in the singular as a pleasant and harmonious 'free play' ('freies Spiel') between understanding and sensory perception, which suspends our everyday relation with things where the understanding actively forms the raw material of perception.[17] But both the creative and perceptive singularity and autonomy of art are countered by a principle of universality and normativity. Thus, Kant claims, the free creation of genius necessarily incarnates a universal aesthetic idea unknowable to the artist, which symbolically expresses the ethical laws of a common world, and the experience of beauty is accompanied by the feeling of necessity.[18] In short, Kant identifies art as at once singular and universal, autonomous and heteronomous, separated and inseparable from common life. According to Rancière, this is the abstract, paradoxical logic on which the aesthetic regime and German aesthetic thinking of the 1790s is founded.

---

15 Rancière, *Le partage du sensible*, 28–31, and 'The Politics of Literature', *SubStance* 103 (2004) 10–24, 13.

16 Rancière, *Le partage du sensible*, 32–33.

17 Immanuel Kant, *Kritik der Urteilskraft*, vol 10 of *Werke in zwölf Bänden*, ed. by Wilhelm Weischedel (Frankfurt a. M.: Suhrkamp, 1974), pp. 132–134.

18 Kant, *Kritik der Urteilskraft*, 249–250 and 157–160.

In Rancière's view, the first and most influential attempt to think through the paradoxes of the aesthetic regime in political terms was Schiller's *Über die ästhetische Erziehung des Menschen*.[19] This work starts out with a brief analysis of the French Revolution, the course of which according to Schiller had revealed a fatal gap between the elites and the common people: while the first were absorbed in vain theoretical discussions, the others satisfied their animal appetites.[20] The remedy that Schiller proposes to close this gap is autonomous art. The logic behind this proposal is simple: if the condition of pleasurable harmony and *equality* between understanding and sense perception in the aesthetic free play is achievable for every individual, it must also be achievable for society as such, and thus must be able to unite the social representatives of understanding and sensuality: the elite and the people. Thus the withdrawal of art from life for Schiller paradoxically promises a state of freedom, equality and pleasure which he called the 'aesthetic state' ('Ästhetischer Staat') in which art and life are no longer separated.[21] This interpretation of Kant implies that the autonomy of art is from the beginning inextricably linked to an idea of a common world in which autonomous art as such has disappeared.

The early romantics and Idealists made this fusion of art and life their political ideal, and subsumed both the good and the true under the idea of beauty. Thus the author of the so-called *Älteste Systemprogramm des deutschen Idealismus* (1796/7),[22] which has often been read as a philosophical programme of romanticism, announces that poetry must again become 'die Lehrerin der Menscheit' and 'so müssen endlich Aufgeklärte und Unaufgeklärte sich die Hand reichen, [...] dann herrscht allgemeine Freiheit und Gleichheit der Geister!'[23] The 'once again' of the 'Systemprogramm' refers to the conception of Greek antiquity as a realisation of the ideal of art as the expression of communal life. This idea had immense importance for German aesthetic thinking in the 1790s. For Schiller, too, the aesthetic state

19 Rancière, *Le partage du sensible*, 39, and 'The Aesthetic Revolution and its Outcomes', *New Left Review* 14 (2002) 133–151.
20 Friedrich Schiller, *Über die ästhetische Erziehung des Menschen in einer Reihe von Briefen*, vol 5 of *Sämtliche Werke*, ed. by Gerhard Fricke and Herbert G. Göpfert (Munich: Carl Hanser, 1980), pp. 570- 669, 580.
21 Schiller, *Über die ästhetische Erziehung*, 667.
22 This manuscript has been attributed to both Hölderlin, Schelling and Hegel. It seems now that Hegel was its original author, but the ideas presented in it were inspired by Hölderlin's early drafts of *Hyperion*. Cf. Christoph Jamme and Helmut Schneider, eds, *Mythologie der Vernunft: Hegels 'ältestes Systemprogramm' des deutschen Idealismus* (Frankfurt a. M.: Suhrkamp, 1984), pp. 43–46. Jamme's and Schneider's book contains a critical edition of the 'Systemprogramm' (pp. 11–14) to which I refer in the following as 'Systemprogramm'.
23 'Systemprogramm', 11–12. 'So the enlightened and the unenlightened finally have to shake hands, [...] then general freedom and equality of spirits will rule!' Translation by Oliver Berghof (2000), http://public.csusm.edu/oberghof/www/translation/hegel.html. Last accessed 28 March 2012.

was to be a recreation of the Greek past on a higher, more conscious level. What for the Greeks was the necessary expression of a shared poetic vision of a common world would for the moderns living in a time of fragmentation and individuality have to be created through the singular moments of autonomous art. This also constitutes the basic logic of the idea of the 'new mythology' proposed by the 'Systemprogramm' and developed by Friedrich Schlegel and Schelling in the following years.[24]

Contrary to what has often been claimed, the 1790s do not just give birth to the solitary genius and the autonomy of art, they also invent the idea of the people as artist. And, more importantly, both ideas are logically developed out of the abstract paradoxes in Kantian aesthetics. Schiller's aesthetic education and the new mythology of romanticism place the two poles of the aesthetic paradox in an historical continuum. They confine the elements of necessity and collectivity to Greek antiquity, while making freedom and singularity the marks of sentimental (Schiller) or romantic (Schlegel) poetry in the modern age. Schiller's *Über die ästhetische Erziehung des Menschen* plays a crucial role in Hölderlin's thinking,[25] but contrary to his teacher's, his work shows an acute awareness of the *aporias* inherent in the democratic promise of autonomous art, and *Hyperion* constitutes one of his most sustained and highly original meditations on them. In a central passage, the protagonist claims that the Heraclitian formula of organic totality 'das Eine in sich selber unterschiedne' expresses the very essence of beauty.[26] But as we shall see, Hölderlin does not think of this unity of separation and wholeness in terms of harmony, but in terms of continuous struggle and tension.

---

24 For a discussion of the subtle differences between these similar ideas see Karl-Heinz Bohrer, 'Friedrich Schlegels Rede über die Mythologie', in *Mythos und Moderne: Begriff und Bild einer Rekonstruktion*, ed. by Karl-Heinz Bohrer (Frankfurt a. M.: Suhrkamp, 1983), pp. 52–82.
25 Hölderlin told Niethammer in a letter dated February 24th 1796 that his proposed contribution to Niethammer's *Philosophisches Journal* was to be called *Neue Briefe über die ästhetische Erziehung des Menschen*. Friedrich Hölderlin, *Sämtliche Werke und Briefe*, 2 vols, ed. by Günther Mieth, 1st edn 1970 (München: Carl Hanser Verlag, 1978), II, pp. 689–690. This contribution was never written, but it is probable that the ideas that it was to deal with were instead worked out in *Hyperion*. Cf. Dieter Henrich, *Der Grund im Bewusstsein: Untersuchungen zu Hölderlins Denken (1794/95)* (Stuttgart: Klett-Cotta, 1992), pp. 266–285.
26 Friedrich Hölderlin, *Hyperion*, in *Werke und Briefe*, I, pp. 575–744, 660. Quotations from this edition will be referred to as *Hyperion* plus page number. 'the one differentiated in itself', Friedrich Hölderlin, *Hyperion*, translated by Willard R. Trask (New York and Toronto: The New American Library, 1965), p. 93. All subsequent English quotations from *Hyperion* are from this edition and will be referred to as Trask plus page number.

Between the Islands of Beauty and the Mainland of Politics

This tension is present in the novel from the very beginning. In the first letters to Bellarmin, Hyperion recounts how he grew up on the beautiful island of Tina. One day, the older Adamas introduces him to the heroic age of ancient Greece in the shape of Homer, Plutarch's *Lives* and the forgotten ruins scattered in the Greek landscape (*Hyperion*, 588–590). This encounter shatters his age of innocence, but replaces its oblivious fullness with ideals that he will faithfully commit himself to realising in the social world. He leaves his parents, defying their prosaic wishes for his future, and goes to Smyrna, where he meets the former sailor Alabanda.

Like Hyperion, Alabanda is seized by the desire to radically transform society, and like his friend he is deeply disappointed with the people's docility under the absolutist Turkish rule. But while Alabanda is part of a secret society dedicated to the violent undermining of the social order and, furthermore, defends the principle of a strong state that can force people to be good,[27] Hyperion does not reserve any place for a state in the coming community (*Hyperion*, 607).[28] And although Alabanda's elitist voluntarism holds some fascination for him, he insists that the force of a few can never engender virtue in the many. But since the present state of inequality has depraved the oppressed to the point where they are blind to their own lack of freedom and unable to recognise the truth of their self-appointed liberators, Hyperion cannot envisage any other means of change than divine intervention. 'Da hilft', he says, 'der Regen vom Himmel allein.' (*Hyperion*, 607)[29]

Meeting Diotima and visiting the ruins of ancient Athens, however, make him realise that the coming community can be built on art. Diotima, who lives on the island of Kalaurea, is the very incarnation of beauty ('Sein

---

27 Both Alabanda's sectarianism and his defence of a strong state link him to the ideas of the French Jacobins.

28 Christoph Prignitz argues that Hyperion's critique of the state is in line with the critique of paternalism and the ideas of a minimal state founded on reason known from liberal *Aufklärer* such as Wilhelm von Humboldt and Immanuel Kant; cf. Christoph Prignitz, *Friedrich Hölderlin: Die Entwicklung seines politischen Denkens unter dem Einfluß der Französischen Revolution* (Hamburg: Helmut Buske Verlag, 1976), pp. 164–168. However, Kant in principle separates state politics from civil society and ethics, as in his famous remark that a state of reason can function even in a society of devils. Cf. Immanuel Kant, *Zum ewigen Frieden: Ein philosophischer Entwurf*, in *Werke in zwölf Bänden*, ed. by Wilhelm Weischedel (Frankfurt a. M.: Suhrkamp Verlag, 1977), repr. 1996, XI, pp. 191–151, 224. Hyperion compares the state to the walls around the garden of society and rhetorically asks Alabanda: 'Aber was hilft die Mauer um den Garten, wo der Boden dürre liegt?' (*Hyperion*, 607) 'But is the wall around the garden of any help when the soil lies parched?' (Trask, 44) What Hyperion desires is not a liberal state, but an organic society, where individual freedom is inseparable from collective *ethos*. The logical consequence of this way of thinking is the dissolution of the state altogether. This radical idea had already been set forth in the 'Systemprogramm' (pp. 11–12) and was to become a common theme in early romanticism.

29 'Only the rain from heaven helps then.' (Trask, 44)

Name ist Schönheit'),[30] and Hyperion's relationship with her is represented as a return to his childhood experience of oneness with nature (*Hyperion*, 630). Diotima is a stranger to words; she prefers singing or remaining silent (*Hyperion*, 632). This silence also invades Hyperion's letters about her, where he often complains about the impossibility of bringing back her presence through writing (*Hyperion*, 631–636).

Following the logic of his definition of beauty as 'das Eine in sich selber unterschiedne', Hyperion's oneness with Diotima is also marked by division. He often finds himself gently refused by his mistress, and his relationship with her becomes one of incessant approach and retreat. In a central passage, he writes:

> So bedürfnislos, so göttlichgenügsam hab ich nichts gekannt. Wie die Woge des Ozeans das Gestade seliger Inseln, so umflutete mein ruheloses Herz den Frieden des himmlischen Mädchens. Ich hatt ihr nichts zu geben, als ein Gemüt voll wilder Widersprüche, […] sie aber stand vor mir in wandelloser Schönheit, mühelos, in lächelnder Vollendung da,… (*Hyperion*, 635)[31]

This passage echoes the description of the ancient statue of a goddess known as the Juno Ludovisi in the important 15th letter of Schiller's *Über die ästhetische Erziehung des Menschen*:

> In sich selbst ruhet und wohnt die ganze Gestalt, eine völlig geschlossene Schöpfung, und als wenn sie jenseits des Raumes wäre, ohne Nachgeben, ohne Widerstand; da ist keine Kraft, die mit Kräften kämpfte, keine Blöße, wo die Zeitlichkeit einbrechen könnte. Durch jenes unwiderstehlich ergriffen und angezogen, durch dieses in der Ferne gehalten, befinden wir uns zugleich in dem Zustand der höchsten Ruhe und der höchsten Bewegung, und es entsteht jene wunderbare Rührung, für welche der Verstand keinen Begriff und die Sprache keinen Namen hat.[32]

What Schiller describes through the example of the Greek statue is of course nothing other than the specific experience of autonomous art. By alluding to Schiller's statue in his description of Diotima, Hyperion suggests that she is a living incarnation of autonomous art offering Hyperion an essentially private

---

30 *Hyperion*, 629. 'Its name is beauty.' (Trask, 65)
31 'Such freedom from wants, such divine content I have never found before. As the ocean swells about the shores of happy isles, so the peace of the heavenly maiden flowed about my restless heart. I had nothing to give her except a mind full of wild contradictions […] but she stood before me in changeless beauty, effortless, in smiling perfection.' (Trask, 71)
32 Schiller, *Über die ästhetische Erziehung des Menschen*, 618–619. 'The whole figure reposes and dwells in itself, a creation completely self-contained, and as if existing beyond space, neither yielding nor resisting; here is no force to contend with force, no frailty where temporality might break in. Irresistibly moved and drawn by those former qualities, kept at a distance by these latter, we find ourselves at one and the same time in a state of utter repose and supreme agitation, and there results that wondrous stirring of the heart for which mind has no concept nor speech any name.' Friedrich Schiller, *On the Aesthetic Education of Man in a Series of Letters*, translated by Elizabeth M. Wilkinson and L.A. Willoughby (Oxford, Clarendon Press, 1967), p. 109.

pleasure far from the world of politics.[33] But just as Schiller saw the signs of
the Athenian people's freedom in the features of the statue, Hyperion sees
Diotima's beauty as a confirmation of the possibility of a return of a community expressing its freedom and collective identity through art. Diotima
convinces him that he must bring the promise of free art to the mainland by
becoming the people's aesthetic educator (*Hyperion*, 654–669). With this idea,
the first volume of *Hyperion* ends.

At the beginning of the second, Hyperion receives a letter from Alabanda inciting him to join the fight against the Turkish army, which has begun
on the mainland. Hyperion instantly decides to participate in this revolutionary action, which, as Hannah Arendt says, before anything else always at-
tests to the greatest human faculty, the ability to realise freedom in a new
beginning.[34] The older Hyperion's account of the arrival of the letter, however, is heavy with dire foreboding, inscribing the tragic end in the new beginning. His premonitions particularly concern Diotima and correspond to
her own sense that Hyperion's absence will kill her. At their departure, he
writes retrospectively: 'Diotima stand, wie ein Marmorbild, und ihre Hand
starb fühlbar in meiner. [...] und [ich] stand wie ein Betender, vor der hol-
den Statue.' (*Hyperion*, 682)[35] Bearing in mind the reference to Schiller's statue, this is a significant choice of words disclosing the philosophical logic
behind the sentimental figure of a lover's death from grief. Diotima is the
incarnation of the attraction/repulsion of the autonomous art work. The
separation of the lovers marks a dislocation in her being towards the pole of
repulsion symbolised by her stone-like impenetrability. In other words, she
dies as presence and private pleasure and turns into a sign, a promise of a
future community like the ruins of antiquity scattered in the Greek landscape.

The parting of the lovers thus functions as a dramatization of the logic
of the political promise of autonomous art: it must die as art separated from
communal life to be re-born in a state, where nothing separates the two.
Schiller tried to solve this paradox by envisaging a gradual, historical development between the poles of autonomy and heteronomy. But in Hölderlin's
novel no aesthetic education allows art to cross the void between the island
of private singularity and the mainland of universal politics. Not because
Hyperion does not try. His letters from the battlefields recount how he gathers his troops of mountaineers to tell them about the greatness of ancient
Greece, but despite his efforts to mediate between the ruins of the past and
the actions of the living, it becomes all too clear that his project has failed,

33 This political isolation is further stressed by the fact that Kalaurea remained independent during the Ottoman occupation of Greece.
34 Hannah Arendt, *On Revolution* (New York: Penguin Books, 1963), repr. 1991, p. 35.
35 'Diotima stood like a marble statue and I felt her hand die in mine. [...] and I stood like a
supplicant before that lovely statue.' (Trask, 113)

when his men massacre the innocent inhabitants of Misistra (*Hyperion*, 694–700).

The novel offers two ways of interpreting this failure. Hyperion at first blames his troops' lack of ability to convert their aesthetic education into virtuous action: 'Es war ein außerordentlich Projekt, durch eine Räuberbande mein Elysium zu pflanzen.' (*Hyperion*, 699)[36] The readiness with which Hyperion draws this conclusion reveals that its elitist premise, the ungenerous view of the people, which was already latent in his discussions with Alabanda in Smyrna, was never far from the surface. The other explanation for the failure centres on the relationship between men and gods (or, in Idealist terms, the absolute). The young Hyperion's letters from the battlefield show a growing tendency towards valuing his current adventures more highly than those of the ancients. At one point he writes:

> Diotima! Ich möchte dieses werdende Glück nicht um die schönste Lebenszeit des alten Griechenlands vertauschen, und der kleinste unsrer Siege ist mir lieber, als Marathon und Thermopylä und Platea. Ist's nicht wahr? Ist nicht dem Herzen das genesende Leben mehr wert, als das reine, das die Krankheit noch nicht kennt? Erst wenn die Jugend hin ist, lieben wir sie, und dann erst, wenn die verlorne wiederkehrt, beglückt sie alle Tiefen der Seele. (*Hyperion*, 696)[37]

In Hölderlin's cosmology, the ancients were as close to the gods as humanly possible, and the degradation of antiquity therefore equals *hubris*. From that perspective, the disaster at Misistra is the gods' *nemesis*. As Hyperion writes to Diotima: 'Bei der heiligen Nemesis! Mir ist recht geschehn.' (*Hyperion*, 699)[38] In the following he also often compares himself to King Oedipus, Sophocles' tragic hero, who is quoted in the epigraph of the second volume of *Hyperion*. It is important to note that the category of *hubris* in Hölderlin's tragic thinking, which he developed in *Der Tod des Empedocles* (1797–99), while writing the second half of *Hyperion*, and his later translations of Sophocles, cannot be understood as Christian sin or moral transgression. Rather, for Hölderlin, *hubris* designates an admirable attempt to approach the unlimited by overcoming the positive forms of the given world. The tragic hero is the favourite of the gods, and only his (or her) great love of truth brings him (or her) too close to the absolute, which for Hölderlin is not accessible for man, and *nemesis* is the dramatic experience of this inaccessibility.[39] The young Hyperion's attempt to

---

36 'It was indeed a remarkable undertaking, to establish my Elysium with the help of a robber band!' (Trask, 129)

37 'Diotima! I would not change this budding happiness for the most beautiful life that was ever lived in ancient Greece, and the smallest of our victories is dearer to me than Marathon and Thermopylae and Plataea. Is it not true? Is not life recovering health more cherished than the pure life that has not yet known sickness? Not until youth is gone do we love it, not until what has been lost returns does it rejoice all the depths of the soul.' (Trask, 126)

38 'By sacred Nemesis! I have got what I deserved.' (Trask, 129)

39 Thus the relationship between the tragic hero and the gods is, as Panthea says in *Der Tod des Empedocles*, '[ein] Streit / Der Liebenden' ([a] lovers' quarrel). Hölderlin, *Werke und Briefe*, II,

establish an ideal, aesthetic community, then, is *hubris*, not because it implies the forgetting of the ancients – on the contrary, as the above quotation shows, he aspires to revive ancient Greece in new forms – but because this community is too perfect.

Lawrence Ryan points out that the older Hyperion's letters reveal a changing attitude towards his former actions due to a resignation – 'O hätte ich doch nie gehandelt!' (*Hyperion*, 582)[40] – towards reconciliation at the end of the novel, when he informs Bellarmin that he is 'ruhig' (*Hyperion*, 734).[41] For Ryan, this reconciliation does not imply that the older Hyperion now regards the insurrection as an appropriate means of realising his ideals, but only that he accepts its personal consequence, suffering.[42] But by interrupting the monologue of the older man, the letters of the young Hyperion and Diotima from the time of the uprising invite the reader to consider whether the joyful affirmation of becoming they transmit can really be subsumed under the calm, disillusioned wisdom of experience. Hyperion's use of a tragic vocabulary – not least the concept of *hubris* with its positive connotations in Hölderlin's thinking – to describe the course of events tempts us to answer this question in the negative. The point disclosed by this reference is not that revolutionary action cannot realise Hyperion's ideals, but that they cannot be realised at all. This does not disqualify the attempt. On the contrary, the failure of the revolution seen strictly from the point of view of tragedy testifies to the nobility of the intent. The reason for the older Hyperion's calmness, then, is not his acceptance of his youthful mistakes, but his recognition of the truth of new beginnings regardless of their less than perfect endings.

The two explanations of the failed uprising brought into play by the novel contradict each other. On the one hand, blaming the uneducated people for not following the example of their enlightened leaders reveals an elitist prejudice that confirms the 'myth of the apolitical German' whose artistic ideals separate him from common people and the social world. From this point of view, the Greek struggle for freedom (and the French Revolution, which is, of course, its allegorical reference) was doomed from the outset. On the other hand, Hyperion's use of the vocabulary of tragedy along with the affirmative vitality of his earlier letters conveys a positive outlook by celebrating the human ability to make new beginnings. Even though this ability

---

p. 19, ll. 146–147. For a lucid introduction to Hölderlin's theory of tragedy, including the concept of *hubris*, see Wolfgang Schadewaldt, 'Hölderlins Übersetzung des Sophokles', in Schadewaldt, *Hellas und Hesperien: Gesammelte Schriften zur Antike und neueren Literatur in zwei Bänden* (Zurich and Stuttgart: Artemis Verlag, 1960), II, pp. 261–275.

40 'Oh that I had never acted!' (Trask, 22). Cf. e.g. David Constantine, *Hölderlin* (Oxford: Clarendon Press, 1988), p. 98.

41 'at peace' (Trask, 160). Cf. Ryan, *Hölderlins 'Hyperion'*, 198.

42 Ryan, *Hölderlins 'Hyperion'*, 178–179.

is most explicitly celebrated in relation to Hyperion himself, the novel also implicitly recognises it in the masses. For Hyperion and Alabanda are not the architects of the insurrection, they join a democratic emancipation already begun by ordinary people. That the people would ever seek to liberate themselves was inconceivable from the elitist viewpoint of the two friends, who agreed in Smyrna that the people were slavish even to the point of not realising their own slavish condition. Thus, the novel contains a fundamental ambivalence in the interpretation of both the revolution and the people, which, I will argue in conclusion, is closely connected to its ambivalent view of art – in particular the art of writing.

The Ambivalences of Writing

For Lawrence Ryan, Hyperion's progress towards a synthesis of past and present, action and spirit is mediated by writing. To evaluate this interpretation, let us return to the decisive moment, when Hyperion commits himself to revolutionary action. As we recall, this decision is prompted by the arrival of Alabanda's letter. When Hyperion leaves the island, Diotima turns into a statue, symbolically announcing that the lovers are now entering a world of absence at the mercy of signs. From now on they will communicate through letters. As the further development of the political adventures show, these letters are unreliable messengers.

After the catastrophe at Misistra, Hyperion writes two letters to Diotima announcing that he plans to die in battle. Her answer never reaches him. However, he survives and writes to Diotima suggesting that they move to the Alps. With the prospect of the lovers resuming their private existence, Alabanda leaves, resigning himself to the revenge of the secret society which he has abandoned. Meanwhile, Diotima herself has died, but her farewell note only reaches Hyperion a few moments after Alabanda's departure. The letter that *does* find him, however, is his father's announcement that he disowns Hyperion because of his participation in the uprising. Abandoned, he starts wandering the earth, 'heimatlos und ohne Ruhestätte' (*Hyperion*, 702).[43]

Hyperion's political efforts are thus entirely bound up with the materiality of the written word. This must be taken into account when assessing the meaning of his future commitment to the art of writing, beginning with his declaration after his convalescence: 'Ich will mich rein erhalten, wie ein Künstler sich hält' (*Hyperion*, 709),[44] echoed by Diotima's death bed prophecy that 'die dichterischen Tage keimen dir schon' (*Hyperion*, 733).[45]

43 'homeless and without a resting place' (Trask, 132).
44 'I will keep myself pure, as an artist keeps himself.' (Trask, 138)
45 'Your days of poetry are already germinating.' (Trask, 159)

The move from politics to pure art alluded to in these sentences and understood by Ryan to constitute the apex of Hyperion's personal education, is
disturbed by the novel's dramatization of writing that does not separate it
from the orbit of politics, but tie the two together.

   To understand this paradox it is useful to remember Plato's *Phaedrus*,
where Socrates describes the nature of writing by opposing it to the spoken
word planted by the teacher in the soul of the student.[46] The written word,
Socrates explains, is a mere copy of the spoken word removed from its
sender, or as he says, its *father*. This orphan-hood of the written word entails
a double flaw: at one and the same time, Socrates says, it speaks too little
and too much. It speaks too little, because you cannot ask it what it means.
And it speaks too much, for since it travels the world without a father to
guarantee its meaning, it does not know to whom it should and should not
speak.[47] As Rancière has noted, this idea of writing as the unruly words of
anyone at all destined to no-one comes to be associated with the autonomous words of literature in the aesthetic regime of art around the time of
Hölderlin's novel. Autonomous literature is mute because it does not speak
the instrumental language of rationality, and it speaks too much because it
addresses anyone unaccompanied by any poetological rules.[48]

   For Plato, both the spoken and the written word have a parallel in the
world of politics. In his ideal state, everybody has a proper place based on a
specific harmony of thinking, doing, and speaking. This state is ruled by philosophers, who are born to look into the world of ideas hidden to common
men. While the teacher's word to the pupil is congruent with such a system,
the written word threatens to disturb it because the fatherless letters of
thought can accidentally fall into the hands of those who have no business
in politics and make them leave their places. Plato has a name for this kind
of illegitimate disturbance of the natural order: democracy.[49]

   The two modes of language and their ties to politics outlined by Socrates are both present in Hölderlin's novel. Even though Hyperion's and Alabanda's utopia is not a hierarchy but a state of equality, both share with Plato the basic ideal of a harmonic congruence between inner and outer world,

---

46 Both Hansjörg Bay and Wolfram Groddeck have detected traces of the Platonic critique of
    writing in the novel. But Groddeck does not at all and Bay does only in passing relate this to
    politics. Hansjörg Bay "'Das Zeichen zwischen mir und dir": Schriftlichkeit und Moderne im
    Hyperion', in *Hölderlin Jahrbuch* 34 (2004–5) 215–245; Wolfram Groddeck, '"Hörst Du? Hörst
    Du? Diotima's Grab!" Zur Aporie der Schriftlichkeit in den *Hyperion*-Briefen', in *Hyperion –
    Terra Incognita*, 176–189.
47 Plato, *Plato in Twelve Volumes*, translated by Harold N. Fowler (Cambridge: Harvard University
    Press, 1925), IX, p. 275.
48 Jacques Rancière, *La parole muette: Essai sur les contradictions de la littérature* (Paris: Hachette, 1998),
    pp. 81–89.
49 Plato, *The Republic*, ed. by Francis MacDonald Cornford (New York and London: Oxford
    University Press, 1941), repr. 1968, pp. 279–286.

which Hyperion envisions as the correspondence between the art work and the *ethos* of the community. And despite their love of freedom, they agree that their superior ideals qualify them to educate the people. Alabanda draws the 'Platonic' consequence of this, when he defends the rule of an enlightened state, and although Hyperion rejects this idea, his aesthetic utopia cannot free itself from the spectre of inequality. In line with this elitism, Hyperion addresses his poetic letters to Bellarmin in the spirit of the Socratic word: 'Aber nur dir, mein Bellarmin, nur einer reinen freien Seele wie die deine ist, erzähl' ich's. So freigebig, wie die Sonne mit ihren Strahlen will ich nicht seyn; meine Perlen will ich vor die alberne Menge nicht werfen.' (*Hyperion*, 646–647)[50] This wish of controlling the circulation of the written word is contradicted both by the drama of the novel and by the very act of reading a book that has travelled time and space to reach anyone but the fictitious Bellarmin. In Hyperion's story the mute chatter associated with written words is consistently allied with a democratic principle of contingency and disruptiveness. The eloquence of the half buried architraves make him leave his father, the books of antiquity make him dream of revolutions, the ruins of Athens and Diotima's silence inspire him with the ideal of an aesthetic community, and Alabanda's letter makes him cross from the island of autonomous art to the mainland of political struggle before he fittingly ends the novel walking the earth like a fatherless letter.

Hölderlin's novel thus dismantles Schiller's idea of a smooth transition from autonomous art to aesthetic politics by playing out two contradicting scenarios of its interruption against each other. The first scenario finds its model in the private singularity of beauty which Hyperion experiences with Diotima and which holds a promise of universal equality and freedom. He leaves the island of art as the prophet of this promise only to learn that the people cannot understand it. But this destiny was already inscribed in the Kantian definition of aesthetic beauty as the experience that cancels out understanding. There is nothing to understand, no positive law to abstract from the empty universality of art. Seen from this point of view, what Hölderlin dramatizes in the failure of the popular insurrection is an elitist interpretation of the 'failure' of autonomous art itself. This interpretation is congruent with the 'myth of the apolitical German', which is affirmed in Hyperion's will to withdraw his artful letters from the world and reserve his wisdom for Bellarmin.

The second scenario finds its form in the letters written by Hyperion during the insurrection, expressing the joy of freedom. His adventure is the political culmination of the series of minor emancipations caused by the

---

50 'But only to you, my Bellarmin, only to a pure, free soul like yours, do I tell it. I will not be as lavish as the sun with its rays; I will not cast my pearls before the unknowing multitude.' (Trask, 82)

chatter of mute art that animate the movements of his life. In this sense, *Hyperion* is the celebration of autonomous art's ability to lead anyone away from his or her fixed place in the social order and the governance of the enlightened elite. This ability prevents that art can ever become life in the Schillerian sense. For the uncontrollability of the meanings and directions of aesthetic art is not only the precondition of Hyperion's free wanderings, it is also the guarantee that art cannot be reduced to the fixed mirror of a social state without ceasing to be art.

The conflict between these two versions of the art of writing and their contradicting ties to elitist and democratic politics is not neatly overcome by any reflective synthesis in Hölderlin's novel, which ends with 'Nächstens mehr', promising new beginnings and committing itself to the endless wanderings of literature and democratic politics. The meanings and perspectives of these contradictions cannot be contained in the ideas of autonomous art as an antidote to politics related to the 'myth of the apolitical German'. But neither are they exhausted by the recent debates about the political content of Hölderlin's later work (1800–6) in the context of German aesthetic thinking of the 1790s, which have often exclusively been concerned with evaluating the utopia of an aesthetic community, which some have repudiated as proto-totalitarian,[51] while others have defended it in the form of an idea of aesthetic art as the medium for disinterested constructions of common values in modern societies.[52] By locating the political meaning of Hölderlin's work neither in the logic of withdrawal nor in the idea of a total union between art and life, but in the dynamic interchange between the two extremes, Rancière's approach can, I think, contribute to a fuller appreciation of the complexities and inner contradictions of Hölderlin's literary politics and its relation to German aesthetics of the 1790s. This essay has highlighted some of the ways in which these complexities are played out in *Hyperion*. Hopefully it has thereby succeeded in making a modest case for Hölderlin's only novel as a valuable point of departure for a re-reading of his mature work from a political point of view.

---

51 For example, Philippe Lacoue-Labarthe and Jean-Luc Nancy, *Le mythe nazi* (Paris: Éditions de l'Aube, 1991), repr. 2005.
52 For example, Manfred Frank, *Der kommende Gott: Vorlesungen über die Neue Mythologie* (Frankfurt a. M.: Suhrkamp, 1982).

Événements de circonstance
The Classical Tradition in the Age of Revolution

Ian Macgregor Morris / Uta Degner

> Salut, Peuple Français... C'est sous la dictée, pour ainsi dire, de vos actions et de vos sentiments, que vont parler Léonidas et ses compagnons. Les combats des Thermopyles sont devenus pour vous, après un espace de temps de deux mille deux cents soixante et onze ans, un événement de circonstance.
> (C. D'Estaing, *Les Thermopyles: Tragédie de Circonstance*, 1791)

> Hail, People of France... It is, as it were, thanks to your actions and feelings that Leonidas and his companions have found their voice. For you, the battle of Thermopylae has become, after a space of two thousand two hundred and seventy-one years, a highly topical event.[1]

When the revolutionary admiral, Charles d'Estaing, described the Battle of Thermopylae of 480 B.C. as 'un événement de circonstance', he was not indulging in mere rhetoric. Rather, he was drawing upon, and in turn developing, a complex tradition that stretched across national boundaries and political ideologies, and was deeply rooted in the cultural consciousness of eighteenth-century Europe. The relevance antiquity carried for the actors of the revolutionary age was a very real one.

The eighteenth-century engagement with antiquity was complex and, in some cases, absolute. What had previously been the 'Quarrel of Ancients and Moderns', a debate primarily centred on classical texts, became a key battleground of the *philosophes*. Yet despite a recent surge in interest in what certain English-speaking scholars have labelled 'Reception Studies', the Classical Tradition remains one of the most misunderstood features of eighteenth-century culture.[2] As Jonathan Israel has so eloquently shown, the Enlightenment can only be understood as a pan-European phenomen-

---

1 C. D'Estaing, *Les Thermopyles: Tragédie de Circonstance* (Paris: n. pub., 1791), p.16. Translated by Ian Macgregor Morris.
2 The explosion of interest in the *Nachleben* of classical texts over the last fifteen years has been greatly influenced by what can be termed the Bristol School of Reception Theory, initiated by Charles Martindale. However, their use of the terminology of Hans Robert Jauss' *Rezeptions-ästhetik* is problematic, owing much to deconstruction theory. As we do not share this methodological approach, we prefer the term 'Classical Tradition', which serves as a generic term for

on: constructs such as the 'French' or 'Scottish' Enlightenments, while useful when examining questions on a micro-scale, become a hindrance when considering the greater picture.[3] In the long eighteenth century the Classical Tradition was by definition pan-European, and what today would be termed interdisciplinary. It broke the boundaries of genre, ideology, creed, nation and language.[4] Thus, for example, the development of the historiography of Rome in the late seventeenth and early eighteenth centuries was an endeavour which brought together English Protestants, French Catholics and Scottish Jacobites into an academic community which read and critiqued each other's work.[5] Many central figures moved between the spheres of scholarship, art and politics: Robert Wood, having returned from his archaeological exploits in the Near East, found himself apologising for the lengthy delay in publishing his eagerly anticipated *magnum opus* on Homer with the memorable retort that he was busy drawing up the treaty with France. This widespread engagement with antiquity was, therefore, a particularly pertinent facet of Enlightenment culture, and one which can highlight the interaction between apparently diverse aspects of the history, art and thought of the period. It was not, of course, uniform; but it was interdependent. More-

---

the study of the 'Wirkungsgeschichte' of Antiquity without implying any specific theoretical a priori.

3 In discussing the influence of the seventeenth-century Dutch Enlightenment on the European Enlightenment, Israel remarks that 'there is scarcely any mention of such a thing [...] in the existing historiography. But the fact that so many historians have passed over the Dutch context in complete or virtual silence is not, of course, in any way a proof of its marginality'. Israel goes on to show that an understanding of the Dutch context is 'in fact indispensable to any proper grasp of the subject [...] of the European High Enlightenment as a whole.' Jonathan Israel, 'The Early Dutch Enlightenment as a Factor in the Wider European Enlightenment', in *The Early Enlightenment in the Dutch Republic – 1650–1750,* ed. by Wiep van Bunge (Leiden: Brill, 2003), p. 215. The same can be said of the Classical Tradition, in which the role of, and works written in, 'smaller' countries have been ignored. However, as Israel suggests in the case of the Dutch, all these cultures played a central role in the philosophic and cultural battles of the period. To dismiss them is to throw away one vital piece of the great puzzle, and thus risk misrepresenting the whole.

4 The organisation of modern scholarship, to some degree, hinders understanding of the Classical Tradition as a whole. The politics and practices of the various disciplines inevitably result in, indeed necessitate, the prioritisation of certain forms of evidence and methodologies. Despite the rhetoric of interdisciplinarity, few scholars have either the training, or the time, to cross disciplinary boundaries in any meaningful way. For the study of the Classical Tradition this is especially problematic, because the developments which characterised it in fields as diverse as poetry and archaeology were always interdependent. To prioritise one field at the expense of the others is to remove it from its context. As a result, the Classical Tradition is all too often dismissed as rhetoric and adornment. It is only when examined across a range of fields and disciplines that the full complexity, consistency and pervasiveness of the Tradition can be seen.

5 See Gareth Sampson, 'The Rise and Fall of the Roman Historian: the Eighteenth Century in the Roman Historical Tradition', in *Reinventing History: the Enlightenment Origins of Ancient History,* ed. by James Moore, Ian Macgregor Morris and Andrew J. Bayliss (London: Institute of Historical Research, 2008), pp. 187–218.

over, as the eighteenth century progressed the ancient world appeared increasingly *relevant* to the modern, in a multitude of ways. So much so, that in
the age of revolution calls such as D'Estaing's were the norm, and imbued
with levels of meaning which remain difficult for the historian to access. Indeed, it was in the wake of the revolutionary fixation with antiquity that
Benjamin Constant felt impelled to stress the difference of the past, and so
helped to initiate a very different relationship with the ancient world in the
nineteenth century.[6]

   In order to illustrate the above, we will briefly consider two themes,
from their generation in the work of mid-eighteenth-century British Whigs
to their realisation in the political culture of the France of the Revolutionary
period: the figure of the Spartan king Leonidas as the model of classical 'patriotism', and the link between ancient sites and the relevance of the ancient
past for the present. We will then conclude with a consideration of how
these two themes were reinvented and transformed in the death throws of
the Revolution by a German poet who sought a very different kind of revolution. Space prevents a survey of the development of these ideas, and thus
our concentration must be on their first establishment, and then their recurrence in the Revolution. The intention here is to demonstrate that it is only
possible to understand the Revolutionary period's engagement with antiquity by taking this long pan-European view. The point that Revolutionary
uses of antiquity were developments of longstanding models which were
created in very different contexts reveals both the continuities from pre-
Revolutionary thought, and the extent to which the Classical Tradition
broke boundaries throughout the Enlightenment and Revolutionary period.

   The first of these themes concerns a political model drawn from antiquity: the Spartan King Leonidas, with whom we began. Famed for his sacrifice at the battle of Thermopylae, Leonidas had long stood in the
pantheon of classical heroes. In ancient, medieval and Renaissance texts he
repeatedly appears as an exemplar of virtue, albeit as one amongst many.
However, in the eighteenth century Leonidas ceased to be merely an example of ancient virtue, and became *the* model of a form of heroic sacrifice for
the community, the 'Patriot' par excellence. The key moment in this trans-

---

6   Constant's famous speech, 'The Liberty of the Ancients compared with that of the Moderns',
    delivered at the *Athénée Royal*, can be regarded as a turning point in the Moderns' understanding of the Ancients. See *Benjamin Constant: Political Writings*, ed. and translated by Biancamaria
    Fontana (Cambridge: Cambridge University Press, 2002), pp. 309–328. In developing a theme
    first suggested by Chateaubriand, Constant stressed the incompatibility of ancient models for
    the modern world, and condemned the imitation which, he claimed, characterised the Revolution. The shift in the relationship with antiquity was of course gradual and driven by contemporary political concerns, but it could be said that while in the eighteenth century thinkers used
    antiquity to challenge the status quo, in the nineteenth century they used antiquity to legitimise
    it. See Ian Macgregor Morris, 'Navigating the *Grotesque*: or, Rethinking Greek Historiography',
    in Moore et al., *Reinventing History*, 247–290, especially pp. 258–260.

formation came with the publication of an epic poem in 1737 by a young merchant named Richard Glover. Glover's *Leonidas* was an instant success, spawning several editions, stage adaptions, translations and pictorial representations. The poem has been repeatedly dismissed by modern scholarship, and cast as little more than a party political manifesto. However, the text itself does not support the suggestion that it was composed for a particular political faction. Glover certainly had political concerns in his composition, but they were not partisan. During the years in which Glover was composing his poem, Lord Bolingbroke, who moved in the same social circles as the young poet, was developing his notion of the 'Patriot King', the ruler who is a father, even a servant, to his people.[7] Glover's Leonidas proves the ultimate Patriot King in his virtues and his actions. Moreover, the poem suggests the power of classical models, not merely as illustrative of virtues, but as agents of change in their own right.[8] The idea that political theory should be supported by historical *exemplum* would be a central feature of the eighteenth-century engagement with antiquity.

Glover's *exemplum* is no simplistic eulogy of patriotism. It presents a concrete vision not only of the virtues of the Patriot King, but of the purpose and nature of those virtues, in a manner that makes it relevant to all those wielding political authority. The character of Leonidas certainly represents the high-flown eulogies to 'liberty' familiar from much eighteenth-century poetry. But supporting this idealism is a firmer basis. The hallmark of Leonidas is not that he placed love of country over love of family, but a recognition that any division between the two is misleading, that one who dies for his country *is* dying for his family. The idea that the separation of

---

7   For an in-depth consideration of Glover's poem, see Ian Macgregor Morris, *The Age of Leonidas: Hellenism and the Classical Tradition in the Enlightenment* (forthcoming), and 'To make a new Thermopylae: Hellenism, Greek Liberation, and the Battle of Thermopylae', *Greece & Rome* 47 (2000) 211–14. The argument that Glover wrote on behalf of a political faction has been made, but not substantiated, by the following: George Saintsbury, *Cambridge History of English Literature*, 15 vols (Cambridge: Cambridge, 1907–1927), X, p. 149; Eric Rothstein, *Restoration and Eighteenth Century Poetry* (Boston: Routledge and Kegan Paul, 1981), p. 205; Lucy Sutherland, *Politics and Finance in the eighteenth century* (London: Hambledon, 1984), p. 78; Christine Gerrard, *The Patriot Opposition to Walpole: politics, poetry, and myth, 1725–1742* (Oxford: Oxford University Press, 1994), p. 80.

8   This is a notion which can be traced to antiquity itself, epitomised by Xenophon's *Cyropaedia*; it was summed up in the early eighteenth century by Maurice Ashley-Cooper, the younger brother of the Earl of Shaftesbury, in his comments on Xenophon's work: 'Hints in the Course of the Story, and the Observations that may be made upon them seem to me to let one more into political Knowledge, than most of the Books and Pamphlets that are now written upon that Subject.' 'Preface', in *Cyropaedia: or the Institution of Cyrus*, 2 vols (London: John Noon, 1728), I, p. 37. Ashley's reading of Xenophon proved highly influential on Glover. On Ashley and his translation of Xenophon, see Ian Macgregor Morris, 'Creating the Enlightenment Prince: Maurice Ashley's translation of the *Cyropaedia* of Xenophon', in *Ancient Greece in Eighteenth-century Britain: Essays on Translation and Commentary in a Tradition of Philosophy, Politics, and Culture* (= a special edition of the *Annals of Scholarship*), ed. by Martha K. Zebrowski (forthcoming).

the private and public spheres was damaging to society would prove a central tenet of the radical thinkers who venerated classical Sparta in the later eighteenth century.[9]

This line of thinking is heavily influenced by both Xenophon and Bolingbroke. Glover's vision, of a publicly minded ruling elite and citizen body, is common enough in early-modern thought. Yet, while this may appear moderate, his presentation was revolutionary. In choosing a Greek, rather than a Roman hero, Glover was aligning himself with the increasing number of thinkers who were turning to the more radical implications of classical Greece. The notion of Rome was always tainted by associations with the Church, while Greece was unambiguously pre-Christian. Furthermore the Greek city-states were, in any modern sense, anti-monarchic: Leonidas may have been a king, but it was a curious form of dual kingship, with two kings ruling concurrently and restricted by a constitution. For those seeking an alternative to modernity to counter the power of Church and King, Greece offered what has been described as a 'philosophical arsenal'.[10] While it would be going too far to describe Glover as either anti-monarchic or anti-Christian, the choice of a Greek hero did allow the creation of a patriotism shorn of these associations, and which would in turn carry significant implications for the Revolutionary Leonidas.

Glover reinforced the radical implications of his subject with a radical style. His imitation of Homer constituted a conscious rejection of the norms of neoclassical, and thus the outwardly monarchic Virgilian, epic practice. His characters, Leonidas included, show a level of character development more akin to the emerging genre of the novel, than to traditional epic.[11] This carries one of the central themes of the poem: that the virtues of Leonidas are not inborn, but consciously chosen and developed. He is inherently noble, certainly, but his heroism is characterised by a hesitancy, which renders his final sacrifice all the more noble. It is deliberately chosen, not impulsive: it is the sacrifice of a philosopher.

---

9   On this tradition see Ian Macgregor Morris, 'The Paradigm of Democracy: Sparta in the Enlightenment', in *Spartan Society*, ed. by Thomas Figueira (Swansea: Classical Press of Wales, 2004), pp. 339–362; Haydn Mason: 'Sparta and the French Enlightenment', in *Sparta in Modern Thought: Politics, History and Culture*, ed. by Stephen Hodkinson and Ian Macgregor Morris (Swansea: Classical Press of Wales, 2012), pp. 71–104.

10 Peter Gay, *The Enlightenment*, 2 vols (London: Knopf, 1966–69), I, pp. 32–44.

11 The classic statement on the difference between character in epic and novel can be found in Mikhail Bakhtin, *The Dialogic Imagination*, ed. by Michael Holquist, translated by Michael Holquist and Caryl Emerson (Austin: University of Texas Press, 1981), especially pp. 3–40. Bakhtin suggests that the epic is monologic, in that it presents one moral standpoint; and that its characters are fully developed and all action is externalised. In contrast, the novel is dialogic, presenting and even debating, contrasting moral standpoints, it presents character development, and much of the action is internalised. In this sense, Glover's poem is novelistic.

That such a model would prove popular with an eighteenth-century audience, well versed in the classics, should not be surprising. The themes Glover established in association with Leonidas would prove enduring. And yet, what is perhaps most surprising is, that, despite the very different contexts, and the very different political persuasions of later authors, the model Glover established changed little.

Glover's vision of Leonidas soon made an appearance within a very specific political context. In 1742 the Dutch poet and statesman Willem van Haren published a poem under the same name.[12] Van Haren clearly knew of Glover's poem, but sought to draw on Glover's model for the very specific purpose of attacking the incumbent government of the Dutch Republic.[13] In the ongoing struggle between the States General – the body which represented the seven provinces – and the House of Orange, the Orangists saw an opportunity in the States General's failure to honour the treaty with Maria Theresa of Austria. It was in this scenario that Van Haren's pamphlet appeared. There was a concerted campaign, presumably by the Orangist party, to distribute the poem. In three days, so we are told, the poem sold 100,000 copies.[14] Such a number, in the context of the Netherlands of the early 1740s, is staggering. A mere week later, excerpts from the poem appeared translated into English in the *Gentleman's Magazine* (12, 1742, p. 156). The poem had its desired effect, humiliating the government into dispatching an army. Few poems, it was later remarked, have managed to raise an army of 20,000 men.[15]

The theme of the poem was a potent one. It describes the speech Leonidas makes to the Spartans when deciding to march to Thermopylae in the knowledge that he will not return. The text in Van Haren's poem is reminiscent of a similar speech in Glover's poem, with both pieces stressing the connection between liberty, patriotism, and virtue. In both versions, Leonidas castigates those in Sparta who refuse to march to face the approaching tyrant and defend both their own and their allies' freedom. It has been suggested that each character in Van Haren's poem is but a thinly veiled figure from the contemporary conflict, and the 'betrayal' of Maria Theresa appears

---

12 On Van Haren, see: Reinder Meijer, *The Literature of the Low Countries* (The Hague: Nijhoff, 1978), pp. 166–168; Johan van Vloten, ed., *Leven en Werken van Willem en Onno Zwier van Haren* (Deventer: A. Ter Gunne, 1874), especially pp. 134–137; Jan te Winkel, *De ontwikkelingsgang der Nederlandsche letterkunde*, 7 vols (Haarlem: F. Bohm, 1907–1927), V, pp. 349–363; Wisse Smit, *Kalliope in de Nederlanden*, 2 vols (Groningen: Wolters-Noordhoff, 1983), II, pp. 349–392; Macgregor Morris, *The Age of Leonidas*.

13 On Van Haren's reading of Glover, see Dirk Christiaan Nijhoff, 'De Staatsman-Dichter Willem van Haren', *Nederland* 3 (1901) 183.

14 Kornelius ter Laan, *Letterkundig woordenboek voor Noord en Zuid* (s'Gravenhage: G.B. van Goor Zonen, 1952), pp. 302–303; Philipp Christiaan Molhuysen and Petrus Johannes Blok, eds, *Nieuw Nederlandsch biografisch woordenboek*, 10 vols (Leiden: Sijthoff, 1930), VIII, p. 690.

15 Meijer, *The Literature of the Low Countries*, 167.

as dishonourable and cowardly. The model already established in Glover's version served as the ideal template, although the politics behind the poems remains quite different: Glover had been highly critical of the excessive power of monarchs, while Van Haren was supporting the claims of a Prince striving to challenge parliamentary power. Glover's Patriot-King acts as servant to his people, while Van Haren uses that moderate vision of kingship to justify his prince's power in the face of a corrupt oligarchy. Yet Van Haren could only use Leonidas in this way because Glover had established him as the model of benign rule, dedicated to the common good. Once the idea that such benign rule by a Patriot King was established, the very notion Glover had created to be a critique of royal power becomes a tool for its re-establishment in a different context. Nevertheless, while the purpose of the model is quite different, the model *itself* remains unchanged. Leonidas, and the virtues he embodies, are the same.

Despite the very different ends in mind, Van Haren's use of Glover's Leonidas served to reinforce that model. The emergence of such a similar vision of the Spartan in such a different context ensured its survival. Moreover, both poems enjoyed considerable success beyond their own countries. Glover's poem, alongside a commentary upon it, was quickly translated into French, and drew praise from the Abbé Prevost, who published a summary of the poem in his journal, *Le Pour et Le Contre*; German translations soon followed, prompting ecstatic praise from the poet Klopstock. Van Haren's greatest foreign admirer was Voltaire, who penned a eulogy to the Dutchman.[16] Such widespread recognition by some of the leading literary figures of the period helped to ensure that the vision of Leonidas they had generated remained current, even as the poets themselves fell out of favour in their own countries.

While the second half of the eighteenth century witnessed an increasing number of references to Leonidas, it was in the Revolutionary period that the Spartan would come to the fore. A series of works, poetic, philosophical and scholarly had both legitimised and developed the Leonidas of Glover as a patriotic prototype.[17] These lent themselves to revolutionary interpretation: both Glover and Van Haren had presented virtue as a quality which, by definition, strove for liberty. Leonidas' first revolutionary appearances came in the works of the early philhellenic writers, such as the Comte de Choiseul-Gouffier, seeking to 'reignite' what they believed was the latent pa-

---

16 See Van Vloten, *Leven en Werken*, 160–161; Roger Oake, 'Political Elements in Criticism of Voltaire in England', *Modern Language Notes* 57 (1942) 351–354.
17 Key here are Abbé de Mably's *Observations sur les Grecs* (1749; revised as *Observations sur l'histoire de la Grèce* in 1766) and Jean-Jacques Barthélemy's *Les Voyages du jeune Anacharsis en Grèce* (1788).

triotic virtue of the modern Greeks.[18] It is little wonder, then, that in the early years of the French Revolution a number of theatrical productions appeared, both supporting and condemning the events in France, which sought to bring the Spartan into the furore of contemporary events. D'Estaing's *Les Thermopyles: Tragédie de Circonstance* appeared in 1791, and suggested an enduring relevance far more literal than Glover or even Van Haren. Yet the principle is clearly drawn from the tradition they established. This can also be seen in the supposed claim by General Dumouriez, on the eve of the Battle of Valmy in 1792, that he was Leonidas, and that Valmy was France's Thermopylae.[19] The same year an English poet used the figure of Leonidas to condemn the Revolution: John Roberdeau's *Thermopylae, or Invasion Repulsed* reveals its finale in the title, which sees the Greeks celebrate victory even as Leonidas himself falls. Such a deviation from both Glover, and indeed history, could also be seen the following year in Loaisel de Treogate's *Le Combat des Thermopyles ou l'école des guerriers*, in which Leonidas appears as a democratic general dreaming of a kingless future, securing victory with his death.

As the Revolution turned into an Empire, Glover's patriot developed accordingly. A string of lavish new editions of Glover's epic were produced, the first in thirty years, decorated with engravings emphasising the themes of the poem. As the threat of invasion loomed in 1803, the fiery orator Robert Hall called the English to arms by insisting that now, in the face of the 'tyranny' of Napoleon, they stood in 'the Thermopylae of the Universe'.[20] Broadsheets were produced under the title 'A Briton's Payer', seeking to recruit volunteers to resist the invader, comprised entirely of lengthy quotations from Glover, with only the appropriate nomenclature changed: so 'Grecians' became 'Britons', and 'Xerxes', the Persian King, became 'Buono'.[21] Yet perhaps the most powerful rendering of Leonidas began as a republican ideal, and was completed as a memorial to Napoleon. Jacques-Louis David's *Leonidas aux Thermopyles* has been described as the most famous artwork on any Spartan subject, and the greatest representation of his republican ideals. Certainly, the Leonidas of David is a powerful rendering of republican ideology, but it is also directly based on the model created by Glover, and David was certainly aware of the text.[22]

18 Marie-Gabriel-Auguste-Florent Choiseul-Gouffier, *Voyage Pittoresque de la Grèce*, 2 vols (Paris: n. pub., 1782). On Choiseul's use of Leonidas, see Macgregor Morris, 'To make a new Thermopylae', 222–223, and *The Age of Leonidas*.
19 Elizabeth Rawson, *The Spartan Tradition in European Thought* (Oxford: Clarendon, 1969), p. 285.
20 Robert Hall, *The Sentiments Proper to the Present Crisis* (London: Whittington, 1803).
21 *The Briton's Prayer. Address to the VOLUNTEERS of GREAT BRITAIN, armed in Defence of their RELIGION, their COUNTRY, and their KING* (London: Ginger, 1803).
22 Indeed, it can be shown that David had used Glover's poem, or at least the Abbé Prevost's paraphrase of it. In his 'Explication' of the poem, published in 1814, David describes details

Each retelling was very much part of the tradition established by Glover, concentrating on the theme of noble sacrifice for the community as the
necessary prerequisite for liberty and virtue. Yet they developed the themes.
The victory described by Roberdeau and Treogate was a literal realisation of
the moral victory implied by Glover, while the democratic credentials are an
attribution drawn from the *philosophe* Mably, whose influential works had envisioned Sparta as truly democratic.[23] The philosophic nature of the sacrifice, so evident in D'Estaing and David, has its origin in both Glover's text
and the Enlightenment fascination with the philosopher as hero.[24]

In each version, the notion of 'Patriotism' carries much the same connotations. The virtue of patriotism was in many ways *the* virtue of eighteenth-century rhetoric. Throughout the history of eighteenth-century politics, many factions adopted the term as a proof that they sought to serve
the public good: thus, the opposition to Robert Walpole's government in
1730s England – the very faction for which Glover has been accused of
writing – gloried in the label 'Patriots'. Van Haren insisted on the patriotic
nature of the Orangist cause, a theme which would run through the successful Orange revolution of 1747–48; and yet, a generation later the anti-Or-
angist revolutionaries who drew the Dutch Republic into its death throws
proudly termed themselves 'Patriots'. The mid-century *philosophes*, especially
Rousseau and Mably, had developed the notion of Spartan patriotism into a
philosophical paradigm, and while their key sources were ancient, the influence of the vision created and propagated by Glover and Van Haren cannot
be ignored.[25] For the Revolution, such a model served as both an inspiration and a legitimisation. The extent of the Jacobins' devotion to Sparta is
certainly open to question, as even Chateaubriand, the first to portray them
as hankering after a new Sparta, was quick to realise.[26] However, Saint-Just's
vision of reforming France with Laconic measures suggests a genuine interest, and reflects Mably's conclusion that the greatest achievement of the

---

which could only be drawn from the Englishman's work. See Macgregor Morris, *The Age of
Leonidas.*

23 Mably's vision of Sparta as democratic was not as untenable as modern visions of Sparta might
suggest. See Macgregor Morris, 'Paradigm of Democracy', and Mason, 'Sparta and the French
Enlightenment', especially pp. 78–80.

24 See Gay, *Enlightenment*, 82; and Katherine Carson, 'Socrates Observed: Three Eighteenth-Century Views', *Diderot Studies* 14 (1971) 273–281.

25 While the extent of the *philosophes'* reading of these two poets is hard to determine, their availability in French and popularity with certain French writers suggests that were certainly
known. Moreover, the congruence between the vision of Leonidas in the poets, and Sparta
in the *philosophes*, is too strong to ignore.

26 Chateaubriand, having suggested that the Jacobins had sought to 'recall Sparta from her ruins',
admits that most of them did not even know who Lycurgus was. See Ian Macgregor Morris,
'From Ancient Dreams to Modern Nightmares: Classical Revolutions in Enlightenment
Thought', in *Lumières et histoire*, ed. by Alicia Montoya, et. al. (Paris: Champion, 2010),
pp. 301–321.

Spartan law-giver Lycurgus was not the laws themselves, but his reforming of the 'manners' of the people.[27] This was the point and purpose of the Revolutionary vision of Leonidas: not merely as rhetoric, but as an agent for reform and change.

It is here that we see the remarkable consistency of the Classical Tradition in a wide variety of political contexts. The model itself emerged virtually unchanged from that created by Glover: the battle of Thermopylae itself was transformed into a victory, but the character, actions and purpose – and most centrally, the virtues – of Leonidas remained. What the writers of the period did, however, was to stress the *relevance* of Leonidas to the Revolution. It is not the classical model, but the significance it carries, which changes. While for Van Haren, Leonidas had *represented* the virtue which the Dutch Republic had lost, for D'Estaing the Revolution had *resuscitated* that virtue. The revolutionaries had not imitated – they had completed. The virtue of the Spartans and the French were not merely similar, but were one and the same. In this way, the ideal of the Patriot King became the reality of the Revolutionary Citizen. The later uses of Leonidas, be they counter-revolutionary or Napoleonic, all stressed this immediacy.

The apparent paradox of revolutionaries adopting a model formulated by monarchists should not confuse us. While Glover and Van Haren envisioned a Patriot 'King', that monarch was strictly constitutional, and, in a true Spartan sense, was a citizen first and foremost. The Revolutionary writers, far from rejecting the Classical Tradition, were embracing it with even greater ardour than its creators. To do this, they drew upon a tradition which spanned much of Europe and crossed ideological boundaries. Indeed, it was the very divergent nature of the tradition which gave it such a power and relevance in the first place; and it is only in light of this pan-European nature that we can understand it.

The second theme we wish to consider follows a similar path, although it is very different in its nature. It began in the thought of the scholar-traveller Robert Wood.[28] Like Glover, Wood was a Whig, also closely associated with Pitt the Elder. Yet his fascination with antiquity centred on the past as a place. He spent several years exploring, and indeed discovering ancient sites and cities. His rediscovery of Palmyra, a moment immortalised by the neoclassical painter Gavin Hamilton, would become an iconic image to the Romantic travellers. And while the lavishly illustrated volumes he published

27 See Macgregor Morris, 'Paradigm of Democracy'.
28 On Wood see Terence Spencer, 'Robert Wood and the Problem of Troy in the Eighteenth Century', *Journal of the Courtald and Warburg Institutes* 20 (1957) 75–105; David Constantine, *Early Greek Travellers and the Hellenic Ideal* (Cambridge: Cambridge University Press, 1984); Ian Macgregor Morris, 'Shrines of the Mighty: Rediscovering the Battlefields of the Persian Wars', in *Cultural Responses to the Persian Wars: Antiquity to the Third Millennium*, ed. by E. Bridges et al. (Oxford: Oxford University Press, 2007), pp. 239–249.

of sites such as Palmyra and Balbec would inspire a revolution in architecture, as he explored these sites he also developed a quite novel way to understand them. He realised that any classical text could only be fully appreciated within its topographical context:

> The Iliad has new beauties on the banks of the Scamander, and the Odyssey is most pleasing in the countries where Ulysses travelled and Homer sung [...]. The classical ground not only makes us always relish the poet, or historian more, but sometimes helps us to understand them better.[29]

From this he concluded that the key to understanding the past lay in the present: in a pioneering attempt in archaeology and ethnography, he turned to the modern landscape and modern cultures to explain the ancient. Moreover, the ancient texts and remains in turn could help us to understand the modern. Brought together, both could be made whole again.[30]

Wood never completed his masterpiece on Homer, in which he had hoped finally to realise his blend of ethno-archaeology. His frustration to reconcile ancient and modern led him continually to delay publication, and the posthumous volume which eventually appeared is but a poor shadow of his vision as laid out in his manuscript diaries.[31] But the vision itself was captivating: Wood had fused the seeds of Romanticism with Enlightenment rationalism, and suggested a philosophical approach which offered much more than dusty antiquarianism. The surge in travel to classical sites beyond the Grand Tour was greatly influenced by Wood. Travellers began to consider ancient and modern, not merely in terms of crude comparison, but as ways to understand them as a whole. In Italy, the likes of William Hamilton, Richard Payne-Knight and the Baron D'Hancarville considered discoveries from Pompeii in the light of local religious practices;[32] in Greece travellers such as Pierre Guys conducted ethnographies ancient and modern.[33] By the end of the eighteenth century, the ideologies of Philhellenism centred on notions of the connections between past and present, and from these to

29 Robert Wood, *The Ruins of Palmyra* (London: [s.n.], 1753), Preface, [no pagination].
30 For discussions of concepts of the past and of historicity, see Reinhart Koselleck, *Futures Past: On the Semantics of Historical Time*, translated by Keith Tribe (New York: Columbia University Press, 2004), Maike Oergel, *Culture and Identity: Historicity in German Literature and Thought 1770–1815* (Berlin and New York: de Gruyter, 2006) and Moore et al., *Reinventing History*.
31 Cf. Wood's diaries, which are held at the Institute of Classical Studies London.
32 Hamilton and Payne-Knight believed that they could trace contemporary religious practice to ancient rituals. On Hamilton see David Constantine, *Fields of Fire: A Life of Sir William Hamilton* (London: Weidenfeld and Nicolson, 2001); on Payne-Knight see Bruce Redford, *Dilettanti: The Antic and the Antique in Eighteenth-Century England* (Los Angeles: Paul Getty Museum, 2008); on D'Hancarville see James Moore, 'History as Theoretical Reconstruction? Baron D'Hancarville and the Exploration of Ancient Mythology in the Eighteenth Century', in *Reinventing History*, ed. by Moore et al., 137–167.
33 See Constantine, *Early Greek Travellers*, 147–168.

programmes of regeneration and revolution. Once more, the ancient past was *relevant*.

Yet the most literal, and absolute realisation of Wood's ideas appeared in the revolutionary works of Constantin-François Volney. Volney had travelled extensively through the Near East, and developed his own interpretation of the relevance of antiquity. While Wood's project was scientific, Volney's was philosophical and political. In his *Les ruines, ou méditation sur les révolutions des empires*, published in 1791, Volney developed the revolutionary potential of Wood's thesis. Imagining himself amidst the ruins of Palmyra, the author falls into a reverie while contemplating the fall of past civilisations, and the implications this carries for the future:

> Pregnant, I may truly call you [the ruins of antiquity], with useful lessons, with pathetic and irresistible advice to the man who knows how to consult you. A while ago the whole world bowed the neck in silence before the tyrants that oppressed it; and yet in that hopeless moment you already proclaimed the truths that tyrants hold in abhorrence: mixing the dust of the proudest kings with that of the meanest slaves, you called upon us to contemplate this example of Equality.[34]

In his dream he is confronted by a spirit which guides him through the past and future, and reveals how an understanding of the former can lead to a realisation of the latter. Volney's evocation of Wood is reinforced by his development of the latter's ideas. Where Wood had sought to use past and present to understand classical texts and the forms of ancient sites, Volney hoped to use this combination of past and present as a template for the future. Much as other revolutionary writers were doing with the patriotic model of Leonidas, Volney was stressing the relevance of the past as an active agent for revolutionary change: the Classical became now.

It is therefore no coincidence that the two themes discussed above emerge in the thought of one of the most important philhellenic and pro-Revolutionary authors of the German language at the time: Friedrich Hölderlin. For Hölderlin and his time, Revolution meant not (only) the Revolution in Paris, but a new kind of morally informed philosophy in practice, of which the events following 1789 were only the first, still imperfect signs. It is in this sense that in 1797 Hölderlin proclaims to his friend Johann Gottfried Ebel a 'future revolution of convictions and modes of thought and imagining that will make everything hitherto blush with shame'.[35] In Ger-

---

34 Constantin François Volney, *The Ruins: or A Survey of the Revolutions of Empires*, translated by James Marshall (London: T. Tegg, 1811), p. vi. On Volney's use of Wood, see Macgregor Morris, 'Ancient Dreams to Modern Nightmares', 311–314.

35 Letter to J.G. Ebel, 10 January 1797, in Friedrich Hölderlin, *Sämtliche Werke*, 8 vols, ed. by Friedrich Beißner (Stuttgart: Kohlhammer, 1948–1985), VI (1968): *Briefe*, ed. by Adolf Beck, pp. 228–230, 229: 'Ich glaube an eine künftige Revolution der Gesinnungen und Vorstellungsarten, die alles bisherige schaamroth machen wird', translated by Christopher Jenkin-Jones in Uta Degner, 'Dichtende Wolken/Authoring Clouds', in *Katharina Grosse, shadowbox*, ed. by Cube Kunsthalle (Köln: Buchhandlung Walter König, 2009), pp. 70–75, 73. On the pre-1789

many, too, parallels were drawn between the Republican French Army and the resistance of the Greeks against the Persians.[36] Glover's epic had proved particularly popular, with three full-length translations being published, and drawing ecstatic praise from Klopstock. In 1793 Schiller published a translation of an extract from 'the newest London edition' of Glover's *Leonidas* in his journal *Neue Thalia*, 'one of the most beautiful scenes' ('[e]ine der schönsten Stellen') of the poem. Schiller chooses

> [den] Abschied des Helden von seiner Gattin und seinen Kindern. Als er, nach dem Spruch des Orakels: dass Lacedämon sich gegen die hereinströmende Macht des Persers nur durch den Tod eines seiner Könige schützen könne; *freywillig* sein Leben dem Vaterlande dargeboten hatte, musste sein Herz noch einen schweren Kampf bestehn. Er war geliebter Gatte und zärtlicher Vater. Indem seine Seele im vollen Gefühl der Erfüllung einer großen Pflicht den eignen Beyfall, und die Dankbarkeit der Mitwelt und Nachwelt vorausgeniesst, zieht ihn das Bild seiner verlassnen Gattin, und seiner jammernden, bald verwaisten Kinder von der hohen Bahn des Ruhms, die seine patriotische Tugend wandelt, in den stillsten Kreis der häuslichen Sorge, herab, und nur der Gedanke: Lo! Thy country calls, hebt ihn über diese überwallenden Empfindungen.[37]

Schiller emphasises that Leonidas acts not out of natural necessity, but 'freywillig', out of free will. In the second part of his essay on the sublime, *Fortgesetzte Entwicklung des Erhabenen* (*On the Pathetic*), which appeared in the subsequent issue of the same journal and which follows Kantian ideas, he judges this free will as an aesthetic dimension. The case of Leonidas is almost unique

---

meanings of 'revolution' still detectable in Hölderlin's use of the term, see Reinhart Koselleck, 'Historical Criteria of the Modern Concept of Revolution', in Koselleck, *Futures Past*, 43–57; on the German context see Gerhard Kurz, *Mittelbarkeit und Vereinigung: Zum Verhältnis von Poesie, Reflexion und Revolution bei Hölderlin* (Stuttgart: Metzler, 1975), pp. 2–15; and Pierre Bertaux, *Hölderlin und die französische Revolution* (Frankfurt a. M.: Suhrkamp, 1969). An overview of scholarship on Hölderlin's position *vis-à-vis* the Revolution can be found in Laura Anna Macor, *Friedrich Hölderlin: Tra illuminismo e rivoluzione* (Pisa: ETS, 2006), pp. 13–59.

36 Cf. Gotthold Friedrich Stäudlin in *Fortgesezte Schubart'sche Chronik für 1792*, 22 May, p. 333; cited in Günter Mieth, *Friedrich Hölderlin: Dichter der bürgerlich-demokratischen Revolution*, 2nd edn (Würzburg: Königshausen und Neumann, 2001), pp. 25 and 202.

37 'Der Abschied des Leonidas', in *Neue Thalia* vol. 3, part 1, 1793 (Bern: Herbert Lang, 1969), pp. 75–82, 75–76. The quoted passage occurs in the introductory 'Vorerinnerung'. 'The farewell of the hero from his wife and his children. When he, after the prediction of the oracle that Lacedaemon can protect itself against the inpouring power of the Persian only through the death of one of its kings, voluntarily had offered his life to his fatherland, his heart still had to fight a heavy battle. He was a beloved husband and affectionate father. While his soul was already enjoying the full feeling of acclaim for pursuing a great duty, and the thankfulness of his contemporaries and posterity, the image of his abandoned wife and his mourning, soon to be orphaned children, tears him down from his high avenues of fame, upon which his patriotic virtue is walking, into the still domestic circle, only the thought: "Lo! Thy country calls", lifts him up over these overwhelming emotions.' Translated by Uta Degner. On this and the following cf. Uta Degner, 'Spartanic Verses: Hölderlin and the role of Sparta in German literary Hellenism, c. 1800', in *Sparta in Modern Thought*, 231–251.

in that there is no conflict between the aesthetic and the moral, two categories which for Schiller are usually in conflict:

> Ich denke mir z.B. die Selbstaufopferung des Leonidas bey Thermopylä. Moralisch beurtheilt ist mir diese Handlung Darstellung des, bey allem Widerspruch der Instinkte erfüllten, Sittengesetzes; ästhetisch beurtheilt ist sie mir Darstellung des, von allem Zwang der Instinkte unabhängigen, sittlichen Vermögens. Meinen moralischen Sinn (die Vernunft) *befriedigt* diese Handlung; meinen ästhetischen Sinn (die Einbildungskraft) *entzückt* sie. [38]

Leonidas is an important example, as he shows how we can act for freedom freely even in situations where such action appears impossible. He becomes a figure of orientation, as his behaviour combines morality and freedom: 'Daß Leonidas die heldenmüthige Entschließung *wirklich faßte*, billigen wir; daß er sie fassen *konnte*, darüber frohlocken wir, und sind entzückt.'[39] In providing such examples, poetry has the power to overcome historical reality and 'conceive[s] possibilities'; it is central to revolutions as it presents models of moral action. Two years later, Schiller would place the motif of the battle of Thermoplyae at the centre of one of his best known poems, the cultural reflection *Elegie*.[40]

Hölderlin admired Schiller as his poetic model, and surely read his contributions with care. His approach to revolution – political and aesthetical – is fuelled by the same belief in and the longing for autonomy as a ground for every moral human action that Schiller identifies in Leonidas. Hölderlin draws upon the Spartan model in his poem *Der Tod fürs Vaterland* (Death for the Fatherland) of 1799, a German 'Marseillaise' against the oppressors at home. It is in his famous novel, *Hyperion*, however, that this Spartan model becomes a guiding principle for the central character. An early 'Fragment von Hyperion' appears in the fifth issue of Schiller's journal, two issues after the extract from Glover. When the central character and his friends invoke

---

38 Friedrich Schiller, 'Fortgesetzte Entwicklung des Erhabenen', in *Neue Thalia*, vol. 4, part 4, 1793, pp. 52–73, 57. 'I think, for example, of the self-sacrifice of Leonidas at Thermopylae. Judged morally, this action is a representation to me of the moral law; judged aesthetically, it is a representation to me of the moral capacity, independent of every compulsion of instinct. This action *satisfies* my moral sense (reason); it *delights* my aesthetical sense (the imaginative power).' Friedrich Schiller, 'On the Pathetic', translated by William F. Wertz Jr., in *Schiller, Poet of Freedom*, 4 vols (Washington D.C.: Schiller Institute, 1990), III, pp. 227–253, 245 (stress in the original).

39 Schiller, 'Fortgesetzte Entwicklung des Erhabenen', 61. 'That Leonidas *actually made* his heroic resolution, we approve; that he *could* make it, thereat do we exult and are we delighted.' ('On the Pathetic', 247) Compare also Schiller's comment further down: 'The aesthetical judgment leaves us free, and elevates and inspires us, because already through the mere capacity to will absolutely, already through the mere predisposition to morality, we prove to have evident advantage over sensuousness, because already through the mere possibility to renounce the compulsion of nature, our need for freedom is flattered. [...] There, we swing upward from the real to the possible.' ('On the Pathetic', 247–248)

40 See Manuel Baumbach, '"Wanderer, kommst du nach Sparta..."': Zur Rezeption eines Simonides-Epigramms', *Poetica* 32 (2000) 1–22.

'Wundern griechischer Freundschaft' (miracles of Greek friendship), the
'Phalanx der Sparter' (phalanx of the Spartans) plays a defining role.[41] Hölderlin specifically stresses the imaginative power as the basis and goal of all
revolutionary activities, and the relevance of the Schillerian 'aesthetical
sense'. In accordance with Wood's model and his notion of reading *The Iliad*
in the land 'where Homer sung', Hyperion and his friends gather around
'Homer's Grotto' and evoke ancient figures: the re-volution, as a return to
the past, shows Leonidas as an ideal still valid for the present.[42] By conceiving of the past as an organic development, the present reveals itself as part
of an open process, or better: progress coming from antiquity, turning into
today.

> Lasst vergehen, was vergeht, […], es vergeht, um wiederzukehren, es altert, um sich
> zu verjüngen, es trennt sich um sich inniger zu vereinigen, es stirbt, um lebendiger zu
> leben. […] So verblühen die schönen jugendlichen Myrthen der Vorwelt, die Dich-
> tungen Homers und seiner Zeiten, die Prophezeyungen und Offenbarungen, aber
> der Keim der in ihnen lag, gehet als reife Frucht hervor im Herbste. Die Einfalt und
> Unschuld der ersten Zeit erstirbt, dass sie wiederkehre in der vollendeten Bildung,
> und der heilige Friede des Paradieses gehet unter, dass, was nur Gabe der Natur war,
> wiederaufblühe, als errungnes Eigenthum der Menschheit.[43]

The emphasis on the naturalness of antiquity owes much to Wood's vision of
Homer as a 'faithful' copier of nature.[44] Yet here it is the connection – the
continuity – between ancient and modern which defines the relationship between the two. The link between past and present that was key to both Wood
and Volney, becomes in *Hyperion* a fundamental aspect of humanity. In the
final published version of *Hyperion*, Hölderlin emphasises this connection in
his recourse to identify with figures such as Leonidas at Thermopylae, as Hyperion longs for 'ein Thermopylä, wo ich mit Ehren sie verbluten könnte, all
die einsame Liebe'.[45] That Hyperion later becomes disillusioned with the no-

---

41 Friedrich Hölderlin, 'Fragment von Hyperion', in *Neue Thalia* vol. 4, part 5, 1793, pp. 181–221,
    192. On the Spartan dimension of *Hyperion* see Degner, 'Spartanic Verses'.
42 On the notion of 'revolution' as a return to the past in Wood's thought, see Macgregor Morris,
    'Ancient Dreams to Modern Nightmares', 307–309.
43 Hölderlin, 'Fragment von Hyperion', 213. 'Let pass what passes, […] it passes to recur, it ages
    to rejuvenate itself, it splits up to unite more dearly, it dies to live more vividly. […] So wither
    the beautiful juvenile myrtles of the past, the poetry of Homer and his times, the prophecies
    and revelations; but the germ that lies in them turns out as a ripe fruit in autumn. The inno-
    cence and ingenuity of the first time dies to recur in the most perfect creation, and the holy
    peace of paradise fades so that that which was only the gift of nature blossoms as an achieved
    property of mankind.' (Translated by Uta Degner).
44 Wood's ideas proved hugely popular in Germany; indeed, his book on Homer was published
    in German before its full appearance in English. On Wood's vision of Homer and its influence
    in Germany, see K. Simonsuuri, *Homer's Original Genius: Eighteenth-Century Notions of the Early
    Greek Epic* (Cambridge: Cambridge University Press, 1979), and Constantine, *Greek Travellers*.
45 Hölderlin, *Sämtliche Werke*, III: *Hyperion*, p. 151. 'a Thermopylae where I could bleed […] to
    death with honour'; Friedrich Hölderlin, *Hyperion, or the Hermit in Greece*, translated by Ross
    Benjamin (New York: Archipelago Books, 2008), p. 203.

tion of recreating ancient virtue does not in any way undermine antiquity's relevance, either as a source of models for emulation or, more crucially, as a defining feature of modernity. It is the modern world that is at fault: the relevance remains.

Hölderlin returned to Wood's – and Volney's – 'coincidential' setting of past and present in a later poem, that clearly draws upon the latter:

Lebensalter	*The Ages of Life*
Ihr Städte des Euphrats!	You cities of Euphrates,
Ihr Gassen von Palmyra!	You streets at Palmyra,
Ihr Säulenwälder in der Eb'ne der Wüste,	You forests of pillars in the desert plain,
Was seid ihr?	What are you?
Euch hat die Kronen,	Your crests,
Dieweil ihr über die Gränze	As you passed beyond
Der Othmenden seid gegangen,	The bounds of those who breathe,
Vom Himmlischen der Rauchdampf und	By smoke of heavenly powers and
Hinweg das Feuer genommen;	By fire were taken away;
Jetzt aber siz' ich unter Wolken (deren	But now I sit beneath clouds, in which
Ein jedes eine Ruh' hat eigen) unter	Peculiar quiet comes to each one, beneath
Wohleingerichteten Eichen, auf	A pleasing order of oak-trees, on
Der Heide des Rehs, und fremd	The heath where the roe-deer feed, and strange
Erscheinen und gestorben mir	To me, remote and dead seem[46]
Der Seeligen Geister.[47]	The souls of the blessed.

As Wolfram Groddeck has shown, the scene of the poem is based on the engraved frontispiece from Volney's *Les ruines*, which shows a man meditating in front of the Palmyran ruins, and in his vocabulary even copies Volney's invocation.[48] Here we find the same precepts familiar from revolutionary Philhellenism: the resort to the past in the interest of present and future – and the topographical proximity of the past. The fact that the antique is stressed as 'strange', 'remote' and 'dead' (ll. 12–13), does not deprecate its relevance – as the speaker of the poem shows, his 'now' (l. 9) is completely enclosed by it. That Hölderlin's poem, in contrast to Volney's 'spirit', does not enfold a project for a future revolution, does not mean that it parodies the Enlightenment philosophy of revolution, as Hölderlin scholarship has suggested.[49] Rather, it should be read as a concession to its readers and a licence for their 'imaginative power'. The poem tries to realise *in poetics* what he wants *in politics*: an emancipation and participation of the citizens, exemplified in creating autonomy for the reader. Hölderlin's later poems therefore suspend the

---

46 Friedrich Hölderlin, *Selected Poems and Fragments*, translated by Michael Hamburger, ed. by Jeremy Adler (London: Penguin, 1998), p. 171.
47 Hölderlin, *Sämtliche Werke*, II.1: *Gedichte nach 1800*, p. 115.
48 See Wolfram Groddeck, 'Betrachtungen über das Gedicht *Lebensalter*', in *Interpretationen: Gedichte von Friedrich Hölderlin*, ed. by Gerhard Kurz (Stuttgart: Reclam, 1996), p. 156; see also Uta Degner, *Bilder im Wechsel der Töne: Hölderlins Elegien und 'Nachtgesänge'* (Heidelberg: Winter, 2008), pp. 261–266.
49 See Groddeck, 'Betrachtungen'.

'drawing' of future realities and develop poetic strategies that activate the reader's imaginative capacities towards possibilities. His poetry does not, as Peter Szondi suggests,[50] want to realise in poetics that which has not been realised yet in reality, but uses poetry to create the conditions of the possibilities of revolution. The revolutionary aspect of Hölderlin's later poems lies in the way in which they use the Classical Tradition to show the openness of historical 'becoming'. The temporally open 'now' of *Lebensalter* calls for readers to carry out the revolution in modes of thought and imagining in their own time and their own ways, in the openness of a future (be)coming. The ancient world is an example that shows – even in its strangeness – the convertibility of history, the capacity to break the boundaries of the present. It provided the opportunity to understand the present as temporary. The orientation towards the past allowed possibilities for the future, and created a way out of the agonising present.

In the revolutionary Philhellenism of the early nineteenth century, the two themes originally generated by Glover and Wood come together. Volney's revolutionary development of Wood's ideas fed into the Leonidas-tradition, so that Philhellenes envisioned that the spirit – the virtue itself – of Leonidas lay in the landscape. Thus Chateaubriand melodramatically invoked the ghost of Leonidas amidst the meagre ruins of Sparta, and Byron called upon the modern Greeks to 'make a new Thermopylae'.[51] Such locations, in Philhellenic thought, were the key to the political and cultural regeneration of modern Greece.

In the cases of Glover and Wood, we can see the ways in which the thinkers of the Revolutionary period sought to stress the relevance of the antique. They did not reject the Classical Tradition of the Enlightenment, but neither did they submissively repeat it. These two examples represent the Classical Tradition in action. While they draw on tradition, they are constantly reworking it. They are genuinely revolutionary, because they subvert the tradition whilst maintaining, indeed reinforcing it. The model of patriotic virtue envisioned by Glover remains – indeed, the Leonidas of Treogate and David is remarkably similar to that of Glover. Similarly, the theoretical basis of Wood's scholarship is the philosophical basis of Volney's vision, and serves to generate a revolutionary aesthetics for Hölderlin. The subversion lies in the re-interpretation not of the models themselves, but in their

---

50 Peter Szondi, 'Der Fürstenmord, der nicht stattfand – Hölderlin und die französische Revolution', in *Einführung in die literarische Hermeneutik: Studienausgabe der Vorlesungen*, vol. 5 (Frankfurt a. M.: Suhrkamp, 1975), p. 426.
51 Macgregor Morris, 'To make a New Thermopylae', and 'Liars, Eccentrics and Visionaries: Early Travellers to Sparta and the Birth of Laconian Archaeology', in William G. Cavanagh, Chrysanthi Gallou and Mercourios Georgiadis, eds, *Sparta and Laconia: From Prehistory to Premodern* (London: British School at Athens, 2009), pp. 387–395.

relevance to the contemporary world. Here the Classical Tradition is revealed as, quite literally, breaking boundaries.

Detours of Knowledge

Aspects of Novalis' Aesthetic Epistemology[1]

Peter Krilles

After several decades of debate on the possibility of distinguishing different, mutually exclusive realms of knowledge,[2] the idea of one culture of knowledge seems to prevail over a restriction of knowledge to the apparently objective realm of hard science.[3] However, it becomes increasingly difficult to establish a distinction between what could be called 'knowledge' and any representation of 'reality'. In order to stay scientifically relevant, actual conceptions of knowledge need certainly not be normative, but still have to feature a dimension that exceeds the contingence of mere individual points of view.

In Foucault's discursive perspective, knowledge does not just have a relative and constructed character. It also allows for a profoundly historical approach to knowledge: history can be read as a scale of different notions of knowledge that are part of and arise from different discursive cultures. As a consequence, the debate about the number of epistemological cultures or about a narrow or wide notion of knowledge has itself to be placed in a history of the organisation of knowledge.[4]

Certain periods of the overwhelmingly long history of knowledge paradigms[5] are particularly significant for actual epistemological matters like the debate on the connection between aesthetics and epistemology. One such period is the late eighteenth century. The years after the Kantian philosoph-

---

1 I wish to thank Maike Oergel for her inspiring comments on previous versions of this paper.
2 Pethes and Reinalter summarise the different aspects of this debate. Cf. Nicolas Pethes, 'Literatur- und Wissenschaftsgeschichte. Ein Forschungsbericht', *IASL* 28 (2003) 181–231 and Helmut Reinalter, ed., *Natur- und Geisteswissenschaften – zwei Kulturen?* (Innsbruck/Wien: Studien-Verlag, 1999).
3 Cf. Bernhard J. Dotzler and Sigrid Weigel, eds, *'fülle der combination': Literaturforschung und Wissenschaftsgeschichte* (Munich: Fink, 2005). Theoretical conceptions such as Foucault's discourse analysis, Luhmann's systems theory or Deleuzian philosophy are the central references in this debate.
4 Foucault points out the major importance of Early German Romanticism in this history. Cf. Michel Foucault, 'Le 'non' du père', in *Dits et Ecrits 1954–1988*, 2 vols (Paris: Gallimard, 2001), I, pp. 189–203, 202.
5 Cf. the introduction in Michael Wood, *Literature and the Taste of Knowledge* (Cambridge: Cambridge University Press, 2005).

ical and the French socio-political revolutions are a time of crisis with regard to, amongst other things, the organisation of human knowledge.[6] At the same time, thinkers like Friedrich Schlegel, Hölderlin and Novalis contribute to the constitution of new, dynamic epistemological paradigms at a moment in history when the classical, taxonomic order of reality and knowledge loses its dominant influence. This paper aims to show the important role which Early German Romanticism, and especially the work of Novalis, play in this epistemological shift.

In his fragments and notes, especially in *Das Allgemeine Brouillon*, Novalis establishes a new relationship between knowledge and aesthetics. Dealing with the question of knowledge and aesthetics in Novalis is illuminating both from an historical and a systematic point of view. Firstly, Early German Romanticism is highly significant for the discursive situation that arises around 1800. Novalis' ideas on knowledge have to be considered as an important step not only for the redefinition of the organisation of scientific knowledge, but also for the evolution of modern literary studies and research. Secondly, Early German Romanticism has hence a systematic importance, dealing with concepts still discussed nowadays, as for example the relationship between fact and fiction, or the phenomenon of interdisciplinarity.

In his *Notes for a Romantic Encyclopaedia*, or, more precisely, in what Novalis calls *Encyclopedistics*, Novalis elaborates on a conception of knowledge that has to be considered as a radical split from epistemological paradigms of Enlightenment. A comparison between the main features of French encyclopaedia and Novalis' encyclopaedic project shows how the vision of the latter differs radically from Enlightenment culture. The two projects are separated by the turning point of Kantian philosophy. If some of the most important problems brought up by Kant are already present in the writings of D'Alembert and Diderot, the – pre-Kantian – solution of the French encyclopaedists differs from the paradigms which early German Romantics will argue for.

Moreover, Novalis' *Encyclopedistics* outline the importance of a genuinely aesthetic approach to knowledge. Traditionally, aesthetics, which generally means fictional, 'untrue' paradigms, are not part of knowledge; this is not the case in D'Alembert's conception since French Encyclopaedia does have an aesthetic dimension.[7] However, the organisation of knowledge is still characterised by the normative rule of rationality.

---

6   Cf. Gabriele Brandstetter and Gerhard Neumann, eds., *Romantische Wissenspoetik* (Würzburg: Königshausen and Neumann, 2004), pp. 9–11.

7   The theory and practice of cross-references plays an important role in this context as Kilcher shows. Cf. Andreas B. Kilcher, *mathesis und poiesis: Die Enzyklopädik der Literatur 1600–2000* (Munich: Fink, 2003), pp. 252ff.

This paper focuses on Novalis' vision of knowledge in relation to two important contexts: on the one hand, French Encyclopaedia, the central epistemological reference at the end of the eighteenth century, and on the other, German philosophy, especially Kant and Fichte. The central problem that arises from the Kantian shift in epistemology is the question of the range of human knowledge and, in particular, the question of its foundation in view of its restricted character. The Early German Romantics drew radical consequences from Kant's critical project: for them, a fundamental void opens up where Kant tries to find a transcendental founding principle of knowledge. The Romantics do not fill this void by an absolute approach to knowledge, which is characteristic, for example, of Fichte's philosophy. Novalis puts forward a dynamic conception of knowledge that overcomes normative distinctions between the realm of the hard sciences and aesthetics without synthesising them in a superior unity.

Encyclopaedia versus *Encyclopedistics* – D'Alembert versus Novalis: the Break-up of the Order of Knowledge at the End of the Eighteenth Century

Novalis refers in his writings to multiple epistemological paradigms. Novalis' *Notes for a Romantic Encyclopaedia* are not only influenced by apparently obsolete, mystical paradigms associated with the Renaissance, especially with Paracelsus and Böhme.[8] Novalis also deals with contemporary paradigms of epistemological matters: with Kantian and post-Kantian thought (Fichte) and with French Encyclopaedia. In fact, in *Das Allgemeine Brouillon* Novalis explicitly cites D'Alembert's *Discours préliminaire*, and the passage he chooses indicates some of the essential epistemological shifts that characterise the late eighteenth century.

D'Alembert's and Diderot's *Encyclopédie* pursues two aims. On the one hand, it evokes the original sense of the word 'encyclopaedia': the chain of knowledge. On the other hand, French Encyclopaedia is a central step in the evolution of the modern sense of encyclopaedia meaning a work that outlines human knowledge in total.[9] In agreement with these two aspects, French Encyclopaedia is characterised by a double organisation: firstly, there is an alphabetical arrangement of different articles on diverse subjects. Secondly, the general system organising these different realms of knowledge is laid down in the famous tree of knowledge called 'mappemonde'. D'Alem-

---

8   Cf. Paola Mayer, *Jena Romanticism and its Appropriation of Jakob Böhme: Theosophy, Hagiography, Literature* (Montreal: McGill-Queen's University Press, 1999).

9   For etymological aspects cf. Ulrich Dierse, *Enzyklopädie: Zur Geschichte eines philosophischen und wissenschaftstheoretischen Begriffs* (Bonn: Bouvier, 1977).

bert's and Diderot's notion of knowledge[10] is highly ambiguous: the infinite character of human knowledge contrasts with the unity of its system of representation. Diderot and D'Alembert emphasise the difficulty of their project due to the immense amount[11] and the historical, potentially infinite and even arbitrary, character of knowledge.[12] Nevertheless, they aim to build up an exhaustive and unified system of knowledge ('refermer en un système qui soit un, les branches infiniment variées de la science humaine'[13]) that will one day be complete.[14] It is one of the central characteristics of French Encyclopaedia that the two aspects are inextricably bound to one another: each note of the *Encyclopédie* implicitly actualises the rational philosophical basis that the 'mappemonde' expresses,[15] an organising principle that Foucault calls 'double representation' ('représentation redoublée') meaning a general feature of the classical *episteme*.[16] The useful dimension and the universal grasp of the French Encyclopaedia result from this ambiguous double organisation of knowledge that makes it possible to easily include new information and findings, without having to change the system as a whole, assuring the unity of human knowledge. Human knowledge is thus founded on a rational ground that does not change even though concrete knowledge is profoundly historical and potentially infinite.

The encyclopaedic project of Novalis differs radically from the French model, which is already evident from its fragmented structure and form.

---

10 While Diderot's and D'Alembert's visions of knowledge have some aspects in common, they are at the same time very different. Cf. Thomas L. Hankins, *Jean d'Alembert – Science and the Enlightenment* (New York et al.: Gorden and Breach, 1990), pp. 66–103. For the encyclopaedic tradition in general cf. Richard Yeo, *Encyclopaedic Visions: Scientific Dictionaries and Enlightenment Culture* (Cambridge: Cambridge University Press, 2001).

11 Cf. Denis Diderot, 'Encyclopédie', in *Œuvres complètes*, vol. 7, ed. by John Lough and Jacques Proust (Paris: Hermann, 1976), pp. 174–262, 175.

12 Cf. Claudia Moscovici, 'Beyond the Particular and the Universal: D'Alembert's *Discours préliminaire* to the Encyclopédie', *Eighteenth-Century Studies* 33 (2000) 383–400.

13 Jean le Rond d'Alembert, *Discours préliminaire de l'Encyclopédie* (Paris: Vrin, 2000), p. 84. 'To encompass the infinitely varied branches of human knowledge in a truly unified system.' Jean le Rond d'Alembert, *Preliminary Discourse to the Encyclopedia of Diderot*, ed. and translated by Richard N. Schwab (Chicago: The University of Chicago Press, 1995), p. 5. Cf. Diderot, 'Encyclopédie', 174.

14 Cf. D'Alembert, *Discours*, 159. For Diderot this finished character is even constitutive of an encyclopaedia. Cf. Diderot, 'Encyclopédie', 182.

15 Reason forms the centre of the French system of knowledge and is personified by the philosopher who oversees it: 'l'ordre encyclopédique de nos connaissances [...] consiste à les rassembler dans le plus petit espace possible, et à placer, pour ainsi dire, le philosophe au-dessus de ce vaste labyrinthe dans un point de vue fort élevé d'où il puisse apercevoir à la fois les sciences et les arts principaux.' (D'Alembert, *Discours*, 109). 'The encyclopedic arrangement of our knowledge [...] consists of collecting knowledge into the smallest area possible and of placing the philosopher at a vantage point, so to speak, high above this vast labyrinth, whence he can perceive the principal sciences and the arts simultaneously.' (D'Alembert, *Discourse*, 47).

16 Cf. Michel Foucault, *Les mots et les choses: Une archéologie des sciences humaines* (Paris: Gallimard, 1966), pp. 77–78.

Das Allgemeine Brouillon consists of 1151 notes written in 1798 and 1799 about multiple subjects. In Novalis' epistemological project, the two principles of organisation that characterise the French model, alphabetical order and the tree of knowledge as a pre-established system of knowledge, disappear. Rather than being a concrete encyclopaedic project, Novalis' text gathers the 'material' in view of what he calls *Encyclopedistics* and lays down the principles of a 'total-science' ('Totalwissenschaft'). In comparison to D'Alembert, totality is no longer the starting point (cf. the tree of knowledge) and the end point (as the material result) of an encyclopaedic project. Novalis turns epistemological totality into the utopia of the obligatorily unfinished perfect book of all books, a new Bible. 'Mein Buch soll eine scientifische Bibel werden – ein reales und ideales Muster – und Keim aller Bücher.'[17] He thus shifts it to the level of the concrete practice of establishing knowledge: totality does not constitute Novalis' project but turns into the endlessness of a radically interdisciplinary approach. Novalis includes highly heterogeneous elements in one 'system' that starts to vacillate and cannot be called a system anymore ('Systemlosigkeit in ein System gebracht').[18] In fact, the main purpose of *Encyclopedistics* is to create connections between the different sciences that man separates artificially: 'Die größesten Wahrheiten unsrer Tage verdanken wir dem Contact der lange getrennten Glieder der Totalwissenschaft.' (*Werke*, 509, Fragment 199)[19] In spite of a tendency in critical discussions to talk about Novalis' work in terms of an encyclopaedia,[20] Novalis' epistemological project is not an encyclopaedia in the sense that he gives this term himself,[21] rather it is an epistemologically relevant

---

17 Novalis, *Werke, Tagebücher und Briefe*, vol. 2, ed. by Hans-Joachim Mähl and Richard Samuel (Munich: Hanser, 1978), p. 599, Fragment 557, in the following as *Werke*. 'My book shall be a scientific Bible – a real, and an ideal model – and the seed of all books.' Novalis, *Notes for a Romantic Encyclopaedia: Das Allgemeine Brouillon*, translated and ed. by David W. Wood (Albany: State University of New York Press, 2007), p. 99, fragment 557; in the following as *Notes*.

18 Novalis, *Werke*, 200, Fragment 648. 'An authentic philosophical system [...] must systematize systemlessness.' Novalis, *Fichte Studies*, translated and ed. by Jane Kneller (Cambridge: Cambridge University Press, 2003), p. 187, fragment 648. According to Kilcher, Novalis' project belongs to an encyclopaedic paradigm he calls 'texture' that comes into existence at the very end of the eighteenth century and that replaces the paradigm of the 'alphabet' to which French Encyclopaedia belongs. Kilcher explains that Romantic epistemology organises knowledge in fragmented networks and not in an alphabetical, i.e. pragmatic and arbitrary but rational system. Cf. Kilcher, *Enzyklopädik*, 177–178, 323.

19 'We owe the most sublime truths of our day to contact with the long-separated elements of the total-science' (*Notes*, 30, fragment 199).

20 Cf. for example Gerhart Baumann. 'Novalis, Dichtung und Enzyklopädie: Unendliche Annäherungen', in *Skizzen* (Freiburg i.Br.: Rombach, 2000), pp. 25–35.

21 Cf. Novalis' definition of encyclopaedia (with reference to Werner): 'eine richtige Ordnung und Aufzählung der Kenntnisse, die man zur Erreichung eines Zwecks, nöthig hat.' (*Werke*, 634, Fragment 670). 'a correct ordering and enumeration of the knowledge necessary for the attainment of a *goal*' (*Notes*, 124, fragment 670).

poetic and unsystematic method of organising reality and human knowledge.

The difference between Novalis and D'Alembert is primarily due to the (post-Kantian) problems of the representation and foundation of knowledge. Kant reveals the realm of human knowledge to be fundamentally limited.[22] At the end of the eighteenth century, it becomes increasingly difficult to represent knowledge, since the foundation of knowledge eludes the grasp of human medial and intellectual faculties. Novalis shows, for example, that the origin of human knowledge is no longer available to mankind. According to D'Alembert, however, the search for the origin of the sciences constitutes the first step of the encyclopaedic project. 'Le premier pas que nous ayons à faire dans cette recherche, est de [...] remonter jusqu'à l'origine et à la génération de nos idées.'[23] Novalis points out that there is no longer one clearly definable beginning or a graspable *telos* of human activity. According to Novalis, absolute beginnings are imaginary: 'Keinen abs(oluten) Anfang giebts nicht – er gehört in die Kategorie d(er) imaginären Gedanken.' (*Werke*, 699, Fragment 1000)[24]

The problem of (the absent) origin and of the foundation of human knowledge has two central dimensions: the problem of self-consciousness and the question of the relationship between human intellect and sensibility. Kant founds human knowledge in transcendental subjectivity,[25] which is a mode of human self-consciousness that is not directly accessible to human beings. Nevertheless, it assures the foundation of human knowledge in the fundamental identity of the subject, and thus constitutes Kant's solution to the epistemological problem his critical project brought up. For Fichte,[26] as for the early German Romantics, this solution is not satisfactory since the self can never be described as one entity because of the inevitable double structure of self-consciousness ('Ich bin ich', *Werke*, 8, Fragment 1).[27] Whereas Fichte tries to find an absolute foundation of human knowledge – cf. the first sentence of his *Wissenschaftslehre* of 1794: 'Wir haben den abso-

---

22 For Kant, human knowledge is limited insofar as mankind can never access what constitutes objective reality: the thing-in-itself is inaccessible to the human mind and human knowledge is limited to the realm of phenomena.
23 D'Alembert, *Discours*, 84. 'The first step which lies before us in our endeavor is to [...] go back to the origin and generation of our ideas.' (D'Alembert, *Discourse*, 5).
24 'There is no such thing as an absolute beginning – it belongs in the category of imaginary thoughts.' (*Notes*, 173, fragment 1000).
25 Kant exposes this subjectivity in the transcendental deduction of the categories and calls it the 'synthetic unity of apperception'. Cf. Immanuel Kant, *Kritik der reinen Vernunft* (Hamburg: Meiner, 1998), § 16, in particular, B 141–B 142.
26 Cf. Dieter Henrich, 'Fichtes ursprüngliche Einsicht', in *Subjektivität und Metaphysik: Festschrift für Wolfgang Cramer*, ed. by Dieter Henrich and Hans Wagner (Frankfurt a. M.: Klostermann, 1966), pp. 188–232.
27 'I am I.' (*Fichte Studies*, 4, fragment 1)

lut-ersten, schlechthin unbedingten Grundsatz alles menschlichen Wissens *aufzusuchen.*[28] – in an absolute subjectivity, in Novalis' writings any knowledge about the self always implies the separation of the self, so that self-consciousness can hardly be considered the foundation of human knowledge. This position radically opposes Novalis to both (post-)Kantian philosophy and the French encyclopaedists. According to D'Alembert, human sensibility makes us conscious of ourselves: sensations tell us that we exist; more precisely, they presuppose the existence of a self-conscious principle of reason, 'principe pensant qui constitue notre nature, et qui n'est point différent de nous-mêmes'.[29]

The question of the possible connection between the realms of human sensibility and intellect is one of the key problems in Kantian philosophy and later German Idealism. D'Alembert acknowledges the problem early on: 'Pourquoi supposer que nous ayons d'avance des notions purement intellectuelles, si nous n'avons besoin, pour les former, que de réfléchir sur nos sensations?'[30] He resolves it by means of a metaphysical construction: according to D'Alembert, the relationship between the self and the world is ensured by an 'instinct' superior to reason:

> [...] n'y ayant aucun rapport entre chaque sensation et l'objet qui l'occasionne, ou du moins auquel nous la rapportons, il ne paraît pas qu'on puisse trouver, par le raisonnement, de passage possible de l'un à l'autre: il n'y a qu'une espèce d'instinct, plus sûr que la raison même, qui puisse nous forcer à franchir un si grand intervalle.[31]

In conjunction with double representation, D'Alembert's 'instinct' ensures the unity of a systematic approach to potentially infinite and arbitrary knowledge.

The passage about this *fundamental* role of instinct is precisely the one Novalis cites from D'Alembert's *Discours.* Just a few notes later he takes up the question and lays down his own, *historical* conception of instinct: 'Mit Instinkt hat der Mensch angefangen, mit Instinkt soll der Mensch endigen. Instinkt ist das *Genie im Paradiese* – vor der Periode der *Selbstabsonderung*(,)

---

28 Johann Gottlieb Fichte, *Grundlage der gesamten Wissenschaftslehre (1794)* (Hamburg: Meiner, 1997), p. 11. 'Our task is to *discover* the primordial, absolutely unconditioned first principle of all human knowledge.' Johann Gottlieb Fichte, *Science of knowledge*, translated and ed. by Peter Heath and John Lachs (Cambridge: Cambridge University Press, 1991), p. 93.

29 D'Alembert, *Discours*, 85. '[T]hinking principle which constitutes our nature and which is in no way distinct from ourselves' (D'Alembert, *Discourse*, 8).

30 D'Alembert, *Discours*, 85. 'Why suppose that we have purely intellectual notions at the outset [innate ideas], if all we need do in order to form them is to reflect upon our sensations?' (D'Alembert, *Discourse*, 7)

31 D'Alembert, *Discours*, 85–86. '[S]ince there is no connection between each sensation and the object that occasions it, or at least the object to which we relate it, it does not seem that any possible passage from one to the other can be found through reasoning. Only a kind of instinct, surer than reason itself, can compel us to leap so great a gap.' (D'Alembert, *Discourse*, 8–9)

Selbsterkenntniß.' (*Werke*, 536, Fragment 340)[32] In view of the fact that human existence is condemned to the realm of separation ('*Selbstabsonderung*'), absolute principles such as self-knowledge or instinct appear as being no longer accessible to mankind and turn into dynamic, historical processes. Novalis thus restrains human knowledge to an infinite approximation, which he illustrates by the image of the *perpetuum mobile*:

> Jede W(issenschaft) hat ihren Gott, der zugleich ihr Ziel ist. So lebt eigentlich die Mechanik vom Perpetuo mobili – und sucht zu gleicher Zeit, als ihr höchstes Problem, ein *Perpetuum mobile* zu contruiren. [...] Die Phil(osophie) sucht ein erstes und einziges Princip. Der Mathem(atiker) die Quadratur des Zirkels [...]. Der *Mensch* – *Gott*. [...] Über die Hindernisse der Auflösung jeder dieser Aufgaben. (Approximationsprincipe. Hierzu gehört auch das *absolute Ich*.) (*Werke*, 530, Fragment 314)[33]

Once the foundation of human knowledge becomes fragile and turns into a historical dynamic, the problem of the representation of knowledge arises. It is in this context that Novalis points out the epistemological relevance of an aesthetic order of knowledge.

The Reassessment of Imagination and the Aesthetic Order of Knowledge in Novalis' Project of Encyclopaedistics

In contrast to the French model of organising knowledge, Novalis turns to imagination as a central aspect of his encyclopaedic project. D'Alembert's vision of imagination is limited in two ways. Firstly, imagination appears as bound to the principle of imitation: D'Alembert defines imagination as 'the talent of creating by imitating'[34]. Secondly, imagination does not occupy a central place in the system of human faculties and knowledge. One could say that imagination is subordinate to the reign of double representation. According to D'Alembert, it is under the control of human understanding ('entendement') and thus a secondary matter in comparison to the key faculty of reason:

> Si nous plaçons la raison avant l'imagination, cet ordre nous paraît bien fondé et conforme au progrès naturel des opérations de l'esprit: l'imagination est une faculté

---

32 'Man began with instinct – and he will end with instinct. Instinct is the *genius in paradise* – before the period of self-separation and self-knowledge.' (*Notes*, 51, fragment 340)

33 'Every science has its God, that is also its goal. Thus mechanics actually lives by the *perpetuum mobile* – and seeks at the same time to construct, as its highest problem, a *perpetuum mobile*. [...] Philosophy seeks a first and single principle. The mathematician, the squaring of the circle [...]. *The human being – God.* [...] On the obstacles that hinder a solution to every one of these problems. (Approximation principles. The *absolute ego* belongs here as well.)' (*Notes*, 46–47, fragment 314)

34 D'Alembert, *Discourse*, 51. '[L]e talent de créer en imitant' (D'Alembert, *Discours*, 111). Cf. also D'Alembert, *Discours*, 102.

créatrice; et l'esprit, avant que de songer à créer, commence par raisonner sur ce qu'il voit et ce qu'il connaît.[35]

As in the case of 'instinct', D'Alembert's conception of knowledge is based on a 'naturally' ('progrès naturel') rational approach. In the writings of Novalis, the three central human faculties are the same as in the works of Bacon and the French encyclopaedists: memory, reason, and imagination. But Novalis transfers imagination to the heart of his epistemological conception: 'Gedächtniß ist directer (pos[itiver]) Sinn – Verstand – indirecter (neg[ativer]) Sinn. Die Einb[ildungs]Kr[aft] ist das würckende Princip – Sie [...] soll (äußrer) directer und (innrer) indirecter Sinn zugleich werden.' (*Werke*, 532, Fragment 327)[36]

While this reassessment of imagination reflects a general tendency in eighteenth-century European thinking,[37] Novalis highlights three specific aspects that constitute its epistemological impact: the substitution of the in-between for the (absent) centre, the productive potential of imagination and its medial functioning. Novalis situates imagination between the two other central human faculties. This in-between-position is one of the most important figures in the philosophy of Early German Romanticism. The in-between-position becomes the highest possible approximation to the (absent) positive synthetic unity. As does Schlegel, Novalis explains this by means of the metaphor of hovering: 'Sollte es noch eine höhere Sfäre [als das Nur-Seyn, P.K.] geben, so wäre es die zwischen Seyn und Nichtseyn – das Schweben zwischen beyden – Ein Unaussprechliches.' (*Werke*, 11, Fragment 3)[38] Human imagination does no longer ensure the possibility of absolute synthesis as it does in Kant's first version of the *Critique of Pure Reason*.[39]

---

35 D'Alembert, *Discours*, 111. 'Placing reason ahead of imagination appears to us to be a well-founded arrangement and one which is in conformity with the natural progress of the operations of the mind. Imagination is a creative faculty, and the mind, before it considers creating, begins by reasoning upon what it sees and knows.' (D'Alembert, *Discourse*, 51)

36 'Memory is a direct (positive) sense – Intellect – an indirect (negative) sense. Imagination is the effective principle – The imagination will become simultaneously an (outward) direct sense, and an (inward) indirect sense.' (*Notes*, 48, fragment 327)

37 Cf. Gabriele Dürbeck, *Einbildungskraft und Aufklärung: Perspektiven der Philosophie, Anthropologie und Ästhetik um 1750* (Tübingen: Niemeyer, 1998).

38 'Should there be a still higher sphere, it would be the sphere between being and not-being. – The oscillating between the two. – Something inexpressible.' (*Fichte Studies*, 6, fragment 3)

39 In the restricted context of this essay, we cannot recount the many challenges and problems of this point. In fact, there is a debate about the role imagination plays in Kantian philosophy, a debate that is connected to the different versions of the *Critique of Pure Reason*. Whereas imagination seems to guarantee the synthetic unity of the Kantian system in the first version (1781), things considerably change in the second one (1784), where some kind of rationalisation of imagination – and thus of the whole system – takes place. Heidegger is one of the critics who analyses the differences between the two versions. Cf. Martin Heidegger, *Kant und das Problem der Metaphysik*, 6 edn (Frankfurt a. M.: Klostermann, 1998). Cf. also Reinhard Loock, *Schwebende Einbildungskraft: Konzeptionen theoretischer Freiheit in der Philosophie Kants, Fichtes und Schellings* (Würzburg: Königshausen and Neumann, 2007) and Wilhelm Metz, *Kategoriende-*

Not synthesis but the oscillating ('Wechsel') of imagination, the fluctuation from one element to its opposite, now appears as the highest level of human activity and knowledge: 'Die Einbildungskraft ist das verbindende Mittelglied – die Synthese – die *Wechselkraft*.' (*Werke*, 94, Fragment 246)[40] Oscillation and hovering are some of the theoretical conceptions and metaphors the early German Romantics share with Fichte. As a matter of fact, Fichte established a connection between the dynamic of hovering oscillation and the functioning of imagination.[41] However, if imagination appears as a central human faculty in Novalis' writings, it does not play this central role in Fichte's philosophy. In fact, Fichte deals with imagination in the second part of the *Science of Knowledge*, i.e. not in the part that is dedicated to the foundation of knowledge.[42] Concerning the main features of imagination, both Fichte and Novalis, characterise imagination as an *active* principle of *creation*. For Novalis this is the most important difference between imagination and the other human faculties: 'Das Gefühl, der Verst(and) und d(ie) Vernunft sind gewisserweise passiv [...] – hingegen ist die Einbildungskraft allein *Kraft* – allein das Thätige – das Bewegende.' (*Werke*, 74, Fragment 212)[43] According to this conception, imagination not only serves as an organising principle of reality and knowledge, but it creates them. From an epistemological point of view, one can say that in Novalis' conception, the basis for the human organisation of knowledge is not simply to be represented on grounds of a universal and absolute principle – it has to be constructed.

The position of the in-between, the hovering between extremes cannot be expressed according to Novalis, it is 'inexpressible' ('ein Unaussprechliches'), which raises the problem of medial representation. According to Novalis, language and representation in general are no longer reliable means

---

duktion und produktive Einbildungskraft in der theoretischen Philosophie Kants und Fichtes (Stuttgart-Bad Cannstatt: Frommann-Holzboog, 1991).

40 'The imagination is the binding mediator – the synthesis – the *power of change* [*Wechselkraft*].' (*Fichte Studies*, 84, fragment 246)

41 Cf. Fichte, *Grundlage*, 134ff.

42 More precisely, imagination does not interfere in the fundamental part of Fichte's *Science of Knowledge* and it is not situated at the level of the empirical self (cf. Metz, *Kategoriendeduktion*, 209–210). It is, however, precisely this empirical level on which Novalis situates imagination. Cf. Gabriele Rommel, 'Imagination in the Transcendental Poetics of Novalis', in *The Romantic Imagination: Literature and Art in England and Germany*, ed. by Frederick Burwick and Jürgen Klein (Amsterdam/Atlanta: Rodopi, 1996), pp. 95–122, 103. According to Kilcher, this is the reason why there is no need for an aesthetic order in Fichte's conception of knowledge. Cf. Kilcher, *Enzyklopädik*, 13. Several critics show that, according to Fichte, imagination is dominated by reason. Cf. Loock, *Einbildungskraft*, 227, and Lore Hühn, 'Das Schweben der Einbildungskraft: Zur frühromantischen Überbietung Fichtes', *Deutsche Vierteljahrsschrift* 70.4 (1996) 569–599. This is another central difference between Fichte and Novalis.

43 'Feeling, understanding and reason are in a way passive [...] – imagination on the other hand is the only *power* – the only active one – the moving one.' (*Fichte Studies*, 65, fragment 212)

of describing reality and knowledge: 'was kann durch das Medium der Sprache *wahr* seyn?' (*Werke*, 12, Fragment 11)[44] Language and visual representation are indispensable for establishing and expressing human knowledge, but they are profoundly deficient as they are limited to the realm of mere reflection throwing back a distorted version of the true relationships. According to Novalis, human knowledge can never transcend the level of these deficiencies. Imagination, however, provides a decisive advantage over representation: it launches dynamic processes. This is what makes imagination a 'higher organ' and a 'poetic sense' (*Werke*, 357, Fragment 206). Dynamic and constructive activity replace the search for the absolute:

> Durch das freywillige Entsagen des Absoluten entsteht die unendliche freye Thätigkeit in uns – das Einzig mögliche Absolute, was uns gegeben werden kann und was wir durch unsere Unvermögenheit ein Absolutes zu erreichen und zu erkennen, finden. Dies uns gegebene Absolute läßt sich nur negativ erkennen, indem wir handeln und finden, daß durch kein Handeln das erreicht wird, was wir suchen. (*Werke*, 181, Fragment 566)[45]

If there is no access to the synthetic centre of human knowledge, passive faculties can no longer establish knowledge. Knowledge has rather to be established by actions, by dynamic processes that human beings institute themselves. Novalis substitutes the creation of knowledge for the pure organisation of given and metaphysically confirmed knowledge with the (knowledge-generating) activities of human imagination.

This reassessment of imagination is the basis on which Novalis establishes an aesthetic order of knowledge. *Encyclopaedistics* is revealed to be a poetic method of notation and of organising knowledge. Several aspects of this poetic method have a structure similar to imagination: the principle of analogy and heterogeneity, the role of combinatorics, which concerns the question of the infinite and of contingence, and Novalis' theory of passage and transition. In one of his notes Novalis points out that his encyclopaedic method relies essentially on the principle of analogy: 'ENC[YCLOPAEDISTIK]. *Analogistik*. Die Analogie – als Werckzeug, beschrieben und ihren

---

44 '[W]hat can be *true* through the medium of language?' (*Fichte Studies*, 7, fragment 11) At the end of the eighteenth century, this question is directly linked to the problem of representation ('Darstellung'). We cannot resume the highly productive debate on these issues in our restricted context. One can say that the major epistemological principles Novalis points out in *Das Allgemeine Brouillon* are central features of a new conception of *Darstellung*. As far as epistemological matters are concerned, the difference between classical approaches to knowledge and Romantic paradigms can be grasped in the different approaches to form – as it can be opposed to knowledge as content – and to medium, in which this normative distinction no longer works. Cf. Kilcher, *Enzyklopädik*, 177.

45 'Unending free activity in us arises through the free renunciation of the absolute – the only possible absolute that can be given us and that we only find through our inability to attain and know an absolute. This absolute that is given to us can only be known negatively, insofar as we act and find that what we seek cannot be attained through action.' (*Fichte Studies*, 168, fragment 566)

mannichfaltigen Gebrauch gezeigt'. (*Werke*, 556, Fragment 431)[46] Novalis
uses analogy as an instrument and does not implement Renaissance paradigms of a metaphysical world vision based on analogy.[47] He does, however,
believe in an absolute order of the universe that makes analogical thinking
possible, but for Novalis this absolute order is not accessible anymore.
'Analogistics' is a way to establish similarities between heterogeneous elements. The aim of this activity forms the heart of Novalis' *Encyclopedistics*,
the creation of productive combinations of different sciences. The use of
analogies and contrasts ('Contraste – sind *inverse* Aehnlichkeiten', *Werke*,
476, Fragment 32)[48] is a poetic method that makes it possible to discover
the epistemological potential of the in-between-position. The purpose of its
use is the *approach* of the absolute and infinite ('Alle Vereinigung des *Hetero-
génen* führt auf ∞', *Werke*, 690, Fragment 935)[49] and not the *realisation* of a
synthesis on a higher level. With this conception of heterogeneity, Novalis
places his epistemological project in the context of late eighteenth-century
dialectic thinking and, more precisely, in a line of conceptions that do not
emphasise a synthesis of the opposites but the heterogeneous dynamic of
contrast itself.[50]

Infinity is a central paradigm of combinatorial analysis. Novalis, indeed,
does refer to the *ars combinatoria* of Leibniz, a universal scientific method
that allows the hormonious structure of the world to be described. According to Leibniz, this structure is granted by the theorem of pre-established
harmony. Novalis radically modifies this central aspect of Leibniz' philosophy by inverting the status of harmony. It is most striking that the inversion
Novalis carries out when he refers to Leibniz' pre-established harmony is
exactly the same as in the case of D'Alembert's 'instinct'. Whereas Leibniz'

---

46 'ENCYCLOPEDISTICS. *Analogistics*. Analogy – described as an instrument, and its myriad
uses outlined.' (*Notes*, 67, fragment 431)
47 Analogy is possibly the most important Novalisian epistemological paradigm associated with
Renaissance thinking (for the general importance of analogy in the Renaissance *episteme* cf.
Foucault, *Mots*, chapter 2). Mystical thinkers like Böhme found their analogical procedures
on the basis of an all underlying unity and correspondence between inside and outside or
the self and the world. Cf. Gerald Funk et al., 'Symbole und Signaturen. Charakteristik und
Geschichte des Ähnlichkeitsdenkens', in *Ästhetik des Ähnlichen*, ed. by Gerald Funk et al.
(Frankfurt a. M.: Fischer, 2001), pp. 7–34. What is central for Novalis is not this unity, but
the epistemological potential of Renaissance practices and proceedings in the context of establishing an 'open epistemology.' Cf. Waldemar Fromm, 'Die Sympathie des Zeichens mit dem
Bezeichneten. Ähnlichkeit in Literatur und Sprachästhetik um 1800', in *Ästhetik des Ähnlichen*,
35–67, 40.
48 'Contrasts – are *inverse* similarities.' (*Notes*, 5, fragment 32)
49 'Every union of the *heterogeneous* leads to ∞.' (*Notes*, 166, fragment 935)
50 Referring to Schlegel, Maike Oergel summarises this conception as follows: 'The dynamic
dialectical process is not so much the path to the eventual solution, but the main event itself.'
Oergel, *Culture and Identity: Historicity in German Literature and Thought 1770–1815* (Berlin: de
Gruyter, 2006), p. 82.

pre-established harmony is the foundation of knowledge, Novalis turns it into a state yet to be achieved: 'Die praestabilirte Harmonie wird der Erfolg, oder die Constitution der vollk[ommenen] moralischen Welt seyn.' (*Werke*, 654, Fragment 750)[51] According to Novalis, combinatorial procedures, therefore, do not express a harmonions order but Novalis wants to use them as poetic principles, which create dynamic knowledge about the world.

The last aspect of Novalis' aesthetic order of knowledge concerns his theory of passage or transition. Novalis himself calls it a '[t]heory of *contact – of transition*'.[52] *Encyclopedistics* establishes relationships between heterogeneous elements of knowledge, which opposes him to the French encyclopaedists and to the classical system of representation. Instead of founding a new static system of organising knowledge, Novalis wants to concentrate on the poetic activity of the imagination that allows the creation of interspaces of transition and passage. For Novalis passage and transition result directly from the use of imagination: 'Aller Transitus – alle Bewegung ist Wircksamkeit der Einbild(ungs)Kr(aft).' (*Werke*, 96, Fragment 249)[53] In his notes, he describes imagination as being the faculty of an in-between, a moment in which a transition between heterogeneous elements is established: 'sich im Moment des Übergehens von Einem Gliede zum andern schwebend zu erhalten und anzuschauen' (*Werke*, 316, Fragment 13).[54]

New Epistemological Paradigms

The reassessment of the epistemological potential of imagination and the aesthetic ordering of knowledge bring up new epistemological paradigms at the end of the eighteenth century. These paradigms are an important step in the history of modern and even contemporary cultures of knowledge. What are the most important aspects of this conception of knowledge?

Firstly, heterogeneous elements can now be brought into contact with one another. According to Novalis, classical oppositions like knowledge and belief or science and aesthetics no longer structure the human relationship with knowledge. For Novalis, knowledge can never be separated from a form of belief (cf. *Werke*, 610, Fragment 601) and the traditional distinction between science and aesthetics is no longer valid. In Novalis' thinking, knowledge appears as one culture whose unity is not pre-established but has to be created in dynamic and heterogeneous processes.

---

51 'Preestablished harmony will be the result or constitution of the perfect moral world.' (*Notes*, 139, fragment 750)
52 *Notes*, 115, fragment 634. 'Theorie der *Berührung* – des *Übergangs*' (*Werke*, 622, Fragment 634).
53 'All transition – all movement is the efficacy of imagination.' (*Fichte Studies*, 86, fragment 249)
54 'to persist, at the moment of transition from one element to the other, in a hovering and to contemplate itself.' (My own translation.)

Secondly, Novalis does not have a conception of *absolute* knowledge. Knowledge becomes relative and can never transcend the highly deficient level of medial representation. Like human consciousness, knowledge is described by Novalis as a dynamic of oscillation ('Wechsel').[55] The particularity of Novalis' conception consists of the pursuit of finding absolute knowledge without transcending the level of human deficiency. According to Novalis, knowledge constitutes itself in terms of processes, as a movement between illusion and truth and not as the establishment – or rather representation – of absolute truth: 'Die Mittelresultate des Processes sind die Hauptsache – das zufällig gewordene – oder gemachte Ding – ist das Verkehrt Beabsichtigte.' (*Werke*, 610, Fragment 601)[56] Imagination is the central human faculty, it is the force of the in-between.

As a consequence, and thirdly, knowledge becomes dynamic ('Processes', 'gewordene') and contingent ('zufällig'). Knowledge is constituted in social practices that establish distinctions between illusion and truth. It is, once again, human imagination that creates both illusion and truth (cf. *Werke*, 87, Fragment 234) and, thus, reality. Synthesis – and what corresponds most to it on the level of human activity: the passage of the in-between – is now bound to both illusion and truth:

> Alle Illusion ist zur Wahrheit so wesentlich, wie der Körper der Seele – Irrthum ist das nothw[endige] Instrument d[er] Wahrheit – Mit dem Irrthum mach ich Wahrheit [...]. Alle Synth[ese] – alle Progression – oder Übergang fängt mit *Illusion* an [...].' (*Werke*, 610, Fragment 601)[57]

Novalis' works form an important step towards modern and even contemporary conceptions of cultures of knowledge. The latter share some central characteristics with Novalis' conception: the medial, constructed, dynamic character of knowledge and the impossibility of establishing a clear distinction between the so-called 'two cultures' of science and aesthetics. Novalis' approach to knowledge is on the one hand constructivist, which arises from the rapprochement of contemporary and Romantic epistemological paradigms.[58] On the other hand, there still is a conception of (an original) unity

---

55 'D(as) Bewußtseyn ist die Sfäre des Wissens. / Was für eine Beziehung ist das Wissen ? Es ist ein Seyn außer dem Seyn, das doch im Seyn ist.' (*Werke*, 10, Fragment 2). 'Consciousness is the sphere of knowledge. [...] What kind of a relation is knowledge? It is a being outside of being that is nevertheless within being.' (*Fichte Studies*, 5, fragment 2)

56 'The intermediate results of this process are the most important – while that which has come about by chance – or is fashioned by chance – is the inverse of what is intended.' (*Notes*, 106, fragment 601).

57 'All illusion is as essential to truth, as the body is to the soul – Error is the necessary instrument of truth – I create truth with error [...]. All synthesis – all progression – or transition, begins with *illusion*.' (*Notes*, 106, fragment 601)

58 Cf. for example Ferris' rapprochement of Novalis and Deleuze. Cf. David S. Ferris, 'Post-Modern Interdisciplinarity: Kant, Diderot and the Encyclopedic Project', *Modern Language Notes* 118 (2003) 1251–1277.

behind it: Novalis does not abandon all notion of synthetic and absolute truth in general. However, there is an important inversion of point of view: the starting point and the *telos* of organising knowledge is not this true unity anymore, but human knowledge, i.e. relative, historical, constructed knowledge that always appears as a combination of truth and illusion since it is impossible to access any absolute perspective.

Challenging Time(s)

Memory, Politics, and the Philosophy of Time in Jean Paul's *Quintus Fixlein*

Dirk Göttsche

I.

The late eighteenth century marks a significant threshold in the cultural history of time, effectively a revolution in European discourses about time, temporality and history, which culminated during the 1790s, in the wake of the French Revolution. But while the French Revolution acted as a catalyst for the new sense of living in an age of accelerated change and crisis, it was in fact preceded – and indeed facilitated – by the 'discovery of time'[1] in late Enlightenment thought, and in particular by the temporalization of historical thought ('Verzeitlichung', in Reinhart Koselleck's terms),[2] which filtered into exploring the historicity of all areas of knowledge and experience.[3] Releasing history from the eschatological framework of religious interpretation, this temporalization of history gave rise to the modern sense of critical time, to the notion of 'Zeitgeschichte' (of the present day reflecting and shaping history), and to historicist philosophies of history (from Herder to Hegel), which can be seen as both an expression and a containment of the newly discovered dynamics of history, since they sought to give secular meaning to the disturbing experience of radical change and the sense of living in an age of transition.

This pervasive dynamic of 'Verzeitlichung' also informs the rise of anthropology and empirical psychology in late eighteenth-century scholarship and literature. Writers such as Wieland, Moritz, Jean Paul, Mereau, Tieck, Novalis, Brentano, and Goethe began to explore the anthropology of time, in other words, the temporality of human life, the historicity of personal identity, and the perception and construction of time in the human

---

1 Stephen Toulmin and Jane Goodfield, *The Discovery of Time* (London: Hutchinson, 1965).
2 Reinhart Koselleck, *Vergangene Zukunft: Zur Semantik geschichtlicher Zeiten* (Frankfurt a. M.: Suhrkamp, 1979), pp. 34, 321; English translation: *Future Pasts: On the Semantics of Historical Time*, translated by Keith Tribe (Columbia SC: Columbia University Press, 2004).
3 For a more extensive discussion see Dirk Göttsche, *Zeit im Roman: Literarische Zeitreflexion und die Geschichte des Zeitromans im späten 18. und im 19. Jahrhundert* (Munich: Fink, 2001).

mind, with its 'distension' (in Paul Ricoeur's reading of Saint Augustine)[4] between the present moment, memory and anticipation. This anthropology of time culminated in Kant's understanding of time as the pure form of sensible intuition ('reine Form der sinnlichen Anschauung')[5] and in the temporalization of self ('Verzeitlichung des Selbstbewußtseins')[6] in Romanticism. Moreover, the modern notions of critical time and historicity also made social time a crucial issue in late eighteenth-century writing, long before the industrial revolution and capitalism led to a radical re-organization and rationalization of time in modern German culture. In writers such as Jean Paul and Goethe,[7] engagement with the anthropology of time and the new sense of critical time go along with a moral philosophy of time, which critiques the use of time in the society of the period and revalidates the significance of time for individual happiness as well as the resolution of political and social crises.

The 'discovery of time' thus affects all areas of late eighteenth-century experience and discourse. The German verb 'zeitigen', which dictionaries translate uneasily as 'bring about' or 'produce',[8] gives poignant expression to this modern sense of all-pervasive temporality and historicity by suggesting that whatever man or nature create is effectively produced by time, seen as a single force penetrating all aspects of the universe, or as Jean Paul notes: 'Zeitigen ist fast die Übersetzung von Temporisieren'.[9] Similarly, Koselleck highlights the transition from polyhistoric notions of multiple histories to the idea of one singular universal process of History in late eighteenth-century historicism.[10]

---

4 Paul Ricoeur, *Time and Narrative*, 3 vols, translated by Kathleen McLaughlin and David Pellauer (Chicago: University of Chicago Press, 1984–88), I, pp. 16–22.

5 Immanuel Kant, *Werke in zehn Bänden*, ed. by Wilhelm Weischedel (Darmstadt: Wissenschaftliche Buchgesellschaft, 1983), III, p. 79 (*Kritik der reinen Vernunft*, A31).

6 Manfred Frank, *Das Problem 'Zeit' in der deutschen Romantik: Zeitbewußtsein und Bewußtsein von Zeitlichkeit in der frühromantischen Philosophie und in Tiecks Dichtung* (Munich: Winkler, 1972), p. 15.

7 See for example Goethe's novel *Wilhelm Meisters Wanderjahre* (Göttsche, *Zeit im Roman*, 406–432).

8 See for example *Collins German – English, English – German Dictionary*, unabridged, ed. by Peter Terrell et al., 4th edn (Glasgow: Harper Collins, 1999), p. 953; *Langenscheidts Handwörterbuch Englisch*, part II: *Deutsch – Englisch*, by Sonia Brough, ed. by the Langenscheidt-Redaktion, 5th edn (Berlin, Munich: Langenscheidt, 1999), p. 1449; *The Oxford-Duden German Dictionary: German – English / English – German*, ed. by the Dudenredaktion et al., 2nd edn (Oxford: Oxford University Press, 1999), p. 845.

9 'Produce almost translates as temporalize'. Jean Paul's works are cited in the text in German, giving series, volume and page numbers in the Hanser edition: Jean Paul, *[Sämtliche] Werke*, ed. by Norbert Miller (Munich: Hanser, 1974–89). Here Jean Paul, *Werke*, II/2, p. 982. All unreferenced translations are my own.

10 See Reinhart Koselleck and Horst Günther, 'Geschichte', in *Geschichtliche Grundbegriffe: Historisches Lexikon zur politisch-sozialen Sprache in Deutschland*, ed. by Otto Brunner, Werner Konze, and R. Koselleck, 8 vols (Stuttgart: Klett-Cotta, 1971–97), II, pp. 593–717, 647–678. – This may be the appropriate place to note the very different mapping of the semantic field in German

One of the most striking stylistic features of the new, critical sense of time and history in German literature during the 1790s is the emergence of a metaphoric of time, a system of metaphors which express the period's heightened awareness of historical crisis and of both political and epistemological challenge in terms of temporal experience. Jean Paul's works provide ample evidence of this metaphoric, well before it became wide-spread during and after the era of Napoleonic occupation. In the preface to his novel *Siebenkäs* (1796), for example, Jean Paul calls the 'Zeitungsmacher' (the journalist) a 'Zeitevangelist' (I/2, 20); in *Flegeljahre* (1804/05), Vult's diary is classed as 'Zeitstück' (I/2, 996); in *Briefe und bevorstehender Lebenslauf* (1799) satirical criticism of the times uses the 'Zeitmann' family as an allegorical foil (I/4, 931ff.); and political critique in Jean Paul's essays after 1800 abounds with temporal metaphors of historicity such as 'Zeittäuschung', 'Zeit-Flucht', 'Zeitfeinde' (I/5, 999, 1015, 1144), 'Zeit-Hoffnungen', 'Zeit-betrachtungen', and 'Zeitmenschen' (II/3, 269, 424, 691).[11] These later and more obviously political examples of Jean Paul's metaphoric of time coincide with the wave of 'Zeitgeist' essayism during the period of Napoleonic occupation, which reflects the overwhelming experience of accelerated change: 'Wer die letzten zwanzig Jahre gelebt hat, der hat für Jahrhunderte gelebt', as Ernst Moritz Arndt puts it in the first volume of his *Geist der Zeit* (1806).[12] It is thus not coincidental that neologisms such as 'Zeitgeschichte' and 'Zeitgeist' often originate around or just after 1800, when this political metaphoric of time first emerged, which was later to be elaborated further by the Young German writers and the language of political liberalism during the 1830s.[13]

German literature plays a crucial role in the emergence of the new, modern sense of temporality and historicity in the late eighteenth century, reflecting and promoting it not just in terms of themes and motifs, but also in the transformation of literary styles and genres.[14] Arguably the most direct response to temporalization and historical crisis in German literature during 1790s is the emergence of the 'Zeitroman', the social and political

and English. The lack of English equivalents to German derivations of 'Zeit', such as 'zeitigen', 'Zeitgeschichte', 'Zeitreflexion', 'Zeitkritik', 'Zeitgeist', or 'Zeitroman', suggests that in English time, temporality and history remain largely separate concepts, while in German the revolution in temporal and historical thought in the late eighteenth century has resulted in the cross-mapping of these three aspects of 'Verzeitlichung' in the interrelated meanings of the noun 'Zeit' and its derivations.

11 See Göttsche, *Zeit im Roman*, 140.
12 'Those who have lived through the past twenty years, have lived for centuries.' Ernst Moritz Arndt, *Ausgewählte Werke in 16 Bänden*, ed. by Heinrich Meisner and Robert Geerds (Leipzig: Max Hesse, not dated), IX, p. 49; also see Göttsche, *Zeit im Roman*, 274–284.
13 See Wulf Wülfing, *Schlagworte des Jungen Deutschland: Mit einer Einführung in die Schlagwortforschung* (Berlin: Erich Schmidt, 1982).
14 See Göttsche, *Zeit im Roman*, 65–200.

novel, which was specifically designed to represent and critique the experience of accelerated historical change, reflect the impact of political history on private life, explore individual involvement in 'making history', and intervene in political controversy as well as wider cultural debate.[15] August Lafontaine's *Klara du Plessis und Klairant* (1794), Friedrich Ludwig Textor's *Paul Roderich* (1794), Therese Huber's *Die Familie Seldorf* (1795/96), Friedrich Maximilian Klinger's *Geschichte eines Teutschen der neusten Zeit* (1798), and Johann Weitzel's *Lindau oder der unsichtbare Bund* (1805) are just some early examples of this new departure in genre history.[16] Although Jean Paul did not participate in the creation of the 'Zeitroman', he developed the most extensive *poetics* of time in German literature around 1800. His persistent engagement with time, temporality and historicity reflects the universal impact of 'Verzeitlichung' in German literature of the period and marks a crucial threshold on the road from *Empfindsamkeit* (the proto-Romantic counter strand in later German Enlightenment, normally translated into English as sensibility) to Jena Romanticism. Jean Paul's poetics of time transform *Empfindsamkeit*'s obsession with human mortality and social time into an all-encompassing dialectic of time, which anticipates the transcendental dialectic of time in Novalis or Friedrich Schlegel, but rejects the Romantic temporalization of self and the Romantic philosophy of history.[17] Jean Paul's poetics of time, i.e. his both critical and literary engagement with the individual's experience and awareness of time, with the philosophy of time, and with the period's political history, epitomize the multiple links between these seemingly separate sites of temporalization during the 1790s and early 1800s, while also confirming his singular position in German literature around 1800, as he participates critically in idealist, Classicist and Romanticist debates – which he does from the perspective of advanced late Enlightenment scepticism and empiricism.

15 See Göttsche, *Zeit im Roman*, 200–405.
16 August Heinrich Julius Lafontaine, *Clara du Plessis und Clairant: Eine Familiengeschichte französischer Emigrierten*, ed. by Evi Rietzschel (Munich: Beck, 1986); [Friedrich Ludwig Textor], *Leben, Abentheuer und Heldentod Paul Roderichs des Democraten: Eine Geschichte aus dem gegenwärtigen Kriege, von seinem aristocratischen Vetter beschrieben* (Frankfurt a. M., Leipzig: Neue Buchhandlung, 1794); Therese Huber, *Die Familie Seldorf*, 2 parts in 1 vol, ed. by Magdalene Heuser (Hildesheim: Olms, 1989); Friedrich Maximilian Klinger, *Geschichte eines Teutschen der neusten Zeit*, in *Werke*, 12 vols (Königsberg: Friedrich Nicolovius, 1809–16), II; [Johann] Weitzel, *Lindau oder der unsichtbare Bund: Eine Geschichte aus dem Revolutions-Kriege* (Frankfurt a. M.: Bernhard Körner, 1805).
17 Also see Ralf Berhorst, *Anamorphosen der Zeit: Jean Pauls Romanästhetik und Geschichtsphilosophie* (Tübingen: Niemeyer, 2002), pp. 6–68.

II.

As a case study of the period's fascination with temporality and historicity, the main body of this essay will combine an overview of Jean Paul's philosophy and poetics of time with brief analysis of his *Leben des Quintus Fixlein* (1796), a seemingly random collection of pieces enigmatically subtitled 'aus funfzehn Zettelkästen gezogen; nebst einem Musteil und einigen Jus de tablette' ('Musteil' is a widow's right to fifty percent of the food in her deceased husband's estate, and 'Jus de tablette' are the forerunners of the modern stock cube).[18] The comedy of the collection's subtitle exemplifies Jean Paul's pervasive humour, which also reflects his scepticism about any set truths or (Enlightened or idealist) philosophical systems; and his extensive use of metaphor is the mark of a poetic imagination which constantly explores connections between seemingly unrelated areas of knowledge. The book opens with two quasi-prefaces, a 'Billet an meine Freunde' (Letter to my friends), which contains Jean Paul's famous suggestion of three paths towards greater happiness – 'drei Wege, glücklicher (nicht glücklich) zu werden' (I/4, 10)[19] – and the preface to

---

18 'Life of Quintus Fixlein, extracted from 15 card index boxes, together with a Musteil and some Jus de tablette' (also see editor's note in I/4, p. 1141). Like several of Jean Paul's works the book was never fully translated into English, but Thomas Carlyle, one of the chief promoters of German-English cultural transfer in the nineteenth century and a keen admirer of Jean Paul, included the central piece, the Fixlein idyll, in his translation of two Jean Paul 'romances' in 1827: *German Romance: Specimens of its Chief Authors; with Biographical and Critical Notices. By the Translator of Wilhelm Meister, and Author of the Life of Schiller*, 4 vols, III: Jean Paul Friedrich Richter (Edinburgh, London: William and Charles Tait, 1827). And two of the allegories, 'The Moon' and 'The Death of an Angel', saw multiple translations and publications during the nineteenth century, making these ostensible 'romances' the most widely published texts by Jean Paul in English (along with 'Gothic' pieces such as 'The New Year's Night of an Unhappy Man' and 'The Atheist's Dream'). See Eduard Berend, *Jean-Paul-Bibliographie*, neu bearbeitet und ergänzt von Johannes Krogoll (Stuttgart: Klett, 1963), pp. 75–81; also J. W. Smeed, 'Carlyles Jean-Paul-Übersetzungen' *Deutsche Vierteljahrsschrift für Literatur und Geistesgeschichte* 35 (1961) 262–279. This popular British reception thus seems to limit Jean Paul to stereotypical perceptions of German sentimentalism and 'Romanticism', whereas Jean Paul's highly self-reflexive, ironic and philosophical style of writing is specifically designed to undercut such discursive clichés.

19 Carlyle translates the full passage as follows: 'Of ways for becoming happier (not happy) I could never inquire out more than three. The first, rather an elevated road, is this: To soar away so far above the clouds of life, that you see the whole external world, with its wolf-dens, charnel-houses, and thunder-rods, lying far down beneath you, shrunk into a little child's garden. The second is: Simply to sink down into this little garden; and there to nestle yourself so snugly, so homewise, in some furrow, that in looking out from your warm lark-nest, you likewise can discern no wolf-dens, charnel-houses, or thunder-rods, but only blades and ears, every one of which, for the nest-bird, is a tree, and a sun-screen, and rain-screen. The third finally, which I look upon as the hardest and cunningest, is that of alternating between the other two.' (*Life*, 116) In the notes to this chapter quotations from Carlyle's English translation will be cited from the following facsimile edition, using the abbreviation *Life* and page number: Jean Paul Friedrich Richter, *'Army-Chaplain Schmelzle's Journey to Flaetz' and 'Life of Quintus Fixlein'*, translated by Thomas Carlyle, introduction by Wulf Koepke (Columbia SC: Camden House, 1991).

the second edition of 1801, written in 1796,[20] where humour and self-reflexive narrative temporalize the genre by providing the story of a journey meant to result in the production of the preface rather than the finished product. This is only the first instance of his technique of temporalization in the form of open-ended, fragmentary writing.

In a poignant example of the 'Kontrastspannungen' (the contrasts and tensions)[21] which characterize his writing throughout, this ironic preface is complemented with the first of three allegorical narratives, which draw on the rhetoric of *Empfindsamkeit* and on cosmological imagery to explore the temporality of human life. This first allegory, 'Die Mondfinsternis' (Eclipse of the Moon) is followed in the 'Musteil für Mädchen' by two further related allegories, 'Der Tod des Engel' and 'Der Mond, eine phantasierende Geschichte', which all link back to the initial preface's first path towards happiness, the path which leads 'in die Höhe' (upwards) and achieves happiness through (spatial and/or psychological) distance from the daily world of malice, death and danger, 'die ganze äußere Welt mit ihren Wolfsgruben, Beinhäusern und Gewitterableitern' (I/4, 10).[22]

By contrast, the book's central narrative, the idyll *Des Quintus Fixlein Leben bis auf unsere Zeiten*, illustrates the second path towards potential happiness, which escapes the hardships and worries of existence by undercutting them:

> [...] herabzufallen ins Gärtchen und da sich so einheimisch in eine Furche einzunisten, daß, wenn man aus seinem warmen Lerchennest heraussieht, man ebenfalls keine Wolfsgruben, Beinhäuser und Stangen, sondern nur Ähren erblickt, deren jede für den Nestvogel ein Baum und ein Sonnen- und Regenschirm ist. (I/4, 10)[23]

While the cosmological world of the metaphysical allegories in the book's first part imagines movement beyond the constraints of earthly reality, the idealized microcosm of the idyll, which sees the humble teacher Fixlein advance through deputy headship of his school to the secure position of pastor in his home village, married man and father, excludes the challenges of human existence and political history through a change of perspective.[24] It moves conflict beyond the horizon to celebrate enjoyment of the present moment in line with the narrator's 'Lebensregel' (his moral rule): 'Jede Minute, Mensch, sei

20 See Sabine Straub, '"Vorrede zur Vorrede": Aus Jean Pauls unveröffentlichten Materialien zur "Geschichte meiner Vorrede zur zweiten Auflage des Quintus Fixlein"', *Jahrbuch der Jean-Paul-Gesellschaft* 44 (2009) 18–32, 21.
21 Gerhart Baumann, 'Jean Paul: "Des Luftschiffers Giannozzo Seebuch"', in *Die Wissenschaft von deutscher Sprache und Dichtung: Methoden, Probleme, Aufgaben. Festschrift F. Maurer*, ed. by Siegfried Gutenbrunner et al. (Suttgart: Klett, 1963), pp. 399–423, 414.
22 For a translation, see note 19 above.
23 For a translation, see note 19 above.
24 See Brigitte Langer, *Jean Pauls Weg zur Metapher: Sein 'Buch' 'Leben des Quintus Fixlein'* (Frankfurt a. M.: Peter Lang, 2003), p. 31.

dir ein volles Leben!' (I/4, 185)[25] By setting his idyll *within* contemporary society (rather than in a pastoral Arcadia outside history), Jean Paul reinvents
the genre as a critique of the temporal and historical world.[26] Fixlein's social
rise is ironically the result of a series of coincidences, errors, and confusions,
which Jean Paul invents to critique the failures of corporative administration
in the Holy Roman Empire. In line with his definition of the idyll as 'epische
Darstellung des *Vollglücks* in der *Beschränkung*' (I/5, 258),[27] *Quintus Fixlein*
combines realist representation of petit-bourgeois existence with its poetic
idealization through a focus on 'Himmelfahrten des gedrückten Lebens' (I/
5, 257; also see I/4, 71)[28] and holidays – religious and school holidays, birth-
days, ecstatic moments of love, and other breaks in the bourgeois calendar.
Given the irreconcilable difference between '*bürgerliche[s]* Leben' and ideal humanity (I/4, 184), such idealization necessarily relies on irony or humour, in
line with Jean Paul's definition of humour as 'das umgekehrte Erhabene',
which 'vernichtet nicht das Einzelne, sondern das Endliche durch den Kon-
trast mit der Idee' (I/5, 125).[29]

The book's third part opens with one of Jean Paul's most important theoretical essays, 'Über die natürliche Magie der Einbildungskraft', which
presents arguably the fullest account of his anthropology of time, while it
also provides a poetological comment on the Fixlein idyll. A further essay
on the moral philosophy of love ('Es gibt weder eine eigennützige Liebe
noch eine Selbstliebe, sondern nur eigennützige Handlungen')[30] separates
two satirical pieces (the official Josuah Freudel's complaint about always
being in the wrong place at the wrong time, and headmaster Florian Fälbel's
account of a disastrous school trip), which put the petit-bourgeois world of
the Fixlein idyll and its celebration of happy moments into critical perspective. These satires of German provincialism and narrow-mindedness form
the opposite pole to the cosmological allegories of love which precede the
Fixlein idyll in the book's symmetrical composition, and this contrapuntal
arrangement is underlined symbolically by their dedication to male readers
('für Mannspersonen'), whereas the sentimental allegories – placing tradi-

25 'Be every minute, Man, a full life to thee!' (*Life*, 300)
26 Also see Ralph-Rainer Wuthenow, 'Nachwort', in Jean Paul, *Leben des Quintus Fixlein* (Stuttgart:
    Reclam, 1987), pp. 313–327, 316–317; Götz Müller, *Jean Pauls Ästhetik und Naturphilosophie*
    (Tübingen: Niemeyer, 1983), pp. 195–203; Kurt Wölfel, '"Ein Echo, das sich selber in das
    Unendliche nachhallt": Eine Betrachtung von Jean Pauls Poetik und Poesie', in *Jean Paul-Stu-
    dien*, ed. by Bernhard Buschendorf (Frankfurt a. M.: Suhrkamp, 1989), pp. 259–300, 260–261.
27 'This [the idyll] is the epic presentation of *perfect happiness within limits*.' [Jean Paul,] *Horn of
    Oberon: Jean Paul Richter's School for Aesthetics*, introduction and translation by Margaret R. Hale
    (Detroit: Wayne State University, 1973), p. 186.
28 'heavenly ascents from an oppressed life' (*Horn of Oberon*, 185).
29 'Humour as the inverted sublime annihilates not the individual but the finite through its con-
    trast with the idea.' (*Horn of Oberon*, 88)
30 'There is no selfish love nor love of self, there are only selfish actions.'

tional gendering in ironic perspective – are meant to be for girls ('für Mädchen'). The book's third part thus mirrors the collection's compositional
structure as a whole by combining heterogeneous and contrasting pieces
which are linked through multiple cross-references and intertextual echoes.
Rather than following a linear 'Bewegung des Denkens'[31] the deliberate ran-
domness and pointedly non-teleological structure of the composition points
to the quasi-encyclopaedic texture of Jean Paul's writing,[32] reflected in the
motif of the 'Zettelkasten' (the filing box), which the narrator uses for the
chapter headings, echoing Fixlein's own 'Zettelkasten' archive of childhood
memories.[33] One of the central themes linking the short prose pieces in the
Quintus Fixlein collection is Jean Paul's (partially oblique) engagement with
time, temporality and 'Zeitgeschichte'.

III.

The starting point for Jean Paul's engagement with time – both in biographical and in philosophical and literary terms – is human mortality and the col-
lapse of religious metaphysics.[34] His much-cited death vision of 15 November 1790 marks the transition from the satirical writing of his youth to his
mature works and the emergence of his poetics of time at the intersection of
anthropology and metaphysics. The vision of his own death makes the awareness of time the basis of self-awareness and personal identity, while it also
generates a moral philosophy of time, based on revalidation of life:

> Wichtigster Abend meines Lebens: denn ich empfand den Gedanken des Todes, daß
> es schlechterdings kein Unterschied ist ob ich morgen oder in 30 Jahren sterbe, daß

---

31 'a movement of thought'; Langer, *Jean Pauls Weg zur Metapher*, 187.
32 Andreas Kilcher, *'mathesis' und 'poiesis': Die Enzyklopädik der Literatur 1600 bis 2000* (Munich:
    Fink, 2003), p. 382, also see pp. 124–127 on *Quintus Fixlein*.
33 In the *Quintus Fixlein* collection such poetological reference to encyclopaedic intertextuality is –
    paradoxically – part of Jean Paul's approach to small prose (*Kleine Prosa*). Interestingly, the
    book's third part is entitled 'Jus de tablette' (stock cubes), which suggests that the collection's
    short pieces are concentrated food for thought requiring the reader's active participation if they
    are to become palatable broth. Resonating with the period's poetics of the aphorism and the
    fragment, this is essentially the same idea that Peter Altenberg was to use some one-hundred
    years later in outlining the poetics of his modernist prose sketches, which he defined as 'Ex-
    trakte des Lebens' (extracts of life), ironically comparing them to Liebig's stock cubes. See
    Peter Altenberg, 'Selbstbiographie', in *Auswahl aus seinen Büchern* von Karl Kraus (Frank-
    furt a. M.: Insel, 1997 [Vienna: Schroll, 1932]), p. 59. Also see Dirk Göttsche, *Kleine Prosa
    in Moderne und Gegenwart* (Münster: Aschendorff, 2006), pp. 65–68; for the late eighteenth-
    century context of Jean Paul's short prose see *Kleine Prosa: Theorie und Geschichte eines Textfeldes
    im Literatursystem der Moderne*, ed. by Thomas Althaus, Wolfgang Bunzel and Dirk Göttsche
    (Tübingen: Niemeyer, 2007), pp. ix-24, 45–54.
34 For a more comprehensive account of Jean Paul's poetics of time see Göttsche, *Zeit im Roman*,
    115–141.

alle Plane und alles mir davonschwindet und daß ich die armen Menschen lieben sol, die sobald mit ihren Bisgen Leben niedersinken [...].[35]

Moving beyond this existential and moral legacy of *Empfindsamkeit*, Jean Paul's death vision culminates in the realization that God is dead, as reflected poignantly in the 'Rede des toten Christus vom Weltgebäude herab, daß kein Gott sei' in his novel *Siebenkäs* (I/2, 270–275).[36] This turn from Enlightened scepticism to radical nihilism, which Ralf Simon has recently seen as anticipating Nietzsche, generates the key problematic in Jean Paul's writing, namely 'contrafactual production of meaning [Sinn]',[37] his attempt to project and sustain a metaphysical frame of reference against the despair of nihilism by giving meaning to life through ceaseless writing.

It is ultimately his continued belief in the metaphysical origin of the soul and hence the metaphysical needs of the individual which transforms the nihilism of his death vision into the fundamental dialectic of mortality and immortality, time and eternity, the finite world of time and history, and the timeless infinite beyond and above, which marks the core dynamic in his philosophy of time. In Ralf Berhorst's summary:

> Der Diskurs über die Unsterblichkeit der Seele und die Fortsetzung des Lebens nach dem Tode verdeutlicht seine [Jean Paul's] Vorstellung einer unaufhebbaren Grenze zwischen Endlichkeit und Unendlichkeit. Diese ist gleichbedeutend mit der Differenz zwischen Zeit und Geschichte einerseits und dem ersehnten Ideal der Zeitlosigkeit und Ewigkeit andererseits.[38]

However, Berhorst's view that Jean Paul regards time as purely negative, as exclusively 'nichts' and 'vernichtend',[39] echoes older research in suggesting that the author's literary engagement with time and temporality was effectively a struggle *against* time.[40] Such one-sided reading overlooks the validation of time in his moral philosophy of time, and it fails to acknowledge the fact that the difference between time and eternity initiates a dialectical movement, which integrates Jean Paul's poetic visions of immortality and eternity in the universal dynamic of 'Verzeitlichung'. Early Romanticism construes

---

35 'Most important evening of my life: since I experienced the thought of death, that it simply does not make any difference whether I die tomorrow or in thirty years time, that all my plans and everything fades away for me, and that I should love the poor people who sink down so soon with what little life they have.' Cited from *Jean Paul 1763–1963* (= Sonderausstellungen des Schiller-Nationalmuseums, catalogue 11), ed. by Bernhard Zeller (Marbach: Schiller-Gesellschaft, 1963), p. 18.
36 'Dead Christ's Speech from the Top of the World lamenting that there is no God.'
37 Ralf Simon, 'Jean Pauls Idyllentiere oder Hermeneutik der Welt-als-Idylle', *Jahrbuch der Jean-Paul-Gesellschaft* 44 (2009) 63–80, 74–75.
38 Berhorst, *Anamorphosen der Zeit*, 1. 'The discourse about the immortality of the soul and the continuation of life after death illustrates Jean Paul's idea of an unsurmountable barrier between the finite and the infinite. This is synonymous with the difference between time and history on the one hand, and the longed-for ideal of timelessness and eternity on the other.'
39 Berhorst, *Anamorphosen der Zeit*, 43.
40 For a fuller discussion see Göttsche, *Zeit im Roman*, 116, note 146.

the dialectic of time as progressive 'Einheit von Einheit und Differenz'[41] based on the Romantic philosophy of history and temporalization of the idealist concepts of identity and self-awareness. By contrast, Jean Paul's antithetical dialectic of 'Zeit und Ewigkeit' (I/5, 65) cannot conceive of *Einheit der Zeit* (I/1, 722) within the temporal world. The crucial role of ecstatic moments in his writing, as symbolic approximations of eternity, only serves to reinforce the fundamental temporality and historicity of human life. Grounding his philosophy of time in anthropology, Jean Paul maintains that even 'in *Arkadien* würden wir nach *Utopien* schmachten' (I/3, 222), 'selbst im 2ten Leben [...] nach aller Möglichkeit unsrer Natur nicht anders selig werden als durch die Perspektive einer 3ten [Zukunft]'[42]. There is no escape from the dialectic of time in Jean Paul's world, and this dialectic is productive, producing the conditions both for our happiness and our misery.

The allegorical parables in the first part of the *Quintus Fixlein* collection illustrate this cross-mapping of metaphysics and anthropology in Jean Paul's philosophy of time. The eclectic imagery of his allegories, which blends philosophical, religious and sentimental symbolism into a poetic language of his own, anticipates the early Romantic project of a 'new mythology'.[43] The allegory 'Der Tod eines Engels' (Death of an Angel) links the realms of mortality and immortality, the historical world 'below' and eternity 'above' through a narrative double-bind: as a soldier on a battle-field experiences death as rebirth to a second life in 'Eden', the sympathetic angel of man's last hour ('Engel der *letzten* Stunde') decides to take his place on earth (I/4, 45), suffering the burden of physical existence and man's metaphysical yearning, aggravated by the death of the soldier's beloved wife from grief. At her grave, the soldier's body finally fails the angel; he dies in turn and is

41 Manfred Engel, *Der Roman der Goethezeit*, vol. 1: *Anfänge in Klassik und Frühromantik: Transzendentale Geschichten* (Stuttgart: Metzler, 1993), p. 328; 'unison of unity and difference'.

42 Jean Paul, *Sämtliche Werke: Historisch-kritische Ausgabe*, Abt. III: *Briefe*, ed. by Eduard Berend (Berlin: Akademie-Verlag, 1956–64) II, p. 280. 'In Arcadia we would still yearn for Utopia.' 'Even in a second life our nature would not allow us contentment without the prospect of a third future.'

43 For a relevant discussion of Romanticism's 'new mythology' see Heinz Gockel, *Mythos und Poesie: Zum Mythosbegriff in Aufklärung und Frühromantik* (Frankfurt a. M.: Klostermann, 1981), pp. 321–337; Manfred Frank, *Der kommende Gott: Vorlesungen über die Neue Mythologie* (Frankfurt/M.: Suhrkamp, 1982), pp. 153–187; for Herder's influence on Jean Paul's 'new mythology' see Hans Esselborn, '"Denn der Unendliche hat in den Himmel seinen Namen in glühenden Sternen gesäet": Die astronomische Metaphorik des Unendlichen bei Jean Paul', in *Geschichtlichkeit und Gegenwart: Festschrift H. D. Irmscher*, ed. by Hans Esselborn and Werner Keller (Cologne: Böhlau, 1994), pp. 209–228; on the angel allegories in Romanticism and Jean Paul see Monika Schmitz-Emans, 'Engel in der Krise: Zum Engelsmotiv in der romantischen Ästhetik und in Jean Pauls Roman *Der Komet*', *Jahrbuch der Jean-Paul-Gesellschaft* 38 (2003) 111–138; on Jean Paul's poetic fascination with the moon Karl-Heinz Rofkar, '*Silberküste einer andern Welt –*': *Jean Paul und der Mond: Eine lexikographische Anthologie seiner metaphorischen, parabolischen, allegorischen und symbolischen Selenismen* (Bielefeld: Aisthesis, 2000).

kissed back into eternal life by his brother, the angel of birth ('Engel der ersten Stunde'; I/4, 49). The sentimental play with the interchangeability of birth and death, the visualization of men's 'first' and 'last' hours as angels, and the cross-stitching of temporality and eternity in the motif of the death angel's rebirth through death in life inform the story with a metaphysical dialectic of time, which – giving a Romantic turn to typical motifs of *Empfindsamkeit* – centres on love as the universal principle of synthesis: it is out of love for humankind that the death angel seeks embodiment in life; and it is love for the deceased which makes the lovers yearn for re-unification through death (I/4, 47–48). In line with the collection's essay against egotism and its metaphysical definition of love as the magnetic 'Universalgeist' (universal spirit) of the moral world (I/4, 223), love is construed paradoxically as both the agent and the antidote of temporality, since it reflects man's '*Sinn des Grenzenlosen*' (his innate sense of the infinite; I/4, 200), the most powerful force of temporalization in Jean Paul and his equivalent to the Romantic concept of *Sehnsucht* (infinite yearning).

The 'fantastic story' 'Der Mond' (The Moon) presents a variation on the same theme, again symbolizing temporality and eternity as two co-existing 'worlds' linked through love, death, and man's metaphysical yearning. Protected by the invisible angel of the future, the young couple Eugenius and Rosamunde take their sick two-year-old child into the mountains, the symbolic sphere of the sublime, in yet another 'Himmelfahrt des gedrückten Lebens'. As first the child, then the father and finally the mother die, their upward journey turns into an allegory of everyman's course through life to death 'auf der ewigen Bergstraße durch die Zeit' (I/4, 38).[44] The allegory's narrative introduction with its antithetical gravestone inscriptions – 'Ich gehe vorüber' and 'Hier finden wir uns wieder' (I/4, 52)[45] – prepares the ground for the motif of metaphysical 'Wieder-holung' (repetition in Kierkegaard's sense),[46] the loving family's eventual reunification in the realm of eternity, symbolized by the moon. In this allegory, the temporal world and its beyond are linked not only by love and 'unendliche Sehnsucht' (I/4, 60), but also through dreams, which are seen – again in line with Jean Paul's essay on the natural magic of imagination – as yet another human faculty that transcends the confines of every-day existence. The allegory's lovers – and hence the temporal world and eternity – communicate through their interlocking dreams (I/4, 60–61).

The cultural criticism, which informs the allegorical parables through the sentimental motif of painful mortality, the symbolic representation of

---

44 'on the eternal mountain road through time'.
45 'I'm passing through.' – 'Here we meet again.'
46 Søren Kierkegaard, *Fear and Trembling; Repetition*, ed. and translated with an introduction and notes by Howard V. Hong and Edna H. Hong (Princeton NJ, Chichester: Princeton University Press, 1983).

history as war, and the injustices ('Ungerechtigkeiten'; I/4, 48) which the characters suffer, is the main theme in the third allegory, 'Die Mondfinsternis'. In this text, Jean Paul turns his poetic vision of a metaphysical and utopian 'Welt über der Erde' (world above Earth), which is nevertheless defined by its relationship with the historical and temporal world through birth and death (I/4, 38, 41), into a critical allegory of his age. However, where Novalis's historical allegories are based on the Romantic philosophy of history, Jean Paul critiques eighteenth-century history in moral terms as a period of crisis in the eternal struggle between good and evil, between the 'Genius der Religion' (genius of religion), turned 'Genius der Tugend' (genius of virtue), and the 'böse Genius des achtzehnten Jahrhunderts' (the eighteenth century's evil spirit) (I/4, 39, 41–42), which thrives on materialism (money) and power (symbolized by marriage rings; I/4, 40) and which heroic virtue is unable fully to defeat.

The Freudel and Fälbel satires in the collection's third part complement this epic perspective on eighteenth-century cultural history by a microscopic critique of the narrow-minded petit-bourgeois mentality and egotism represented by their narrator-protagonists. In contrapuntal references both to the metaphysical dialectic of time in the allegories and the moral philosophy of time in the *Quintus Fixlein* idyll, the satires represent eighteenth-century philistinism as failure to acknowledge the natural dynamic of time in daily life. Freudel's complaint about always being in the wrong place at the wrong time is combined with a pedantic regime that organizes life according to the calendar and the clock and thus fails to live the moment to the full. The fact that he spends his wedding night studying a wedding calendar and his diary rather than with his wife (I/4, 212), throws the horror of pedantic time-management into comic relief and confirms the moral lesson: 'Mache deine Gegenwart zu keinem Mittel der Zukunft' (I/4, 185).[47] Similarly the ruthless schedule which headmaster Fälbel imposes on his school trip – although it is supposed to be his students' holiday – destroys enjoyment of the moment for himself, his daughter and his pupils, who are given as little time as freedom. Failure to appreciate time and to use it appropriately thus features prominently in the satire's cultural critique, which Jean Paul's literary alter ego summarizes by reaffirming the value of the seeming 'Kleinigkeiten' of daily life: 'Unsere Gedanken ausgenommen, aber nicht unsere *Handlungen*, kriecht alles über Sekunden, jede große Tat, jedes große Leben zerspringt in den Staub der Zeitteile [...]' (I/4, 232).[48] Throughout Jean Paul's writing, the second, or more generally the moment, reflects the characters' experience of their world, oscillating precariously between the nihilist

---

47   'Do not make the Present a means of thy Future.' (*Life*, 300)

48   'Excepting our thoughts, but not our actions, everything crawls over seconds, each great deed, each great life disperses into the dust produced by the fragments of time.'

perception of the present as a fragile 'Dunstkügelchen der Zeit' (a little drop of vapour; I/1, 306), a 'spitze Augenblick [...] zwischen den beiden zusammenstoßenden Ewigkeits-Meeren' of the past and the future (I/6, 1117)[49] – and as a counterpoint to this, celebration of the living moment and the ecstatic moment of metaphysical experience. An example of the latter is the rare 'Augen-Blick' of love between Fixlein and Thienette, which gives their mediocre lives the gloss of the ideal ('idealische Mondschein'; I/4, 199): 'Jede Minute wurde ein Föderationsfest, und jede Sekunde wurde der Vorsabbat dazu.' (I/4, 112)[50]

IV.

In the central *Quintus Fixlein* story the political context of Jean Paul's philosophy of time is more obvious. This humorous idealization of petit-bourgeois happiness is set not only within contemporary society, but also specifically in the wake of the French Revolution. Oblique references to this political context include a passing comment on the September massacres of 1792 (I/4, 107) and Fixlein's poodle, 'der wegen der französischen Unruhen mit andern Emigranten aus Nantes fortgelaufen war' (I/4, 70),[51] which links the idyll in a humorous way to French revolutionary terror and the popularity of French aristocratic emigrants as victims of 'Zeitgeschichte' in the popular fiction of the period. The narrator also comments on the rejuvenating effect of change – 'weil man das Leben allezeit von der letzten Revolution an datiert, wie die Franzosen von der ihrigen an' (I/4, 102)[52] – and concludes with the sentimental hope for peace in the on-going Coalition Wars against the French republic (I/4, 191). It is clear therefore that the *Quintus Fixlein* idyll is to be seen as one of Jean Paul's literary responses to the French revolution and the politics of his time. The unlikely idealization of petit-bourgeois life and its small world, which culminates in the ironic 'Lebensregel' 'bleibe zu Hause' (I/4, 185–186),[53] resonates with the political and cultural upheaval of the early 1790s and is part of German literature's attempts during this period to reframe and rethink Enlightenment ideals in the light of the French revolution's descent into terror and civil war.

The idyll's oblique relationship to political history – and to the temporal world of historicity more widely – is given humorous illustration in Fixlein's

---

49 'a pointed moment [...] between the two colliding oceans of eternity'.
50 'Every minute was a Federation-festival, and every second a Preparation-Sabbath for it.' (*Life*, 192)
51 'with his Shock, which, by reason of the French convulsions, had, in company with other emigrants, run off from Nantes' (*Life*, 130).
52 'Great changes – in offices, marriages, travels – make us younger; we always date our history from the last revolution, as the French have done from theirs.' (*Life*, 178)
53 'Keep at home' (*Life*, 300).

delight in outdated newspapers. He asks the local baron's servant for 'den vorigen Jahrgang des Hamburger politischen Journals' for comfort on dreary autumn evenings, in order to read last year's news: 'was sich etwan gutes Neues in der politischen Welt zutrage – im vorigen Jahr' (I/4, 80).[54] Resonating with ironic comment on Germany's historical belatedness, Fixlein's reading combines naive curiosity with the appreciation of the seemingly useless 'Achtung für alle Makulatur' (I/4, 88) and historical scholarship, the urge to rescue 'historisch[e] Belege der Zeit' (I/4, 80).[55] The motif, however, that last year's news have turned into waste-paper and food for aesthetic and antiquarian pleasure, reflects in an ironic way the experience of accelerated political change in the wake of the French Revolution. This is particularly obvious, when Fixlein spends Christmas Eve 1791 reading about the previous winter's military campaigns and warming to military victories and political hopes, which have since been disappointed for 'die Leute in der Stadt, die nur die neuesten Zeitungen hielten' (I/4, 88).[56] Jean Paul's self-reflexive and humorous narrative thus creates constant friction between the idyll's generic setting outside time and history, and its oblique engagement with both political history and the challenges of human temporality, increasing awareness of both.

Indeed, the idyll's realism is reflected throughout in temporal leitmotifs and precise indications of temporal setting as constant reminders of progress through time. The story starts with Fixlein's summer holidays in 1791 and moves through 'einzelne helle Marientage [...] aus dem in Alltagsschlacken vererzten Leben Fixleins' (I/4, 101)[57] until May 1794, when the narrator-biographer joins his character, encouraging the reader to open the calendar of 1794 next to his book (I/4, 164) so as to witness the climax of the story, Fixlein's crisis and recovery. Dates, indications of time and clock motifs[58] punctuate the narrative and serve as timely reminders of the temporality of human life and the management of time in the social calendar. Jean Paul's real concern, however, is with the individual's experience and

---

54 'In gloomy harvest evenings, he could now sit down and read for himself what good news were transpiring in the political world – twelve months ago.' (*Life*, 145)
55 'respect for all waste-paper'; 'historical documents of the time' (*Life*, 158, 145).
56 'the people in the town, who got only the newest newspapers' (*Life*, 157–158).
57 'As it is but a few clear Ladydays, warm Mayday-nights, at the most a few odorous Rose-weeks, which I am digging from this Fixlienic Life, embedded in the dross of week-day cares.' (*Life*, 177)
58 There is the 'Stutzuhr' (I/4, 92), which Fixlein inherits from the Baroness Aufhammer as a token of his luck and his newly found social security, and its 'Uhr-Affe', which regularly reminds Fixlein of his 'frohe Zeit' (I/4, 98); satirical comment compares Fixlein's academic projects with '*Konzertuhren*' in contrast with the 'dumme plumpe *Turmuhren*' of his day-job (I/4, 83); ironic sentimentalism contrasts the '*Wasseruhr* fallender Tränen' with the '*Blumenuhr*' of happiness (I/4, 190); the narrator's 'Lebensregeln' reflect appropriate use of time with reference to the clock (I/4, 185); a church clock is the key symbol in Fixlein's gothic vision of death (I/4, 178–179).

awareness of time. The motif which most clearly temporalizes the idyll is Fixlein's *'fixe* Idee' (I/4, 11)[59] that he will die prematurely aged 32 ('im zweiunddreißigsten Jahre am Kantatesonntag'; I/4, 97) like his father and his male ancestors before him. The narrative's temporal symbolism therefore revolves around the 'Kantatesonntag', the fourth Sunday after Easter of the years 1792 to 1794, as Fixlein's uncertainty about his exact age[60] first makes him anxious, then reassures him that he is meant to live, until the discovery that he actually turned 32 in 1794 triggers a nervous breakdown, which exposes him to a nihilist vision of death, comically echoing Jean Paul's own seminal experience of mortality. In the grotesque gothic imagery of his fever, Fixlein dreams of a malfunctioning church clock, which fails to stop striking the midnight hour, and of meeting the Grim Reaper, until he is released through the sentimental vision of rebirth (I/4, 178–179).

The eventual cure of his delusion ('Todes-Wahn'; I/4, 140) through the imagination exemplifies Jean Paul's anthropology of time and his fascination with childhood memory. In an imaginary re-enactment of the past, Fixlein is made to relive his earlier crisis as an eight-year old, who was 'gerade an dem Kantatesonntag, wo man seinen Vater aufs Leichenbrett band, vor Kummer krank und nur durch sein Spielzeug geheilt' (I/4, 97).[61] This time, toys from his dead brother's cabinet, his 'Depositenkasse der Zeit' (I/4, 170),[62] take Fixlein's imagination back into childhood as the one time which we never forget and which therefore helps to define our identity: 'ein[e] himmlisch[e] Zeit, die wir nie vergessen, die wir ewig lieben und nach der wir noch auf dem Grabe zurücksehen' (I/4, 182–83).[63] Drawing on late eighteenth-century fascination with spontaneous, involuntary memory, for example in the works of Karl Philip Moritz,[64] this re-enactment of childhood memory puts Fixlein back on track in the history of his life, restoring his self-confidence along with his sense of time and freeing him of his 'närrische Todesfurcht' (I/4, 183).[65]

---

59 'fixed idea' (*Life*, 116).
60 In order to protect Fixlein against the threat of death at the age of 32, his mother deliberately keeps him in the dark about his exact age (which makes Fixlein's archive of childhood memories, based on her account, even more ironic) and seems to suggest that he turned 32 in 1792 (rather than two years later). It is only when Fixlein marks his inauguration as village pastor by having the top of the church spire replaced that documents preserved in the old church top reveal his true age to him.
61 'When a boy he had fallen sick of sorrow, on the very Cantata-Sunday when his father was lying in the winding-sheet, and only been saved from death by his playthings.' (*Life*, 171)
62 'deposit bank of time'.
63 'this conflagration-place and Golgatha of a heavenly time, which none of us forgets, which we love for ever, and look back to even from the grave' (*Life*, 296).
64 See Göttsche, *Zeit im Roman*, 80–87; Helmut Pfotenhauer, *Literarische Anthropologie: Selbstbiographien und ihre Geschichte – am Leitfaden des Leibes* (Stuttgart: Metzler, 1987), pp. 99–100, 113–14.
65 'silly fear of death'.

Fixlein's cure thus illustrates the crucial role of memory for personal identity – 'Ohne Erinnerung [...] gibts kein Ich', as Emmanuel argues in *Hesperus* (I/1, 1127)[66] –, and it reflects the cross-mapping of memory and imagination in Jean Paul's anthropology of time. In the appended essay on the natural magic of imagination Jean Paul draws on the eighteenth-century distinction between reproductive and productive imagination to define memory (Gedächtnis) as *'eingeschränktere* Phantasie' (I/4, 195).[67] At the same time, he gives Kant's understanding of imagination (Einbildungskraft) as transcendental synthesis[68] a psychological and critical turn and also temporalizes it by linking the transformative power of the imagination to the past and the future: 'So zieht das Fernrohr der Phantasie einen bunten Diffusionsraum um die glücklichen Inseln der Vergangenheit, um das gelobte Land der Zukunft.' (I/4, 197)[69] This temporalization of the imagination[70] through memory and anticipation results from man's metaphysical '*Sinn des Grenzenlosen*', his infinite yearning for infinite space and infinite time ('einen unendlichen *Raum* und eine unendliche *Zeit*'; I/4, 200), which puts the present in critical perspective. In the human mind, the temporal sequence of past, present and future ('*Zeit* in ihrem Dreiklang von Vergangenheit, Gegenwart und Zukunft'; I/6, 601) translates into a complex dynamic, which places the present moment between memory ('*Erinnerung*') and anticipation or hope ('*Hoffnung*'), 'den beiden Polen des elliptischen Gewölbes der Zeit' (I/3, 221),[71] temporalizing self-awareness and potentially also personal identity.

In Jean Paul's anthropology of time, the 'distention' of the mind'[72] and its movement between the present moment, memory and anticipation is thus the psychological equivalent to the overarching dialectic of time with its endless movement between temporality and eternity, the finite and the infinite. This analogy also informs his conception of childhood memory. Although he is well aware of painful childhood memories – such as those of Fixlein's friend and later wife Thienette, who still suffers from the 'Winterlandschaft und Eisregion ihrer verjammerten Jugend' (I/4, 169)[73] –, Jean Paul conceives of childhood memory as the memory of infinite expectation and hope and therefore as a prime site of man's metaphysical yearning: it is the 'Andenken an unsere damalige kindliche Erwartung eines unendlichen

66 'There is no "I" without memory.'
67 'restrained imagination'.
68 Kant, *Werke*, III, p. 148 (*Kritik der reinen Vernunft*, B151).
69 'The telescope of fantasy thus draws a colourful halo of diffusion around the happy islands of the past, around the promised land of the future.'
70 See Berhorst, *Anamorphosen der Zeit*, 68, 73.
71 'the two poles in the elliptical vault of time'.
72 'distentio animi' (see note 4).
73 'the winter landscape and ice region of her sorrow-wasted youth' (*Life*, 276).

Genusses', the memory of 'grenzenlose Hoffnungen', which links childhood memory to our 'Sinn des Grenzenlosen' (I/4, 202, 92)[74] and makes memory ('*Erinnerung*') – in one of Jean Paul's most famous aphorisms – 'das einzige Paradies, aus welchem wir nicht getrieben werden können' (II/3, 820).[75] Fixlein's cure through his imaginary return to childhood ultimately restores his sanity by reconnecting him to his sense of the future. Restoring the balance between memory and anticipation also makes possible a return to the enjoyment of the living moment – 'Jede Minute, Mensch, sei dir ein volles Leben!' (I/4, 185) –, which marks the centre of the idealization of provincial philistinism in the idyll's moral philosophy of time.

Fixlein's story thus provides oblique illustration of Jean Paul's anthropology of time and of his theory of memory. It is obviously Fixlein's mediocrity and moderation, his 'temperiertes Temperament' (I/4, 188), which prevents his crisis from turning tragic and secures the idyllic 'Vollglück in der Beschränkung'. Part of his comically inadequate engagement with human temporality is his involuntary travesty of the ancient art of memory (ars memoriae) in his 'Zettelkästen' archive of childhood memories (I/4, 83). Echoing the ancient spatial concept of memory as an archive of images while also mimicking baroque techniques of encyclopaedic scholarship, Fixlein records the details of his childhood on 'kleine Blätter' (little pieces of paper) in chronological filing boxes, in order to learn more about his exact age, but also to simply enjoy remembering: 'Wollt er sich nach einem pädagogischen Baufron-Tag einen Rastabend machen: so riß er bloß ein Zettelfach, einen Registerzug seiner Lebensorgel, heraus und besann sich auf alles.' (I/4, 84)[76] The irony of this travesty of the mnemonic tradition lies not just in Fixlein's obsession with complete, accurate and systematic memory, but also in the fact that he relies on his mother's accounts of his childhood rather than his own memories for this 'perspektivische Aufriß seiner kindlichen Vergangenheit' (I/4, 83).[77] Fixlein's treatment of memory as a commodity – 'durchnehmen' (rehearse) is one of the expressions used for his technique of remembering (I/4, 90) – ignores the discoveries of late eighteenth-century psychology, the new poetics of autobiographical writing and Jean Paul's own interest in the temporality of memory, in other words, in the transformation of memories over time and the dialectical interaction between the present which remembers and the past which is remembered.[78]

---

74 'remembrance of our former childish expectations of infinite pleasure'; 'boundless hopes'; 'our sense of the infinite'.
75 'Memory is the only paradise from which we cannot be expelled.'
76 'Whenever he chose to conclude a day of pedagogic drudgery by an evening of peculiar rest, he simply pulled out a letter-drawer, a register-bar in his Life-hand-organ, and recollected the whole.' (*Life*, 150)
77 'this perspective sketch of his early Past' (*Life*, 150).
78 See Göttsche, *Zeit im Roman*, 130–132.

Searching the loft in his mother's house and browsing through his discarded toys similarly serves to contain rather than unleash the incalculable dynamic of memory (I/4, 84–85).

Rather than engaging in retrospective self-reflection, which would promote the temporalization of self, Fixlein safeguards his idyll by treating childhood memories as aesthetic objects or commodities; only in his illness is he for once overpowered by childhood memory. He does not get any further in terms of understanding the temporality of self than wondering why 'ihm die Kinderspiele an Kindern nicht so gefielen als die Schilderungen derselben, wenn das Kind, das sie getrieben, schon aufgeschossen vor ihm stand' (I/4, 85).[79] By contrast, the narrator comments on Fixlein's art of memory in the light of Jean Paul's anthropology of time and his awareness of the historicity of personal identity. For example, the poetological motif of 'Fernrohr der Phantasie' (I/4, 197)[80] is given a temporal turn in the imagery used to represent Fixlein's celebration of childhood memory on Christmas Eve 1791, when he looks 'aus der Ferne von zwanzig Jahren in die stille Stube seiner Eltern hinein' (I/4, 90).[81] The scene resonates with the metaphysical theme of childhood memory as memory of infinite expectation (in this case the boy's anticipation of Christmas), but it also presents a poetic model of the hermeneutics of memory. Looking back at his happy childhood, when his father and his brother were still alive, Fixlein rediscovers 'die schönen Jahre seiner Kindheit aufgedeckt, frisch, grün und duftend' underneath the 'Schnee der Zeit'. And yet this past is locked inside the family home, into which he as an adult has to look from the outside, penetrating the 'Fenster-Flora' of ice on the window pane which separates the past and the present, or more accurately: the remembered past and its presence in memory (I/4, 90). The floral frost patterns on the window thus symbolize both the passage of time and the role of memory in the natural magic of the imagination, which counteracts the threat of mortality: 'O es ist schön, daß der Rauch, der über unserem verpuffenden Leben aufsteigt, sich wie bei dem vergehenden Spießglas in neuen, obwohl poetischen Freuden-Blumen anlegt!' (I/4, 90)[82] The beautiful ice patterns symbolize the idealization of

---

79 'He wondered that the real sports of children should not so delight him, as the emblems of these sports, when the child that had carried them on was standing grown up to manhood in his presence.' (*Life*, 152–153)

80 'telescope of fantasy'.

81 Carlyle translates the passage as follows, leaving out one sentence and changing the concluding metaphor: 'And now he shook away the snow of Time from the winter-green of Memory; and beheld the fair years of his childhood, uncovered, fresh, green, and balmy, standing afar off before him. From his distance of twenty years, he looked into the quiet cottage of his parents, where his father and brother had not yet been reaped away by the sickle of Death.' (*Life*, 160)

82 'Oh, it is nice that the smoke which rises above our life as it puffs away, settles in new, albeit poetic flowers of joy, very much like fading antimony.' Carlyle omits this sentence in his translation.

the past from the perspective of the present, but they also mark the insurmountable barrier which separates the present from the past and highlights the historicity of life.

On the level of Jean Paul's poetics of time, this symbolic representation of the hermeneutics of memory illustrates the spatial rendering of time in his imagery, imagining the past as a room into which we look through the window of time. Jean Paul's writing is characterized throughout by the two complementary techniques of temporalizing space and translating temporal experience into spatial categories (*Verzeitlichung des Raumes – Verräumlichung der Zeit*), often drawing on the archive of relevant cultural symbolism. To give just a few examples, there is the metaphor of 'Gewölbe der Zeit',[83] extending between memory and hope (I/3, 221); the sentimental allegory of the moon as the site of immortality and eternity; conventional metaphors such as the wheels of fortune and time ('So rollen seine Minuten auf lauter Glücksrädern über die zwölf Tage'; I/4, 145),[84] 'Strom der Zeit' (I/4, 182), 'Vorhang der Zukunft' (I/4, 177) and 'Ringe der Ewigkeit' (I/4, 142);[85] images drawing on the catena aurea tradition such as the 'garland' of Fixlein's childhood years (I/4, 67), the 'Blumenkette' of his happy days (I/4, 165), the 'ewige Reihe' (chain of being), which temporalizes the universe (I/4, 191), or in the nihilist variant, the 'glass pearls' of our days, which slip off our lives' thread, rolling into the grave (I/4, 87). Finally there is the garden metaphor – Fixlein's 'Hauptallee langer Jahre' (I/4, 97); '[d]ie nebeneinander aufblühenden Lusthaine seiner vier Karnikularwochen' (I/4, 81) –, which is given a poetological turn, when the narrator sees himself 'vor einem wichtigen Platze dieser Geschichte' (I/4, 96) or presents himself as a bee-keeper, who distributes the story's flowers 'in verschiedene Zeiten', 'damit es in allen Kapiteln blühe' (I/4, 151).[86] Such imagery ultimately reflects the cross-mapping of space and time in Jean Paul's dialectic of time as antithetical movement between temporality and eternity as well as between the finite and the infinite, triggered and sustained by man's metaphysical 'Sinn des Grenzenlosen'.

---

83 'vault of time'.

84 'Thus roll his minutes, on golden wheels-of-fortune, over the twelve days' (*Life*, 242). This example blends the metaphors 'Rad der Zeit' and 'Glücksrad'.

85 'stream of time'; 'curtain of Futurity'; 'Ring of Eternity' (*Life*, 296, 289, 237).

86 In terms of the different semantic mapping of temporal experience in German and English, it is interesting to note that Carlyle clearly struggled to translate Jean Paul's cross-stitching of time and space and reduced or deleted some of his spatial metaphors of temporality and historicity: 'the same long vista of years' (*Life*, 171); 'The thickset blooming grove of his four carnicular weeks, and the flying tumult of blossoms therein' (*Life*, 146); 'a most important circumstance in this History' (*Life*, 170); 'An author is a sort of bee-keeper for his reader-swarm; in whose behalf he separates the Flora kept for their use into different seasons, and here accelerates, and there retards, the blossoming of many a flower, that so in all chapters there be blooming.' (*Life*, 250–251)

V.

Jean Paul's poetics of time thus inform even the most unlikely of texts, such as the allegories, idylls and satires of his *Quintus Fixlein* collection. Jean Paul reflects and promotes the late eighteenth-century dynamic of temporalization in a plethora of temporal motifs, which punctuate his narrative and cross-reference philosophical, anthropological, moral, and political thought about time. Jean Paul's modern sense of critical time is at the very heart of his writing and of his critique of political and cultural history in the wake of the French Revolution. In his poetic universe, this critical sense of time incorporates experiences of suspended time (such as the ecstatic moments of metaphysical experience), deceleration (such as in the Fixlein idyll) and discontinuity (for example in his critique of memory). But such counterpoints to the period's sense of accelerated change and its emergent philosophies of history only serve to underline – dialectically and often in an ironic way – the all-pervasive temporality and historicity of modern life, which Jean Paul's writing never ceases to explore and reflect. Challenging time is just one of the literary devices in his response to the challenging times which he witnessed.

Xavier de Maistre and Angelology

David McCallam

In February 1790 on the eve of the Turin Carnival a young sub-lieutenant of his Sardinian majesty's army, Xavier de Maistre, was put under strict house arrest for his involvement in a duel with a fellow officer, one Patono de Meïran.[1] The house arrest was to last for forty-two days. In this time, de Maistre, a budding *littérateur*, decided to write an ironic story about his internment in the manner of Laurence Sterne's *Sentimental Journey*. This was to become his fantastical *Voyage autour de ma chambre*. Begun in 1790, the text was put down and picked up in dilatory fashion over the course of the next four years until it was finally finished in 1794. It was subsequently published in 1795 in Lausanne under the supervision of the author's elder brother, comte Joseph de Maistre, the radical counter-revolutionary, who would publish his own, more influential, *Considérations sur la France* in Neuchâtel in 1797. Xavier de Maistre's text thus bears the traces – sometimes overtly, sometimes obliquely – of the increasing revolutionary violence and radicalism of the years of its composition. It is clearly marked by the military annexation of his Savoy homeland by revolutionary France in 1792 as well as by his own engagement in the bloody, unsuccessful counter-offensive launched by Sardinian troops in the summer of 1793. Less explicitly, it is also redolent of a growing sense of exile experienced at this time at various garrison postings in Piedmont and at the Sardinian court in Turin, an exile that seemed increasingly irreversible to de Maistre as news of the Terror in France intermittently reached him.

Yet, on a first reading, the *Voyage autour de ma chambre* seems little concerned with contemporary events. Its room is, after all, a familiar enclosed space, a cocoon of *ancien régime* civility, a homely bulwark against the revolutionary turmoil beyond its walls. Moreover, the journey made around it is not polemical or particularly picaresque; it is polite, mildly erotic, ironic, a discursive meandering which decentres the reading experience in a series of Sternean shifts of perspective. As Daniel Sangsue puts it, it is literally an 'ex-centric' narrative, a dizzying and fantastical journey around ('autour') and

---

1   Cited in Xavier de Maistre, *Voyage autour de ma chambre*, ed. by Florence Lotterie (Paris: Flammarion, 2003), p. 45. All subsequent references to the text in the body of the essay will be to this edition. For further references to de Maistre's life, see Alfred Berthier, *Xavier de Maistre: Étude biographique et littéraire* (Paris: Emmanuel Vitte, 1921; repr. Geneva: Slatkine Reprints, 1984).

not in ('dans') the room.[2] And this ex-centric narration is told by what might be called a 'concentric' narrator, revealing variously superposed layers of feeling and reason as he goes, but, like Roland Barthes's famous image of the text as 'onion',[3] exposing in the last analysis no unequivocal core or kernel, no secret or irreducible principle to his travels or his person.

However, any further thorough-going 'postmodern' interpretation of his narrative is frustrated by the narrator's claim to two principal personas or psychic drives according to what he calls his 'système de *l'âme et de la bête*' (*Voyage*, 52, his italics) – his 'system of the soul and the beast'. It is important here to establish that this system of 'âme-bête' is not a banal reprise of the classical Cartesian or Pascalian dualism of mind and matter, of immaterial soul and material body. In the *Voyage autour de ma chambre*, the narrator's 'âme' and his 'bête' are both forms of spirit, of intelligence. Theirs is a distinction of quality, not of nature. Schematically, the 'âme' is characterized by its celestial aspirations, by its associations with pure light and rarefied air. Composed of the 'rayons purs de l'intelligence' (*Voyage*, 52), at home in the 'vastes plaines du ciel' (*Voyage*, 60),[4] it habitually soars skywards towards a realm of neo-platonic ideas or divine beauty, playing on the sense of a vertical, ethereal 'transport' which is, of course, the only movement or 'transport' allowed to the officer imprisoned in his small room.[5] His 'bête' or beast, on the other hand, is earthy and sensual. It is identified with lower, animal impulses, with what Florence Lotterie calls the 'automatismes qui régissent les gestes de la vie quotidienne' (*Voyage*, 32).[6] Unlike the solitary lofty soul, the beast is a massy, social mind negotiating everyday interactions in the material world. Yet crucially, like the image of the layers of the Barthesian 'onion', soul and beast, 'âme' and 'bête', are not discrete entities, but are inextricably joined to one another 'par je ne sais quel lien secret' (*Voyage*, 60),[7] concentrically imbricated into one another, performing a sort of psychic symbiosis that constitutes the narrator's being in the world. In this

2   Daniel Sangsue, *Le Récit excentrique: Gautier, de Maistre, Nerval, Nodier* (Paris: José Corti, 1987), p. 165.
3   Roland Barthes, 'Le style et son image', in *Œuvres complètes*, 4 vols (Paris: Seuil, 2002), III, pp. 980–981.
4   'Pure rays of intelligence', 'vast plains of the sky'. Unless indicated otherwise, the translations are my own.
5   As has been noted before, the narrator's figurative soaring skywards has as its paradigm the author's personal experience of a celebrated, pioneering balloon flight undertaken on 6 May 1784 at Chambéry, less than a year after the first manned flights rose from Versailles and the Tuileries. For de Maistre's personal account of this 'sublime' aeronautic experience that only 'an angel or a fool' would attempt to put into words (*Voyage*, 31), see his 'Lettre contenant une relation de l'expérience aérostatique de Chambéry', in *Œuvres inédites de Xavier de Maistre: premiers essais, fragments et correspondance*, ed. by Eugène Réaume, 2 vols (Paris: A. Lemierre, 1877), I, pp. 21–39.
6   'Automatic reflexes which govern the gestures of our everyday lives'.
7   'By an inscrutable secret link'.

sense, it would be more appropriate to talk of a duo, rather than a dualism.[8] Nonetheless, the narrator declares that a discernible hierarchy obtains between his constitutive faculties. He writes: 'il faut que l'âme ait une certaine supériorité sur la bête pour être en état de faire la distinction' (*Voyage*, 52);[9] that is, the soul has to be superior to the beast in order to make a distinction in the first instance between their relative operations. Society, and its civilizing process, have then as their goal the public consecration of this hierarchy: to enshrine the pre-eminence of the spiritual over the bestial by domesticating the beast and liberating the soul.

This is, however, where events in the external world intervene in this intimate metaphysical relationship and upset its equilibrium. For, Xavier de Maistre seems to imply, the Revolution represents both socially and politically the unnatural and highly undesirable ascendency of the beast over the soul. It institutes the reign of the animal, the base, the 'mechanical', taking this last word in its Shakespearean sense too of the lowest social orders. It is the regime of the masses, where mass signifies both a ponderous, earthbound heaviness, the opposite of the soul's empyrean flight, and large numbers of people gathered together, manifest in the revolutionary assemblies, clubs, crowds and mobs, forming the dreaded crowd ('foule') – a word that comes up time and time again, and always with negative connotations, in de Maistre's text. This inversion of what the author might see as the 'natural' order is also translated into explicit political terminology, with the 'legislative' beast now overruling the 'executive' soul (*Voyage*, 53). What is worse, as the Revolution steadily becomes a secularizing juggernaut, at its most extreme in the radical dechristianizing phase of the Terror (September 1793 to January 1794), the Church is no longer able to offer institutional support or ecclesiastical authority to the beleaguered soul, to provide its largely aesthetic spirituality with the complementary spirituality of revealed religion. For orthodox Catholics, like Xavier de Maistre, the risen Christ is henceforth denied them as the privileged intermediary between men and God. In such dire circumstances, and despite some of the misgivings found in the apostolic teachings of Saint Paul,[10] true believers such as de Maistre have to summon up other heavenly intercessors to protect the soul or 'âme', in both its aesthetic and religious senses here, since both are threatened by the Revolution's increasingly militant secularism. First and foremost among the

---

8   See Gilbert Durand, 'Le voyage et la chambre dans l'œuvre de Xavier de Maistre', *Romantisme* 2.4 (1972) 76–89, 80. Durant writes: 'La duplication n'est pas l'antithèse, elle est dualitude plus que dualité', i.e., 'Duplication is not antithesis, it is complementary duet more than antagonistic duality'.

9   'The soul has necessarily a certain pre-eminence over the beast in order to be able to distinguish itself from the latter'.

10 See, for example, Colossians 2. 18; or his denunciation of fallen angels, especially Satan, Ephesians 6. 11–12.

second rank of heavenly intermediaries are, of course, the angels. As Harold
Bloom has shown, invoking angels is a classic millenarian recourse,[11] for in
times of imagined social disintegration, the angelic host offers a fixed, eternal hierarchical order submissive to the will of the one true Lord, that is, the
very socio-political model for an absolutist society of orders.[12] Invoking angels is therefore all the more attractive to those counter-revolutionaries who
were at this time quick to equate the Revolution itself with the advent of
Hell on Earth, often in prose of suitably apocalyptic violence.[13] Yet, the lure
of the angelic is all the stronger for de Maistre, insofar as the rare essence
which characterizes his notion of 'soul' corresponds to the disincarnate nature of angels as 'pure spirit'[14] as they were defined by Catholic doctrine
following the teachings of the 'Angelic Doctor' himself, Saint Thomas Aquinas.

So the basic contention of this study is that, in the *Voyage autour de ma
chambre*, de Maistre evokes certain representations of the angelic in both art
and literature in order symbolically to restore the dominion of the soul over
the beast. This amounts to obliquely offering fictional inspiration and spiritual succour to the forces of political and military counter-Revolution. Yet it
will also be contended that in appealing to these cultural representations of
angels, de Maistre comes up against a fundamental ambivalence inherent in
the figure of the angel which goes no small way towards destabilizing, even
undermining, the ideological use to which he wants to put his angelic figures.[15]

To look first at art, de Maistre, who was himself a proficient landscape
painter, has his narrator consider a number of prints and paintings decorat-
ing the walls of his room. These variously depict a scene from Goethe's *Werther*; an image of 'le malheureux *Ugolin*' ('the unfortunate Ugolino'), a
damned soul from Dante's Hell; Nicolas d'Assas, a French hero of the Seven Years war who died valiantly in an ambush; and a pregnant black woman betrayed and sold into slavery by her colonial lover (*Voyage*, 79–80, 85).

---

11 Harold Bloom, *Omens of Millennium: Gnosis of Angels, Dreams, and Resurrection* (New York: River-
    head Books, 1996), pp. 3–9.
12 See Peter Marshall and Alexandra Walsham, 'Migrations of angels in the early modern world',
    in *Angels in the Early Modern World*, ed. by Peter Marshall and Alexandra Walsham (Cambridge:
    Cambridge University Press, 2006), pp. 1–40, 8. This hierarchical vision of the angel world is
    the product above all of the influential text, *On the Celestial Hierarchy*, written by the Syrian
    monk, Pseudo-Dionysius, around 500 CE and widely circulated in a ninth-century Latin trans-
    lation.
13 See Darrin M. McMahon, *Enemies of the Enlightenment: The French Counter-Enlightenment and the
    Making of Modernity* (Oxford: Oxford University Press, 2001), pp. 92–95.
14 Marshall and Walsham, 'Migrations of angels', 6.
15 The radical ambivalence is also inherent in the 'literariness' of de Maistre's text, in the way it
    foregrounds its own modes of signification, reflecting Sternean or perhaps Diderotian influen-
    ces. See Malcolm Cook, '*Le Voyage autour de ma chambre* by Xavier de Maistre', *Australian Journal
    of French Studies* 38 (2001) 158–165.

These are popular tropes culled from a variety of aesthetic movements of sensibility in late eighteenth-century Europe (for example, 'Sturm und Drang' in Germany, Rousseauism in France); movements which de Maistre at once emulates and gently ironizes here. These appeals to the narrator's sensibility are succeeded by a painting representing an Alpine shepherdess tending her flock in a florid meadow. The timeless joy of this pastoral idyll is, however, suddenly destroyed by the violent intrusion of the revolutionary wars. 'Le demon de la guerre' or demon of war appears – the product not of the painting itself but of the narrator's troubled imagination, as History routs Nature. The narrator pictures the scene with increasing horror: 'Déjà les soldats s'avancent; je les vois gravir de montagnes en montagnes, et s'approcher des nues. – Le bruit du canon se fait entendre dans le séjour élevé du tonnerre' (*Voyage*, 86).[16] In other words, the revolutionary beast has invaded the natural heights that were previously the exclusive preserve of the lofty, sensitive soul. And it is from this scene of desolation, that the narrator turns to the artistic figure of the angel, more specifically, to two portraits by the Italian master, Raphael. One is a self-portrait revealing a face 'ouverte, sensible, spirituelle' (*Voyage*, 91);[17] the second is that of the artist's seductive mistress. As the painter is to be identified with the soul, so his lover comes to represent the beast. Yet Raphael, more than any other Renaissance master, also evokes the angelic. Described by the narrator as 'ce flambeau céleste, ce génie divin […] un dieu' (*Voyage*, 91–92),[18] his well-attested personal grace, his early death and religious masterpieces such as the Mond Crucifixion, the Coronation of the Virgin (both 1502–1503), not to mention his stunning 'The Freeing of Saint Peter' (1514) – the saint sprung from his prison cell by an angel – all make him a pre-eminent cipher for the more general aesthetic humanization of angels realized by the Italian Renaissance.[19] Moreover, as the deuterocanonical Book of Tobit makes clear, Raphael is also the name of one of the seven Archangels of the Lord. In fact, his angelic intervention in Tobit's son, Tobias's, dangerous journey to Media has been described as 'the Bible's most affecting account of human-angel interaction'.[20] He is also a prominent angelic presence in later apocryphal or gnostic texts of the early Christian church, such as the controversial Book of Enoch.

---

16 'Already the soldiers advance, I see them climbing from mountain to mountain, and approaching the clouds. The noise of cannon sounds in thunder's elevated abode'.

17 'Open, sensitive, spiritual'.

18 'This celestial flame, this divine genius […] a god'.

19 On this Renaissance trend, see Bloom, *Omens of Millennium*, 43.

20 See Tobit 5–12. The citation is from Marshall and Walsham, 'Migrations of angels', 4. Raphael also painted his angelic namesake accompanying Tobias in a panel picture now held in the San Domenico church, Naples.

There are, however, some problems with the choice of angelic model here, as the narrator himself has to admit. Firstly, and more esoterically, against the strictures of Saint Thomas Aquinas, Raphael in the Book of Tobit is an angel who eats and drinks; that is, he is an angel who seriously compromises his nature as pure spirit, thereby contravening the Church's teachings on angels. More explicitly, as the narrator recognizes, Raphael the artist was wont to give in to far baser animal urges. As Giorgio Vasari alleges in his sometimes unreliable *The Lives of the Artists*, Raphael died as a result of the sexual excesses demanded of him by his mistress,[21] the supposed model for the portrait, the *Fornarina* or bakerwoman, the very image hanging alongside the artist's self-portrait in the narrator's room. In fact, the very thought of the artist's nyphomaniacal mistress leads to one of the more openly erotic passages of the *Voyage autour de ma chambre*, in which the beast firmly re-establishes its ascendency over the soul, with the narrator dreaming of dying the same voluptuous death as Raphael in the arms of his 'belle Romaine' (*Voyage*, 92), his 'beautiful Roman' mistress. Consequently, this passage was prudishly struck from later editions of the novel on the insistence of de Maistre himself.

In literature his choice of angelic model proves to be equally ambivalent. Perusing the books in his library, the narrator is again transported figuratively 'depuis le fin fond des Enfers jusqu'à la dernière étoile fixe au-delà de la voie lactée, jusqu'aux confins de l'univers, jusqu'aux portes du chaos'[...] (*Voyage*, 114).[22] That is, he soars again into the soul's realm, his imagination empowered by a select band of authors – Homer, Milton, Virgil and Ossian – all literary references dear to contemporary European sensibility movements. And of these mythopoeic writers, the narrator dwells on the most angelic, or rather angelological, John Milton. Thus he joins the poet in his celestial flight, clinging metaphorically to the hem of his flowing robe 'au moment où il s'élance dans le ciel, et qu'il ose approcher du trône de l'Éternel' (*Voyage*, 115).[23] To the narrator, it is as though Milton himself partook of the angelic flight of his creations. Yet from these heavenly heights, the narrator cannot help but fall with Milton's angels into the very pits of Hell, where he attends on 'la foule des esprits rebelles' (*Voyage*, 115), the 'crowd of rebel spirits', that unruly, raucous assembly of fallen angels gathered there. Interestingly, this is the very same 'Pandaemonium' or convocation of devils that Joseph de Maistre was to choose in his *Considérations sur la France*

---

21 Giorgio Vasari, *The Lives of the Artists*, translated by George Bull (London: Penguin Books, 1965), pp. 312, 320.

22 'From the farthest depths of Hell to the last star fixed beyond the Milky Way, on to the outer edge of the universe, up to the very gates of chaos'.

23 'At the very moment when he takes off into the sky, and dares to approach the throne of the Eternal'.

to represent the French National Convention 'séant dans un manège et con-voquant tous les esprits mauvais'.[24]

Yet Xavier de Maistre in his *Voyage autour de ma chambre* owns rather to a deep fascination, bordering on admiration, for the chief of the fallen angels, for Lucifer turned Satan. He writes: 'j'avoue que la fermeté qu'il [Satan] montre dans l'excès du malheur et la grandeur de son courage me forcent à l'admiration malgré moi' (*Voyage*, 116).[25] The singling out of the fallen angel par excellence, the satanic 'bad eminence', may well have initially been a means of consoling the enemies of the Revolution in their extreme adver-sity, that is, recognizing the existence of a force of character capable of over-coming the extreme misfortunes ('l'excès du Malheur') experienced in the Emigration and indirectly attributed to anti-revolutionary nobles, clergy and other readers in the opening chapter of the *Voyage autour de ma chambre*. Yet in doing so, de Maistre inadvertently identifies with their revolutionary op-posite, with Satan the celestial rebel, the implacable dissenter from divine authority. The narrator acknowledges reluctantly Satan's revolutionary stat-ure: 'c'est un vrai démocrate, non de ceux d'Athènes, mais de ceux de Paris' (*Voyage*, 116),[26] but adds that even this cannot cure him of his prejudice in Satan's favour. Moreover, in strictly religious terms, de Maistre is borrowing here from more than just an ambivalent model: he is borrowing from an antithetical Protestant puritan-republican text, one in which not only Satan, but all the angels, fallen and 'unfallen', so to speak (including the very prom-inent Raphael), are in no way the disembodied will-less instruments of God's bidding, as the angels of the Catholic Church are prescribed to be. Milton's host eat, drink, know angelic sexual pleasure, speak and sing heart-ily, and if undying, can still wound one another, as Michael does Lucifer.[27] This last is not only embodied, he is moreover endowed with an all-too-hu-man psychological complexity as well as an intractable, steely free will. And, of course, he uses this free will precisely to damn himself, just as the revolu-tionaries have done in the eyes of the refractory Church and the political counter-Revolution. In this sense, Milton's Satan is less angelic than he is Promethean; but as either fallen angel or new Prometheus, he proves to be a subversive, countervailing figure for de Maistre's angelology.

---

24 Joseph de Maistre, *Considérations sur la France*, ed. by Jean-Louis Darcel (Geneva: Éditions Slaktine, 1980), p. 105. 'Sitting in a riding school and convening all the evil spirits'. The riding school in question is that of the Tuileries palace where the National Assembly relocated after the royal family's forced removal to Paris in October 1789.

25 'I confess that the fortitude that he [Satan] shows in his extreme misfortune, and the grandeur of his courage, compel my admiration despite myself'.

26 'He's a true democrat, not of the Athenian kind, but of those in Paris'.

27 See Robert H. West, *Milton and the Angels* (Athens, GA: University of Georgia Press, 1955); see also Bloom, *Omens of Millennium*, 38–39; and Joad Raymond, '"With the tongues of angels": Angelic Conversation in *Paradise Lost* and seventeenth-century England', in *Angels in the Early Modern World*, 256–281.

This might in part be attributed to the popularity, even ubiquity, of Milton's *Paradise Lost* as a reference point for French writers of the late eighteenth century, well before the Romantic obsession with all things infernal and satanic. From its first unexpurgated French translation by Louis Racine in 1755, and in those that followed, such as Le Roy or Beaulaton's rhyming verse translations of 1775 and 1779 respectively,[28] Milton's 'Archangel ruined', his chief fallen angel, was taken not just as a religious, but increasingly as a secular, model of transcendental agency. In a way, he was seen more and more as superhuman rather than supernatural. To cite but one example: Sébastien-Roch Nicolas Chamfort, in his *Maximes et pensées, caractères et anecdotes*, published posthumously in the same year as de Maistre's *Voyage autour de ma chambre*, cites a contemporary (who could just as easily be Chamfort himself) saying: "'J'ai vu peu de fiertés dont j'ai été content. Ce que je connais le mieux en ce genre, c'est celle de Satan dans le *Paradis perdu*'".[29] If Chamfort, the ardent revolutionary, identifies with Satan, then de Maistre's championing of this same figure will clearly do little, once again, to raise the soul over the beast.

In the context of the 1790s counter-Revolution, the most pressing question raised by Milton's angels, especially his fallen ones, is that of human (or angelic) free will in the face of divine providence. More specifically, how can counter-revolutionaries embrace the force or further the cause of divine providence when this operates, by its very definition, beyond their power? What is more, as Joseph de Maistre was to claim, their best efforts may prove counter-productive and be doomed to fail by the very agency – divine providence – that they are attempting to assist. Hence in the famous opening passage of his *Considérations sur la France*, the chief ideologist of the counter-Revolution responds to this vexed question with a series of paradoxes:

> Nous sommes tous attachés au trône de l'Être suprême par une chaîne souple, qui nous retient sans nous asservir. [...] Librement esclaves, ils [des êtres libres] opèrent tout à la fois volontairement et nécessairement: ils font réellement ce qu'ils veulent, mais sans pouvoir déranger les plans généraux.[30]

Some have seen here evidence only of an embarrassment in reconciling such diametrically opposed positions as those of divine omnipotence and human

---

28 For Milton's place in late eighteenth-century French literature, see Jean Gillet, *Le Paradis perdu dans la littérature française de Voltaire à Chateaubriand* (Paris: Klincksieck, 1975).

29 Sébastien-Roch Nicolas Chamfort, *Maximes et pensées, caractères et anecdotes* (Paris: Gallimard, 1970), p. 300. "'I have seen few instances of pride which have pleased me. The best I know of in this style is Satan's in *Paradise Lost*'".

30 Joseph de Maistre, *Considérations sur la France*, 63. 'We are all attached to the throne of the Supreme Being by a supple chain which restrains us without subjugating us. [...] Freely enslaved, [such] free beings act at once out of volition and out of necessity: they genuinely do what they want but without being able to disrupt the general designs of Providence'.

freedom;[31] others might see a more naïve articulation of what was to be one
of the central preoccupations of contemporary German idealism.[32] But it is
also possible to read in Joseph de Maistre's paradoxes a genuine expression
of what he perceives to be the impenetrable mystery of providential design.
This would seem to be supported by the fact that Xavier de Maistre articu-
lates the self-same paradox in his fiction: our only freedom is in chains, or
rather it resides in acknowledging the necessity of our chains. This is the lesson of his later tale, *Les Prisonniers du Caucase*, published in 1825, in which the
hero, Major Kascambo, is only able to flee captivity by keeping his chains
on.[33] The same appears to be true for the narrator of the *Voyage autour de ma
chambre*, who exclaims on his eventual liberation from detention: 'C'est au-
jourd'hui donc que je suis libre, ou plutôt que je vais rentrer dans les fers!'
(*Voyage*, 133).[34] To move freely in society requires him submitting to chains
of another less obvious sort. Hence both Joseph de Maistre's counter-revolutionary philosophy and Xavier de Maistre's fantastical fiction maintain that
freedom is necessarily conditional and relative. This, then, is the gross error
of the revolutionary beast: to seek absolute freedom, to decree an idealized
and abstract liberty which for both de Maistres, drawing undoubtedly on Edmund Burke here, is nothing other than a licence for bloody anarchy.

Admitting himself to be increasingly troubled, even terrified, in the
presence of crowds, the narrator of the *Voyage autour de ma chambre* has a
dream or vision of just such bloody anarchy. In this dream ('songe') a polite
social gathering is suddenly interrupted by 'un ours blanc, un philosophe,
un tigre, ou quelque autre animal de cette espèce' (*Voyage*, 103).[35] Without
dwelling too long here on the jarring juxtaposition of bears, tigers and *philosophes* as interchangeable revolutionary beasts, the narrator recounts how
this 'animal' gets up on stage, calls to all present to take up arms and to slit
the throats of those occupying the best seats in the house, declaring: 'vous
êtes *libres*, arrachez votre roi de son trône et votre Dieu de son sanctuaire!'
(*Voyage*, 104, his italics).[36] What perhaps is most odd about this gruesome
vision is that the bloodthirsty revolutionary creature characterizes his audi-

---

31 For example, E. M. Cioran, 'Joseph de Maistre: An Essay on Reactionary Thought', in *Ana-
themas and Admirations*, translated by Richard Howard (London: Quartet Books, 1992), pp. 22–
78, 32.

32 For example, the relationship between necessity and freedom in Schelling's *Identitätsphilosophie*
and between freedom and the 'cunning of reason' in Hegel.

33 For more on this point, see Gilbert Durand, 'Le voyage et la chambre', 79. It is interesting to
note that in this article, referring to de Maistre's *La Jeune Sibérienne* (1825), Durand sees in this
eastern tale the workings of a deeper myth, that of the story of Hagar in the Bible (Genesis 16,
21), essentially the story of Hagar and the angel, hence 'une Angélologie [...] un mythe de
l'ange' (84) – 'an Angelology [...] a myth of angels'.

34 'It is thus today that I am free, or rather that I take up my chains again'.

35 'A polar bear, a *philosophe* [natural free-thinker], a tiger or some other animal of this sort'.

36 'You are *free*, throw down your king from his throne and your God from his shrine'.

ence in exactly the same way as the counter-revolutionary narrator does: as the unfortunate and wretched of the earth. Both similarly offer practical solutions for the miserable condition in which their audience finds itself. 'Malheureux humains!' cries the revolutionary – rise up (*Voyage*, 103); 'malheureux', declares the narrator – read this book, its fantastical consolations are 'indépendant[es] de la fortune' (*Voyage*, 41).[37] Whether urging an absolute freedom to cast off social chains (the revolutionary beast) or recommending the diverting exercise of a more conditional liberty (the counter-revolutionary soul), the implied objective of both freedoms is to seek out happiness, magically to transform 'malheur' into 'bonheur', misery into joy.

It is obvious, however, that we are dealing with two distinct, opposed forms of happiness here.[38] The narrator tries to recapture a lost happiness enjoyed in the company of his coquettish mistress or his dead friend, surrounding himself with the material comforts reminiscent of this former life (bed, valet, dog, coffee, etc). This happiness is profoundly conservative: it always wants things to stay the same. The other happiness, sought by the revolutionary, is more a utilitarian happiness of the greatest number, born of the knowledge of past misery and in the hope of future bliss. It is a radical, reforming happiness that demands that things change. And both of these forms of happiness take inspiration in the 1790s from a selective reading of Jean-Jacques Rousseau's *œuvre*. The first happiness, the narrator's, is that of Rousseau's *Les Rêveries du promeneur solitaire* – a major intertext here.[39] It is the eternal present of Jean-Jacques's solitary pastoral idyll on the isolated île de St Pierre in the lac de Bienne, described rhapsodically as

> un état où l'âme trouve une assiette assez solide pour s'y reposer tout entière et rassembler là tout son être, sans avoir besoin de rappeler le passé ni d'enjamber sur l'avenir; où le temps ne soit rien pour elle, […] tant que cet état dure celui qui s'y trouve peut s'appeler heureux, non d'un bonheur imparfait, pauvre et relatif […] mais d'un bonheur suffisant, parfait et plein, qui ne laisse dans l'âme aucun vide qu'elle sente le besoin de remplir.[40]

---

37 'Unfortunate humans!' […] 'Wretches' [the book's consolations are] 'independent of your fortune'.

38 The obligatory reference here is Robert Mauzi, *L'Idée du bonheur dans la littérature et la pensée françaises au XVIIIᵉ siècle* (Paris: Armand Colin, 1960).

39 See, for example, the narrator's reference to happy painters of nature taking 'solitary walks' (*Voyage*, 55) or praise of 'idleness' (*Voyage*, 67–68). See also Marie Wellington, '*Voyage autour de ma chambre* et les Lumières: un enchaînement', *Neuphilologische Mitteilungen* 91.3 (1990) 379–387, 380.

40 Jean-Jacques Rousseau, *Les Rêveries du promeneur solitaire* (Paris: Gallimard, 1972), p. 101. 'A state in which the soul finds a seat solid enough to settle completely there and gather all its being about itself, without needing to recall the past or step into the future; where time is nothing […] and, for as long as this state endures, s/he who finds himself or herself there may be called happy, not with an imperfect, impoverished and relative happiness […] but with a sufficient, perfect and complete happiness, leaving no void in the soul which it feels the need to fill'.

The second happiness is that promised in Rousseau's *Du contrat social*, at least
as this is interpreted in the political messianism of Robespierrist revolutionaries such as Antoine de Saint-Just.[41] In his address to the National Convention of 3 March 1794 on the redistribution of property confiscated from the
'enemies of the Revolution' to be given to 'destitute patriots', Saint-Just fa-
mously declared that these redistributive laws were formulated so that Europe might

> apprenne que vous [members of the Convention] ne voulez plus un malheureux ni
> un oppresseur sur le territoire français; que cet exemple fructifie sur la terre; qu'il y
> propage l'amour des vertus et le bonheur. Le bonheur est une idée neuve en Eu-
> rope![42]

The first form of happiness is, then, an angelic utterance of a soul in reverie,
already no longer of this world; the second is affirmed by the unwavering revolutionary zealot, by the ironically nicknamed 'Archangel of the Revolution',
bent on changing the world.

Clearly Xavier de Maistre identifies happiness first and foremost with
soulful Rousseauist reverie; he promotes a version of this in the *Voyage autour de ma chambre*, as though engaged in a belated attempt to reclaim Rousseau from his distorted ideological exploitation by certain revolutionary factions. Just as in Rousseau's *Rêveries*, happiness for de Maistre is above all a
wistful memory, the immaterial solace of counter-revolutionary exile. Indeed, the very condition of exile informs his nostalgic representations of
happiness, just as it informs his (and his brother's) notion of a necessarily
conditional freedom. Both physically and metaphysically, exile is the epitome of conditional freedom: to have definite limits placed on one's liberty,
to be free only as long as one does not return to the place where freedom
was given meaning, the place where freedom was initially granted and realized. In a paradox worthy of Joseph de Maistre, exile is this: to be free from
freedom – in contradistinction to incarceration or enslavement which constitute a negation or total absence of freedom. So exile sadly means living at
a remove from the de Maistrean ideal of a perfect coincidence of divine
providence and human free will. Exile is proof that God and the counter-
revolutionary are not willing the same thing. Or rather, it proves that God
and the counter-revolutionary are not willing the same thing *yet*; for Joseph
de Maistre responds to exile by projecting this idealized state of divine-hu-
man order into the future, in his prophesies of a Bourbon Restoration. In

---

41 For this collective political happiness in Rousseau, see Mauzi, *L'Idée du bonheur*, 140–141; for
   Saint-Just's political messianism, see Michael Burleigh, *Earthly Powers: Religion and Politics in
   Europe from the Enlightenment to the Great War* (London: HarperCollins, 2005), pp. 91–93.
42 Cited in Bernard Vinot, *Saint-Just* (Paris: Fayard, 1985), p. 284. 'Learn that you [members of
   the National Convention] no longer want a single pauper or a single oppressor on French soil;
   that this example may flourish over the earth; that it may spread the love of virtue and happiness. Happiness is a new idea in Europe!'

contrast, Xavier de Maistre, in his *Voyage autour de ma chambre*, seems to prefer a projection into the past, to be always looking back over his shoulder at
an Eden lost. Geographically, this is a royalist Savoy independent of France;
historically, it is the *ancien régime*. Here again, in reference to Eden, he (and
we) come up against the deep ambivalence revealed in the figure of the angel. The archetype of all exiling, Eden is the preserve of the angels, but entry
into it is also blocked by them, by the fiery sword-wielding cherubim of the
Book of Genesis (Genesis 3. 24).

Thus in the face of a Revolution that is akin to a second 'Fall' from
grace, Xavier de Maistre retreats into an alternative, ethereal universe. This
is the haven of *ancien régime* civility and aesthetic pleasure cultivated in his
'room', characterized by all that is otherworldly and angelic. It is a haven
delicate to the point of evanescence; in fact, so delicate that the Revolution
raging outside its walls cannot be kept out forever. The 'room' ultimately
proves porous or purely imaginary. The Revolution enters, or worse still, is
found to have been always already there, lurking in the form of the insidious
beast that shadows the narrator's contemplative soul. Under the influence
of the ever-present beast, the soul is thus doomed, just as the beautiful Raphael turns into the baleful Lucifer (a figure at once abhorred and strangely
admired). And by the same process, the home, his 'room', becomes only
another form of exile.

In conclusion, then, when Xavier de Maistre comes to write his sequel
to the *Voyage autour de ma chambre*, that is, his *Expédition nocturne autour de ma
chambre* – begun in 1799 but not finished until 1823 – he does away with the
ambivalent 'soul-beast' distinction; he does away too with angels, preferring
to place his faith in the stars, lost in contemplation before the sublimity of a
starlit night, and ultimately letting himself be guided north by the pole star.
Here stars serve as a metonymic figure of astronomy, positing a notion of
revolution as a cyclical, cosmic and conservative phenomenon, the very opposite of the linear, man-made, progressive-radical revolution begun in
1789. The stars to which Xavier de Maistre's narrator is drawn reject the
Revolution and shine instead as an unequivocal reminder of Providence at
work in the world.[43] They are stars that also lead the author into yet deeper
exile, to Russia, to the army of the Tsar, and into the arms of his reactionary
brother.

---

43 Xavier de Maistre, *Expédition nocturne autour de ma chambre*, in *Œuvres complètes du comte Xavier de
    Maistre* (Paris: Garnier Frères, 1911), pp. 113–209. Hence the narrator, rudely evicted from the
    'chambre' of his original *Voyage* by encroaching revolutionary violence, settles in the 'rue de la
    Providence' (*Voyage*, 116), i.e., 'Providence Street', from where he addresses the pole star,
    declaring 'je crois à une providence divine qui conduit les hommes par des moyens inconnus'
    (*Voyage*, 186–187). 'I believe in a divine providence which leads men on by unknown means'.

Introducing the *Songs* with Inspiration
William Blake, Lavater, and the Legacy of Felix Hess

Sibylle Erle

Most of us know, or have read, Willliam Blake's *Songs of Innocence and of Experience*. The *Songs of Innocence* date from 1789, but were issued again in combination with the *Songs of Experience* in 1794, the same year in which Blake launched his creation myth, *The Book of Urizen*. The subtitle on the title-page of the combined *Songs* reads: 'Shewing the two contrary states of the human souls'.[1] Against a backdrop of flames, the plate depicts the expulsion of Adam and Eve from Paradise. The design states what the *Songs* are about: a transition from innocence to experience, from childhood to adulthood, from the world of paradise to the world we live in. The idea that Blake prefers to express himself through contraries, such as text and image or contrary emotions, is, again, articulated in *The Marriage of Heaven and Hell* (1790) where it says: 'Without Contraries is no progression. / Attraction and Repulsion, Reason and Energy, Love and Hate, are necessary to Human existence' (E, 34). Applied to the *Songs*, a reading experience which produces progress is one during which readers remain actively involved. Readers will grow if they try to understand the connections between the two sets of songs and their treatments of similar ideas.[2] The *Songs* have been discussed alongside eighteenth-century children's books. Critics such as Heather Glen stress how innovative Blake's approach to teaching children was. His ironic attitude confronts the reader with a 'disconcerting inconclusiveness'. Glen concludes that there is 'no direction'.[3] Each of the sets, *Innocence* and *Experience*, is memorably introduced through a frontispiece, depicting a shepherd and a small child in one and a bard and an angel in the other, as well as an introductory poem, each of

---

1   *The Complete Poetry and Prose of William Blake*, newly revised edition, ed. by David V. Erdman and Harold Bloom (New York, London, Toronto, Sydney and Auckland: Double Day Anchor Books, 1988), p. 7, to be abbreviated as E plus page number.
2   Blake favoured dialectics to 'suggest the possibility of an objective, impartial view of contraries', cf. Edward Larrissy, *William Blake* (Oxford: Blackwell, 1985), p. 7. For interpretations of the different pairs and combinations, see William Blake, *The Songs of Innocence and of Experience*, ed. by Andrew Lincoln (London: Tate Gallery Publications for The William Blake Trust, 1991).
3   Heather Glen, *Vision and Disenchantment: Blake's Songs and Wordsworth's Lyrical Ballads* (Cambridge: Cambridge University Press, 1983), p. 19.

which dramatizes a different kind of author-muse relationship. Reading the *Songs* as children's literature, however, has led to an over-emphasis on the text.

Not only the *Songs*, but also *Europe* (1793), *The Book of Urizen* and *The Song of Los* (1795) open with scenes of invocation. In the 1790s Blake is experimenting with a new concept of inspiration, because rather than use the classical trope as an explanation, he adapts these scenes in order to establish the poet as an original source of poetic truth. In the past, the opening sequence (text and image) of *Innocence* has been interpreted as a 'symbolic account' of how Blake wrote poetry.[4] Whereas in *Innocence* the account is personal and immediate, in *Experience* it is formulaic and abstract and, therefore, sanctioned rather than original. Zachary Leader discusses the transition from child to cherub and piper to bard and stresses that, while in *Innocence* the adult is 'prepared to join the child's game',[5] in *Experience* 'child and shepherd-youth stare straight ahead. Gone is the human contact of the earlier frontispiece'.[6] This essay argues that Blake's understanding of inspiration was shaped by his friendship with the Swiss-born painter Henry Fuseli, who introduced him to a new artistic model, one which replaced divine with original and human creativity.

The Swiss pastor Johann Caspar Lavater, author of *Essays on Physiognomy* (1789–98), is important for our understanding of the development of Blake's thought in the 1790s.[7] Whereas Swedenborg, who also influenced Lavater,[8] is a well-established source, Lavater is still neglected.[9] When Blake was putting together the *Songs of Innocence*, he was annotating Swedenborg's *Divine Love and Divine Wisdom*, but he was also reading it alongside Lavater's

---

4   Eric Donald Hirsch, Jr., *Innocence and Experience: An Introduction to Blake* (New Haven: Yale University Press, 1964), p. 173.
5   Zachary Leader, *Reading Blake's Songs* (London: Routledge and Paul Kegan, 1981), p. 73.
6   Leader, *Reading*, 131.
7   Joseph Viscomi writes that Blake's short 'philosophical tractates' are evidence of 'just how influenced Blake was by Lavater and the aphoristic form'. Cf. *Blake and the Idea of the Book* (Princeton, N.J.: Princeton University Press, 1993), pp. 195, 197.
8   Ernst Benz explains how Swedenborg's ideas of a universal, physiognomical language shaped Lavater's approach to physiognomy. 'Swedenborg and Lavater: The Religious Foundation of Physiognomy: The Art of Judging Character from Facial Features' (1938), translated by Alfred Heron, *The New Philosophy* 104.1–2 (2001) 59–116. Swedenborg was widely read and commented on in eighteenth-century Germany. Othmar Tobisch documents Lavater's engagement with Swedenborg and concludes, with respect to the afterlife, that Lavater could not agree with Swedenborg. Cf. Othmar Tobisch, 'Lavater and Swedenborg', *The New-Church Review* 40.4 (1933) 210- 233. I thank James Wilson, Librarian of the Swedenborgian Society, for these essays.
9   Magnus Ankarsjö synthesizes the existing debates about Moravian, Swedenborigian and Unitarian influences in his *William Blake and Religion: A New Critical View* (Jefferson, NC, and London: McFarland & Company, 2009). Peter Otto discusses embodiment and transcendence with reference to Locke and Swedenborg, but not to Lavater, in his *Blake's Critique of Transcendence: Love, Jealousy, and the Sublime in The Four Zoas* (Oxford: Oxford University Press, 2000).

Aphorisms on Man (1788) and engraving plates for both *Aphorisms on Man* and *Essays on Physiognomy*. What appealed in Swedenborg was the notion of parallel worlds, a material and a spiritual one, and the connection he said existed between them: 'Swedenborg's view of the two worlds as discrete but connected by correspondence and influx can at times accommodate Blake's desire for a synthesis of both and at other times appear to contradict it.'[10] William and Catherine Blake attended the Swedenborg conference in East Cheap in London in April 1790 where they met some extraordinary people. David Worrall, while drawing attention to the life and work of Dorothy Gott, points out: 'the poems in which Blake ironizes several contemporary prophetic rhetorics were preceded by his meeting a woman who already commanded the prophetic mode.'[11] This mode, and especially the kind of inspiration associated with Old-Testament prophecy, can be linked to Lavater as well. The influences of Lavater and Swedenborg may be converging, but Blake's interest in Lavater was profound because it was personal.[12] In the late 1780s, Blake was asked by his employer, the publisher Joseph Johnson and possibly Henry Fuseli, who was Lavater's friend, to engrave four plates for *Essays on Physiognomy*; and he worked alongside Fuseli, who was preparing *Aphorisms on Man* for publication. Carol Louise Hall, in *Blake and Fuseli*, argues that Fuseli introduced Blake to a number of European thought traditions, among them Lavater's new approach to the ancient art of face-reading.[13]

Not only had Fuseli been trained as a theologian, he supported the use of physiognomy from an artistic point of view. He thought it was useful. In one of the prospectuses advertising *Essays on Physiognomy* Fuseli writes, for example, 'Artists in all Branches of Design will be furnished with innumer-

---

10 Morton D. Paley, '"A New Heaven Is Begun": Blake and Swedenborgianism', in *Blake and Swedenborg: Opposition Is True Friendship*, ed. by Harvey F. Bellin and Darrell Ruhl (New York: Swedenborg Foundation, 1985), pp. 15–34, 18.

11 David Worrall, 'Blake, the Female Prophet and the American Agent: The Evidence of the 1789 Swedenborg Conference Attendance List', in: *Blake and Conflict*, ed. by Sarah Haggarty and Jon Mee (Basingstoke: Palgrave Macmillan, 2009), pp. 48–64, 50.

12 Keri Davies argues along these lines. Due to his Moravian upbringing, Blake would have been familiar with Moravian hymns. This explains the similarities between, for example, 'O Jesu, sweet and mild' and 'The Lamb', from *Innocence*. Keri Davies, 'Lost Moravian History of William Blake's Family: Snapshots from the Archive', *Literature Compass* 3.6 (2006) 1297–1319, 1298.

13 Carol Louise Hall, *Blake and Fuseli: A Study in the Transmission of Ideas* (New York and London: Garland Publishing, 1985), p. 5. In response to Hall Matthew Green writes that not Lavater's style but his 'philosophy could have been far more significant to Blake's work than has hitherto been thought'. Cf. Matthew Green, 'Outlining the "Human Form Divine": Reading Blake's Thoughts on Outline and Response to Locke alongside Lavater and Cumberland', *European Romantic Review* 15.4 (2004) 511–532, 513.

able Hints respecting the Principles and the Improvements of their Art.'[14] Blake, who thought of himself as a poet as well as a painter, would naturally have been interested in what Fuseli had to say. *Aphorisms on Man*, moreover, the work which Blake both read and annotated, presents Lavater's physiognomical principles in a much more comprehensible manner than *Essays on Physiognomy*. Lavater was sharply criticized for his belief that physiognomy would, sooner or later, develop into an empirical science. In his annotations Blake acknowledges this, 'there is a strong objection to Lavaters [*sic*] principles', (E 600), but he is also keen to agree with Lavater:

> Man is bad or good. as he unites himself with bad or good spirits. […] it is impossible to know God or heavenly things without conjunction with those who know God & heavenly things. therefore, all who converse in the spirit, converse with spirits. […] this Book is written by consultation with Good Spirits because it is Good.' (E 600)

For Lavater the spiritual and the material were ultimately inseparable. The question for me is this: how much of Lavater's approach did Fuseli relate to Blake?

In *Aussichten in die Ewigkeit* (1768–73) Lavater explores ideas about the life of the soul and the nature of the eternal body. He states, for example, that the resurrected body resembles Christ's body. He talks about 'Selbstausbreitungskraft' (force of self-expansion)[15] and 'Zusammendrängbarkeit' (ability to contract), then explains that the resurrected body can expand and contract like light, and without ever losing its characteristic shape.[16] Man will be resurrected as a 'light-body', able to communicate without words and through a flexible, new body alone.[17] Much later, we find these ideas about the condition of the soul in the afterlife repeated in a series of letters, written in 1798 for the Tsarina Maria Feodorovna. The soul, Lavater writes, experiences very differently from the material body. Everything is determined by the senses, but what the soul experiences is of much better quality, because after death and resurrection the material world appears completely different to the 'disembodied soul'.[18] Souls, according to Lavater, can communicate through letters with the living. They can dictate them to a light-enabled mind ('Lichtfähiger Geist').[19] Given its superior sensory organs, it

---

14 David H. Weinglass, ed., *Prints and Engraved Illustrations by and after Henry Fuseli: A Catalogue Raisonné* (Aldershot: Scolar Press, 1994), p. 97.

15 All translations into English are my own.

16 Johann Caspar Lavater, *Aussichten in die Ewigkeit, in Briefen an Herrn Johann Georg Zimmermann, Königlichen Großbritannischen Leibarzt in Hannover*, 3 vols (Hamburg: Buchhändler Gesellschaft, 1768–73), II, p. 67.

17 Karl Pestalozzi, 'Lavaters Utopie', in *Literaturwissenschaft und Geschichtsphilosophie: Festschrift für Wilhelm Emrich*, ed. by Helmut Arntzen et al. (Berlin and New York: de Gruyter, 1975), pp. 283–301, 288–290.

18 Johann Caspar Lavater, *Briefe an die Kaiserin Maria Feodorowna: Über den Zustand der Seele nach dem Tode* (St. Petersburg: Kaiserliche Öffentliche Bibliothek zu St. Petersburg, 1858), p. 26.

19 Lavater, *Briefe an die Kaiserin Maria Feodorowna*, 48.

is easy for the soul to find such a person. To prove all this, Lavater says, he will share such a letter with the Tsarina. He does not know who sent it, but it arrived one day after he finished his previous letter to her, on 15 November 15, 1798. Lavater, in other words, allows a soul to tell the Tsarina how it is able to 'talk' through another person: 'Wie der Papillon über den Blumen schwebt, so schweben wir oft, nicht immer, über den Häuptern der Guten.'[20] The anonymous writer explains that some people have eyes sensitive enough to perceive this kind of communication as a light radiating from another person's head. This is what we might call a halo. Then this writer explains how he/she went about dictating a letter for Lavater. Whenever a 'disembodied soul' finds a pious person ('Frommguten'), it reads their minds, assesses the light it contains, and then directs their thoughts:

> Ich schwebe über Ihm [...] Ich wirke auf Ihn. Ich errege Gedanken in Ihm. Er schreibt sie – nach meiner Stimmung, Leitung, Bestrahlung. [...] Er schreibt, was ich von Ihm geschrieben wünsche. Ich schreibe durch Ihn. Alle meine Gedanken werden die Seinigen. Es ist Ihm wohl beim Schreiben.[21]

Before this writer ends, he/she reminds Lavater that he, too, is a recipient of such thoughts. Lavater must have wondered why he had never been contacted directly. A possible explanation is that he had long since accepted that he was not pious enough: that is, the light inside his mind was not pure enough to receive spiritual thoughts.

Lavater's belief, that in order to be a good physiognomist he first had to know himself, is expressed in the frontispiece to *Aphorisms on Man*, designed by Fuseli and engraved by Blake. It shows a muse floating over a writer who is lost in thought and holding a pen. At first sight, this is a scene typical of the classical model, because the figure seems to be listening to a possibly divine source of inspiration. However, the supposed muse holds a tablet with the Greek Socratic inscription 'Know thyself', which would imply that the figure – not the muse – is responsible for the impending act of creative production. When handing over the design, Fuseli must have given Blake instructions to help with its execution, because this is a fairly rough sketch. Did Fuseli and Blake have a conversation about the nature of artistic inspiration? Ruthven Todd, who first discussed the sketch, noted that Fuseli, half-way through, changed his mind; he decided to omit the wings of the muse. Todd quotes Alan Cunningham who quotes Fuseli as saying regarding the angels in a painting done for his Milton Gallery that they should

---

20 'Like the butterfly hovers over flowers, we hover often, not always, over the heads of the virtuous.'
21 Lavater, *Briefe an die Kaiserin Maria Feodorowna*, 47–48. 'I hover over him [...] I influence him. I incite thoughts in him. He writes them down – after my mood, instruction, emission. [...] He writes what I want him to write. I write through him. All my thoughts become his own. He enjoys writing.'

"'rise without wings'".[22] Significantly, this suggests that Fuseli broke with tradition. While the wings would have indicated that the muse is an angel, the lack of wings means that it is defying gravity because of the nature of its body. Leader, analyzing how the adult-figure responds to the 'child on the cloud', argues that leaving out the wings in the frontispiece to *Innocence* calls attention to 'the divinity of children or innocents in this world'.[23]

According to Robert Essick, Fuseli chose to depict a moment of 'transmundane inspiration' both in the minds of the author and the translator.[24] I have argued elsewhere that the frontispiece might represent an externalization of the writer's thoughts.[25] The inscription on the tablet is, therefore, a description rather than a prompt. This makes it, as far as Fuseli is concerned, another attempt to gain distance from John Locke's model of the mind. It has already been noted that Blake's response to Lockean psychology is less dismissive or negative than tends to be assumed. Steve Clark has argued that both (Blake and Locke) are part of 'a common tradition of radical Protestantism'.[26] Blake knew that the mind had to reconstruct external reality, while processing information: 'the opposition is not [...] between a "quiescent blank slate" and an "exuberantly active mind", but between labour within severely restricted bounds and the effortless mode of simultaneous perception implied by Blake's own doctrine of innate principles'.[27] Blake, I think, revisits a well-worn formula in an attempt to come to terms with the nature of original inspiration. When discussing the effect of the disappearance of the child in *Innocence*, Leader, recalling Wicksteed who argued that 'the Child is now something within',[28] notes that it echoes Lavater's explanation of genius: 'like the apparition of an angel, it comes not, but is suddenly present, leaves not, but is gone. Like the apparition of an angel, it moves us to the marrow'.[29] The reason the muse disappears is that the piper 'takes on the child's way of seeing and speaking'.[30] The question of how creative the mind can be haunts Blake's early poetry. At the beginning of *Europe,* Blake evokes the Lockean mind through the image of a 'cavern'd Man' who pieces together the outside world by means of 'Five windows'

22 Ruthven Todd, 'Two Blake Prints and Two Fuseli Drawings', *Blake Newsletter* 5.3 (1971–72) 173–181, 174.
23 Leader, *Reading*, 73.
24 Robert N. Essick, *Commercial Book Illustrations: A Catalogue and Study of the Plates engraved by Blake after Designs by other Artists* (Oxford: Clarendon, 1991), pp. 40–41.
25 Sibylle Erle, *Blake, Lavater and Physiognomy* (London: Legenda, 2010), p. 97.
26 Steve Clark, "Labouring at the Resolute Anvil": Blake's Response to Locke', in: *Blake in the Nineties*, ed. by Steve Clark and David Worrall (London: Macmillan, 1999), pp. 133–152, 134.
27 Clark, "Labouring at the Resolute Anvil"', 137–138.
28 Joseph Hartley Wicksteed, *Blake's Innocence and Experience: A Study of the Songs and Manuscripts* (London: J.M. Dent, 1928), p. 81.
29 Leader, *Reading*, 70.
30 Leader, *Reading*, 70.

(E 60), which, like the senses, are his sole information leads. The passage is told by a fairy; but it turns out that the various creative processes are intertwined. To start with, the author of the poem is curious. He catches the fairy and says: 'How know you this said I small Sir? where did you learn this song?' (E 60). When there is no answer, this poet contents himself with an account of the material world; later, when the fairy responds, it laughs and says: 'I will write a book on leaves of flowers, / If you will feed me on love-thoughts, & give me now and then / A cup of sparkling poetic fancies' (E 60), to which the poet adds:

> I took him home in my warm bosom: as we went along
> Wild flowers I gatherd; & he shew'd me each eternal flower:
> He laugh'd aloud to see them whimper because they were pluck'd.
> They hover'd round me like a cloud of incense: when I came
> Into my parlour and sat down, and took my pen to write:
> My Fairy sat upon the table, and dictated EUROPE. (E 60)

The poet's muse, no doubt, is an unreliable, if not mischievous joker. What interests me in this passage is the implied coexistence of spiritual and material elements in the poet's day-to-day experience. The poet is writing down what the fairy is telling him, but on his way home he also notices that he is surrounded by leaves of eternal flowers.[31] According to the fairy, these leaves might themselves be carriers of text. The Fairy is 'dictating' *Europe*, and I wonder whether it is reading off the floating leaves. So the earlier, random act of cruelty might actually be a precondition for the creative act itself. The imagery of floating eternal spirits, as I have argued above, can be traced back to Lavater, to his ideas about the spiritual world and the ways in which its inhabitants communicated with the living.

There is a sense that, as his work on physiognomy progressed, Lavater decided to withhold some of his findings, because he differentiates between two very different audiences. Whereas the first comprises his friends, whom he trusts, and people who he reckons are able to use his insights in a responsible manner, the second, much bigger, group is the wider reading public, which, from Lavater's point of view, is not sensitive or developed enough to put his approach into practice. So, on the one hand, Lavater pushes for extended versions of *Physiognomische Fragemente* to be translated into French and English, but, on the other hand, he decides to produce separate physiognomical rules, which he publishes privately and in small octavo volumes.

---

31 Plate iii, from which this passage is taken, is only in two of the known copies, which makes its connection with the rest of the poem tenuous. Detlef Dörrbecker draws attention to Milton's invocation of a muse, and the fact that Blake creates a 'lighthearted version of the forest imagery encountered in the ensuing prophecy', and argues that 'the plucking of the wild flowers, "with its sexual connotations"', resonates with 'Blake's characterization of Enitharmon's equation of love and sin in the prophecy proper'. Cf. *The Continental Prophecies*, ed. by Detlef W. Dörrbecker (London: Tate Gallery Publications for The William Blake Trust, 1995), p. 283.

These rules seem to be revealing all: the shapes (eyes, foreheads, eyebrows, noses, mouths, and ears) which embody human character. In place of a preface Lavater addresses his specially chosen friends. He forbids them to share his rules with anyone and says, if they did or, worse still, printed them, they would betray him. One of the few surviving copies is in the Staatsbibliothek Berlin.[32] This copy is inscribed with a personalized dedication: 'Mit des Verfassers Einwilligung seiner lieben Schwester Mary zum Andenken gegeben' (With the author's agreement given to his dear sister Mary as a memento). It is signed and dated '4. d. 13.X.96'. According to its title, *Vermischte Physiognomische Regeln. Manuscript für Freunde. mit einigen charakteristischen Linien. Erstes Hundert* (Miscellaneous Physiognomical Rules. Manuscript for Friends. with some characteristic lines. The First Hundred), composed in 1798, Lavater envisaged these rules to be only the beginning. We do not know if he sent a copy to Fuseli in London. What he did send was the manuscript which Fuseli edited, translated and published as *Aphorisms on Man*. While Fuseli tried hard to hide behind Lavater, he says that there was going to be a second volume of aphorisms 'not indeed by the same author', but him, the editor,[33] and brushed over the extent to which he changed the manuscript, Blake approaches the work very differently. He acknowledges that it inspired him, by writing onto the first page: 'for the reason of these remarks see the last aphorism' (E 583), and adds, in response, his comments.[34] I think, working for Fuseli quickly moved beyond matters to do with artistic collaboration, because the men realized that they shared a deep emotional bond. This was first suggested by David Erdman who writes that, when they met in 1787, Fuseli might have been something of a 'spiritual comforter' to Blake who had just lost his younger brother Robert.[35] Robert's dying, according to Blake's Victorian biographer Alexander Gilchrist, was a prolonged and traumatic affair.[36] The reason Fuseli was sympathetic towards Blake is that he, too, had lost a very dear friend: Felix Hess, who, like Robert, had died from tuberculosis. Did Fuseli tell Blake about Lavater's conviction that the souls of the deceased would stay close to their former friends? Fuseli may have told Blake that Lavater, who had been even closer to Hess, had been desperate after his death. He could sense that Hess was there, but he could not see him.

32 Staatsbibliothek Berlin, Ms. Germ. Oct. 424.
33 Johann Caspar Lavater, *Aphorisms on Man*, translated from the original manuscript of the Rev. John Caspar Lavater [by Henry Fuseli] (London: Joseph Johnson, 1788), p. vi.
34 Sibylle Erle, 'Leaving their mark: Lavater, Fuseli and Blake and their imprint on *Aphorisms on Man*,' *Comparative Critical Studies* 3.3 (2006) 347–369.
35 David V. Erdman, *Blake: Prophet against the Empire*, 3rd rev. edition (Princeton, N.J.: Princeton University Press, 1977), p. 141.
36 Alexander Gilchrist, *The Life of William Blake*, 1st edn 1863, ed. by W. Graham Robertson (New York: Dover Publications, 1998), p. 60. Blake saw Robert in his visions and communicated with him all his life (Gilchrist, *Life*, 70–71).

There is plenty of evidence for Robert's continued presence in Blake's life. In a poem composed during a walk near Felpham in 1802 Blake relates how he is being accompanied by angels and demons, as well as his father and brothers:

> With my Father hovering upon the wind
> And my Brother Robert just behind
> And my Brother John the evil one
> In a black cloud […]. (E 721)

Such mixed company is also typical of Swedenborg's experiences, who recorded the conversations he had with angels and demons in his dream diary. The difference is that Robert is said to have contributed to artistic production. Robert is normally ascribed an important role in Blake's invention of illuminated printing, the technique used to print the *Songs*. G.E. Bentley emphasizes that Robert was a 'fellow spirit and even […] a spiritual guide' to Blake.[37] Robert also appears in *Milton* (1804–18), a work which incorporates the two picture-plates 'Robert' and 'William'. Robert, David Erdman has argued, 'is the spiritual component of Blake's psyche [...] yet he is one with William'; and since the plates are not next to each other, we ought to think of them as illustrating the progress from one state of being into another, that is, they depict the transition from the material to the spiritual realm.[38] Marsha Keith Schuchard, when considering the impact of Robert's death, notes that Blake 'benefited from the "substantialised spiritualism" of Animal Magnetism to not only focus his vision but communicate with the spirit of Robert.'[39] Blake managed to focus the faculty of vision. I am, however, less sure if he achieved this on his own. At least in the first half of the 1790s, Blake's thinking and writing betrays a dialogue, or rather exchange, between the spiritual and material worlds. Poetic vision is not something which an artist receives *gratis* from a helping muse. It manifests itself during artistic production and depends on sensitivity and consciousness.

Fuseli is an important mediator because he may also have introduced Blake to a theological debate. The debate was triggered by the Enlightenment's attempts to find rational explanations for the afterlife and the immortality of the human soul. Part of this tradition is the question of the nature of the human soul and how it should be represented. Lavater had sketched Hess on his deathbed and asked Fuseli to work up the drawing. In his reply Fuseli announced to Lavater that he had doubts about the purpose

---

37 G.E. Bentley Jr., *The Stranger from Paradise: A Biography of William Blake* (New Haven and London: Yale University Press, 2001), p. 6. See also Bentley, *Blake Records*, 2nd edn (New Haven and London: Yale University Press, 2004), pp. 44–45.

38 David Erdman, 'The steps (of Dance and Stone) that order Blake's *Milton*', *Blake Studies* 6.1 (1973) 73–87, 81.

39 Marsha Keith Schuchard, *Why Mrs Blake Cried: William Blake and the Erotic Imagination* (London: Pimlico, 2007), p. 205.

of such a portrait: 'Verkennest du deines Freundes Kleid für ihn selbst?'
(Do you mistake your friend's clothes for your friend?)[40] Fuseli accepted
the power attributed to images generally, but mocked Lavater, who believed
that a good portrait evoked or rather created presence. In a letter written in
1766 (two years earlier) he asked Lavater if he was fed up with him: Lavater
has only a little spark of love ('geringe Funke von Zuneigung'), which sends
only small rays over his name and image ('einen kleinen Strahl über meinen
Namen und Bildness').[41] Fuseli is reproaching Lavater for his neglect by
suggesting that there is an emotional connection between Fuseli and his
portrait in Lavater's possession.

I cannot say for certain that Fuseli read *Aussichten in die Ewigkeit,* but his
preoccupation with age and death, which found its way into his own poetry,
produced similar imagery, that is, imagery of friendship continuing beyond
death. In 'Zweite Ode an Lavater' (Second Ode to Lavater), written in
1802–03, shortly after Lavater's death, Fuseli is looking back on his life with
confidence. He sees a good future ahead of him and wonders if Lavater is
still a part of it:

> Tue den siebten Teil von dem, was du tun kannst, so sagte,
> Als seinem Arm ich entfloh, mein nun unsterblicher Freund.[42]
> Tat ich den siebenten Teil von dem, was ich tun konnte?
> Schwebst du itzt um mein Haupt, sag es, unsterblicher Freund?
> Sechzig Jahre entfloh'n, mein Haupt ist silber, der Zunge
> Elfenbeinerne Mauer fällt in Fragmente zerknirscht. (ll. 1–6) [43]

As well as reflecting on the diminishing powers of his poetic vision, he had
tried to be a poet as well as painter, Fuseli asks if Lavater is 'hovering' over
him and is still keeping an eye on him. Lavater had always been a supportive
friend. He had, for example, sponsored Fuseli during his studies in Rome in
the 1770s. Tensions between them, however, flared up when Fuseli made
drawings for *Physiognomische Fragmente* and Lavater criticized them. He told Fuseli what changes he had to make. Fuseli soon had enough: 'Deine und meine
Imagination mögen dieselbe sein; aber um ihre Bilder auszuführen, muß sie
in meinem und nicht in deinem Kopf aufflammen.'[44] He uses flame imagery,
which represents energy, to point out that to paint anything the image had to
be forged in his own mind. It could not be put there by Lavater. In the extract

---

40 *Heinrich Füsslis Briefe,* ed. by Walter Muschg (Basel: Benno Schwabe, 1942), p. 143.
41 *Füsslis Briefe,* 127–128.
42 This is a motto which Lavater gave to Fuseli after their study tour. Hall, *Blake and Fuseli,* 24.
43 Johann Heinrich Füssli, *Sämtliche Gedichte,* ed. by Martin Bircher and Karl S. Guthke (Zurich:
     Orell Füssli Verlag, 1973), p. 90. 'Do the seventh part of that which you can do, so said / As I
     departed from his arms, my now immortal friend. / Did I do the seventh part of what I was
     able to do? / Are you now hovering over my head, tell me, immortal friend? / Sixty years have
     departed, my hair is silver, the tongue's / Ivory wall falls into crumbled pieces.'
44 *Füsslis Briefe,* 166. 'Your and my imagination may be one and the same; but to execute its
     images, it has to flame up in my head and not in yours.'

quoted above, Fuseli deliberates if Lavater is making good use of his new soul-body. Is he, indeed, going to assist him? My impression, given Fuseli's attempts to emancipate himself from Lavater, is that Fuseli's poem is tongue-in-cheek. Fuseli challenges literary convention, because he both defends and insists on the power of his own imagination. This, of course, is a familiar Romantic stance. Could it be that Fuseli's stories prompted Blake to reconsider the handed-down theory of inspiration?

Fuseli and Felix Hess had been keen readers of English literature, an interest which dates back to their days at the *Collegium Carolinum* in Zurich. It was especially the translation of Milton's *Paradise Lost* by their teacher, the historian and literary critic Johann Jakob Bodmer, which whetted their appetites. Before their paths separated, the three friends spent a few months of intensive study together at the house of the theologian Johann Joachim Spalding in Pomerania. It was after this visit that their friendships changed forever: Hess and Lavater returned to Zurich and Fuseli left for England. Lavater describes this at the beginning of a 'new chapter' in his attempt at a biography of Hess:

> Denn nunmehr sahe sich mein seeliger Freund allein an der Hand seines Herzensfreundes, mit dem er alle seine Einsichten, seine Angelegenheiten und Absichten bis ans Ende seines Lebens zu theilen gesonnen war. Nein – ohne Schmerzen der heissesten Liebe, ohne bange Zurückwünschung dieser goldenen Stunden kann ich es nicht niederschreiben, was mir da sein redliches, für Wahrheit und Tugend so entschlossnes Herz für grosse Absichten entdekte [*sic*], für mächtige Ermunterungen gab ... O mögte ich sie ganz wiederum geniessen, die in meinem bebenden Andenken unsterbliche Nacht, wo der Mond unsern einsamen Wagen, als ein feyrlicher [*sic*] Zeuge, beleuchtete, – die heilige Nacht, wo er meine Hand, die in der seinigen ruhte, mit einer ihm selbst ungewohnten Zärtlichkeit drückte, und seine offenen Augen vom Himmel auf mich richtete, und mit einer unausprechlich herzlichen Stimme, die ewig unvergeßlichen Worte aussprach: 'Wills Gott, Lavater! wir wollen alles thun! wir wollen Hand in Hand schlagen, Wahrheit und Tugend unter den Menschen auszubreiten. Wir wollen einander nicht verlassen! Laßt uns Ein Herz und Eine Seele – Lavater! Ein Herz und Eine Seele seyn!' – Ich muß die Feder niederlegen ... Ach! mein Gott! warum hast du diesen Freund von meiner Seite genommen –⁴⁵

---

45 Johann Caspar Lavater, *Denkmal auf Johann Felix Heß, weyland Diener Göttlichen Wortes* (Zürich: [n. pub.], 1774), pp. 23–24. 'Because from now on my departed friend was the only one holding the hand of his bosom friend, with whom he decided to share all his insights, his affairs and intentions until the end of his days. No – it is impossible for me to write down, without the pains of the most intense love, without the anxious wish for those golden hours to return, what intentions his honest heart, set on truth and virtue, revealed to me, what powerful encouragements it gave ... O if only I could enjoy again this immortal night which quivers in my memory, in which the moon, as if a solemn witness, illuminated our lonely carriage, – the holy night, in which he took my hand into his, and pressed it with unfamiliar tenderness, and his open eyes turned from the sky to me, and he spoke with an inexpressibly cordial voice, the eternally unforgettable words: "With God's help, Lavater! We will do everything! We will join hands, and spread truth and virtue among people. We will never leave each other! Let us be

But Hess and Fuseli stayed in touch.[46] Judging from Fuseli's letters to Lavater, he sent several volumes to Zurich, among them an edition of poems by Thomas Gray and Laurence Sterne's *Sentimental Journey*, the latter probably for Hess to translate.[47] They both admired the work of Sterne, and Hess even undertook a translation of Sterne's sermons, which tells us a lot about their interest in the literature of sensibility as well as in parody and satire.[48] In the biography Lavater includes a letter by Hess, which accompanied his translation:

> Ich habe mich mit der Uebersetzung derselben versündiget. Doch kann ich mich entschuldigen; Ich that es meinem Füeßli zu gefallen, und, ohne stolz zu seyn, konnte ich es selbst fühlen, daß dieser Verfasser unter meinen Händen weniger verlieren würde, als sein Tristram Shandy unter der unverschämten Feder seines deutschen Uebersetzers verloren hat.[49]

Lavater reports that Hess, like Fuseli, was studying English while at Spalding's, which again suggests that the two men had a lot in common.[50] Once back in Zurich, life was not easy. Hess had a weak constitution and fell seriously ill. During the last months of his life, Lavater spent hours sitting at his bed. When Hess died on 3 March 1768, he said goodbye to his wife and then turned to his friend: 'Lavater! Von dir nehme ich nicht Abschied – Lobe mich nicht nach meinem Tode – Sage genau, was ich gewesen bin! Präcis! –'.[51]

Lavater was left with the task of describing the life and death of what seems to be the dearest person he had ever lost. In 1774 he published the biography *Denkmal auf Johann Felix Heß, weyland Diener Göttlichen Wortes*, which consists of a blend of description, shared memories and edited letters. *Denkmal* is about Hess, whose love-letters are beautiful, but also about Lavater, the editor whose presence overshadows the book. It is interesting that Lavater did not fulfil Hess's wish. Earlier on in *Denkmal*, in the section containing Hess's letters to his bride, Lavater interrupts, because Hess is about to reveal a humiliating incident. He cannot allow him to continue:

> Ich muß es nicht um meines seeligen Freundes, sondern um des Publikums willen. Es würde mir nicht vergeben, was er mir gewiß vergeben, was er mich vermuthlich entdecken heissen würde. [...] Aber ich bin zu schwach, zu blöde, zu sehr im Gedrän-

---

one heart and one soul – Lavater! To be one heart and one soul!" – I have to put my pen down ... O! My God! Why did you take this friend away from my side – .'

46 Lavater, *Denkmal,* 174.
47 *Füsslis Briefe,* 142, 145.
48 Hall, *Blake and Fuseli,* 36–37.
49 Lavater, *Denkmal,* 180. 'My imperfect translation of these has occasioned me no little shame. But I have this excuse: I did it to oblige Fuseli, and, without being proud, I could feel (within myself) that this author would lose less in my hands than his Tristram Shandy lost through the impudent pen of his German translator.'
50 Lavater, *Denkmal,* 8.
51 Lavater, *Denkmal,* 146–147. 'Lavater! I won't say goodbye to you – Don't praise me after my death – Say exactly what I have been! Precisely! –'

ge der menschlichen Urtheile; Ich habe schon vieles mitgetheilt, welches sich nur durch die Bitte des Seeligen, und die Nutzbarkeit, die ich demselben zutraue, entschuldigen läßt.[52]

Lavater is concerned that the reader might get the wrong idea. There are things that have to stay between friends and remain secret. This is despite Hess telling him, as he admits, that he thought it would be useful if Lavater wrote about his mistakes ('meine Fehler').[53]

After Hess's death Lavater became increasingly interested in accounts of miracles. This interest turned him into a target for public ridicule, but Lavater was adamant and continued to investigate the authenticity of visions and the credibility of self-styled faith-healers and mystics, among them Swedenborg. He published *Aussichten in die Ewigkeit*, and despite the failed attempts to contact him in the late 1760s, Lavater's belief in Swedenborg remained unwavering. In 1785 he writes:

> [...] diese Visionen waren seiner individuellen Natur angemessen; sie richteten sich nach dem Medium, durch welches gesehen ward. Das aufrichtigste Auge sieht gelb durch ein gelbes Glas. Auch selbst Geister können anders nicht, als nach dem Medium wirken, das sich ihnen darstellt. Sie sprechen deutsch mit Deutschen, französisch mit Franzosen. So erscheinen sie auch Jedem in der möglichen Gleichförmigkeit seiner Natur.[54]

According to Lavater, whether or not a person can engage with the spiritual world, depends on the physical condition of their bodies. To be a medium, the body has to be receptive. Lavater is quite specific when he discusses the optical potential of the eye and the powers of human perception. When he talks about the 'uniformity' of the medium's 'nature', he means that a spirit or ghost cannot gain any access, if body and soul are not in harmony. This position is in direct contradiction with the contemporary views on body-soul relationships, because according to the empiricist-mechanistic model, body and soul were not only two different entities, but what a man 'is' depended almost entirely on experience or exposure to the natural world.

The 'Introduction' to *Innocence* is about a piper who meets a child which asks him for a song (E 7). The song is piped, sung, and, according to the

---

52 Lavater, *Denkmal*, 64–65. 'I have to do this not for the sake of my departed friend but for that of the audience. They would not forgive me, what he would surely forgive, what he would probably tell me to reveal. [...] But I am too weak, too stupid, too far immersed in the press of human judgments; I have already communicated a lot of things, which can only be excused because it heeds the request of the departed and because I believe in its usefulness.'
53 Lavater, *Denkmal*, 149.
54 *Johann Kaspar Lavater's [sic] ausgewählte Schriften*, ed. Johann Kaspar Orelli (Zurich: Druck und Verlag von Fr. Schultheß, 1841), p. 273. '[...] these visions were suited to his individual nature; they conformed to the medium through which they were being seen. The most honest eye sees yellow through a yellow glass. Even ghosts cannot but act through the medium which is at their disposal. They speak German with Germans, French with the French. In the same way they appear to everyone in accordance with that person's nature.'

piper, written down, so that 'Every child may joy to hear' (l. 20) it. Piping
can be associated with breathing, which as opposed to the piping of the
wind, embodies the rhythms of the body.[55] The rhythm remains a shapeless
mood, until the point when the child asks to hear a 'song about a Lamb' (l.
5). Now the song acquires a subject matter; meaning is created further by
means of melody. Stanza 3 adds the next layer – words. This is the point
where the moment of inspiration stops. The child disappears and the now
self-motivated piper sits down to write. There is no more singing or hum-
ming. All we can hear is the 'hollow reed' (l. 16) moving across the page:
'And I stain'd the water clear, / And I wrote my happy songs' (ll. 18–19).
Critics have discussed the implications of the reed, staining the water in order to 'to make ink' and produce a material object,[56] or to create a metaphor for human understanding and 'a mutually educative experience'.[57] The
latter, Williams's interpretation, is positive, because it links the stain with the
cloud, thus delineating: 'these parallel images suggest that the song is
"stained" from the first stanza rather than simply descending into the stain
of print in the last.'[58] Williams, in other words, addresses the theme of inspiration, but I still think that this poem is about mental processing and artistic
embodiment, because if we assume a connection between cloud and stain,
then both could potentially obscure meaning. The piper's confidence and
satisfaction, moreover, rest on the knowledge that the children he is writing
for will be able to 'hear' (l. 20) – not read – his songs.

The 'Introduction' to the *Songs of Experience* is very different (E 18), because the reader is told to listen: 'Hear the voice of the Bard!' (l. 1). Not
only has the shepherd been promoted to bard, who knows about 'Present,
Past, & Future', 'Whose ears have heard / The Holy Word' (ll. 2–4; E 18),
he is ready to deliver his songs. He urges the listener, 'the lapsed soul' (l .6),
not to turn away as time is running out. What he has to offer is more important than immediate earthly existence: 'The starry floor / The watry
shore / Is giv'n thee till the break of day' (ll. 18–20). Instead of demonstrating the process of song-writing, this 'Introduction', like its frontispiece, addresses the reader directly. It is not clear who or what is the Bard's source.
Larrissy suggests that it 'could either be the original sentiments of the Bard;
or else a form of words prompted by the "Holy Word"'. Is the Bard 'speak-

---

55 Larrissy writes: 'Piping recalls the breath of inspiration. [...] It is as if some spiritual essence of
    innocence were directing itself into the form of pipe music. This is already a descent from the
    formless to the formed, though the form taken seems free and benign.' Larrissy, *William Blake*,
    26.
56 Glen, *Vision and Disenchantment*, 66.
57 Nicolas M. Williams, *Ideology and Utopia in the Poetry of William Blake* (Cambridge: Cambridge
    University Press, 1998), p. 59.
58 Williams, *Ideology*, 58.

ing from "Dictation"', or is he a 'prophet-turned-priest'?[59] The source of
inspiration seems to have become more abstract. The child has been replaced with 'The Holy Word' (l. 4), and yet this only increases the authority
and urgency with which the poem confronts the reader. The frontispiece
shows two figures, looking expectantly at the reader. Their gazes create sus-
pense because they do not speak. Embodying silence, they create a gap between text and image.

Perhaps the answer lies in the frontispieces to the *Songs*. The shepherd
in the frontispiece to *Innocence*, surrounded by sheep, is looking up and is
concentrating very hard (Fig. 1). Lincoln comments that 'his upward glance
emphasizes his coming to consciousness. He doesn't share the child's
smile'.[60] How are we to interpret these facial expressions? The design follows the frontispiece of *Aphorisms on Man*, because the figure is holding a
pipe but is not playing on it. In the frontispiece to *Experience* the shepherd is
placed in front of sheep but against a much barer background (Fig. 2). He
has no pipe, but holds the arms of a cherub who is sitting on his head like a
hat. It is as if the Bard, figuratively speaking, extends his mind with that of
another. Leader regrets that this frontispiece lacks 'human contact',[61] but
thinking back to *Aphorisms on Man* and 'the contrary states' represented in
the *Songs*, it seems that what the two frontispieces allude to is man's double
nature: an artist can be introverted, focused on what is going on inside him
as well as extrovert and aware of what is wrong with the world outside him.
This dynamic is already introduced in 'To the Muses' (E 417) from *Poetical
Sketches* (1783). In the first stanza Blake describes the status quo: 'Whether
on Ida's shady brow, / Or in the chambers of the East, / The chambers of
the sun, that now / From antient melody have ceas'd' (ll. 1–4). At the end
of the third stanza, he moves from bemoaning fading memories and echoes
to accusing the muses: 'Fair Nine, forsaking Poetry!' (l. 12). Blake ends with
deploring the state of contemporary poetry by wondering how they could
have abandoned poetry: 'How have you left the antient love / That bards of
old enjoy'd in you! / The languid strings do scarcely move! / The sound is
forc'd, the notes are few!' (ll. 13–16). There are no good sounds left to celebrate; something needs to be done. An illustration which may depict the
classical situation of poet and muse appears in Blake's illustration to Thomas Gray's 'The Progress of Poesy', dating from c.1797–98: a poet, sitting,
harp-in-hand, is pausing, and looking at what the muse above him is, literally, pouring out. The figure of the muse combines light, a rainbow, and human features. All these are reminiscent of Lavater's light-bodies. In the
1790s, I think, Blake advances the idea of a different kind of inspired poet.

---

59 Larrissy, *William Blake*, 68–69.
60 Lincoln, *Songs of Innocence and of Experience*, 142.
61 Leader, *Reading*, 131.

Fig. 1: Blake, *Songs of Innocence and Experience: Shewing the Two Contrary States of the Human Soul,*
Copy T, plate 2 (copyright the Trustees of the British Museum)

Fig. 2: Blake, *Songs of Innocence and Experience: Shewing the Two Contrary States of the Human Soul*, Copy T, plate 28 (copyright the Trustees of the British Museum)

The Book of Urizen, stylistically very different from the *Songs*, starts with a 'Preludium', in which an invisible narrator, possibly Blake, explains that what he is about to relate is something he has heard. It is not pleasant, but 'dark visions of torment'. Still, he is glad, because he is ready and strong: 'Eternals I hear your call gladly, / Dictate swift winged words, & fear not / To unfold your dark visions of torment.' (ll. 5–7; E 70) The source of inspiration is an unspecified number of Eternals' voices. This does not mean that we are dealing with a confused narrator, which, by the way, is not what can be said about the poem itself. The Preludium plate (Fig. 3) differs from the rest of *The Book of Urizen* because its text is not divided into two columns. The unity, however, is challenged by the two floating figures, which seem to talk to each other rather than to the poet.[62] A similarly confident voice starts off *The Song of Los*: 'I will sing you a song of Los. the Eternal Prophet: / He sung it to four harps at the tables of Eternity. [...] And thus the Song began' (ll. 1–5; E 67). Here the poet relates his vision of Los. He saw him sit and perform what he, the poet, is going to reveal to the reader. As Blake's work progresses, the scenes of invocation change. He constructs author-muse relationships which present the poet as resourceful as well as a reliable source. In the works discussed we see Blake engage with classical tradition, reconsider it after he met Fuseli, and possibly heard about Lavater and Felix Hess, but eventually he turns his back on anything that does not originate in his own mind. The conflict, or opposition, remaining is that which always exists between the poet and the reader, because whether or not a poet is successful depends on the reader. Tackling ambivalence, uncertainty, or ambiguity is and remains the reader's task.[63]

---

62 I do not agree with W.J.T. Mitchell's reading of this plate, because it draws on the inscription to this plate ('Teach these Souls to Fly') used in the *Small Books of Design*: 'So the baby is the reader, or the child he must become to participate in prophetic vision, and the woman is a visionary reader's guide, a sign that the monolithic symmetry of the previous plate is not the whole story.' W.J.T. Mitchell, *Blake's Composite Art: A Study of the Illuminated Poetry* (Princeton, N. J.: Princeton University Press, 1978), p. 144. I believe this interpretation relies too much on a completely different literary context for this plate.

63 In this I agree with Williams who writes that 'perhaps the point of the "Contrary States" is better reflected in the notion that each speaker and each Song migrates undecidably between Innocence and Experience, and that each plate is subject to 'contrary' readings in its interactions with an audience.' Williams, *Ideology*, 61.

Fig. 3: Blake, *The Book of Urizen*, Copy D, plate 2 (copyright the Trustees of the British Museum)

The Contributors

UTA DEGNER

is Assistant Professor in German at the University of Salzburg, Austria. She has published on Hölderlin, including *Bilder im Wechsel der Töne: Hölderlins Elegien und "Nachtgesänge"* (2008), Kafka, Jelinek, Brecht, and Leopardi, and co-edited, with N.C. Wolf, *Der neue Wettstreit der Künste: Legitimation und Dominanz im Zeichen der Intermedialität* (2010).

MELISSA A. DEININGER

is Assistant Professor of French at Iowa State University, USA. She specializes in the Marquis de Sade's political writings, and also works on Hugo and Verne in relation to political crisis. Her research focuses on how literature, art, and architecture are used as propaganda during régime changes in France. She also works with literary genres that emerge from the chaos of these moments, including fantasy and horror stories of the nineteenth century.

CHRISTIAN DEULING

is currently completing his PhD on cultural transfer via the periodical *London und Paris* in the German Department at the University of Nottingham, UK. He has published a number of articles on cultural transfer via periodicals in the Goethezeit and is interested in international journalism around 1800.

SIBYLLE ERLE

is Senior Lecturer in English at Bishop Grossesteste University College in Lincoln, UK. She works on the Romantic period, especially the interface between literature and science, and text-image relationships. She is the author of *Blake, Lavater and Physiognomy* (2010) and is co-editing, with Morton Pale, *The Reception of Blake in Europe*.

DIRK GÖTTSCHE

is Professor of German at the University of Nottingham, UK, and the author of numerous books, *Die Produktivität der Sprachkrise in der modernen Prosa* (1987), *Zeit im Roman: Literarische Zeitreflexion und die Geschichte des Zeitromans im späten 18. und im 19. Jahrhundert* (2001), *Zeitreflexion und Zeitkritik im Werk Wilhelm Raabes* (2000) and *Kleine Prosa in Moderne und Gegenwart* (2006). He is Vice-President of the *Internationale Raabe Gesellschaft* and co-editor of the *Jahrbuch der Raabe-Gesellschaft*. His research areas include German literature of the long nineteenth century, Austrian Modernism, modernist short prose, time, history and memory in German literature, and postcolonial and cross-cultural literary studies.

IMKE HEUER

studied English and History in Hamburg, Perugia, and York, where she completed a PhD on *'The German's Tale': German History, English Drama and the Politics of Adaptation*. She has published and forthcoming articles on Byron's dramas, Georgiana, Duchess of Devonshire and amateur play-writing, and Harriet and Sophia Lee. A visiting fellow at Chawton House Library and the University of Southampton, UK, she is currently preparing a critical edition of Joshua Pickersgill's Gothic novel *The Three Brothers*.

SUSANNE KORD

is Professor of German at University College London, UK. In addition to articles on many aspects of women's literary history and reception, she is the author of seven books on subjects including gender images in recent Hollywood films, women and violent crime in Germany's eighteenth and nineteenth centuries, eighteenth-century women peasant poets in England, Scotland and Germany, German women playwrights, and women's anonymity and pseudonyms. She has received six major awards for her writing, most recently the 2011 *Forum for Modern Language Studies*-prize for best article of the year.

PETER KRILLES

completed his PhD on Novalis at the Sorbonne in Paris, France in 2009.

JAKOB LADEGAARD

is Assistant Professor in Comparative Literature at Aarhus University, Denmark. His research interests focus on the relations between modern literature, cinema, aesthetic theory and politics. His current research project investigates representations of Eastern Europe in Western literature and cinema. Recent publications include *Confronting Universalities: Aesthetics and Politics under the Sign of Globalisation*, edited with M.A. Baggesgaard (2011).

DAVID MCCALLAM

is Reader in French eighteenth-century Studies at the University of Sheffield, UK. His research focuses on the literature and culture of eighteenth-century France, with specific reference to revolutionary politics and the development of earth sciences. Recent publications include *L'Art de l'équivoque chez Laclos* (2008), articles on exploring Vesuvius in the late eighteenth century, Montesquieu's *Lettres persanes*, eighteenth-century Dalmatia as seen by the French, and forthcoming chapters on avalanches and extreme cold in the same period.

IAN MACGREGOR MORRIS

specializes in political culture, the history of ideas, and the classical tradition in the long eighteenth century. Recent publications include a co-edited volume on historiography and political culture, *Reinventing History: The Enlightenment Origins of Ancient History* (2008) and another on uses of the classical past as comparative models for modern societies and institutions, *Sparta in Modern Thought* (2012). His forthcoming monograph, *The Age of Leonidas: Hellenism and the Classical Tradition in the Enlightenment*, considers the process of the classical tradition in eighteenth-century political culture within a pan-European context.

BARRY MURNANE

is Assistant Professor in German Studies at the Martin-Luther-Universität Halle-Wittenberg, Germany. He has published on German literature and culture and Anglo-German cultural transfer from 1750 to the present and has worked extensively on the Gothic, including a monograph on Franz Kafka (2008), and two edited volumes on the German Gothic, *Populäre Erscheinungen* (2011) and *Popular Revenants* (2012). He is currently working on a monograph on the relation between literature and pharmacy in the long eighteenth century.

MAIKE OERGEL

is Associate Professor in German and the Director of the Centre for Translation and Comparative Cultural Studies at the University of Nottingham, UK. She co-edits, together with Glyn Hambrook, *Comparative Critical Studies* and specializes in Anglo-German intellectual and literary history between 1750 and 1900. She has published on the constructions of modern national identity (*The Return of King Arthur and the Nibelungen: National Myth in 19th-century English and German Literature*, 1998) and modernity (*Culture and Identity: Historicity in German Literature and Thought 1770–1815*, 2006), co-edited volumes on counter-cultures (*From Sturm und Drang to Baader-Meinhof: Counter-Cultures in Germany and Central Europe*, 2003) and aesthetics (*Aesthetics and Modernity: From Schiller to Marcuse*, 2012) as well as published on other cultural, intellectual, and literary issues of the Enlightenment and Romanticism.

RENATA SCHELLENBERG

is Associate Professor of German at Mount Allison University in Sackville, Canada. She specializes in post-Enlightenment German literature and has published on topics pertaining to scientific literacy, word and image, and textual strategies in the long eighteenth century. She is currently completing a monograph on collecting culture in eighteenth-century Germanophone Europe.

JUDITH STILL

is Professor of French and Critical Theory at the University of Nottingham, UK. She is the author of *Justice and Difference in the Work of Rousseau* (1993), *Feminine Economies: Thinking Against the Market in the Enlightenment and the Late Twentieth Century* (1997*), Derrida and Hospitality* (2010) *and Enlightenment Hospitality: Cannibals, Harems and Adoption* (2011). She is also the editor of *Men's Bodies* (2003), and co-editor, with M. Worton, of *Intertextuality* (1990) and *Textuality and Sexuality* (1993); with D. Knight of *Women and Representation* (1995) *and Theory-tinged Criticism* (2009); with S. Ribeiro de Oliveira of *Brazilian Feminisms* (1999).

BIRGIT TAUTZ

is Associate Professor of German at Bowdoin College, Maine, USA. A specialist in eighteenth- and nineteenth-century German literature, culture, and philosophy, she is the author of *Reading and Seeing Ethnic Differences in the Enlightenment: From China to Africa* (2007) and editor of *Colors 1800/1900/2000: Signs of Ethnic Difference* (2004). She is currently working on a monograph entitled 'Translating the World: Remaking Late Eighteenth-century Literature between Hamburg and Weimar'.

W. DANIEL WILSON

is professor of German at Royal Holloway, University of London, UK. He researches literature, culture, and history of late eighteenth- and early nineteenth-century German-speaking lands, especially Classical Weimar, and political and gender issues. His major book publications are *Geheimräte gegen Geheimbünde: Ein unbekanntes Kapitel der klassisch-romantischen Geschichte Weimars* (1991), *Impure Reason: Dialectic of Enlightenment in Germany* (ed. with Robert Holub, 1994), *Das Goethe-Tabu: Protest und Menschenrechte im klassischen Weimar* (1999), *Unterirdische Gänge: Goethe, Freimaurerei und Politik* (1999), *Goethes Weimar und die Französische Revolution: Dokumente der Krisenjahre* (2004), and *Goethe Männer Knaben: Ansichten zur "Homosexualität"* (2012).